Helen Keller

by Jane Sutcliffe
illustrations by Elaine Verstraete

On My Own
BIOGRAPHY

 Carolrhoda Books, Inc./Minneapolis

This book is available in two editions:
Library binding by Carolrhoda Books, Inc., a division of Lerner Publishing Group
Soft cover by First Avenue Editions, an imprint of Lerner Publishing Group
241 First Avenue North
Minneapolis, MN 55401 U.S.A.

Website address: www.lernerbooks.com

Library of Congress Cataloging-in-Publication Data

Sutcliffe, Jane.
    Helen Keller / by Jane Sutcliffe ; illustrations by Elaine Verstraete.
        p.   cm. — (On my own biography)
    Summary: Focuses on the early life of a woman who is well known for overcoming her handicaps of being both blind and deaf.
    ISBN: 0–87614–600–0 (lib. bdg. : alk. paper)
    ISBN: 0–87614–903–4 (pbk. : alk. paper)
    1. Keller, Helen, 1880–1968—Juvenile literature. 2. Blind-deaf women—United States—Biography—Juvenile literature. [1. Keller, Helen, 1880–1968. 2. Blind. 3. Deaf. 4. Physically handicapped. 5. Women—Biography.] I. Verstraete, Elaine, ill. II. Title. III. Series.
    HV1624.K4 S88 2002
    362.4'1'092—dc21   2001006585

Manufactured in the United States of America
1 2 3 4 5 6 – JR – 07 06 05 04 03 02

For my mother and my "Teacher," Clarice McCormick — J. S.

For my mother, always.
For Olivia and Megan. Thank you for your
imagination and dedication. — E. V.

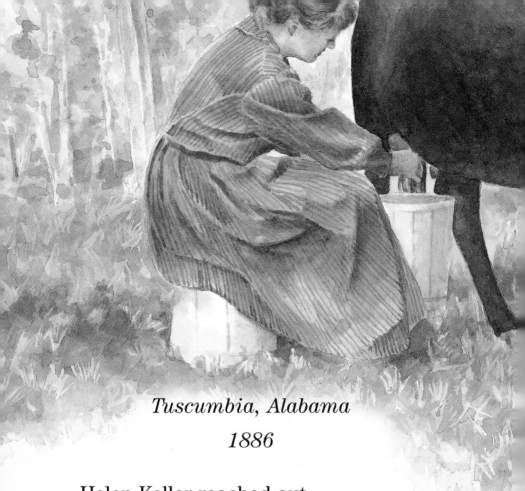

Tuscumbia, Alabama

1886

Helen Keller reached out.

She touched warm, coarse hair.

Her busy fingers moved farther down.

They felt something smooth and wet.

Slap! A hairy tail smacked

into Helen's face.

Helen could not see
her family's milking cow.
But she liked touching it.
Helen Keller had been blind and deaf
for most of her life.
The only way she knew the world was by
touch, taste, and smell.

Helen was born in 1880
in Tuscumbia, Alabama.
When she was just a baby,
she became very sick.
The illness took away
her sight and hearing.
Helen could not hear her brothers'
laughter or her mother's voice.
She could not see her father's smile
or the pretty flowers outside her window.
For Helen, there was only silence
and gray darkness.

To learn to speak,

children need to hear words.

But Helen could not hear anything.

So she could not speak.

Instead, she made motions.

When she wanted her mother,

she put her hand against her face.

When she wanted her father,

she made the motion of putting on

a pair of glasses.

When she was hungry,

she pretended to slice and butter bread.

Helen knew she was different from
the rest of her family.
They moved their lips
when they wanted things.
Sometimes Helen stood between
two people as they talked.
She held her hands to their lips.
Then she tried moving her own lips.
But still no one understood her.

That made Helen angry.

Sometimes she screamed and cried
and kicked for hours.

She threw things and hit people.

But it didn't change anything.

She was still alone
in silence and darkness.

Helen was hard to control.

Her parents didn't know how to help her.

They took her to doctors.

None of the doctors could help Helen
see or hear again.

When Helen was six, a doctor suggested
the Kellers visit Alexander Graham Bell.

Dr. Bell was famous
for inventing the telephone.

He also taught deaf people.

Dr. Bell told the Kellers to write to
Michael Anagnos in Boston.
Mr. Anagnos was the head of
the Perkins Institution for the Blind.
He believed Helen could learn how
to let out the thoughts locked inside her.
Mr. Anagnos promised
to send Helen a teacher.

Helen and Teacher
March 1887

Helen's teacher came to live
with the Kellers that spring.
Her name was Annie Sullivan.
Annie had studied at the Perkins School.
She was nearly blind herself.
Annie needed to control Helen's wild
behavior so she could teach her.
But Helen did not understand
that Annie wanted to help her.
For two weeks, Helen fought with Annie.
She hit Annie and knocked out
one of her front teeth.
She even locked Annie in an upstairs room.
Mr. Keller had to get a ladder
and let Annie out through a window.

Still, Annie did not give up.

Little by little, Helen learned

to trust her new teacher.

Annie began to teach Helen about words.

She spelled words using her fingers.

Her hand formed a different shape

for each letter.

She pressed each shape

into Helen's hand.

When she gave Helen some cake,

she spelled C-A-K-E into Helen's palm.

When Helen held her doll,

Annie spelled D-O-L-L for Helen.

Helen imitated the shapes.

She thought it was a game.

She didn't know that the shapes

spelled words.

After a month, Helen could spell
whatever Annie spelled.
But Helen still did not know that she
was naming the things she touched.

One day Helen and Annie
walked to the well house.
Someone was pumping water.
Annie pushed Helen's hand
into the rushing water.
Helen felt the cool water on one hand.
She felt her teacher's fingers spelling
W-A-T-E-R into her other hand.
Over and over,
Annie spelled the word.
Suddenly Helen stood very still.
All at once she understood!
The liquid flowing over her hand
had a name.
It was W-A-T-E-R!

Everything had a name!

Helen wanted to learn them all.

She ran from one thing to another.

Annie spelled the name of everything

Helen touched.

Then Helen turned and pointed to Annie.

T-E-A-C-H-E-R, spelled Annie.

From then on, Helen's name for Annie

was "Teacher."

That summer, Helen learned

a lot of new words.

She stopped using her old motions.

Her fingers gave her

all the words she needed.

Annie did not teach Helen words
one at a time.
She talked to her in full sentences.
That way, Helen learned more
than just new words.
She learned new ideas.
Helen and Annie took long walks
through the woods and along the river.
Annie gave Helen lessons on the walks.
She showed Helen how seeds sprout
and plants grow.
She made mountains out of mud
and taught Helen about volcanoes.
Sometimes they climbed a tree
and had a lesson there.

Helen was hungry for knowledge.
She wanted to learn everything
Annie could teach her.
Soon Annie started teaching Helen
how to read.
The words were printed in raised letters
for a blind person.

Helen felt the words with her fingers.
She liked to hunt for words she knew.
When she learned to read better,
she read her books over and over.
Her curious fingers wore down
the raised letters.

Helen also learned to write.

She wrote letters to her family and Dr. Bell.

She wrote many letters
to Mr. Anagnos in Boston.

Mr. Anagnos was amazed by how much
Helen had learned.

He published some of Helen's letters.

Reporters began to write about Helen.

Soon she was famous.

People all over the world wanted to know
about the miracle girl.

And Helen wanted to know
all about the world.

Traveling
May 1888

Eight-year-old Helen sat on a train
with her teacher and her mother.
She was going to Boston to visit
the Perkins Institution for the Blind.
Helen wanted to hear all about
the countryside rushing past them.
Annie spelled into Helen's hand
everything she saw outside the window.
She described hills, rivers, forests,
and cotton fields.

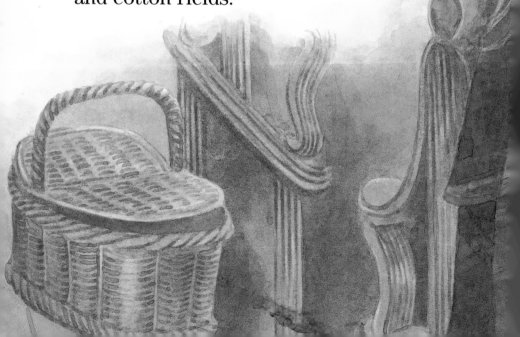

At the Perkins School,
Helen met Mr. Anagnos.
She also met children who knew
how to talk with their fingers.
"What joy to talk to other children in my
own language!" Helen wrote.
Helen also went to the ocean
for the first time.
She had only read about the ocean in books.
Right away, she ran into the water.
Then she tripped on a rock.
The water quickly closed over her head.
The waves tossed her back and forth.

It was as if they were playing
a game with her!
Finally she struggled toward the shore.
She was shivering and gasping for air.
She reached for her teacher's hand.
"Who put salt in the water?" she asked.
No one had told her that
ocean water was salty!

The world was opening up for Helen.

In three years she had learned

to finger spell, to read, and to write.

She even knew some French and Latin.

Everyone was astonished by how much

she had learned.

But Helen wanted to learn so much more.

She wanted to speak like other people.

She wanted to talk to her baby sister.

She wanted her dog to come

when she called.

She begged Annie to help her

find a way to speak.

When Helen was 10 years old,

Annie took her to a school in Boston.

A teacher there taught Helen to read lips

with her fingers.

Helen put her hand on a speaker's lips,
nose, and throat.
She learned to feel the words.
Then she tried to make her own sounds.
But her words never seemed
to come out quite right.

A few years later, Helen entered a school
for the deaf in New York City.
Helen loved New York.
She and Annie rode horses
in Central Park.

She went sledding
with the other students.
Once she climbed to the top
of the Statue of Liberty.

Helen also met many famous people.
When she met the writer Mark Twain,
they became friends at once.
His funny stories made her laugh
until she cried.
Still, one thing always made Helen sad.
She had worked day and night
to improve her speech.
But she had not learned to speak clearly.
Helen decided she would not let her
disappointment stop her from dreaming.

More to Learn

October 1896

At age 16, Helen was a young lady.

She was tall and strong.

She had a clever sense of humor.

She loved to swim and sail.

She could even row a boat herself.

She steered by the scent of the plants
that grew on shore.
Helen had always dreamed
of going to college.
To prepare, Helen entered
the Cambridge School for Young Ladies.

Up to now, Helen had gone to school
with other deaf or blind students.
At this new school, she lived with girls
who could see and hear.
She played games
and took long walks with them.
But everyone at her new school
had to speak to her through Annie.
They did not know how to finger spell.

Annie went to all of Helen's classes.

She spelled the lessons into Helen's hand.

Helen could not take notes

like the other students.

Her hands were "busy listening."

Helen studied hard.

After four years,

she was ready for college.

Helen entered Radcliffe College
in the fall of 1900.
She was the first deaf-blind person
ever to go to college.
As always, Helen wanted to learn
everything she could.
She took many classes.
Writing was her best subject.
She wrote about her first
dunking in the ocean.
She described how even she could see
the dazzle of sunlight on snow.
A magazine editor
heard about Helen's stories.
He knew that people would read them.
They wanted to know about the girl who
had broken out of her silent, gray world.

The editor asked Helen to write
about her life for his magazine.
Helen turned the stories into a book.
Her book was called *The Story of My Life.*
It was published in 1903.
Newspapers praised Helen's book.
Helen's friend Mark Twain wrote
with congratulations.
Helen had wanted so much
to speak to the world!
At last she had found a way.
Her book told the whole world
about her amazing life.

Helen Keller at about the age of 14

Afterword

Helen graduated from Radcliffe College in 1904. She spent the rest of her life helping the deaf and blind. Even though she never learned to speak as clearly as she wanted, she gave lectures to raise money for the American Foundation for the Blind. She wrote articles and books about her life and about her teacher.

Annie Sullivan stayed with Helen until Annie's death in 1936. The two of them had been together for nearly 50 years. A year later, Helen began touring the world on behalf of the blind. By the end of her life, she had traveled to 35 countries.

Helen had been famous almost all her life. From the time she was eight, she had met every president of the United States. She starred in two movies about her life. One of them, *The Unconquered*, won an Academy Award in 1955. A famous play, *The Miracle Worker*, was written about Helen and Annie.

Wherever Helen went, she charmed and amazed the crowds that came to see her. She reminded them that, with hard work, anyone can make a dream come true.

Important Dates

1880—Helen Adams Keller is born in Tuscumbia, Alabama, on June 27.

1881—Helen becomes deaf and blind after an illness.

1887—Annie Sullivan comes to Tuscumbia to teach Helen.

1894—Helen moves to New York City to attend school.

1896—Helen attends the Cambridge School for Young Ladies.

1900—Helen enters Radcliffe College.

1903—Helen's first book, *The Story of My Life*, is published.

1904—Helen graduates from Radcliffe College.

1924—Helen begins work for the American Foundation for the Blind.

1936—Annie Sullivan dies.

1964—Helen is awarded the Presidential Medal of Freedom by President Lyndon Johnson.

1968—Helen dies in Connecticut at age 87 on June 1.

1996—*The Story of My Life* is named one of the New York Public Library's Books of the Century.

Microsoft® Office

Excel® 2007 Programming

Your visual blueprint™ for creating interactive spreadsheets

by Denise Etheridge

1807
WILEY
2007

Wiley Publishing, Inc.

Microsoft® Office Excel® 2007 Programming: Your visual blueprint™ for creating interactive spreadsheets

Published by
Wiley Publishing, Inc.
111 River Street
Hoboken, NJ 07030-5774

Published simultaneously in Canada

Library of Congress Control Number: 2007933273

ISBN: 978-0-470-13230-2

Manufactured in the United States of America

10 9 8 7 6 5 4 3 2 1

Trademark Acknowledgments

FOR PURPOSES OF ILLUSTRATING THE CONCEPTS AND TECHNIQUES DESCRIBED IN THIS BOOK, THE AUTHOR HAS CREATED VARIOUS NAMES, COMPANY NAMES, MAILING, E-MAIL AND INTERNET ADDRESSES, PHONE AND FAX NUMBERS AND SIMILAR INFORMATION, ALL OF WHICH ARE FICTITIOUS. ANY RESEMBLANCE OF THESE FICTITIOUS NAMES, ADDRESSES, PHONE AND FAX NUMBERS AND SIMILAR INFORMATION TO ANY ACTUAL PERSON, COMPANY AND/OR ORGANIZATION IS UNINTENTIONAL AND PURELY COINCIDENTAL.

Contact Us

For general information on our other products and services, please contact our Customer Care Department within the U.S. at 800-762-2974, outside the U.S. at 317-572-3993 or fax 317-572-4002.

For technical support, please visit www.wiley.com/techsupport.

The Roman Theater of Aspendos

Built when Marcus Aurelius was Emperor of Rome (161–180 A.D.), this magnificent theater, faithful to the Greek tradition, nestles into the side of a hill. It is among the best preserved of its era, and concerts and operas are still performed upon its stage today. Its acoustics are quite literally legendary. A favorite story tells how the architect, Zeno, won the king's daughter by creating this masterpiece in which a word murmured from the stage could be heard throughout the arena.

Learn more about Aspendos and its artifacts in *Frommer's Turkey*, available wherever books are sold or at www.frommers.com.

WILEY

Sales

Contact Wiley
at (800) 762-2974
or (317) 572-4002.

PRAISE FOR VISUAL BOOKS ...

"This is absolutely the best computer-related book I have ever bought. Thank you so much for this fantastic text. Simply the best computer book series I have ever seen. I will look for, recommend, and purchase more of the same."

—David E. Prince (NeoNome.com)

"I have several of your Visual books and they are the best I have ever used."

—Stanley Clark (Crawfordville, FL)

"I just want to let you know that I really enjoy all your books. I'm a strong visual learner. You really know how to get people addicted to learning! I'm a very satisfied Visual customer. Keep up the excellent work!"

—Helen Lee (Calgary, Alberta, Canada)

"I have several books from the Visual series and have always found them to be valuable resources."

—Stephen P. Miller (Ballston Spa, NY)

"This book is PERFECT for me —it's highly visual and gets right to the point. What I like most about it is that each page presents a new task that you can try verbatim or, alternatively, take the ideas and build your own examples. Also, this book isn't bogged down with trying to 'tell all' – it gets right to the point. This is an EXCELLENT, EXCELLENT, EXCELLENT book and I look forward to purchasing other books in the series."

—Tom Dierickx (Malta, IL)

"I have quite a few of your Visual books and have been very pleased with all of them. I love the way the lessons are presented!"

—Mary Jane Newman (Yorba Linda, CA)

"I am an avid fan of your Visual books. If I need to learn anything, I just buy one of your books and learn the topic in no time. Wonders! I have even trained my friends to give me Visual books as gifts."

—Illona Bergstrom (Aventura, FL)

"I just had to let you and your company know how great I think your books are. I just purchased my third Visual book (my first two are dog-eared now!) and, once again, your product has surpassed my expectations. The expertise, thought, and effort that go into each book are obvious, and I sincerely appreciate your efforts."

—Tracey Moore (Memphis, TN)

"Compliments to the chef!! Your books are extraordinary! Or, simply put, extra-ordinary, meaning way above the rest! THANK YOU THANK YOU THANK YOU! I buy them for friends, family, and colleagues."

—Christine J. Manfrin (Castle Rock, CO)

"I write to extend my thanks and appreciation for your books. They are clear, easy to follow, and straight to the point. Keep up the good work! I bought several of your books and they are just right! No regrets! I will always buy your books because they are the best."

—Seward Kollie (Dakar, Senegal)

"I am an avid purchaser and reader of the Visual series, and they are the greatest computer books I've seen. Thank you very much for the hard work, effort, and dedication that you put into this series."

—Alex Diaz (Las Vegas, NV)

Credits

Project Editor
Jade L. Williams

Acquisitions Editor
Jody Lefevere

Copy Editor
Marylouise Wiack

Technical Editor
Lee Musick

Editorial Manager
Robyn Siesky

Business Manager
Amy Knies

Sr. Marketing Manager
Sandy Smith

Manufacturing
Allan Conley
Linda Cook
Paul Gilchrist
Jennifer Guynn

Book Design
Kathryn Rickard

Production Coordinator
Adrienne Martinez

Layout
Carrie A. Foster
Joyce Haughey
Jennifer Mayberry
Amanda Spagnuolo
Christine Williams

Screen Artist
Ronda David-Burroughs
Jill Proll

Cover Illustration
Cheryl Grubbs

Proofreader
Broccoli Information Management

Quality Control
Laura Albert

Indexer
Infodex Indexing Services, Inc.

**Vice President and Executive
Group Publisher**
Richard Swadley

Vice President and Publisher
Barry Pruett

Composition Director
Debbie Stailey

Wiley Bicentennial Logo
Richard J. Pacifico

About the Author

Denise Etheridge is a certified public accountant as well as the president and founder of Baycon Group, Inc. She publishes Web sites, provides consulting services on accounting-related software, and authors computer-related books. You can visit www.baycongroup.com to view her online tutorials.

Author's Acknowledgments

I would like to thank all of the people at Wiley who assisted me in writing this book. I would also like to thank Malinda McCain for her assistance. I have said it before and I will say it again, "Malinda, you are the best!"

This book is dedicated to Frederick Douglas Etheridge, Jr.

TABLE OF CONTENTS

TABLE OF CONTENTS

TABLE OF CONTENTS

HOW TO USE THIS BOOK

Microsoft Office Excel 2007 Programming: Your visual blueprint for creating interactive spreadsheets uses clear, descriptive examples to show you how to use powerful Excel macros. If you are already familiar with Excel macros, you can use this book as a quick reference.

Who Needs This Book

This book is for the experienced computer user who wants to find out more about Excel programming. It is also for more experienced Excel users who want to expand their knowledge of the different features that Excel has to offer.

Book Organization

Microsoft Office Excel 2007 Programming: Your visual blueprint for creating interactive spreadsheets has 17 chapters and 2 appendices.

Chapter 1, "Using Macros and Form Controls," shows you how to work with macros in Excel, how to record a simple macro, how to assign macros to the Quick Access toolbar, how to launch a macro, and how to remove a macro from a workbook.

Chapter 2, "Using the Visual Basic Editor," is about the Visual Basic Editor (VBE) that comes with Microsoft Office applications. This chapter shows you how to set up your Visual Basic Editor window to quickly create and modify code modules.

Chapter 3, "Introducing Visual Basic for Applications," introduces you to the essentials of Visual Basic for Applications (VBA). This chapter also covers some VBA programming fundamentals that enable you to use the material in the chapters that follow to create your own Excel macros.

Chapter 4, "Introducing the Excel Object Model," shows you how to work with the Excel Object Model to access the various elements that make up the Excel application. This chapter provides a foundation for the information covered in the remainder of the book, particularly Chapters 9 to 12.

Chapters 5 to 7 build on the VBA programming language by showing you how to work with variables and create arrays. You also learn how to use the various control statements to specify the code that executes when you run a macro. You create dialog boxes using the MsgBox and InputBox functions.

Chapter 8, "Debugging Macros," shows you how to use the various features of the Visual Basic Editor to find programming and logical errors within your VBA code.

Chapters 9 to 12 illustrate how you can use the Workbook, Worksheet, and Range objects to create custom macros. You also learn how to use the corresponding properties and methods associated with these objects.

Chapter 13, "Creating Dialog Boxes and Customizing the Ribbon," shows you how to create a graphical interface for your macros by creating custom dialog boxes and adding items to the Ribbon.

Chapter 14, "Working with Charts," shows you how to create and modify charts from within your macro.

Chapter 15, "Automating Procedures with Excel Events," shows you how to capture user events and use those events to trigger procedures. You also learn how to execute a procedure at a specific time, or how to determine when a specific key sequence is pressed.

Chapter 16, "Building Add-Ins," shows you how to create and load add-ins.

Chapter 17, "Understanding XML," introduces you to Extensible Markup Language (XML). You learn how to open an XML file, create an XML map, import an XML file, and export an XML file.

The appendices are reference sections. After you become familiar with the contents of this book, you can use the appendices to obtain at-a-glance information about VBA statements, functions, constants, and controls used by functions, properties, methods, and RibbonX.

What You Need to Use This Book

Windows Requirements

- 256 megabyte (MB) RAM or higher
- 500 megahertz (MHz) processor or higher
- 2 GB of available hard disk space
- CD-ROM or DVD drive
- Keyboard and pointing device, such as a mouse
- 1024x768 or higher resolution monitor

Microsoft Windows XP with Service Pack (SP) 2, Windows Server 2003 with SP1 or later operating system.

The Conventions in This Book

A number of styles have been used throughout *Microsoft Office Excel 2007 Programming: Your visual blueprint for creating interactive spreadsheets* to designate different types of information.

Courier Font

Indicates the use of VBA and scripting language code, such as tags, attributes, statements, operators, functions, objects, methods, or properties.

Bold

Indicates information that you must type.

Italics

Indicates a new term.

Apply It

An Apply It section takes the code from the preceding task one-step further. Apply It sections allow you to take full advantage of VBA code.

Extra

An Extra section provides additional information about the preceding task. Extra sections contain the inside information to make working with Excel easier and more efficient.

What's on the Web Site

The Web site accompanying this book contains the sample files for the book that you can use to work with *Microsoft Office Excel 2007 Programming: Your visual blueprint for creating interactive spreadsheets.*

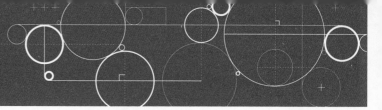

Introducing Excel Programming

As you probably know, Microsoft Excel is an electronic worksheet you can use for a variety of purposes, including the following: maintain lists; perform mathematical, financial, and statistical calculations; create charts; and analyze your data with a PivotTable. Excel can also help you locate data, find trends in your data, and present your data to others.

This book is about automating the tasks you perform in Excel by using Visual Basic for Applications (VBA). You can use VBA to automate those repetitive tasks you perform frequently. For example, if the layout of your monthly report rarely changes, you can use VBA to set up your report each month.

VBA is a programming language; however, you do not have to be a programmer to automate the tasks you perform in Excel. You can also automate a task by using the macro recorder to create a macro. A *macro* is a

recording of the steps you want to automate. You just click a button to turn on the macro recorder and begin performing the steps as you normally would. Excel records each step and creates the VBA code. When you finish, you click the Stop Record button. When you select your macro in the Macro dialog box and click the Run button, Excel plays back the steps you recorded. For example, if you record the steps necessary to create your monthly report, all you have to do each month thereafter is click a button and Excel automatically sets up your report.

With VBA, you can do more that just create macros. You can use VBA to edit macros, create new functions, create custom applications, and create add-ins. For these tasks, you must learn the VBA programming language. This book teaches VBA. It is based on Office 2007; code you write for Office 2007 may not be compatible with earlier versions of Excel.

Introducing Excel Programming

① Click the Developer tab.

Note: *See the section, "Introducing Macros," to learn how to display the Developer tab.*

Use the options in the Code group to automate your tasks.

② Click either of these Record Macro buttons to record a macro.

Note: *See the section, "Record a Macro," for more details.*

③ Click Macros to run a macro.

Note: *See the section, "Run a Macro," for more details.*

- Use the options in the Controls group to add check boxes, fields, and other form controls to your worksheet.

- Use the options in the XML group to work with XML.

④ Click here or press Alt+F11.

Excel moves to the Visual Basic for Applications Editor (VBE).

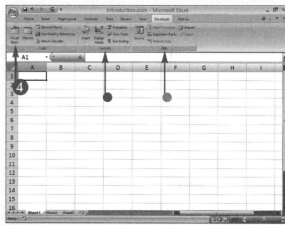

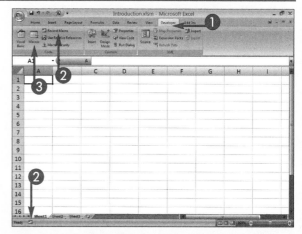

Use the VBE to write and edit code.

Note: See Chapter 2 to learn more about the VBE.

⑤ Click the proper module to access your macros or the VBA code you have written.

⑥ Type or edit your code here.

⑦ Press Alt+F11 to return to Excel.

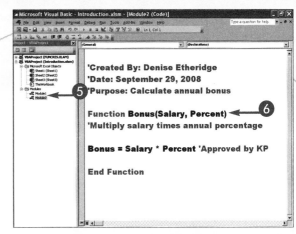

The VBA returns you to Excel.

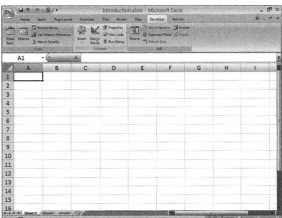

Extra

You can also use Microsoft Visual Studio Tools for the Microsoft Office System (Visual Studio) to develop programs for Microsoft Office products. With Visual Studio, you can write in languages such as Visual Basic .NET, Visual C#, and Managed Extensions for C++. Visual Studio is not part of Microsoft Office; you must purchase it. Microsoft supports both VBA and Visual Studio.

Visual Studio is more difficult to learn than VBA and setting up and using Visual Studio is much more difficult than setting up and using VBA. However, Visual Studio offers better security, a more sophisticated development environment, and built-in Web services.

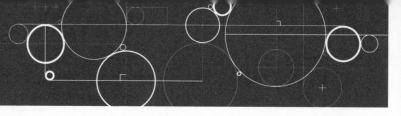

Introducing Macros

You can use macros to automate many of the tasks you perform in Excel. For example, if you frequently format your data in a particular way, you can use Excel's macro recorder to record the steps you use to format your data. You can then play back the recorded steps whenever you want to apply your format. Any series of commands you can execute in Excel, you can also record and play back.

The commands you use to create and execute macros are located on the Developer tab. By default, the Developer tab does not display in Excel. To display it, you must choose the Show Developer Tab in the Ribbon option in the Excel Options dialog box.

You begin recording macros by clicking Record Macro on the Developer tab or by clicking the Record Macro button on the status bar. Both commands open the Record Macro dialog box. For detailed instructions on how to use the

Record Macro dialog box, see the section, "Record a Macro."

When you record a macro, you can record it using an absolute reference or a relative reference. If you record using an *absolute reference*, when Excel plays back your macro, it plays back the exact cells you clicked when you recorded the macro. If you record using a *relative reference*, Excel plays back the relative location of the cells you used when you recorded your macro. Click the Use Relative References button on the Developer tab to record using a relative reference. To learn more about absolute and relative references, see the section, "Record a Macro."

When you save a workbook that has macros, you must save it as a macro-enabled workbook. Excel gives macro-enabled workbooks an .xlsm file extension.

Introducing Macros

SHOW THE DEVELOPER TAB

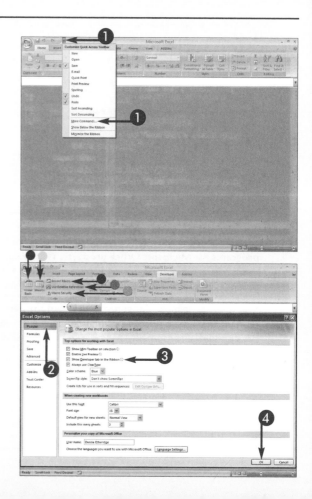

① Click Customize Quick Access Toolbar and then click More Commands.

The Excel Options dialog box appears.

② Click Popular.

③ Click Show Developer Tab in the Ribbon (☐ changes to ☑).

④ Click OK.

The Developer tab appears in the Ribbon.

● Click to record a macro.

● Click to record with a relative reference.

● Click to change macro security.

● Click to run macros.

● Click to open the Visual Basic Editor.

SAVE A WORKBOOK

① Click the Microsoft Office button.

A menu appears.

② Click Save As ➜ Excel Macro-Enabled Workbook.

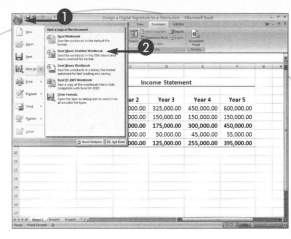

The Save As dialog box appears.

③ Click here and then select the folder in which you want to save your workbook.

④ Type the name you want to give your workbook.

⑤ Click Save.

Excel saves your workbook as a macro-enabled workbook.

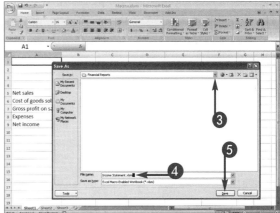

Extra

Because of problems with macro viruses, Excel disables all macros by default when you open a workbook. You can click the Macro Security button on the Developer tab to change the default setting. To learn more about macro security, see the sections, "Set Macro Security," "Create a Digital Signature," and "Assign a Digital Signature to a Macro."

If you have programming experience or aptitude, you can edit Excel macros by using the Visual Basic Editor, which is available by pressing the Visual Basic button on the Developer tab.

You can use the Macro dialog box to run a macro. To open the Macro dialog box, click the Macro button on the Developer tab, press Alt+F8, or place the View Macros button on the Quick Access toolbar.

To place the View Macros button on the Quick Access toolbar, click the Microsoft Office button, and then click Excel Options. The Excel Options dialog box appears. Click Customize. The Customize the Quick Access Toolbar pane appears. In the Choose Commands From field, choose Popular Commands and then click View Macros. Click the Add Button. Click OK. The View Macros button appears on the Quick Access toolbar.

Set Macro Security

Because of increasing problems with computer viruses, specifically macro viruses, the default Excel macro security setting disables all macros when you open a workbook, and allows you to decide on a case-by-case basis whether you want to enable them. This is true whether you created the macros or someone else created them.

You can change the Excel macro security setting. Excel provides four options:

- **Disable all macros without notification:** This option disables all macros and does not provide you with any security alerts to let you know macros exist.

- **Disable all macros with notification:** This is the default setting. It notifies you if macros are present so you can enable them on a case-by-case basis.

- **Disable all macros except digitally signed macros:** This option disables all macros except those digitally signed by a trusted publisher. If the

publisher has digitally signed the macro but you have not opted to trust the publisher, you can enable the macro or trust the publisher. See the "Extra" information in the section, "Run a Macro," to learn how to trust a publisher.

- **Enable all macros (not recommended; potentially dangerous code can run):** This option allows you to run all macros. Because potentially dangerous code can run, Microsoft does not recommend this option.

Changes you make to macro security in Excel do not change the macro security in other Office programs.

Macro creators use digital signatures to verify the safety of the macros they create. You can create your own digital signature by using the Microsoft Selfcert.exe tool, or you can obtain a digital certificate from a commercial certificate of authority vendor. For more information on the Microsoft Selfcert.exe tool, see the next section, "Create a Digital Signature."

Set Macro Security

① Click the Developer tab.

Note: *See the section, "Introducing Macros," to learn how to display the Developer tab.*

② Click Macro Security in the Code group.

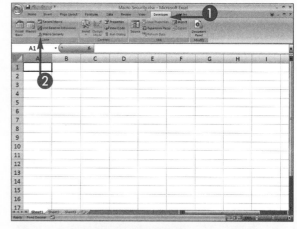

The Trust Center dialog box appears.

③ Click to select a macro setting (○ changes to ●).

④ Click OK.

Excel changes your macro security setting.

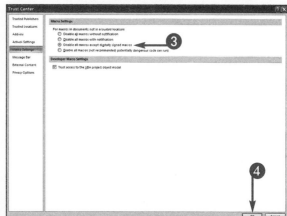

Create a
Digital Signature

I f you create a workbook that contains macros, you should consider using a digital signature. A digital signature provides assurance that the workbook file is valid and no one has altered it. You can create a personal digital signature by using the Microsoft Selfcert.exe tool. Projects signed with digital signatures created with the Selfcert.exe tool only work on computers that have the certificate in their Personal Certificates store.

Digital signatures that you create with the SelfCert.exe tool work well for personal workbooks; however, if you plan to distribute your workbook to users outside your workgroup, you should consider acquiring a commercial digital signature file. When you use a commercial digital signature file, the digital ID attaches to the macro and remains with it; if anyone alters the macro, Excel notifies the user that

someone has changed the macro and therefore the macro should not be trusted.

The most common provider of commercial digital certification is VeriSign, Inc. You can find out more about obtaining a commercial certification from VeriSign at www.verisign.com.

Extra

To view the certificates in your Personal Certificate store, open Internet Explorer. On the Internet Explorer menu, click Tools and then click Internet Options. The Internet Options dialog box appears. Click the Content tab. Click the Certificates button. The Certificates dialog box appears. Click the Personal tab. All of your personal certificates appear.

Create a Digital Signature

① Click Start.

② Click All Programs → Microsoft Office → Microsoft Office Tools → Digital Certificate for VBA Projects.

The Create Digital Certificate dialog box appears.

③ Type the name you want to give your certificate.

④ Click OK.

Excel creates a Personal Digital Certificate.

7

A macro enables you to automate common tasks. You can use a macro to record any series of commands you can execute in Excel. For example, if you frequently apply a certain format to your worksheet, you can record the steps for creating the format and then play them back each time you want to apply the format.

Clicking the Macro Recorder button opens the Record Macro dialog box in which you can name your macro, assign your macro to a shortcut key, and tell Excel where you want to store your macro. You can name your macro anything you want, with the following limitations: the name must start with a letter; it can only contain letters, numbers, and underscores; and it cannot contain any spaces. You can assign any uppercase or lowercase letter to act as the shortcut key.

In the Record Macro dialog box, the Store Macro In field tells Excel where to store your macro. You can choose to store your macro in the Personal Macro Workbook, a New Workbook, or This Workbook. Use the Personal Macro Workbook option if you want to make your macro available to all Excel files. After you have stored a least one macro in the Personal Macro Workbook, the workbook opens whenever you open an Excel file. Use the New Workbook option if you have specialized macros that you want to use with multiple files. If you store your macro in a new workbook, you can use the macros whenever that workbook is open. Use the This Workbook option if you want your macro to be in the workbook in which you are currently working.

Record a Macro

① Click the Developer tab.

Note: See the section, "Introducing Macros," to learn how to display the Developer tab.

● Alternatively, click the Record Macro button on the status bar and skip step 2.

② Click Record Macro in the Code group.

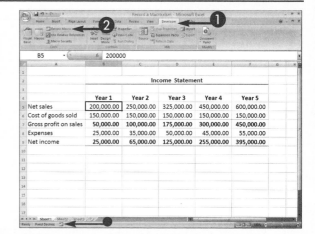

The Record Macro dialog box appears.

③ Type the name you want to give your macro.

④ Type the shortcut key you want to assign to your macro.

Press Shift as you type to assign an uppercase key.

⑤ Click here and then select the workbook in which you want to store your macro.

⑥ Type a description of your macro.

⑦ Click OK.

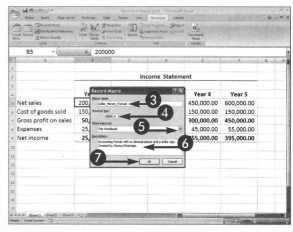

You are now ready to record your macro.

8 Perform the steps you want to record.

This example changes the number format.

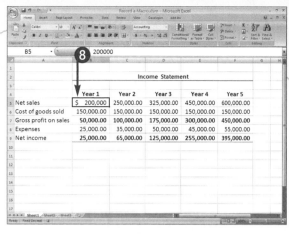

9 Click the Developer tab.

● Alternatively, click the Stop Recording button on the status bar and skip step 10.

10 Click Stop Recording in the Code group.

Excel stops recording your macro.

Your macro is ready for you to use.

Note: *See the section, "Run a Macro," to learn how to run a macro.*

Extra

A macro you create in Excel can have a relative, absolute, or mixed reference. If you use a relative reference, Excel performs the macro based on a relative location. For example, suppose you move up two cells from cell A3 to A1 when creating your macro. When you run your macro, if you are in cell C3, Excel moves up two cells from cell C3 to C1. However, if you use an absolute reference, Excel performs the macro based on the exact cell addresses. For example, suppose again that you move up two cells from cell A3 to A1. When you run your macro, if you are in cell C3, Excel moves from there to the cells you used when you recorded your macro. That is, Excel moves from cell A3 to cell A1.

By default, Excel creates macros with an absolute reference. To create a macro with a relative reference, click the Use Relative Reference button on the Developer tab to toggle the relative reference option on. To create a macro with both a relative and an absolute reference — a mixed reference — toggle the Use Relative Reference on and off as needed as you create your macro.

Assign a Digital Signature to a Macro

A digital signature provides assurance that a workbook file is valid and no one has altered it. There are two types of digital signatures: personal digital signatures and commercial digital signatures. You can create a personal digital signature by using the Microsoft Selfcert.exe tool, or you can purchase a digital signature. Refer to the section, "Create a Digital Signature," to learn how to create digital signatures.

After you create a digital signature, you must attach it to your workbook. Attaching a digital signature is similar to sealing an envelope. If an envelope arrives sealed, you have some level of assurance that no one has tampered with its contents.

Use the Digital Signature dialog box to attach a digital signature. The Visual Basic Editor is a separate Excel

module that you can use to edit your macro. You access the Digital Signature dialog box by opening the Visual Basic Editor. The Digital Signature dialog box lists valid certificates. You can use the Digital Signature dialog box to view certificates and to select the one you want to use.

Unless you have on your computer a valid digital signature certificate for the signature used to sign a macro, Excel removes the digital signature if you modify a macro in a workbook, and you must reattach it. If you are not sure if a workbook has a digital signature, you can check the signature by reviewing the Digital Signature dialog box. If a workbook has a digital signature, the name of the signature appears in the Certificate Name field. If you click the Remove button in the Digital Signature dialog box, Excel removes the digital signature.

Assign a Digital Signature to a Macro

① Click the Developer tab.

Note: *See the section, "Introducing Macros," to learn how to display the Developer tab.*

② Click Visual Basic in the Code group.

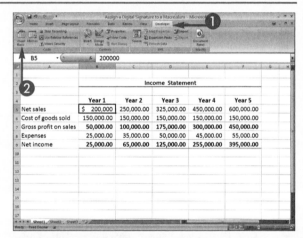

The Visual Basic Editor appears.

③ Click Tools → Digital Signature.

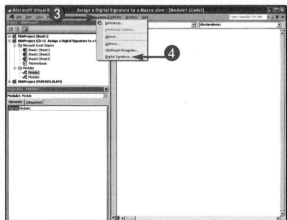

The Digital Signature dialog box appears.

④ Click Choose.

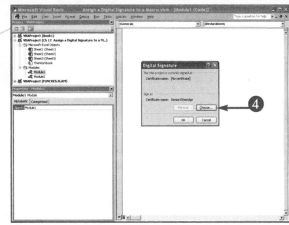

The Select Certificate dialog box appears.

Note: *See the section, "Create a Digital Signature," to learn how to create a digital signature.*

⑤ Click the signature you want to apply.

⑥ Click OK to close the Select Certificate dialog box.

⑦ Click OK to close the Digital Signature dialog box.

Excel attaches the digital signature to your workbook.

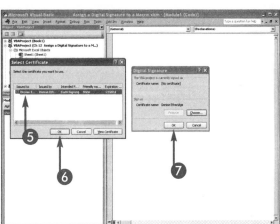

Extra

If you have macro security enabled, Excel displays a warning just below the Ribbon when you open a workbook containing a signed macro. You can click the Options button located next to the warning to open the Microsoft Office Security Options dialog box, where you can indicate that you trust the publisher. Excel then saves the name of the publisher in the Trusted Publishers section of the Trust Center.

If you click the Macro Security button on the Developer tab, the Trust Center dialog box appears. Click Trusted Publisher to display a list of your trusted publishers. If you no longer want to trust macros from a publisher listed on the Trusted Publishers page, click the name of the publisher and then click Remove. The next time you open a workbook with a macro from a removed publisher, Excel again warns you about its macros.

Unless you have your macro settings set to enable all macros, Excel checks all documents you open for macros. See the section, "Set Macro Security," for more information. If you have a file that you do not want Excel to check, you can store it in a trusted location. In the Trust Center dialog box, click Trusted Locations to define a trusted location.

Run a Macro

acros enable you to perform quickly tasks that would normally take multiple steps. When you run a macro, Excel replays the steps you recorded when you created the macro. You can run any macro located in any workbook as long as the workbook in which the macro is located is open. To run a macro, you can press the shortcut key you assigned when you created the macro or you can select the macro from the Macro dialog box.

When you create a macro, you can choose to store it in one of three locations: the current workbook, a new workbook, or the Personal Macro Workbook. By default, the Macro dialog box lists all of the macros in open workbooks. If a macro is stored in the Personal Macro Workbook, the workbook opens as a hidden file each

time you open a file. By default, the macros in the Personal Macro Workbook always appear in the Macro dialog box.

You can use the Macros In field to limit the number of macros listed in the Macro dialog box. To see the macros in any open workbook, including the Personal Macro Workbook, select the All Open Workbooks option. To see the macros from a specific workbook, select the name of the workbook from the Macros In drop-down list. To see global macros stored in the Personal Macro Workbook, select the Personal.xlsb option.

To run a macro from another workbook, the macro must be from a signed source or you must enable all macros. You can set the security setting for macros. See the section, "Set Macro Security," for more information.

Run a Macro

① Select the cells to which you want to apply your macro.

② Click the Developer tab.

Note: *See the section, "Introducing Macros," to learn how to display the Developer tab.*

③ Click Macros in the Code group.

Alternatively, click Alt+F8.

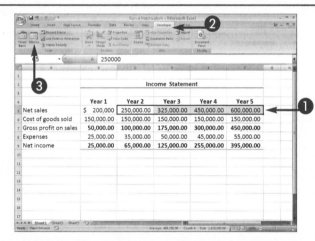

The Macro dialog box appears.

④ If your macro does not appear in the Macro dialog box, click here and then select the workbook that contains your macro.

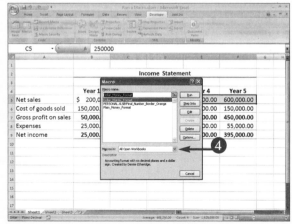

12

⑤ Click the name of the macro you want to run.

⑥ Click Run.

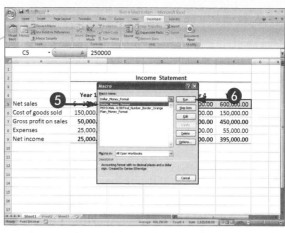

Excel runs the macro.

● In this example, the macro adds dollar signs and removes the decimal places.

You can also run your macro by pressing the shortcut key you assigned when you created your macro.

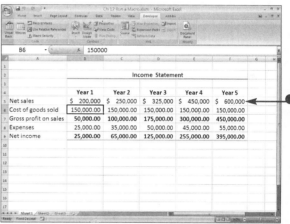

Extra

Excel differentiates between macros listed in the Macro dialog box by placing the name of the workbook that contains the macros in front of the macro name. For example, Excel lists a macro named Sum_Expenses in the Personal Macro Workbook as PERSONAL.XLSB!Sum_Expenses. If the macro Sum_Cells exists in both the Budget.xlsm and Expenses.xlsm workbooks, Excel treats them as two different macros. The Macro dialog box lists them as Budget.xlsm!Sum_Cells and Expenses.xlsm!Sum_Cells.

If you have macro security enabled, the Trust Center checks the macros when you open a workbook to see if the macros are valid. If there are any problems, Excel displays a warning just below the Ribbon. You can click the Options button located next to the warning to open the Microsoft Office Security Options dialog box.

In the Microsoft Office Security Options dialog box, click Help Protect Me from Unknown Content (Recommended) to disable the macros, click Enable the Content to enable the macros, or click Trust All Documents from this Publisher to add the macro publisher to the Trusted Publisher list. Excel does not display a warning when you open workbooks with macros if the publisher is on the Trusted Publisher list.

Create and Launch a Keyboard Shortcut

A keyboard shortcut is a combination of keys you press to execute a command. You can use a keyboard shortcut to launch an Excel macro command. You can assign an uppercase or lowercase key to a macro when you create it, or assign one later by using the Macro Options dialog box. You execute a macro keyboard shortcut by pressing the Ctrl key along with that uppercase or lowercase key. Refer to the section, "Record a Macro," to learn how to create a macro.

Keyboard shortcuts are case sensitive. For example, Excel interprets a lowercase *m* and an uppercase *M* as two different keys. To execute a macro you have assigned to a lowercase letter, press Ctrl plus the letter, such as Ctrl+m. To execute a macro you have assigned to an uppercase letter, press Ctrl and Shift plus the letter, such as Ctrl+Shift+M.

If you assign the same keyboard shortcut to macros in two different workbooks, you may execute the wrong macro if you use the shortcut while you have both workbooks open. Excel cannot discern from which workbook you want the macro. You can use the Macro Options dialog box to reassign one of the conflicting macros to a new key.

You should also be careful not to assign the macro to a keyboard shortcut that Excel uses. If you do, Excel executes your macro instead of the command it created. For example, by default, Ctrl+o opens the Open dialog box. If you assign *o* to a macro, your macro overrides Excel's assignment.

Create and Launch a Keyboard Shortcut

CREATE A KEYBOARD SHORTCUT

1 Click the Developer tab.

2 Click Macros in the Code group.

The Macro dialog box appears.

3 Click the desired macro.

4 Click Options.

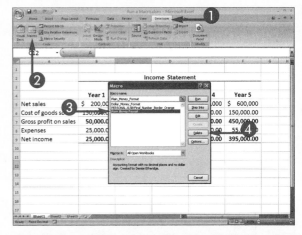

The Macro Options dialog box appears.

5 Type the desired shortcut key.

Press Shift as you type to assign an uppercase key.

6 Type a description.

7 Click OK.

8 Click Close to close the Macro dialog box.

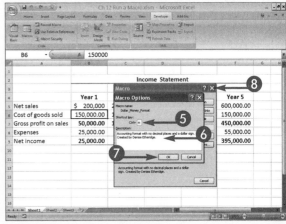

LAUNCH WITH A KEYBOARD SHORTCUT

1️⃣ Select the cells in which you want the macro to execute.

2️⃣ Press Ctrl and the shortcut key.

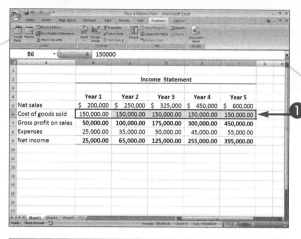

● The macro executes.

3️⃣ Repeat steps 1 and 2 to execute the macro again.

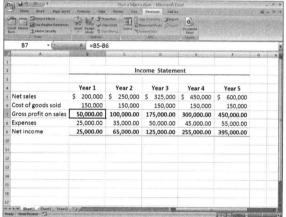

Extra

If you do not use a macro shortcut frequently, it is easy to forget the keyboard shortcut you assigned to your macro. If you forget your keyboard shortcut, you can view it in the Macro Options dialog box.

You can execute a macro by assigning the macro to a picture, clip art, shape, or SmartArt. For example, if you want to assign a macro to a picture, you start by inserting the picture into your worksheet by clicking the Insert tab and then clicking Picture. The Insert Picture dialog box appears. In the Look In field, select the folder in which you stored the picture you want to insert. The pictures in that folder appear. Click the picture you want to insert and then click the Insert button. The picture appears in the worksheet. Click and drag the picture to place it where you want it and then double right-click the picture. A menu appears. Click Assign Macro. The Assign Macro dialog box appears. Click the macro you want to assign to the picture and then click OK. Excel assigns the macro to the picture. Click the picture when you want to execute the macro.

Assign a Macro to the Quick Access Toolbar

You can assign a macro to the Excel Quick Access toolbar. You can execute macros assigned to the Quick Access toolbar using a shortcut key or the Macro dialog box; however, using the Quick Access toolbar means you can access the macros by clicking the appropriate button.

When you add a button to the Quick Access toolbar, you can specify whether it should appear on the toolbar of all Excel workbooks or only on the Quick Access toolbar in the workbook you specify. By default, the button appears in all workbooks. If you have placed your macro in the Personal Macro Workbook, you will probably want your macro button to appear in all workbooks. If your macro is only available to a single workbook, your macro button should only appear on the Quick Access toolbar for that workbook.

You can use the Customize the Quick Access Toolbar pane of the Excel Options dialog box to add a macro button to the Quick Access toolbar. The Customize the Quick Access Toolbar pane has a number of options you can set. You can use the Modify button to specify the button you want to use to represent your macro. You can specify where on the Quick Access toolbar your button appears and whether the Quick Access toolbar appears above or below the Ribbon. You can click the Reset button to return the Quick Access toolbar to its default state.

Deleting a macro does not remove the macro button from the Quick Access toolbar. You use the Remove button on the Customize the Quick Access Toolbar pane of the Excel Options dialog box to remove a macro button.

Assign a Macro to the Quick Access Toolbar

① Click Customize Quick Access Toolbar and then click More Commands.

The Excel Options dialog box appears.

② Click here and then click Macros.

③ Click here and then click the workbook in which the button should appear.

④ Click the macro you want to assign to the Quick Access toolbar.

⑤ Click Add.

● The macro appears in the box on the right. Macros display on the Quick Access toolbar in the order shown here.

● Click to move the macro up.

● Click to move the macro down.

⑥ Click Modify.

● Click if you want the Quick Access toolbar to appear below the Ribbon (☐ changes to ☑).

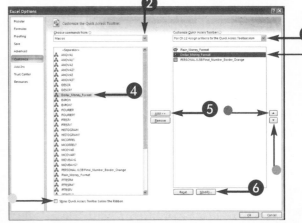

The Modify Button dialog box appears.

7 Click the button you want to use to represent your macro.

8 Click OK to close the Modify Button dialog box.

9 Click OK to close the Excel Options dialog box.

● Click to return the Quick Access toolbar to its default state.

● Click the macro and then click the Remove button to remove a macro.

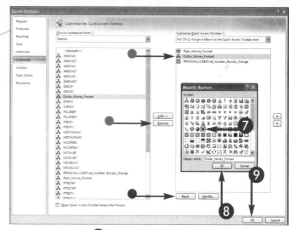

The button appears on the Quick Access toolbar.

10 Click the button to execute your macro.

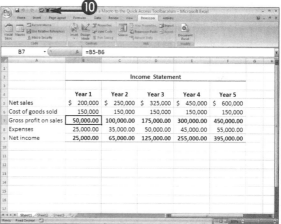

Extra

You can add commands you frequently use to the Quick Access toolbar. Click the Microsoft Office button. A menu appears. Click the Excel Options button located in the bottom-right corner. The Excel Options dialog box appears. Click Customize. The Customize the Quick Access Toolbar page appears. Click the down arrow next to the Choose Commands From field and select All Commands. Click the command you want to add to the Quick Access toolbar and then click the Add button. Click OK. Excel returns you to your workbook, and the command you chose appears on the Quick Access toolbar.

You can add commands you cannot find in the Ribbon by choosing Commands Not in Ribbon in the Choose Commands From field. If a command from a previous version of Excel is not in the Ribbon, you may find it listed under Commands Not in the Ribbon. For example, in previous versions you could format your documents quickly by using AutoFormat. Excel 2007 uses styles, but you can still access AutoFormat through the Commands Not in Ribbon feature.

Delete a Macro

You can delete macros you no longer need by clicking the Delete button in the Macro dialog box. Because the Macro dialog box only displays macros in open workbooks, the workbook that contains the macro must be open before you can delete it.

The Personal Macro Workbook stores macros you want to make available to all workbooks. Excel creates the Personal Macro Workbook when you choose to store your first macro in it. After Excel creates the Personal Macro Workbook, the workbook opens as a hidden file every time you open Excel. To learn more about storing macros in the Personal Macro Workbook, see the section, "Record a Macro."

If your macro is in a hidden workbook such as the Personal Macro Workbook, you must unhide the workbook before you can delete the macro. If you try to

delete a macro from the Personal Macro Workbook prior to unhiding it, Excel displays the following message: "Cannot edit a macro on a hidden workbook, Unhide the workbook using the Unhide command." You can unhide the Personal Macro Workbook and other hidden workbooks by executing the Unhide command on the View tab.

If you unhide the Personal Macro Workbook, make sure you hide it again using the Hide command on the View tab after you delete the macros. Hiding the workbook prevents you from making inadvertent changes to it.

You cannot undo the deletion process, but if you delete a macro by mistake, you can close the workbook without saving. Of course, if you close without saving, you will lose all of the work you have done since saving. Your only other alternative is to re-create the macro.

Delete a Macro

UNHIDE A WORKBOOK

① Click the View tab.

② Click Unhide in the Window group.

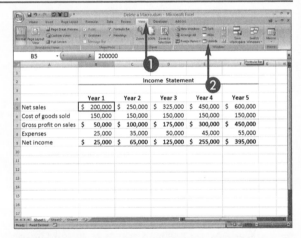

The Unhide dialog box appears.

③ Click the workbook you want to unhide.

④ Click OK.

Excel unhides the workbook.

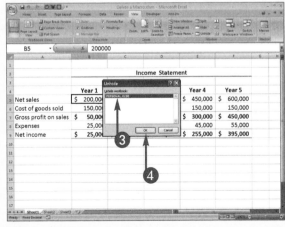

DELETE A MACRO

1 Click the Developer tab.

2 Click Macros in the Code group.

The Macro dialog box appears.

3 Click the macro you want to delete.

4 Click Delete.

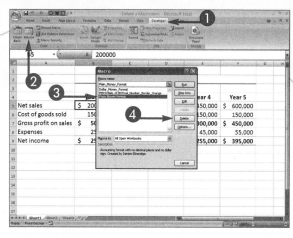

A message box appears, asking you to confirm that you want to delete the macro.

5 Click Yes.

Excel deletes the macro.

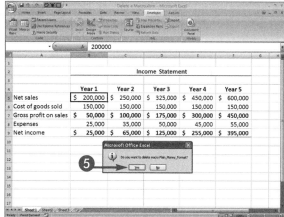

Extra

Typically, you do not share the Personal Macro Workbook with other users. Excel creates a different Personal Macro Workbook for each username on a computer. If you have multiple users on your computer with different usernames, Excel creates a different Personal Macro Workbook for each of them. You can copy a Personal Macro Workbook from one user to another. The Personal Macro Workbook is stored in the XLStart folder and is named PERSONAL.XLSB. In Windows XP, you can usually find the XLStart folder by following this path: C:\Documents and Settings*username*\ Application Data\Microsoft\Excel\XLStart. In Windows Vista, you can usually find the XLStart folder by following this path: C:\Users*username*\ Application Data\Microsoft\Excel\XLStart.

Each user can only have one PERSONAL.XLSB file. If a user already has a Personal Macro Workbook, you should rename the old PERSONAL.XLSB file and place the new PERSONAL.XLSB file in the user's XLStart folder. All files stored in the XLStart folder open when you open Excel, and so both files become available each time the user opens Excel. If you have other files you want to open when you open Excel, place them in the XLStart folder.

Add a Form Control to a Worksheet

Y ou can add controls to a worksheet to make it easier to enter data into a cell. Form controls can help users who are not familiar with Excel and can increase the accuracy of data entry by limiting a user's options. For example, you can add check boxes to your worksheet so it looks like a paper form. You can also add a list box from which users can select an entry.

Excel provides nine controls you can add to a worksheet. You add controls by selecting the control you want from the Forms Control menu. After you add a control, you can adjust its size by dragging the side or corner handles. When you add a control or right-click a control to edit, you are in design mode. In design mode, you can modify the properties and size of the control, but you cannot test its functionality.

When you place a control on a worksheet, it sits on top of the worksheet. You can size it so it appears to be located in a cell, but controls are separate from cells and you can place them anywhere on the worksheet. A control can cover any portion of a cell or range of cells.

After you add controls to a worksheet, you can assign them values. See the section, "Assign Values to a Form Control," for more information on assigning control values. Form control options are located on the Developer tab. See the section, "Introducing Macros," to learn how to display the Developer tab.

Add a Form Control to a Worksheet

➊ Click the Developer tab.

Note: *See the section, "Introducing Macros," to learn how to display the Developer tab.*

➋ Click Insert in the Controls group.

The Forms Control menu appears.

➌ Click to select the control you want to add.

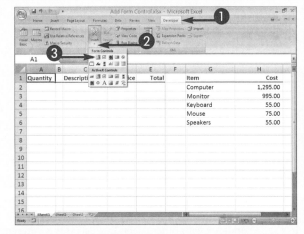

➍ Drag the cursor to create the control.

➎ Drag the handles on the sides and corners to adjust the size.

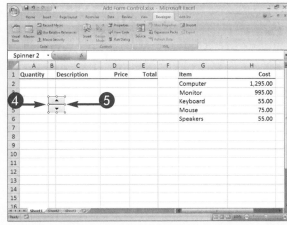

6 Place your pointer on the border of a control and drag the control to change its location.

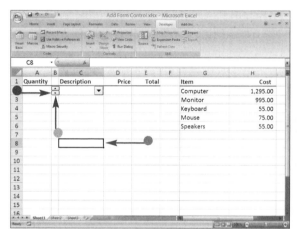

The control appears on the worksheet.

● Right-click the control to place it in design mode.

● To cancel design mode, click any cell in the worksheet.

● To remove a control, right-click the control to select it and then press Delete.

Extra

You can add the controls listed in the following table to your worksheets.

CONTROL	CONTROL NAME	DESCRIPTION
	Button	Runs an associated macro when the user clicks it.
	Combo box	Displays a list of items as a menu.
	Check box	Selects or deselects an option.
	Spinner	Scrolls up and down through a list of numeric values.
	List box	Displays a list of items for selection.
	Radio button	Selects one of a group of items when the user clicks it.
	Group box	Places related controls together.
	Label	Provides information about an associated control.
	Scroll bar	Increases or decreases a value when the user clicks the arrows or drags the bar.

Assign Values to a Form Control

After you add a control to a form, you can assign it the values you want associated with the control. For example, if your worksheet contains a list box, you can assign the list of values that you want to appear when users access the list box. Some controls enable you to define a range of valid numeric values for the control. For example, if you use a spinner, you define the starting value and the maximum value for the control. For combo boxes and list boxes, you can place the options associated with the control in a range of cells. For example, if you use a combo box, you tell Excel the list of values used by the control by entering the range of cells containing the values. The values can be located on another worksheet or even in another workbook, as long as Excel can access the workbook when users view the worksheet that contains the control.

You can link a cell to a control. If you link a cell to a control, the value associated with a user selection becomes the value of the linked cell. If you use a combo box control or list box control, the value in the linked cell is a number that represents the user's selection. Excel assigns the number based on the position of the selected value in your list. If the list contains the values Computer, Monitor, and Keyboard, and the user selects Monitor, the linked cell receives the value 2, because Monitor is second in the list.

With a control such as a check box, you can tell Excel whether you want the option to be initially selected or unselected. Each option — selected or unselected — has a value associated with it.

Assign Values to a Form Control

① Right-click the selected control.

A menu appears.

② Click Format Control.

The Format Object dialog box appears.

③ Click the Control tab.

The available fields are different, depending on the control type.

This example uses a list box.

④ Drag to select a range, or type the range that lists the valid values.

⑤ Click a cell to assign a linked cell.

The value associated with your selection appears in the linked cell.

⑥ Type the number of values in your list.

⑦ Click OK.

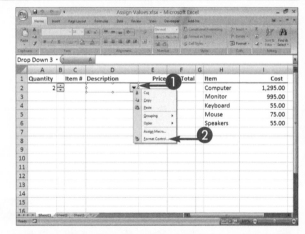

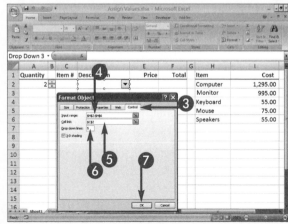

⑧ Select the desired control value.

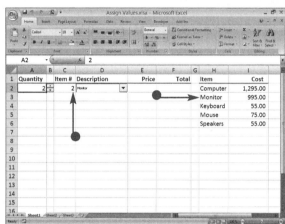

● Excel places a numeric value representing the control selection in the linked cell.

Apply It

When working with a value selected from a list box or combo box control, you may want to use that selection to set the value of another cell. For example, assume you have the following Excel list in cells H2:I4.

Example:
```
Computer      $1295
Monitor       $995
Keyboard      $55
```

You can use the Index function to determine the price, based on the equipment selection. For example, if the user selects Monitor from the control, Excel places a value of 2 in the linked cell. If you want users to find the cost of the selection, you type a formula similar to the following, assuming that C2 is the linked cell:

Example:
```
=INDEX($H$2:$I$4, C2, 2)
```

The Index function actually creates an array of the Excel list and uses the control selection to determine which element in the array to return, in this case the price, The function uses three arguments: Array, Row_num, and Column_num.

Add a Macro to a Form Control

You can assign a macro to any form control on a worksheet. For example, if a user clicks a radio button control, you can have Excel add a postage amount to an invoice.

You can create one macro for each control on a worksheet. You create a macro either by recording a series of keystrokes or by writing a VBA procedure in the Visual Basic Editor. When you select the Assign Macro menu option, Excel automatically creates a new macro with the name of the control followed by an underscore and an event name, such as _Click. Excel assigns the control name to the control when you add it to your worksheet. For example, the first OptionButton control you add to a worksheet is named OptionButton1. If you

create a macro for the option button, Excel gives the macro the name OptionButton1_Click.

The portion of the macro name following the underscore character corresponds to an action, commonly referred to as an *event*. For example, with an OptionButton control, the user clicks the radio button to select the option, and so the event is Click. If you create a macro for a combo box control, Excel assigns Change to the name of the event because you want to execute the macro when the value of the control changes. The event extension tells Excel to monitor the control and execute the macro whenever a user clicks the control.

No matter which option you select — recording or writing VBA — Excel assigns the same name to the macro.

Add a Macro to a Form Control

1 Right-click your control.

A menu appears.

2 Click Assign Macro.

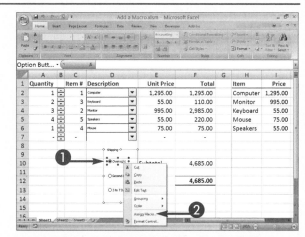

The Assign Macro dialog box appears.

Excel assigns a default macro name for the selected control.

3 Click Record and then record your macro.

Note: See the section, "Record a Macro," for more information.

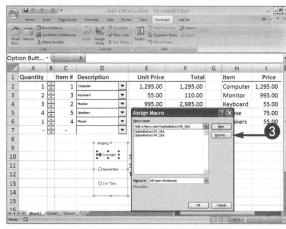

24

④ Click the control with the assigned macro.

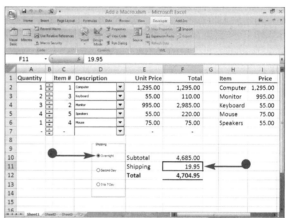

Excel executes the associated macro.

● In this example, Excel assigns postage to the invoice.

Extra

The macros you assign to a control only execute when the corresponding event occurs for the control. For example, you may have a macro assigned to a control that computes the total amount to be paid when the user clicks the control. If you change the values needed to compute the total amount after a user clicks the control, Excel does not update the total until the user clicks the control again.

If you no longer want a macro to be assigned to a control, right-click the control and then click the Assign Macro option. In the Assign Macro dialog box, clear the macro name from the Macro Name field and then click OK. Excel removes the macro assignment from the control, but the macro remains as part of the workbook. To remove the macro from the workbook, click the View tab and then click Macros in the Macros group to display the Macro dialog box. Select the macro you want to delete and then click Delete.

View of the Visual Basic Editor

Ⓐ Project Explorer

The Project Explorer lists all projects. The VBE considers each open workbook and each add-in a project. Microsoft Office arranges projects in the Project Explorer in a tree-like structure. Click plus (+) to show more information. Click minus (−) to show less information. To display the Project Explorer, click View → Project Explorer.

Ⓑ Code Window

Use the Code window to write, edit, and display VBA code. Every VBA object has a Code window that stores the code associated with the object. In the Project Explorer, double-click an object's name to see the associated code. To display the Code window, click View → Code.

Ⓒ Object List Box

The Object List box lists the objects associated with a form.

Ⓓ Procedure List Box

The Procedure List box lists the procedures associated with the selected object.

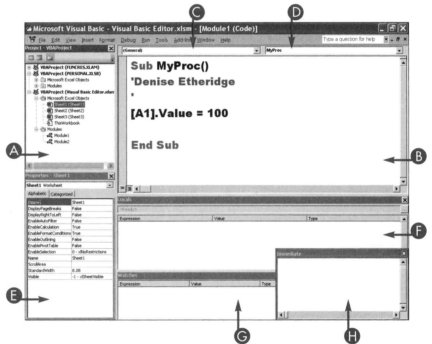

Ⓔ Properties Window

To select an object, click the object name in Project Explorer. To display the Properties window, click View → Properties Window. Use the Properties window to set the properties associated with the selected object.

Ⓕ Locals Window

Use the Locals window to monitor declared variables. To open the Locals window, click View → Locals Window.

Ⓖ Watches Window

Use the Watches window to monitor properties and variables. To display the Watches window, click View → Watch Window.

Ⓗ Immediate Window

The Immediate window returns the results of statements you type into the Immediate window. To display the Immediate window, click View → Immediate Window.

The Visual Basic Editor

Excel provides two ways to create a macro: You can record a macro or you can type Visual Basic for Applications (VBA) code into the Visual Basic Editor (VBE). The VBE is a separate application you use to write and edit VBA code. You can access the VBE through all Microsoft Office applications, including Excel.

You access the VBE by clicking the Visual Basic button on the Developer tab in the Code group, or by pressing Alt+F11. Inside the VBE, you can reposition windows to create the development environment you prefer. You can use the View menu to tell Excel which windows and toolbars you want visible.

Modules

VBA executes procedures in response to a system action or an action performed by a user. A module is a set of procedures that Excel can execute. The VBE stores each macro you create or record as a procedure in a module. The Project Explorer lists each module a project contains. You can add modules by using the steps outlined later in this chapter. When you double-click a module name in the Project Explorer, the contents of the module appear in the Code window. Use the Procedure List box to select the procedure you want to view.

The Project Explorer Window

The Project Explorer resembles the treelike structure used by the Windows Explorer folders pane. When you open the VBE, the VBE opens a VBA project for each open Excel workbook. The VBE names each project VBAProject (*workbook name*). Under the project name, the VBE lists the workbook and each worksheet in the workbook.

When you record a macro, you can choose to store it in the Personal Macro Workbook. Once you have stored a macro in the Personal Macro Workbook, the Personal Macro Workbook opens as a hidden file whenever you run Excel. If the Personal Macro Workbook is open, you can see it listed as a project in the Project Explorer window.

Properties Window

You use VBA code to manipulate objects. Workbooks and worksheets are examples of objects. A property is an attribute of an object. VBA uses attributes to define such things as the name, color, location, or size of an object. The Properties window displays the properties associated with the selected object. To select an object, you click the object name in the Project Explorer window. A module has only one property: its name. Hence, if you select a module, the only property that you see in the Properties window is the module name. Sheets have many properties, and if you select a sheet, you can view and modify the many sheet properties.

To change the properties associated with an object, you simply click the field beside the property and make the desired changes. Some property fields, such as Name, require you to type a value. Other fields have drop-down lists from which you can select the appropriate value. Some properties are read-only. You cannot change read-only properties.

Activate the
Visual Basic Editor

There are two ways to create a macro. One way is to use the macro recorder to record the steps needed to perform the action. The other way is to create the steps by typing the VBA code into the Code window of the VBE. When you use the macro recorder, Excel automatically creates the VBA code for you. You can use the VBE to edit macros you have created with the macro recorder. Often, it is convenient to use a combination of the two methods to create your VBA code: You record part of the VBA code and then you use the VBE to augment or modify your code.

You can use several methods to activate the VBE: You can press Alt+F11 while in Excel; click the Visual Basic button in the Code group on the Developer tab; or click

the Edit button in the Macro dialog box. When the VBE is open, you can open the Code window by pressing Ctrl+R.

If you create your macros using the macro recorder, Excel defines each macro you create as a procedure and stores each procedure in a module. The VBE lists modules in the Project Explorer under the workbook in which they are located.

If the Personal Macro Workbook, Personal.xlsm, contains macros, the project for the Personal.xlsm workbook opens when you access the VBE. You can view and modify all of the macros in the Personal Macro Workbook. See Chapter 1 to learn more about the Personal Macro Workbook.

Activate the Visual Basic Editor

OPEN THE VBE BY USING THE RIBBON

1 Click the Developer tab.

Note: *See Chapter 1 to learn how to display the Developer tab.*

2 Click Visual Basic in the Code group.

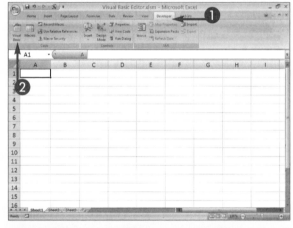

The VBE appears, with the Window layout you last used.

3 Double-click a module name.

Excel shows the macro in the Code window.

● If you placed more than one macro in the module, you can click here and then select the macro you want to see.

Press Alt+F11 to return to Excel.

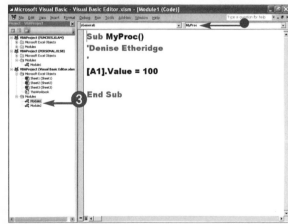

OPEN THE VBE FROM THE MACRO DIALOG BOX

1 Click the Developer tab.

2 Click Macros in the Code group.

The Macro dialog box appears.

3 Click the macro you want to edit.

4 Click Edit.

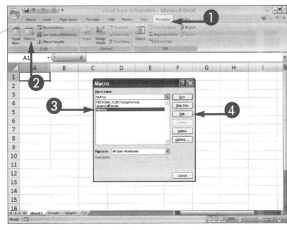

The VBE appears, with the code for the selected macro in the Code window.

Extra

To make the VBE easier to navigate, Microsoft provides shortcut keys. These shortcuts work when the VBE window is open.

SHORTCUT KEY	DESCRIPTION
F1	When you select an item in the Code window and then press F1, the VBE displays online help for the item you selected.
F4	Press F4 to switch to the Property window and display the properties for the selected object. If the Property window is not open, the VBE opens it in the location where you last viewed it.
F7	You select an object by clicking it in the Project Explorer. When you press F7, the Code window for the selected object appears on top of all other Code windows.
Ctrl+G	When you press Ctrl+G, the VBE displays the Immediate window.
Ctrl+R	When you press Ctrl+R, you switch to the Project Explorer. If the Project Explorer window is not open, the VBE opens it in the location where you last viewed it.
Alt+F11	When you press Alt+F11, you toggle between the VBE and Excel.

Open Visual Basic Editor Windows

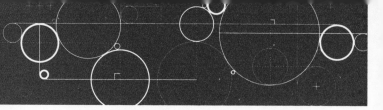

The VBE contains several windows you can use when developing macros. Microsoft provides a basic window setup; however, you can rearrange, resize, remove, and add windows. The most commonly used windows are the Project Explorer, the Properties window, and the Code window. You may also find the Immediate window useful for quickly testing a statement before adding it to your code.

You can select which windows to display and where to display them. The View menu lists the available VBE windows. When you select a window from the menu, that window appears in the location where you last placed it. For example, if you placed the Project Explorer window in the upper-left corner during your previous session, the Project Explorer window reopens in the upper-left corner.

You can move windows by using the standard drag-and-drop feature found in all Windows applications. You can resize a window by dragging its edges.

You can also attach windows to specific locations in the VBE by using the docking feature. When you dock a window, it becomes part of another window attached at the specified location. If you set a window to dock, Excel docks it in the location you specified each time it opens. You can only dock windows on the top, bottom, left edge, or right edge of the screen, application window, or another dockable window. Docking a window does not mean that the window always appears in the VBE.

You can have multiple Code windows open at the same time. You can view multiple Code windows simultaneously by tiling or cascading them.

Understanding the Visual Basic Editor Windows

DISPLAY A WINDOW

1 Click View.

2 Click the window you want to display.

You can choose from the Immediate Window, Locals Window, Watch Window, Project Explorer, or Properties Window.

The selected window appears in the last viewed location.

You can click and drag the window to a new location.

You can close a window by clicking the Close box or by right-clicking and selecting Hide.

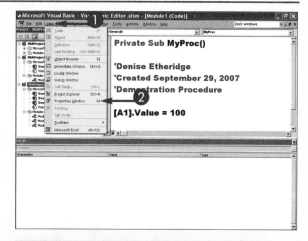

DOCK INDIVIDUAL WINDOWS

1 Click Tools → Options.

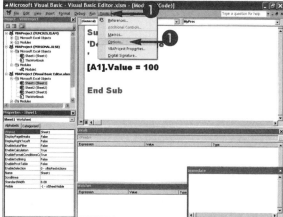

The Options dialog box appears.

2 Click the Docking tab.

3 Click the windows you want to dock (☐ changes to ☑).

4 Click OK.

5 Dock the window by clicking and dragging it to an edge.

Excel moves the window to its new location.

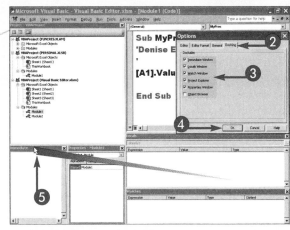

DISPLAY CODE WINDOWS

1 Click Window and then click a tiling option.

You can select Tile Horizontally, Tile Vertically, or Cascade.

The VBE displays your Code windows either tiled or cascading.

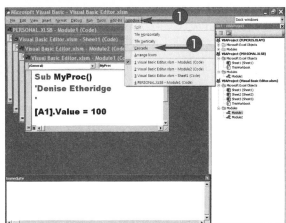

Extra

You can move windows around in the VBE by using the same techniques you use with all Microsoft Windows programs. To move a window, click the title bar and drag it to the desired location. To resize a window, click a corner of the window and drag it to the desired size.

To free up space, you can hide any of the VBE windows. To hide a window, right-click anywhere in the window. In the menu that appears, click Hide.

When you have many lines of code, you may not be able to see all of it at the same time. If you click Window → Split, the VBE splits the Code window so you can view different parts of your code simultaneously. When you split your window, the VBE creates two windows with the same code. You can manipulate each window independent of the other so you can see different parts of your code at the same time.

Set Properties for a Project

You can set the properties, such as the project name and the lock status, for each project you can view in the Project Explorer window. When you lock a project, the project is password-protected so that only people who know the password can view and modify the contents of the project. You can set both the project name and the password in the Project Properties dialog box.

Excel considers each open workbook to be a project when you access the VBE. By default, the VBE gives each project the name VBA Project (*WorkbookName*). You can change the name of a project. Changing the project's name can help distinguish between projects, especially if you have several workbooks open simultaneously. For example, if you have a workbook that contains macros

that perform a specific type of action, you can give your project a name that makes its purpose readily apparent.

If you plan to distribute your workbook to other users, you may want to consider password-protecting your project. If a project is password-protected, the user must enter the password to view or modify any portion of the project. This step can protect VBA code that you do not want others to view or modify. Password-protecting the project does not lock the corresponding Excel workbook, but it can help keep others from viewing and changing your VBA code. Password-protection does not make your code completely secure; there are password recovery utilities on the market that anyone can use to recover your password.

Set Properties for a Project

CHANGE A PROJECT NAME

① Click the project name you want to change.

② Click Tools → *Project Name* Properties.

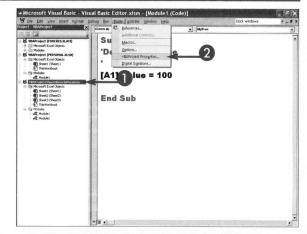

The *Project Name* Properties dialog box appears.

③ Click the General tab.

④ Type the desired project name.

⑤ Click OK.

The project name changes within the Project Explorer window.

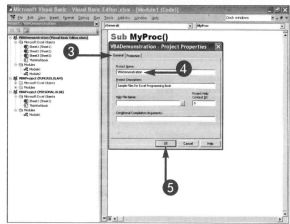

LOCK A PROJECT FROM EDITING

⑥ Click the Protection tab.

⑦ Click the Lock Project for Viewing option
(☐ changes to ☑).

⑧ Type the password required to unlock the
project.

⑨ Type the password again.

⑩ Click OK.

Excel locks your project.

The next time you open the workbook, you
will not be able to view the code unless
you know the password.

OPEN A LOCKED PROJECT

① Save and close your workbook.

② Open your workbook.

③ Press Alt+F11 to open the VBE.

④ Double-click the locked project.

The Password dialog box appears.

⑤ Type the password.

⑥ Click OK.

Excel opens your project.

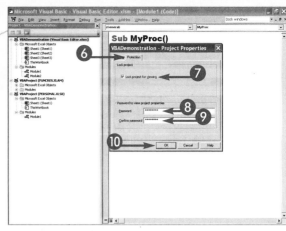

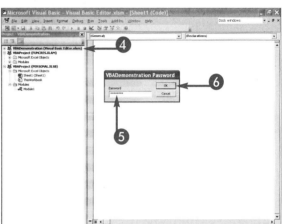

Extra

You can create forms to enable users to interact with macros. If you have multiple workbooks open in Excel,
you can copy modules and forms by using the Project Explorer window. To copy an object, click the object
and drag it to another project. When you release the mouse button, the VBE creates a copy of the selected
module or form in the specified project. By default, the VBE gives the copied module the same name as
the module in the original project. When you copy an object to another project, if one already exists with that
name, the VBE renames the object by adding a number to the end of the name. For example, if you copy
Module2 to a project that already contains a Module2, the copied module name becomes Module21. If you
have a Module21, the VBE names the copied object Module22.

Set Display Options for the Code Window

As you develop your VBA code, you will spend a lot of time interacting with the Code window. You can use the Editor Format tab in the Options dialog box to adjust many aspects of the Code window. These adjustments can make it easier for you to create and debug your VBA code.

You can enter many different categories of text into the Code window. For example, you can use comments to annotate your code. By using the Format Editor, you can adjust the foreground, background, and indicator color for each type of text listed in the Color Text list. When you use colors, it is easier for you to locate a particular type of text when you are creating or debugging your code.

You can use the Font field to select from the fonts installed on your computer. When working with VBA

code, you may find code easier to read if you use a fixed-width font such as Courier New. With a fixed-width font, the characters in the code align vertically, making it easier to detect any spacing problems in your code. Use the Size field to set the size of your font.

The Margin Indicator Bar check box indicates whether a vertical indicator bar appears in the margin when you debug your code. Make sure this option remains selected so you can use the vertical indicator bar to spot the appropriate line of code when you are debugging. The VBE places symbols in the vertical indicator bar to indicate errors and break points. See Chapter 8 for more information on debugging.

As you make changes to the font settings for each of the formatting types, Excel shows you a sample of the changes in the Sample box.

Set Display Options for the Code Window

① Click Tools → Options.

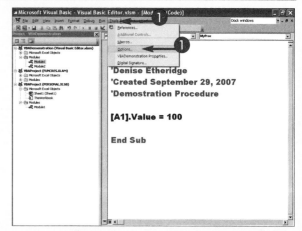

The Options dialog box appears.

② Click the Editor Format tab.

③ Click the type of text for which you want to change the settings.

④ Click here and select a foreground color.

⑤ Click here and select a background color.

⑥ Click here and select an indicator color.

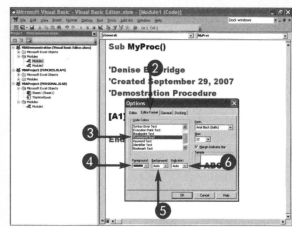

Excel sets the foreground, background, and indicator colors for the category you selected.

● The selection appears in the Sample box.

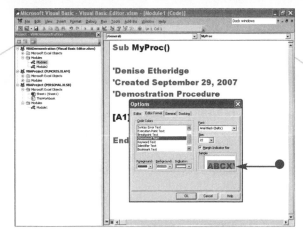

⑦ Click here and select a font.

⑧ Click here and select a font size.

⑨ Make sure the Margin Indicator Bar check box remains selected.

⑩ Click OK.

● The text in the Code window changes to reflect your modifications.

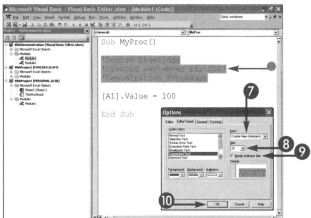

Extra

You can use the Editor tab in the Options dialog box to set the options shown in the table that follows. Click Tools and then click Options to access the Options dialog box.

OPTION	FUNCTION
Auto Syntax Check	Allows the VBE to check the syntax of each line of code immediately after you type it.
Require Variable Declaration	Requires explicit variable declarations within all modules. See Chapter 3 for more information.
Auto List Member	As you type your code, you see a reminder of the next logical value for completing the current statement.
Auto Quick Info	Displays information about functions and their parameters as you type.
Auto Data Tips	Displays the current value of a variable when you place your cursor over the variable while in break mode. See Chapter 8 for more information about debugging your VBA code.
Auto Indent	After you set a tab location, all following lines start at the same tab location. You specify the width of the tabs in the Tab Width field. You can set tabs from 1 to 32 spaces apart.

Add a New Module

When you begin writing code, you will use variables to store information. A *string* is a sequence of characters that does not represent a numeric value. A string can consist of letters, numbers, spaces, and punctuation marks. A variable can hold a number, a string, or some other type of information. When you tell VBA exactly what type of information a variable can contain, you are declaring the variable. A *procedure* is a sequence of code that, when executed, performs an action in Excel. When you record a macro, VBA stores it as a procedure. VBA uses modules to store variable declarations and procedures. Whenever you create a new macro by using the macro recorder, VBA places the procedure in a module and associates the module with the project. The VBE considers every open workbook a project.

When you type VBA code into the VBE, you place it in a module. You can create a module to store your VBA code. As you add new modules to a project, VBA names them Module#. The VBE assigns numbers to the modules, increasing the number by one each time you add a new module. For example, the VBE names the first module in the project Module1, the second Module2, and so on.

The Project Explorer lists all of the modules in a project. When you add a new module, Excel selects that module in the Project Explorer and creates a blank Code window.

You do not have to create a new module for each procedure you add to a workbook. You can add multiple procedures to the same module.

Add a New Module

① Click the project to which you want to add a new module.

② Click Insert → Module.

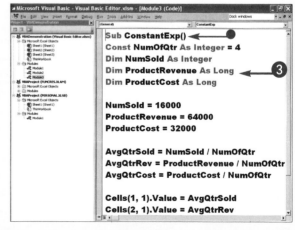

Excel creates a new module and opens the associated Code window.

③ Type the code for your macro.

● This is the macro name.

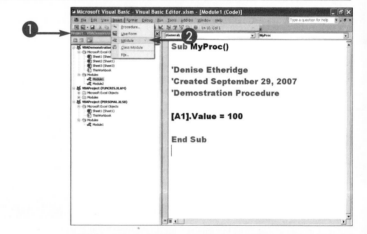

④ Press Alt+F11 to move from the VBE to Excel.

⑤ Click the Developer tab.

⑥ Click Macros in the Code Group.

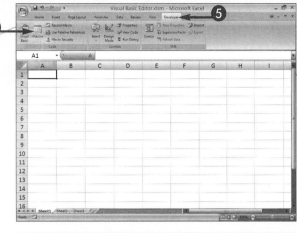

● The Macro dialog box lists all existing macros, including the ones you create in the VBE.

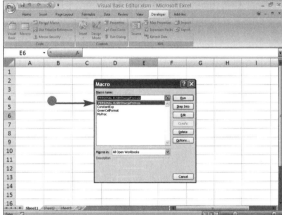

Extra

You can easily change the name of a module. When you create a new module, the VBE automatically names the module Module#, with the number sequentially following the last module you created — for example, Module1, Module2, and so on. If you have a project with several modules, distinguishing one module from another without reviewing the source code can be difficult. You can rename modules with names that reflect the actions that the contents of the module perform.

Use the Properties window to change the name of a module. In the Project Explorer window, click the name of the module you want to rename. Press F4 to move to the Properties window. Type a new name in the Name field and then press Enter. The name of the module changes on the corresponding node in the Project Explorer window.

Remove a Module

You can remove modules from the VBE. Typically, you remove modules that contain procedures you no longer need. When you attempt to remove a module, the VBE gives you the opportunity to export the module to a file before removing it. If there is any possibility that you will need to use a procedure in that module in the future, exporting the module before removing it is good idea.

Exporting a module creates a file with a .bas extension. These files are text files, and you can open and read them with any text editor.

Once you have exported a module, you can use the Import File dialog box to import the module back into the project from which you exported it or into another project. If you have modules you want to share with other programmers, you can export them so the other programmers can import them. When you import a module file, the VBE tries to assign it the same name as the original module. If a module already exists with that name, the VBE adds a sequential number to the end of the module name. Therefore, if you named the original module Module1 and a Module1 exists in the project, Excel names the imported module Module11.

When you remove a module that contains code used by a macro, you can no longer access the macro. If you remove a module that contains code referenced by a procedure in another module, an error message appears when you run the code.

When you delete macros within Excel, Excel removes the corresponding VBA code. If a VBA module does not contain any code, Excel removes the entire module.

Remove a Module

① Click the module you want to remove.

If the Project Explorer is not visible, press Ctrl+R to display it.

② Click File → Remove *Module Name*, where Module Name is the name of the selected module.

The Remove command always contains the name of the selected module.

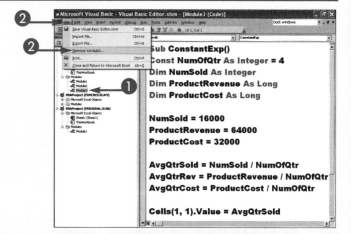

The VBE displays a message, asking whether you want to export the module before removing it.

③ Click Yes to export the module to a file.

Alternatively, click No if you want to delete the module permanently.

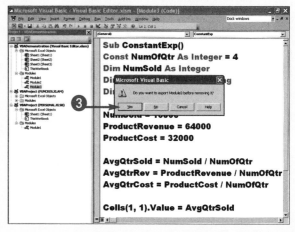

The Export File dialog box appears.

④ Click here and select the folder in which you want to save the module code.

⑤ Type a name for the module code.

⑥ Click Save.

The VBE removes the module from the project and saves the module in the file you specified.

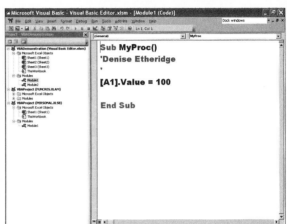

Extra

You do not need to delete a module to save it as a file. If you want to share your code with other VBA developers, you can simply export the module to a file and then distribute the file. To export a macro, you select the module containing the macro and then click File → Export File. The Export file dialog box appears. In the Save In field, select the folder in which you want to save the file. Type a filename in the File Name field and then click Save.

When you export a module to a file, you can import it into any workbook. To import an exported file, click a project name to select the project into which you want to import the file. Click File → Import File. The Import File dialog box appears. Use the Look In field to locate the folder in which you saved the exported module. Click the filename and then click Open. VBA imports the file.

Hide a Macro

You can hide macros so they do not appear in the Excel Macro dialog box. If you create workbooks you intend to share with others, you may want to hide specific macros within your workbook to ensure that users do not inadvertently delete those macros from your workbook.

Because Excel cannot execute a hidden macro from the Macro dialog box, you need to assign the hidden macro to the Ribbon or have another macro call the macro. When you hide a macro, shortcut keys no longer execute the macro.

To hide a macro, open the module containing the macro within the VBE and place the Private statement in front of the Sub statement for the procedure. For example, you

type the following to hide the ChangeText procedure:

```
Private Sub ChangeText().
```

Hiding a macro does not prevent users from viewing or modifying the macro in the VBE. If you want to keep users from accessing the macro, you must password-protect the project containing the macro by changing the properties of the project. See the section, "Set Properties for a Project," for the details on setting project properties. Locking the project prevents users from using the VBE to view and modify the VBA code within that project. To open the project, a user must enter the correct password. Locking a project limits user accessibility, but Excel can still execute any macros in the project.

Hide a Macro

① Click the Developer tab.

② Click Macros in the Code group.

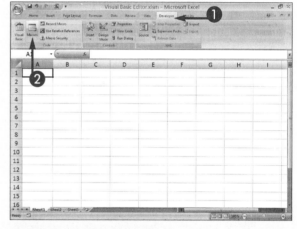

The Macro dialog box appears.

③ Click the macro you want to hide.

④ Click Edit.

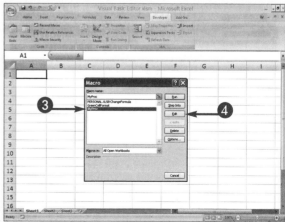

The VBE opens to the macro you selected.

⑤ Type **Private** before the Sub statement.

⑥ Press Alt+F11 to return to Excel.

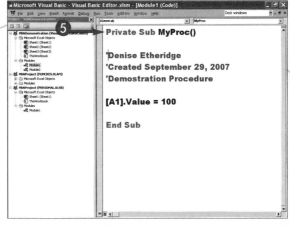

⑦ Repeat steps 1 and 2 to open the Macro dialog box.

The macro no longer displays.

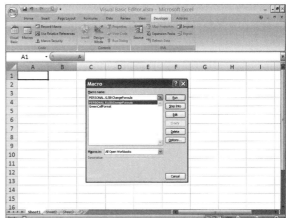

Extra

You should hide macros that are called by other macros if you do not want the user to be able to execute the macro from the Macro dialog box. For example, you have a macro named ChangeCells that calls another macro named AddCellValues. You can hide the AddCellValues macro so users cannot execute the macro from the Macro dialog box. When you mark a procedure as private by placing the Private statement in front of the Sub statement for the procedure, you can only access the procedure within the same code module. In other words, the hidden macro and the procedure that corresponds to the macro calling the hidden macro must be within the same code module.

To make a hidden macro visible again, you need to access the module containing the corresponding procedure within the VBE and delete the Private statement in front of the Sub statement.

Update a Macro

You can update a macro at any time by adding or removing VBA code. After you record a macro, you can record it again to replace it, but you cannot modify it in Excel. The only way to modify your macro is to change the procedure by using the VBE. If you do not know how to read and write the VBA code required for the step you want to add to the macro, this can be quite an undertaking.

Typically, modifying a macro — even one you create with the macro recorder — requires manually specifying the new VBA code you want to add to the macro. You can quickly update an existing macro by recording the code you want to add to the macro and then using the copy and paste features within the VBE to add the new steps to the old macro.

For example, you create a macro that sums the values in a column of cells but you forget to change the formatting of the cell that contains the column total to Currency. You can record a second macro in Excel that formats the column. After you do that, you open the VBE, copy the formatting code you created when you recorded the second macro, and paste it into the procedure for the first macro. When you copy the code, be sure you only copy the portion of the procedure between the Sub and the End Sub statements.

After you copy the code from the second macro into the first macro, you can delete the second macro. You can find out more about deleting macros in Chapter 1.

Update a Macro

1 Click the Developer tab.

2 Click Macros in the Code group.

The Macro dialog box appears.

3 Click your original macro.

4 Click Edit.

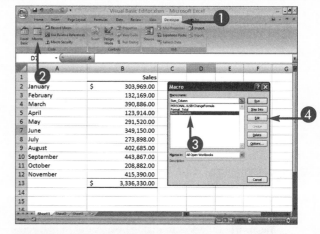

The VBE appears, and opens to the module that contains your macro.

5 Click and drag to select the code in your second macro.

6 Press Ctrl+C to copy the code.

7 Place your cursor at the end of the last line of code in your original macro and then press Enter.

The VBE creates a new line.

8 Press Ctrl+V to paste the code.

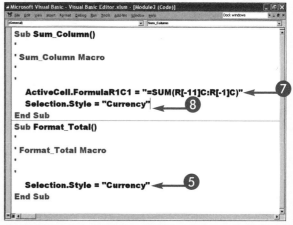

⑨ Click Tools → Macros.

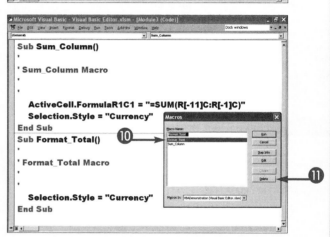

The Macro dialog box appears.

⑩ Select the second macro.

⑪ Click Delete.

The VBE deletes the macro.

Extra

When you view the VBA code for your macro, you may notice that an apostrophe (') precedes several lines. These are called comment lines. Programmers use comments to provide information about the code, such as what the code does, when it was created, and who coded it. When you use the macro recorder to create a macro, any information you type in the Description box appears as a comment.

Example:
```
Sub MyProc()

'Denise Etheridge
'Created September 29, 2007
'Demonstration Procedure

    [A1].Value = 100

End Sub
```

Create Sub Procedures

A block of VBA code that performs a task is a *procedure*. A *Sub procedure* is a special type of procedure that performs a task but does not return a value. Every time you record a macro, Excel creates a Sub procedure. You can view the Sub procedures in the VBE. You can also use the VBE to create Sub procedures.

Every Sub procedure begins with the key word `Sub` followed by the name of the Sub procedure and parentheses. If the Sub procedure does not take any arguments, the parentheses are empty. If the Sub procedure does take arguments, you place the arguments between the parentheses, separated by commas. Sub procedures end with the key words `End Sub`.

Every Sub procedure must have a name. You can name your Sub procedure anything you want as long as you follow these naming rules: The name must start with a letter. The name can contain only letters, numbers, and underscores and cannot contain any spaces. The name cannot be longer than 255 characters. The name cannot be a cell address; for example, you cannot name your Sub procedure A1. Procedure names in VBA are not case-sensitive. The name of your Sub procedure should describe the function the procedure performs. For example, if your Sub procedure prints a sales report, you might want to name it PrintSalesReport or Print_Sales_Report.

You place Sub procedures inside modules. See Chapter 2 to learn more about modules.

Understanding Sub Procedures

① Click Insert → Module.

● The VBE creates a new module.

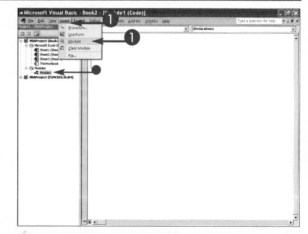

② Type **Sub**.

● The VBE automatically adds the words End Sub.

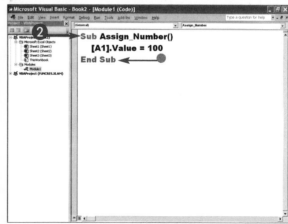

③ Type your procedure name.

④ Type parentheses.

Place arguments between the parentheses separated by commas.

⑤ Type your code.

⑥ Press Alt+F11 to switch from the VBE to Excel, and then run your macro.

Note: *See Chapter 1 to learn how to run a macro.*

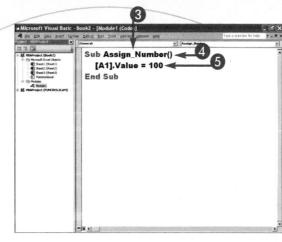

In this example, VBA places the number 100 in cell A1.

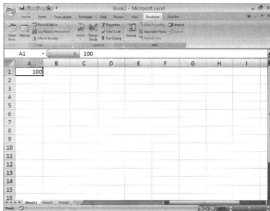

Extra

Glossary

TERM	DEFINITION
Argument	An argument passes information from one procedure to another. An argument can be a constant, a variable, or an expression.
Constant	A value that remains the same.
Function	A type of procedure. This is a block of code that performs a task (usually a calculation) and returns a value.
Expression	A combination of objects, numbers, text, operators, and variables that yield a result. A mathematical equation is an example of an expression.
Procedure	A sequence of code that, when executed, performs a task in Excel. There are several types of procedures.
Sub procedure	A procedure that performs a task but does not return a value.
Variable	A named location where you store information. In the expression x=1, x is a variable that has been assigned the value 1.

Create Functions

You are probably already familiar with functions. Excel has over 300 predefined functions, with SUM being the most commonly used. You use the SUM function to add a list of values. Like a Sub procedure, a function is a special type of procedure. A *function* is a block of code that performs a task — usually a calculation — and returns a value. There are three types of functions: VBA functions, worksheet functions, and custom functions.

VBA functions are provided for your use by VBA. You can use these functions in your code. The MsgBox function is a popular VBA function explained in detail, along with several other VBA functions, in Chapter 7. When executed, the MsgBox function displays a pop-up box with your message. Other VBA functions obtain input from users, execute another program, return the current date, or return the current time.

If an analogous VBA function is not available, you can use Excel's worksheet functions in your code. Chapter 7 explains how to use worksheet functions in detail.

If none of the VBA or worksheet functions suits your needs, you can create a custom function. Every custom function begins with the key word Function followed by the name of the function and parentheses. If your function takes arguments, you place the arguments between the parentheses, separated by commas. Every Custom Function ends with the key words End Function. There are only two ways to execute a custom function: by using the function in a formula or by calling the function from a procedure. Excel lists custom functions under User Defined in the Insert function dialog box. See Chapter 7 for more information on custom functions.

Understanding Functions

1 Click Insert → Module.

● The VBE creates a new module.

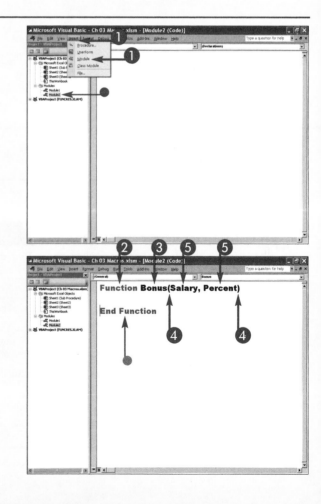

2 Type **Function**.

● The VBE automatically adds the words End Function.

3 Type your procedure name.

4 Type parentheses.

5 Type arguments between the parentheses, separated by commas.

6 Type your code.

7 Press Alt+F11 to switch from the VBE to Excel.

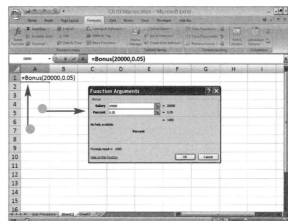

● You can use your function to perform calculations.

Extra

You can create VBA functions you can use within Excel to perform calculations. When you create a public function in the VBE, the function is listed in the Insert Function dialog box that appears when you click Formulas ➜ Insert Function within Excel. The VBE places the functions you create under the User Defined category in the Insert Function dialog box. You can use these VBA functions in your worksheet to create formulas in the same way that you use the built-in functions that are standard with Excel. The VBA functions you create are available in the Insert Function dialog box only when the workbook containing the functions is open. Therefore, if you create a specific function you want to use in all your workbooks, you should add the function to your Personal Macro Workbook, Personal.xlsm, to ensure that it is always available from within Excel. The Personal Macro Workbook always opens with Excel, so any macros and functions it contains are always available. See Chapter 1 for more information on the Personal Macro Workbook.

Comment Your Code

With comments, you can document each step of your code. You can use comments to document such things as the person who created the code, the date when you last updated the code, the purpose of the code, and the purpose of each step of the code. When you are working in a collaborative environment, comments are essential.

In VBA you start a comment by typing an apostrophe ('). When you execute the code, VBA ignores everything after the apostrophe. Comments and code appear in different colors. After you add an apostrophe, the VBE changes the color of the commented text.

You can place an apostrophe anywhere in a line of code, and VBA views the text after the apostrophe as a comment. There is one exception to this rule: If you type an apostrophe within double quotation marks, VBA does

not view it as a comment. For example, VBA would not view the text after the apostrophe in the following example as code: `Saying = "That's Life!"`

Comments only help if they provide enough information to describe the code. A reader should be able to read the comments without studying the code and get a good sense of what the code does. For example, a comment such as "Sums the values" does not provide enough information about the code. Saying "Sums the values in cells A1 and A2 and places the result in cell A3" is better because it describes the actual process.

You can turn several lines of code into a comment by using the Comment Block option on the Edit toolbar. Later, if you want to make the commented lines code again, you can click the Uncomment button.

Comment Your Code

① Double-click the module that contains the code you want to document.

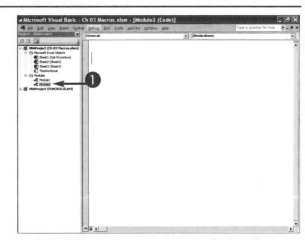

Your code appears in the Code window.

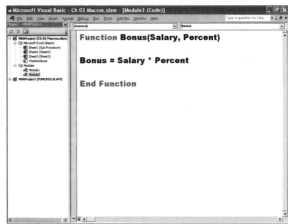

② Type an apostrophe followed by your comments.

You can place your comments anywhere.

③ Press Alt+F11 to switch from the VBE to Excel, and then run the code.

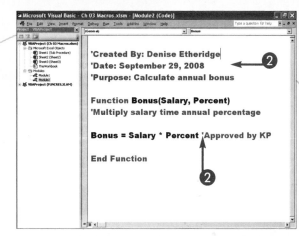

The comments do not affect your code.

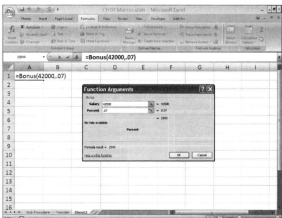

Extra

You can use comments when you are testing your code. If you suspect a line of code is causing your code to run improperly, you can comment it out and run your procedure without it. The process eliminates the need to delete the line of code. You can reactivate the commented-out code by simply removing the apostrophe.

In the VBE, you can use the Edit toolbar to comment out a block of code. To access the Edit toolbar, click View ➔ Toolbars ➔ Edit. The Edit toolbar appears. Select the lines of code you want to comment out. Click the Comment Block button (🔲). The VBE comments out your code. When you run your procedure, the lines of code do not execute. To uncomment the lines of code, select them and then press the Uncomment Block (🔲) button.

Understanding Variables and Data Types

You use variables to store information for later use. The following syntax stores information to a variable.

```
VaribleName = Value
```

VariableName represents the name you give to the variable. The equal sign is the assignment operator. The assignment operator tells VBA you want to assign something to a variable. Value represents what you want to assign to the variable. Once you assign a value to a

variable, VBA retrieves the assigned value whenever you use the variable name. For example, you might make the following assignment:

```
x=2
```

With this assignment, every time VBA sees the variable x, it interprets it to mean 2. You can change the value assigned to a variable many times and at any point in your code.

Variable Names

You can name your variables anything you like; however, you must follow these rules:

- The first character of the variable name must be a letter.

- Your variable name cannot include a space or any of the following: . ! @ & $ or #.

- Your variable name cannot exceed 255 characters.

- Generally, you should not use names that are the same as functions, statements, or methods.

- Your variable name must be unique within its scope.

- You do not need to start each word in your variable name with an uppercase letter; however, that is the convention used in this book. If you develop a convention and use it consistently, you will have an easier time debugging your code.

Data Types

In VBA, a variable can store many data types, including strings, dates, Booleans, and a variety of number types. A *string* is any sequence of characters consisting of any combination of letters, numbers, or punctuation marks. A *Boolean* is a value that is either true or false. A *number* is a value on which you can perform mathematical operations such as addition, subtraction, multiplication, and division.

If you do not declare a data type, VBA assigns the default data type of variant. When a variable is a variant data type, VBA examines the variable to determine if the value is an integer, string, date, Boolean, or other data type. When you change the value assigned to the variable, VBA automatically changes the data type if needed. For example, if you assign x = true, VBA evaluates the expression and determines that x is a Boolean. If you later change the assignment to x = "George", VBA reevaluates the expression and determines x is a string. Having VBA evaluate your variables slows down your code.

When you declare a variable in VBA, you explicitly tell VBA the variable's data type. In other words, if your variable contains an integer, you declare an integer variable. Because declaring a variable makes your code run faster and more efficiently, you should make a habit of declaring variables. To ensure that variables are always properly declared, type Option Explicit as the first statement in your module. If Option Explicit is the first statement in your module, your code will not run if you have any undeclared variables. You must place the Option Explicit statement at the top of each module you create.

Each Excel workbook is a project. Each Sub procedure and function you create is a procedure. You can place multiple procedures in a single module, and you can have many modules in a project. VBA variables can be procedure only, module only, or public. Only the procedure in which the variable resides can use a procedure-only variable. Any procedure in a module can use a module-only variable. Any procedure in a project can use a public variable.

Use the Dim statement to declare a procedure-only variable. You place the statement after the Sub statement but before the procedure code and End Sub statement in a Sub procedure. In a custom function, you place the Dim statement after the Function statement but before the procedure code and the End Function statement. The following example includes several Dim statements to declare procedure-only variables:

Example:
```
Option Explicit

Sub ProcedureOnlyExample()

    Dim EmpLastName As String

    Dim Salary As Long

    Dim StartDate As Date

' Place procedure code here

End Sub
```

When you want to create a module-only variable that any procedure in a module can use, you place your declarations before the first Sub or Function statement in the module. You refer to this area of the module as the declarations area. The example shown here includes several Dim statements used to declare module-only variables.

Example:
```
Option Explicit

    Dim EmpLastName As String

    Dim Salary As Long

    Dim StartDate As Date

Sub ModuleOnlyExample()

' Place module only declarations here.

' Place procedure code here

End Sub
```

When you want to create a public variable that any procedure in your project can use, you place your declarations in the declarations area before the first Sub or Function statement in the module and precede it with the keyword Public instead of Dim.

Example:
```
Option Explicit

    Public EmpLastName As String

    Public Salary As Long

    Public StartDate As Date

' Place module only declarations here

Sub PublicVariableExample()

' Place module only declarations here.

' Place procedure code here

End Sub
```

Reference Cells and Ranges

A s you write your VBA code, you will frequently need to reference cells in an Excel worksheet either to access the information in cells or to put information there. VBA has several methods you can use to reference cells.

One method is the Cells method. When using the Cells method, you use an index to reference a row and column. For example, if you want to reference cell A1, you type the word Cells followed by an open parenthesis, the row reference, a comma, the column reference in quotes, a close parenthesis, a period, and the word Value. The period and the word Value are optional. Both of the following assign the value 1 to cell A1:

`Cells(1,"A").Value = 1, Cells(1,"A") = 1`

When using the Cells method, you can also use numbers to identify the column. The first column in your worksheet is column 1, and each column thereafter is numbered sequentially. To assign the value 10 to cell E1, you would type either of the following:

`Cells(1,5).Value = 10, Cells(1,5) = 10.` Column E is identified by a 5 because it is the fifth column in a worksheet. Using numbers to identify a column is preferable because you can use loops to manipulate your row and column references. To learn more about loops, see Chapter 6.

If you have a simple procedure and you would like to access a cell, you can enclose the cell reference in square brackets followed by a period and the word Value. For example, you can use the following to place the number 25 in cell B3: `[B3].Value = 25.`

Reference Cells and Ranges

1 Click Insert → Module.

● The VBE creates a new module.

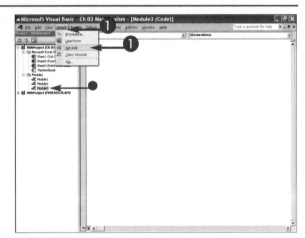

2 Name your procedure.

Note: See the section, "Understanding Sub Procedures," to learn how to name a procedure.

3 Reference a cell by using the Cells method.

● This is a Row reference.

● This is a Column reference.

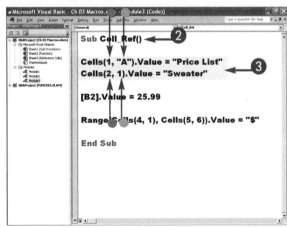

④ Reference a cell by using the cell address.

⑤ Fill a range of cells with a value.

◦ This is the starting cell.

● This is the ending cell.

⑥ Press Alt+F11 to switch from the VBE to Excel, and then run the macro.

Note: *See Chapter 1 to learn how to run a macro.*

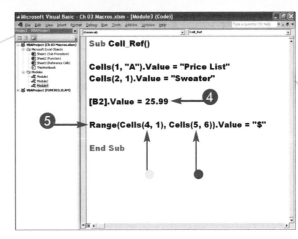

The VBA places the values in the cells you specified.

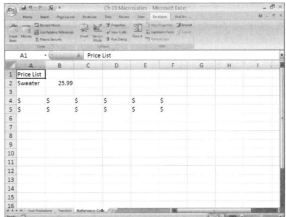

Extra

You can also use the Range property to reference cells. The following table illustrates Range syntax:

SYNTAX	REFERENCE
Range("C4")	Cell C4
Range("B1:B7")	Cells B1 to B7
Range("D1:D8, F1:H2, F7:H8, G2:G6")	Cells D1 to D8, F1 to H2, F7 to H8, and G2 to G6
Range("J:J")	Column J
Range("11:11")	Row 11
Range("L:M")	Columns L to M
Range("14:16")	Rows 14 to 16

Declare Variables

You use a variable to store information for later use. If you are making an assignment to a variable, you should start by declaring the variable. In its simplest form, declaring your variable consists of telling VBA what data type your variable will use.

You can assign one of several data types. Most are listed in the "Extra" section of this task. Generally, if your data consists of text or numbers you do not intend to use in a mathematical calculation, you should declare your data as a string. If your data is numerical data you do intend to use in mathematical calculations, you should use one of the many numeric data types. Use the data type that uses the least amount of bytes but fully accommodates your needs. If you do not declare your variables, VBA assigns a variable type of variant. A variant data type can hold any type of data. However, declaring your variables makes your code run faster. You should declare your variables.

You can declare a variable as procedure only, module only, or public. To learn more, see the section, "Understanding Variables and Data Types." You use a Dim statement to declare a procedure-only or module-only variable. You type the word Dim followed by the variable name, the As keyword, and then the variable type — for example, `Dim EmployeeName As String`. If you are declaring a public variable, you replace the Dim keyword with Public: `Public EmployeeName As String`.

After you have declared a variable, you assign a value to it. Type the variable name, followed by an equal sign and the value you want to assign the variable — for example, `EmployeeName = "John Smith"`.

Declare Variables

① Click Insert → Module.

● The VBE creates a new module.

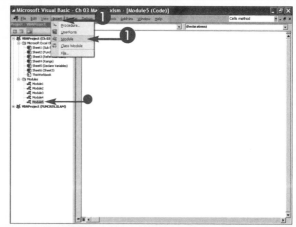

② Type **Option Explicit**.

Note: *See the section, "Understanding Variables and Data Types," for more information.*

● This is the declarations area.

③ Declare your public variables.

④ Declare your module-only variables.

⑤ Name your procedure.

⑥ Declare your procedure-only variables.

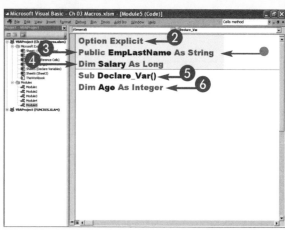

7 Assign values to your variables.

Note: *See the sections, "Work with Numbers" and "Work with Strings," to learn more.*

8 Place the values in cells.

9 Press Alt+F11 to switch from the VBE to Excel, and then run the macro.

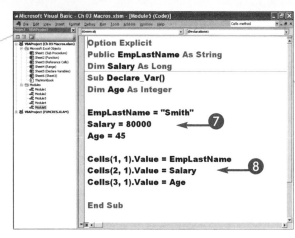

VBA places the values in your variables in the cells you specified.

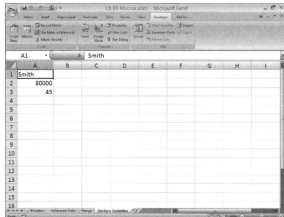

Extra

You should choose the data type that uses the smallest number of bytes but can accommodate your data. Excel provides characters you can use to set the data type for a variable. For example, you can use the following syntax to declare a string: `Dim EmployeeName$`.

DATA TYPE	BYTES USED	RANGE OF VALUE	DECLARATION CHARACTER
Boolean	2 bytes	True or False	
Date	8 bytes	1/1/100 to 12/31/9999	
Double (negative values)	8 bytes	$-1.79769313486231E308$ to $-4.9406564841247E-324$	#
Double (positive values)	8 bytes	$4.94065645841247E-324$ to $1.79769313486232E308$	#
Integer	2 bytes	–32,768 to 32,767	%
Long	4 bytes	–2,147,483,648 to 2,147,483,647	&
Object	4 bytes	Any defined object	
Single (negative values)	4 bytes	$-3.402823E38$ to $-1.401298E-45$	!
Single (positive values)	4 bytes	$1.401298E-45$ to $3.402823E38$	!
String	1 per character	Varies	$
Variant	Varies	Varies	

Work with Numbers

To perform mathematical calculations, you use VBA's seven arithmetic operators: the plus (+), minus (–), multiplication (*), division (/), exponential (^), integer division (\), and Mod operators. You use the plus operator to add, the minus operator to subtract or negate, the multiplication operator to multiply, the division operator to divide, and the exponential operator to raise to a power.

The integer division operator divides two values and returns only the integer portion of the result. VBA discards the remainder when you use this operator. For example, the expression X = 10\3 returns 3. The Mod operator divides two numbers and returns only the remainder. For example, the expression X = 10 Mod 3 returns 1. This operator works well for predetermining if two values divide evenly. If the Mod returns a zero, the values divide evenly.

You can assign the results of a mathematical calculation to a variable, and you can include cells and variables in your calculations. All of the following are valid: A = 5, X = A + 25, X = 5 + 7, X = 9 + Cells(1,1).Value.

When you perform a mathematical calculation in VBA, you must be careful of precedence — the order in which VBA performs calculations. VBA performs calculations from left to right, performing multiplication and division before addition and subtraction. For example, the formula = 3 + 4 * 2 returns 11, VBA multiplies 4 times 2 and then adds 3. If you want to change the order of precedence, use parentheses. Excel calculates numbers in parentheses first. The formula = (3 + 4) * 2 returns 14, VBA adds 3 plus 4 and then multiplies the result by 2.

Work with Numbers

① Click Insert → Module.

● The VBE creates a new module.

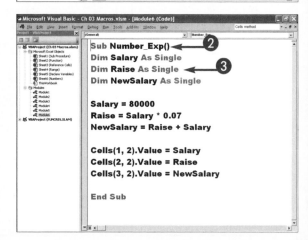

② Name your procedure.

③ Declare your variables.

④ Assign numeric values to variables.

● You can perform mathematical calculations.

⑤ Assign variables to cells.

⑥ Press Alt+F11 to switch from the VBE to Excel, and then run the macro.

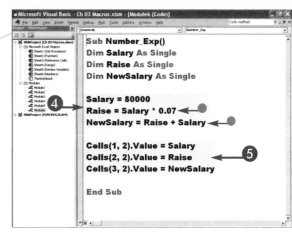

VBA places the values in your variables in the cells you specified.

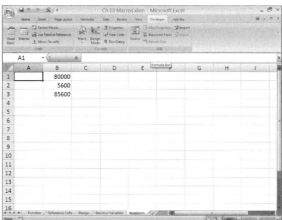

The following table shows the precedence order, from highest to lowest, that VBA uses to evaluate operators in formulas. If the operators in the formula have the same order of precedence, Excel evaluates the equation from left to right.

PRECEDENCE	OPERATORS	SYMBOL
1	Exponentiation	^
2	Minus sign	– (negates a number before any calculations)
3	Multiplication and division	* /
4	Integer division	\
5	Modulus arithmetic	Mod
6	Addition and subtraction	+ –

Work with Strings

You can assign strings to a variable so you can use the string elsewhere in your code. A string is any sequence of characters consisting of any combination of letters, numbers, and punctuation marks. A string can have up to two billion characters. When you declare a string variable, you type the **Dim** keyword followed by the variable name and **As String** — for example, `Dim SampleString As String`.

You can assign a string data type to a variable by typing the variable name followed by an equal sign and then the value you want to assign to the variable within quotation marks. For example, you could use the following syntax to assign the name John Smith to the string variable EmployeeName: `EmployeeName = "John Smith"`.

You can join the contents of two or more strings to create one string. The process of joining strings is called *concatenation.* Use the concatenation operator (&) or the plus concatenation operator (+) to combine strings. Using the concatenation operator is the better choice because the plus concatenation operator can be confused with the plus arithmetic operator. The expression `FirstName = "David"` assigns the string `David` to the variable `FirstName`. The expression `LastName = "Jackson"` assigns the string `Jackson` to the variable `LastName`. The expression `FullName = FirstName + " " + LastName` and the expression `FullName = FirstName & " " & LastName` both return David Jackson. You include the double quotation marks separated by a space (" ") to leave a space between the first and last names.

Work with Strings

① Click Insert → Module.

● The VBE creates a new module.

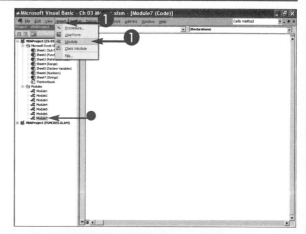

② Name your procedure.

③ Declare your variables.

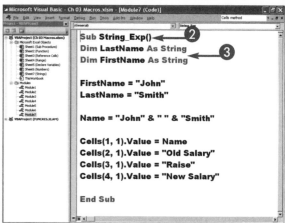

④ Assign string values to variables.

⑤ Concatenate the strings.

⑥ Assign a variable to a cell.

⑦ Assign strings to cells.

You can assign any data type to a cell.

⑧ Press Alt+F11 to switch from the VBE to Excel, and then run the macro.

VBA places the values in your variables in the cells you specified.

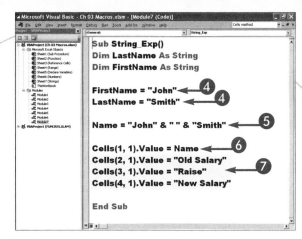

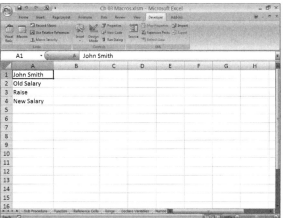

Extra

When you declare a string, you can declare it as a fixed-length or a variable-length string. A fixed-length string can have between 1 and 65,526 characters. When declaring a fixed-length string, you specify the string's maximum length in characters. For example, you can use the following syntax to declare a fixed-length string with a maximum of ten characters: `Dim SampleString As String * 10`.

When concatenating fixed-length strings, there is the potential for exceeding the declared or maximum length of the string. VBA does not extend the size of a fixed-length string to store a larger string. If two joined strings form a string larger than the space allows, VBA truncates the string to fit the allotted space. If each of the strings you want to join is ten characters in length, you must make the variable that receives the concatenated string at least 20 characters in length, or VBA will truncate the string.

Create a Constant

I f you often use a value that never changes, you can declare it is as a constant. For example, there are four quarters in a year. If, in your code, you frequently divide an annual amount by four to get the average quarterly amount, you can store 4 to a constant named NumOfQuarters and use the constant when performing calculations. When you review your code and see the constant name, you instantly know you are dividing by the number of quarters, whereas if you use the number 4, the true meaning of the number would not be as readily apparent. In short, using constants makes your code easier to understand.

You declare constants with a specific data type. In fact, constants use the same data types that variables use. As with variables, if you do not specify a data type for a constant, VBA treats the value as a variant. After you assign a constant a value, you cannot alter the value.

If you want your constant to be available only to the procedure in which it was created, declare your constant after the Sub or Function statement. If you want your constant to be available to all of the procedures in your module, declare your constant in the declarations area. If you want your constant to be available to any procedure in the workbook, declare your constant in the declarations area and use the Public keyword.

Declaration examples: `Const NumOfQuarters As Integer = 4`, `Public Const Region As String = "New York"`

To name your constant, you use the same naming rules as for variables. For more information, see the section, "Understanding Variables and Data Types," earlier in this chapter.

Create a Constant

1 Click Insert → Module.

● The VBE creates a new module.

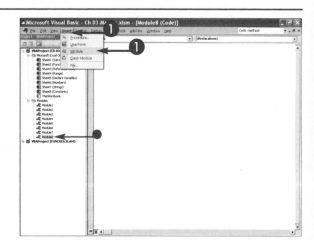

2 Name your procedure.

3 Create your constant.

4 Declare your variables.

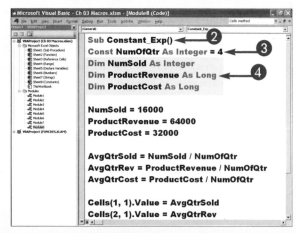

5 Assign values to variables.

6 Use your constant in calculations.

● The results are stored in a variable.

7 Assign variables to cells.

8 Press Alt+F11 to switch from the VBE to Excel, and then run the macro.

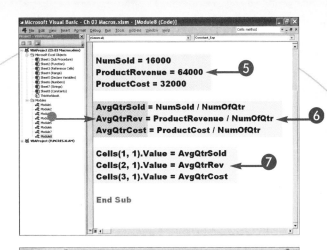

VBA places the values in your variables in the cells you specified.

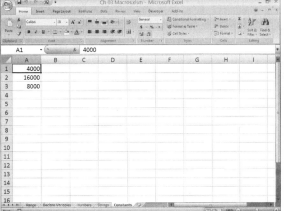

Extra

VBA provides hundreds of built-in constants that you can insert into your code at any point without declaring them. The Excel VBA object model adds over one thousand more, all of which begin with either xl or vb. Each constant has a numeric value. You can use these constants anywhere, and you do not need to know their numeric value to use them. Two of the most commonly used VBA constants deal with inserting carriage returns, vbCrLf, and tab characters, vbTab, in your output. Although each of these constants has a numeric equivalent, you simply type the name of the appropriate constant value in your code. To find a list of all VBA and Excel VBA Object Model constants, press F2 to view the Object Browser and search for Constant. Most of the constant values are self-explanatory, based on the name. Appendix A also includes many of the constant values used in this book. You can also find a listing of constants by typing **constant** in the Help text box.

Discover the Excel Object Model

*O*bjects are the individual pieces of an application. For example, a worksheet is an object, a range of cells is an object, and a chart is an object. You can use the Excel object model to interact with the objects. Using the object model, you can access everything from the entire application to an individual cell in a worksheet. Objects can have properties and methods. You use *methods* to perform actions on objects, such as move an object. You use *properties* to change the characteristics of an object, such as the color of an object.

Excel has an enormous number of objects, properties, and methods, and remembering all of them is virtually impossible. Luckily, the VBE provides a help system to help you quickly locate objects and determine the corresponding methods and properties that are available for the object. You can learn how to work with objects by performing the tasks in this chapter.

Excel Objects

The Excel object model has several hundred objects and thousands of corresponding properties and methods. Each object represents an element of the Excel application. For example, the Application object refers to the entire Excel application, while the Worksheet object refers to an individual worksheet.

Most objects have child objects. A *child object* is an object that is part of a larger object. For example, a Worksheet object is a child object to a Workbook object because worksheets are part of a workbook. All objects in the Excel object model except the Application object is a child of at least one other object. The Excel Application object is the parent of all objects in Excel.

The object model groups common objects into collections. For example, the Workbook object identifies an individual workbook, but the Workbooks collection refers to all open workbooks.

Although the list of available objects is extensive, there are six objects that you use frequently: `Application`, `Workbook`, `Worksheet`, `Chart`, `Range`, and `Dialog`. Because you use these objects frequently, it is a good idea to familiarize yourself with them.

Application Object

You usually need to reference the parent object when referencing the child object. For example, to access the second worksheet in the current workbook, you would type `ThisWorkbook.Worksheets(2)`. The Application object represents the entire Excel program. All other objects are children of the Application object in the Excel object model. The Application object has several properties and methods. Those that return the most common user-interface values, such as the `ActiveCell` property, do not require the use of the Application object in the statement. Both of these statements are valid:

Example:
```
Application.ActiveCell
ActiveCell
```

Workbook Object

Every workbook you open in Excel is a `Workbook` object. Every `Workbook` object is part of the `Workbooks` collection. The `Workbooks` collection is part of the `Application` object. You can use the `Workbook` object methods to do things such as save or close a workbook. See Chapter 9 for more information on working with the `Workbook` object.

Worksheet Object

Every worksheet in Excel is a `Worksheet` object. Every `Worksheet` object is part of the `Worksheets` collection. You can use `Worksheet` methods to do things such as add, delete, or copy a worksheet. See Chapter 10 for more information about working with the `Worksheet` object.

Chart Object

Every chart in a workbook is a Chart object. You can embed a chart in a worksheet or you can place a chart on a chart sheet. The ChartObject object holds Chart objects you embed in a worksheet. Chart objects you place on a chart sheet are part of the Charts collection. All ChartObject objects are part of a ChartObjects object collection. See Chapter 13 for more information about working with charts.

Dialog Object

The Dialog object references each of the built-in dialog boxes available in Excel. Excel stores these dialog boxes in the Dialogs collection. VBA identifies each dialog box by assigning it a constant value. The constant value begins with xlDialog followed by the name of the dialog box. For example, xlDialogSaveAs references the Save As dialog box. You can use the constant value associated with a dialog box to view the dialog box. You view individual dialog boxes by using the Show method. The Dialog object refers to existing dialog boxes. For information on creating dialog boxes, see Chapter 13.

Excel Methods

Each object in the Excel object model has methods. You use methods to perform actions on objects For example, you can use the Copy method to copy a worksheet by copying the Worksheet object and placing it in another location in the workbook.

To use a method with an object, you combine the object name with the method name, as in the following example:

Example:
```
Worksheets(1).CopyAfter:=Worksheets(3)
```

Range Object

The Range object enables you to reference an individual cell or a range of cells. Several different methods and properties use Range objects. See Chapter 11 for more information on the Range object. The following references cell B3.

Example:
```
Range("B3")
```

Excel Properties

Each object in the Excel object model has properties. *Properties* enable you to view or change the characteristics of an object. For example, you can use the Value property to change the value of a cell. You can also use properties to change other aspects of an object. For example, you can use the Hidden property to hide or unhide a worksheet. To change an object property, you combine the object name with the property name and then assign a property, as follows:

Example:
```
Range("A1").Value = 45
```

Object Collections

You can have multiple objects of the same type, such as multiple worksheets in a workbook. To make these objects more accessible, VBA groups them together in an object collection. For example, each Workbook object contains a Worksheets collection. You access a collection in a manner similar to the way you access an array. You use an index value to reference the desired object in the collection. The following code accesses the second worksheet in the Worksheets collection:

Example:
```
Worksheets(2)
```

Glossary

TERM	DESCRIPTION
Object	An element in an application, such as a worksheet, chart, or form. You can use VBA to manipulate objects.
Properties	The characteristics of an object, such as its color, size, or location.
Methods	The actions VBA can perform on an object, such as copy, save, or move. For example, you can use methods to copy, save, or move a worksheet.

Access the Excel Object Model Reference

When you want to know what objects are available to you and the properties and methods associated these objects, you can refer to the Excel Object Model Reference, which is part of the VBA help system. The Excel Object Model Reference provides documentation on every object, method, property, and event in the Excel object model. An event occurs in Excel whenever the user performs any type of action. You can use events to trigger the execution of a procedure by creating event-handling procedures. See Chapter 15 to learn more about events.

The Excel Object Model Reference explains every object, and provides you with sample code. You can cut and paste the sample code into the VBE and then run it in Excel. The Excel Object Model Reference explains each

method, provides you with the syntax for each method, explains the parameters associated with each method, and provides you with sample code for most methods. The Excel Object Model Reference also explains each object property and event and provides you with the syntax and sample code for most properties and events.

When using the Excel Object Model Reference, there are several ways you can access the information you want. You can type the name of an object, method, property, or event into the Search field and the Excel Object Model Reference will bring back a list of topics. Then you can click the topic in which you are interested. You also can select a topic from the Developer Reference Table of Contents, or you can use the Excel Object Model Reference to find the topic you want.

Access the Excel Object Model Reference

① Type a question in the Help field in the upper-right corner of the VBE and then press Enter.

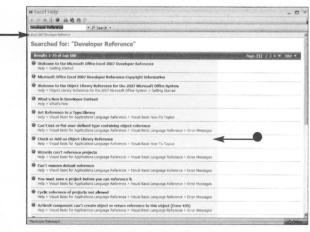

The VBA Help system appears.

● You can select from the options in this menu.

② Click Excel 2007 Developer Reference at the top of the screen under the Search field.

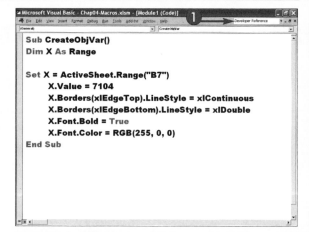

The Developer Reference Table of Contents appears.

③ Click Excel Object Model Reference.

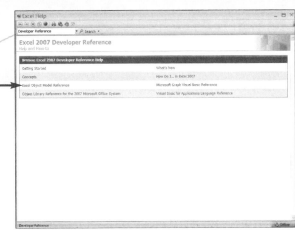

A list of the objects in the Excel object model appears.

④ Click the object for which you want more information.

A screen with links to the properties, methods, and events appears.

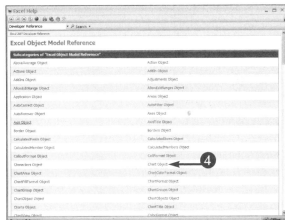

Extra

You can use the Object Browser to access a list of objects, properties, and methods that are available for your use. You open the Object Browser by pressing F2, or by choosing View ⇨ Object Browser from the menu while in the VBE. In the field in the upper-left corner of the browser, select Excel to access the Excel Object Model Reference. Use the Search field in the upper-left corner to search for the object for which you are looking.

If you place your cursor over a keyword in your code and then right-click, a contextual menu appears. Click List Properties/Methods to see a list of properties or methods that you can use with the keyword. Click List Constants to see a list of constants that you can use with the keyword. Click Parameter Info to see a list of parameters.

As you type your code, the VBE provides you with a list of properties, methods, and constants that you can use with the object for which you are creating a command.

Create an
Object Variable

You can reference objects by typing the complete object reference each time you want to reference the object, or you can assign an object to a variable. You assign objects to variables because variable names are usually shorter and easier to remember, and you can change the objects that variables refer to while your code is running. In addition, VBA code runs faster when you use object variables.

You declare object variables in much the same way as you declare a standard variable. You use the Dim statement to declare the variable and the As statement to identify the variable as an object variable. The data type for the variable is the corresponding object type. For example, the statement Dim SampleVar As Worksheet creates an object variable named SampleVar that is a Worksheet object.

After you create an object variable, you assign an object to the variable by using a Set statement. The following statement sets the value of SampleVar to point to Sheet1 in your workbook:

```
Set SampleVar = ActiveWorkbook
    .Worksheets("Sheet1")
```

When you assign an object to a variable, you are assigning a reference to the object to the variable and not the actual object value. For example, when you assign a range to a variable *without* using a Set statement, you are assigning the value in the cell to the variable. When you assign a range to a variable using a Set statement, you reference the actual cells. Assigning a range to a variable by using the Set statement allows you to set properties for the range using the variable.

Create an Object Variable

1. Name your procedure.

2. Declare your object variable.

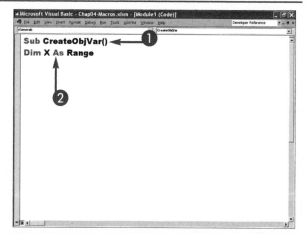

3. Use a Set statement to assign an object to the variable you created.

4. Assign the object properties.

- Assigns a value to a cell.

- Places a single line border at the top of the cell.

- Places a double line border at the bottom of the cell.

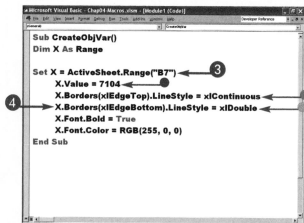

- Makes the font bold.

- Makes the font color red.

5 Press Alt+F11 to switch from the VBE to Excel, and run the macro.

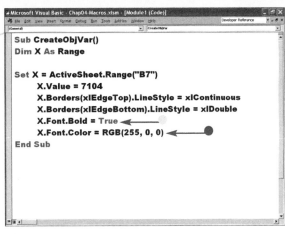

The macro places the value you specified in the cell you specified, adds a single-line border to the top of the cell, adds a double-line border to the bottom of the cell, makes the font bold, and sets the font color to red.

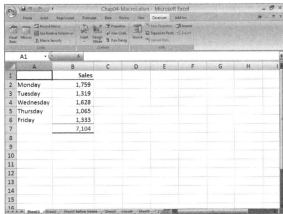

Extra

If you want to refer to the currently selected worksheet, you can use the `ActiveSheet` property. You can use this property in place of an object reference to the worksheet, such as `Worksheets(1)`, which refers to the first worksheet in a workbook. By using the `ActiveSheet` property, you reference the active worksheet at the time your procedure executes. For example, `SheetName = ActiveSheet.Name` assigns the name of the currently active worksheet to the `SheetName` variable.

The `ActiveSheet` property can refer to any type of sheet within a workbook. Therefore, if the currently selected sheet is actually a chart sheet, the `ActiveSheet` property returns a reference to the chart sheet. See Chapter 10 for more information on working with worksheets.

When you create object variables, you are essentially creating object pointers. Unlike a standard variable, which is the name of a memory location containing the variable's value, an object variable actually points to the memory location that stores a pointer to the object. For example, in the following code, `ObjVar` stores the pointer to cell B2 in the worksheet.

Example:
```
Dim ObjVar As Range
Set ObjVar = ActiveSheet.Cells(2, 2)
```

Change the Properties of an Object

You can change the value of an object, its appearance, and other characteristics by modifying the properties associated with the object. For example, when working with a cell on a worksheet, you use the Value property to change the value of the cell. If you want to change the font style, you modify Font object properties, such as Bold, Italic, Underline, and Size.

If you want to make several property changes to the same object, you can create a statement for each property you want to change. For example, you can enter the following statements to change the properties of a cell:

```
ActiveSheet.Range("B7").Value = 7104

ActiveSheet.Range("B7").Borders_
(xlEdgeBottom).LineStyle = xlDouble

ActiveSheet.Range("B7").Borders_
(xlEdgeTop).LineStyle = xlContinuous
```

```
ActiveSheet.Range("B7").Font.Bold = True

ActiveSheet.Range("B7").Font._
Color = RGB(255,0,0)
```

You can simplify these statements by assigning `ActiveSheet.Range("B7")` to an object variable and then referencing the variable for each statement. For example, you can assign `ActiveSheet.Range("B7")` to the variable X.

You can simplify the statements even further by using a `With` statement. Instead of typing the object variable reference, you simply type `With VariableName` followed by each property statement. When you complete your list of property settings, you type `End With` to mark the end of your `With` statement. You can nest your `With` statements to further simplify your code.

Change the Properties of an Object

① Name your procedure.

② Declare your object variable.

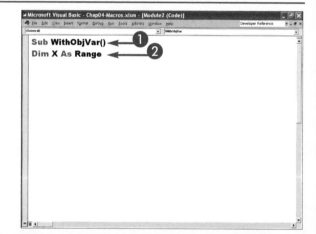

③ Use a `Set` statement to assign an object to the variable you created.

④ Assign the object properties by using a `With` statement.

● Assigns a value to a cell.

● Places a single line border at the top of the cell.

● Places a double line border at the bottom of the cell.

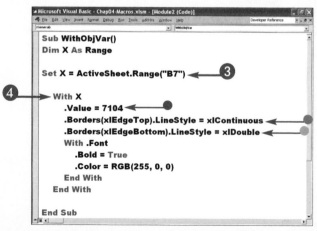

- Makes the font bold.

- Makes the font color red.

5 Press Alt+F11 to switch from the VBE to Excel, and run the macro.

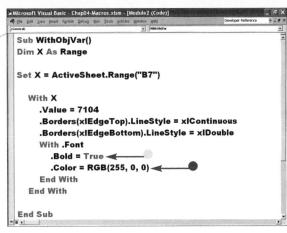

```vba
Sub WithObjVar()
Dim X As Range

Set X = ActiveSheet.Range("B7")

    With X
        .Value = 7104
        .Borders(xlEdgeTop).LineStyle = xlContinuous
        .Borders(xlEdgeBottom).LineStyle = xlDouble
        With .Font
            .Bold = True
            .Color = RGB(255, 0, 0)
        End With
    End With

End Sub
```

The macro places the value you specified in the cell you specified, adds a single-line border to the top of the cell, adds a double-line border to the bottom of the cell, makes the font bold, and sets the font color to red.

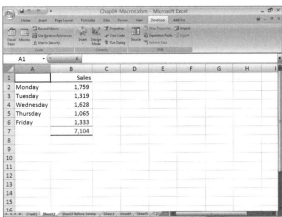

Extra

Some objects, such as the Font object, have a Color property that determines the color of the object. You can use the RGB function to set the font color. When you use this function, you select the desired color by indicating the amount of red, green, and blue in the color. You specify the color values with an integer value between 0 and 255. For example, you type **(0,0,0)** for the color black.

COLOR	RED VALUE	GREEN VALUE	BLUE VALUE
Black	0	0	0
Blue	0	0	255
Cyan	0	255	255
Green	0	255	0
Magenta	255	0	255
Red	255	0	0
White	255	255	255
Yellow	255	255	0

Compare Object Variables

You can use an object comparison to determine if two object variables reference the same object. Unlike standard variables, which actually contain values that you can compare, the object variable does not contain the object, but references it. When you compare two object variables, you are checking to see if they point to the same object. For example, you may want to find out if the currently active worksheet is the first worksheet. If so, you can perform an object comparison.

When you compare standard variables, you use the equals (=) operator to determine if they are the same. For example, `If Value1 = Value2 Then` compares two standard variables. See Chapter 3 for more information on working with standard variables.

When comparing objects, instead of the equals operator, you use the `Is` operator. For example, you write an `If`

`Then` statement to compare two object variables as follows:

```
If ObjVal1 Is ObjVal2 Then
```

This statement looks at the object referenced by `ObjVal1` and checks to see if it is the same as the object referenced by `ObjVal2`.

In addition to comparing two objects, you can also use the `Is` operator to determine if an object variable has an assigned value, as shown in the following example: If `ObjVal1 Is Nothing Then`. This comparison statement returns a value of `True` if the object variable does not point to an object. If the object variable points to an object, the comparison statement returns a value of `False`.

Compare Object Variables

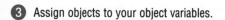

① Name your procedure.

② Declare your variables.

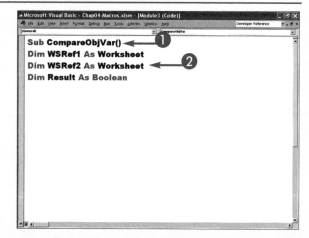

③ Assign objects to your object variables.

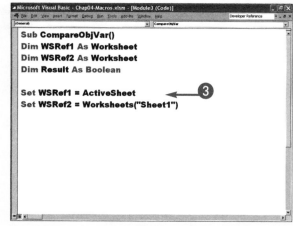

④ Compare the objects and assign the result to a variable.

⑤ Display the result using the MsgBox function.

⑥ Press Alt+F11 to switch from the VBE to Excel, and run the macro.

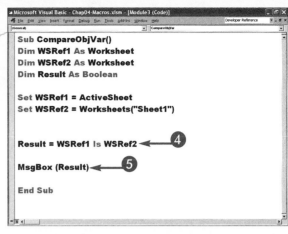

• If you are on Sheet1, the macro returns the value True; otherwise, it returns the value False.

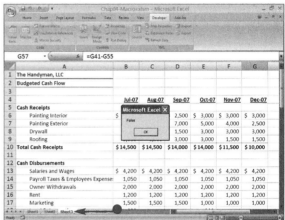

Extra

You can also use the `Is` operator with the `Nothing` keyword to ensure that an object variable points to a valid object. You can compare the value of the object variable to the Nothing keyword by using an `If Then` statement, as shown in the following example. If the `If Then` statement returns a value of `True`, the object variable does not contain a reference to a valid object.

Example:
```
If ObjVar Is Nothing Then
     MsgBox ("Variable does not point to a valid object.")
End If
```

You can use the Nothing keyword to clear the object variable. By doing so, you free up the memory required to store the object pointer in the object variable.

Example:
```
Set ObjVar = Nothing
```

Using an Object Method

You use Excel object methods to modify or perform an action on an object. The Excel object model contains several hundred objects, and each object has a list of methods you can use with it. For example, you can use the Copy method to copy a Worksheet object and then place the copy in another location in your workbook.

To use an object method, you specify the appropriate object, followed by a period and the method you want to use. If the selected method has arguments, you place the arguments after the method.

Example:
```
Worksheet("Sheet2").Copy Before:= Worksheet("Sheet1")
```

In this example, the code copies Sheet2 and places the copy before Sheet1 in the current workbook. `Worksheet("Sheet2")` is the object, `Copy` is the method, and `Before:= Worksheet("Sheet1")` is the argument.

Most methods take arguments. Arguments tell VBA how to modify the object. Usually, at least one argument is required. In this example, the Copy method requires you use either the Before or After argument to tell VBA where to place the copied worksheet. Use the `Before` argument to tell VBA the sheet before which you want to place the copied worksheet. Use the `After` argument to tell VBA the sheet after which you want to place the copied worksheet. See Chapter 10 for more information about copying Excel worksheets.

Using an Object Method

① Name your procedure.

② Declare a Range object variable.

③ Store an object to an object variable.

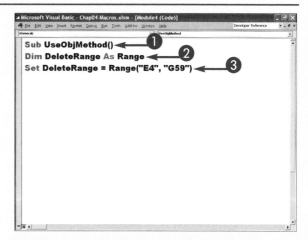

④ Use a method to perform an action on an object.

In this example, you use the Delete method to delete a range.

● The Range object.

● The Delete method.

● Assigns arguments to the method.

This argument is a constant that tells VBA to shift cells to the left after deleting.

⑤ Press Alt+F11 to switch from the VBE to Excel, and run the macro.

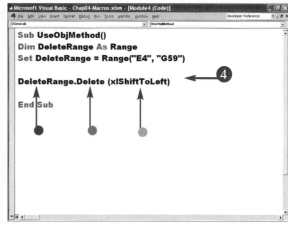

The worksheet before you run the macro.

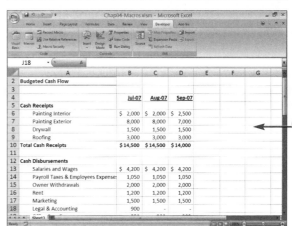

The worksheet after you run the macro.

- The macro deletes the range.

Extra

You can use named arguments with functions, methods, and statements. Using named arguments is an easier way to supply your functions, methods, and statements with the arguments, especially when a large number of arguments are required. If you do not use a named argument, you supply arguments by placing them after the method, enclosed in parentheses and separated by commas in the order VBA expects them. For example, the Worksheet object Protect method has 16 optional arguments. If you do not use named arguments, then calling this property requires a placeholder for each argument to specify a value for the last parameter, as shown in this example:

Example:
```
Worksheets(1).Protect("Excel", , , , , , , , , , , , , ,True,)
```

If you use named arguments, you can provide the arguments in any order. You assign a value to the argument by using a colon followed by an equals sign (:=).

Example:
```
Worksheets(1).Protect Password:= _
"Excel", AllowFiltering:=True
```

Display a Built-in Dialog Box

You can incorporate code into your procedure that opens a built-in Excel dialog box. The Excel object model contains a `Dialog` object for each Excel dialog box. These objects are part of the `Dialogs` collection. You can access each of the Excel dialog box objects by specifying its constant value. The constant value for each dialog box begins with `xlDialog` followed by the name of the dialog box. For example, the constant for the Excel Save As dialog box is `xlDialogSaveAs`.

You can find a complete list of the dialog box constants in the help that comes with the VBE, by typing `XlBuiltInDialog` in the Search field and then clicking `XlBuiltInDialog Enumeration`.

You use the `Show` method to display a built-in dialog box. You cannot access the values that a user places in the fields. You can only determine what the user selects by

looking at the results after the user dismisses the dialog box. You can use arguments to assign values to a dialog box. For example, the Properties dialog box (`xlDialogProperties`) has the following arguments: `Title`, `Subject`, `Author`, `Keywords`, and `Comments`. You can enter the values for these arguments before you open your dialog box. For a list of the arguments associated with each dialog box, type "Built-In Dialog Box Arguments List" in the Search field and then, in the list of options that appears, click Built-In Dialog Box Arguments Lists. If you want to use named arguments to assign values to the arguments, use `Arg1` for the first argument, `Arg2` for the second argument, and continue in this manner. For example, if you are working with the `xlDialogProperties` dialog box, you can use `Arg1` for Title and `Arg2` for Subject.

Display a Built-in Dialog Box

① Create a new procedure.

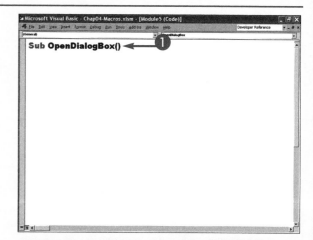

② Type your command.

● The Show method.

● The title.

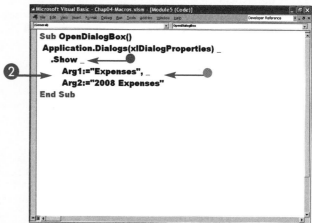

- The subject.

③ Press Alt+F11 to switch from the VBE to Excel, and run the macro.

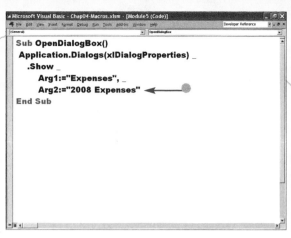

The macro adds the arguments to the dialog box and then opens the dialog box.

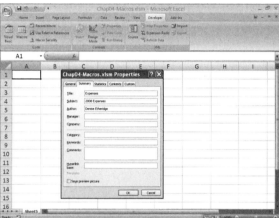

Extra

Excel has hundreds of dialog boxes that display throughout the application. You can display them by using the appropriate constant. The following table lists a few of the most commonly used Excel dialog boxes:

CONSTANT	DISPLAYS
xlDialogFileDelete	The Delete dialog box, where you select files to remove.
xlDialogInsert	The Insert dialog box for adding additional cells to a worksheet.
xlDialogNew	The New dialog box.
xlDialogOpen	The Open dialog box.
xlDialogPrint	The Print dialog box.
xlDialogSaveAs	The Save As dialog box.

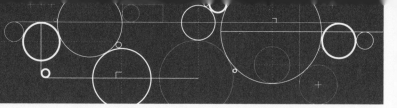

Declare an Array

I f you have a group of related values of the same data type, you can declare them as an array. You declare an array in much the same way you declare other variables and, as with other variables, you can declare arrays as either local or global. You set the scope of an array with the Dim or Public statement. See the section, "Understanding Variables and Data Types," in Chapter 3 for more information about setting the scope of a variable.

You can use arrays to store a group of related data. Using arrays simplifies your code because you can use one variable to store several values. For example, you can declare an array and use it to store all 12 months of the year instead of creating a separate variable for each month.

When you declare an array, you specify the number of elements in the array. For example, the declaration Dim Month(1 To 12) As String declares 12 elements numbered sequentially 1 through 12. In the example, the Month array has 12 elements with a lower bound of 1 and an upper bound of 12.

An element is a data value in the array. You access the elements in an array by using the index value that represents the desired element. Elements are sequentially numbered The lower bound of an array is the lowest index value, and the upper bound of an array is the highest index value. To access the second element of the Month array, use the index value of 2, as in Month(2).

Declare an Array

① Name your procedure.

② Declare your array.

Note: For more information on data types, see Chapter 3.

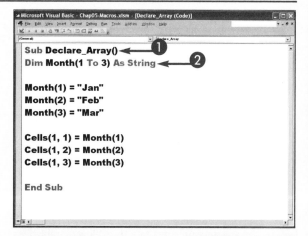

③ Assign values to the array elements.

● A number enclosed in parentheses identifies each element.

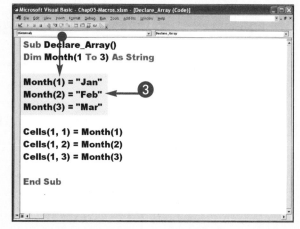

④ Use the Cells method to assign the values in the array to cells in the spreadsheet.

Note: For more information, see the section, "Reference Cells and Ranges," in Chapter 3.

⑤ Press Alt+F11 to switch from the VBE to Excel, and run the macro.

Note: See Chapter 1 to learn how to run a macro.

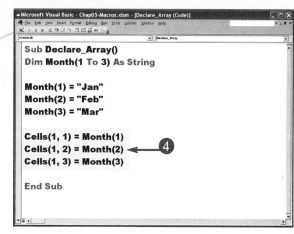

```
Sub Declare_Array()
Dim Month(1 To 3) As String

Month(1) = "Jan"
Month(2) = "Feb"
Month(3) = "Mar"

Cells(1, 1) = Month(1)
Cells(1, 2) = Month(2)     ◄── ④
Cells(1, 3) = Month(3)

End Sub
```

Excel places the values in the array in the specified cell.

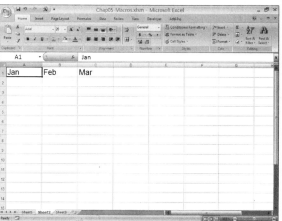

Extra

When you specify the size of an array, you indicate the upper and lower bounds of the array, or the first and last index values. In the example, Dim NewArray(1 To 45), the statement creates an array with 45 elements with a lower bound of 1 and an upper bound of 45. You can omit the lower bound value when you declare an array, as in the example, Dim NewArray(45). If you do not specify the lower bound, VBA assigns a lower bound value of 0. Therefore, the array NewArray actually has 46 elements starting with the first element 0 and ending with the final element 45.

If you want all your arrays to have a lower bound value of 1, place the following statement before any procedures in your module: Option Base 1. Making your arrays one-based is desirable because Microsoft Excel collections are one-based and the arrays that Excel methods and properties return are one-based. If your arrays are also one-based, your code will be easier to debug.

Declare a Multidimensional Array

You can use a multidimensional array to store related values within one array. VBA allows you to create arrays with up to 60 dimensions. However, working with arrays that have more than two or three dimensions can be difficult.

By using multidimensional arrays, you can store related values in one location. For example, you can store team numbers and game scores. The first dimension of the array can contain the team's number, and the second dimension can contain the team's score.

To help envision a multidimensional array, try thinking of a two-dimensional array as a worksheet, with rows and columns. You access each element of the array by specifying two index values. For example, MultiArray(1,2) accesses the value whose first dimension index is 1 and whose second dimension index is 2.

As you add a third dimension to an array, it gains depth. Using the worksheet example, you can add a third dimension to the two-dimensional array to make it resemble a cube. Accessing an element of the array now requires three index values, as in the example, MultiArray(1,2,2).

As with other variables, you use the Dim statement to declare procedure-only arrays and module-only arrays, and the Public statement for arrays that are accessible to the entire workbook.

When you declare a multidimensional array, you indicate the size of each dimension in the array. You do not have to make the dimensions in the array equal. In the example, Dim MultiArray(1 To 4, 1 To 5, 1 To 3), the array contains four elements in the first dimension, five in the second, and three in the third.

Declare a Multidimensional Array

① Name your procedure.

② Declare your array.

③ Specify the range in your Excel worksheet in which VBA will place the contents of your array.

④ Assign values to the array elements.

⑤ Assign the array values to the cells you specified in step 3.

⑥ Press Alt+F11 to switch from the VBE to Excel, and run the macro.

```
        Title(1) = "Team"
        Title(2) = "Score"
        TeamScores(1, 1) = 1
        TeamScores(2, 1) = 2
        TeamScores(3, 1) = 3
        TeamScores(4, 1) = 4            ◄── ④
        TeamScores(1, 2) = 205
        TeamScores(2, 2) = 172
        TeamScores(3, 2) = 289
        TeamScores(4, 2) = 239
        TitleRange.Value = Title
        CellRange.Value = TeamScores ◄── ⑤
End Sub
```

The values in the array appear in cells in your worksheet.

Apply It

You can assign the contents of an array to a series of cells in a worksheet by using the Value property of the Range object. To learn more about the Range object, see Chapter 11. When you create a Range object, you can specify the cells you want to include in the range by using the Set statement. As the macro runs, VBA places any values you assign to the Range object in the corresponding cells in your worksheet.

Example:
```
Dim CellRange As Range
Set CellRange = Range(Cells(2,1), Cells(5,2))
CellRange.Value = TeamScores
```

The Set statement assigns the range of cells to the Range object. You specify the range by using the Cells property to determine the starting and ending cells for the desired range. After you specify the desired range, you assign the contents of an array to the cells in the range by using the Value property.

When you use a multidimensional array, all elements of the array must have the same data type. If you plan to use the array to store different types of values, such as strings and numeric values, you must declare your array as variant.

Example:
```
Dim MultiArray (1 To 4, 1 To 5, 1 To 3) As
Variant
```

79

Convert a List to an Array

By converting a list of values to an array, you can access the individual values quickly using one variable. You can convert a list of values to an array by using a variety of methods.

You can assign values to your array by referencing the index values of each element. Arrays use index values to identify their elements. For example, if an array has ten elements with a lower bound of 1, the third element in the array has an index value of 3. To assign a value to an array, you specify the index values that correspond to the appropriate array element. For example, the following code assigns a value of 45 to the third array element:
`SampleArray(3) = 45`.

With large arrays, assigning values to each element of the array in a statement using the above method can be cumbersome. Using a `For Next` loop is more efficient;

you simply create a `For Next` loop to cycle through the entire array. `For Next` loops work best for adding values either from a series of cells or when values are incremental. See Chapter 6 for more information about working with `For Next` loops.

You can use the `Array` function to add a list of values to an array. The `Array` function adds values to the array by starting at the lower bound of the array and then adding values consecutively. For example, the following code adds the values "One", "Two", and "Three" to SampleArray:
`SampleArray = Array("One", "Two", "Three")`.

You can produce the same results by specifying each element individually; for example, you can assign a value to the first element of the array, as follows:
`SampleArray(1) = "One"`.

Convert a List to an Array

① Name your procedure.

② Declare your array.

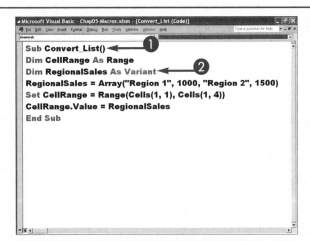

③ Assign values to your array.

④ Set the Range property.

⑤ Press Alt+F11 to switch from the VBE to Excel, and run the macro.

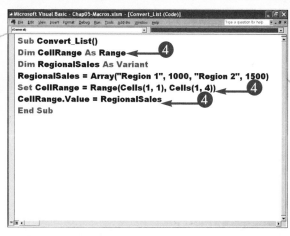

```
Sub Convert_List()
Dim CellRange As Range          ←④
Dim RegionalSales As Variant
RegionalSales = Array("Region 1", 1000, "Region 2", 1500)
Set CellRange = Range(Cells(1, 1), Cells(1, 4))   ←④
CellRange.Value = RegionalSales   ←④
End Sub
```

The values in the array appear in cells in your worksheet.

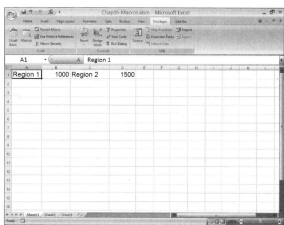

Extra

The Array function uses the variant data type. As a result, you can have different data types in a single array. As shown in the example in this section, you can add both strings and numeric values to the same variable when using the Array function.

You can use the ReDim statement to change the size of the array after you create it. You can also use the Array function more than once in the same procedure to reassign the values in the array. See the section, "Redimension an Array," for more information on resizing an array.

You can use the following code to assign the numbers 1 to 10 to an array. See Chapter 6 for more information on For Next loops.

Example:
```
Sub Assign_Numbers()
Dim X as Integer
Dim RecNo(1 To 10) As
Integer
For X =1 To 10
    RecNo(X) = X
    Cells(X,1) = RecNo(X)
Next
End Sub
```

Redimension an Array

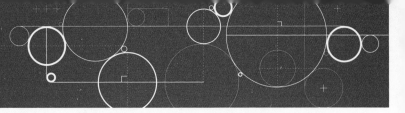

VBA lets you declare two types of arrays: fixed-size and dynamic arrays. When you declare a fixed-size array, you specify the number of elements in the array. For example, the following code creates a fixed-size array with seven elements: Dim NewArray(1,7) As String.

If you do not know how large to make the array when you declare it, you can use a dynamic array. A dynamic array does not have a size until you use the ReDim statement to change the array size. First, use the Dim statement without a size to create a dynamic array — for example: Dim NewArray() As String.

When you are ready to use the array, use the ReDim statement to size the array so you can add values. For example, in the code, ReDim NewArray(1 To 4), an array that was initially declared as a dynamic array with

an unknown number of elements is redimensioned to contain four elements.

VBA does not allow you to redimension a fixed-size array. If you attempt to change the size of a fixed-size array, you receive an "Array already dimensioned" error message. However, if you declare your array as a dynamic array, you can use the ReDim statement multiple times within a procedure to change the size of the array.

Each time you redimension an array, you destroy the existing elements in the array. If you want to preserve the existing values, use the Preserve statement. For example, the statement, ReDim Preserve NewArray(7), instructs VBA to resize the array to seven elements and maintain any existing values. If the array has four values, those values remain the first four values.

Redimension an Array

1. Name your procedure.

2. Declare a dynamic array.

3. Set the initial dimension size.

4. Assign a value to the variable element.

5. Place the contents of the variable in a cell.

6. Redimension the array.

7. Assign values to the variable elements.

8. Place the contents of the variables in cells.

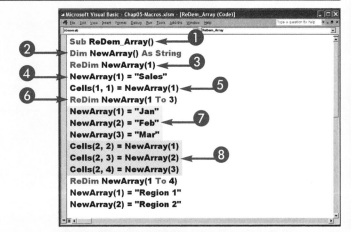

9. Redimension the array.

10. Assign values to the variable elements.

11. Place the contents of the variables into cells.

12. Preserve the first four elements and add space for three more.

13. Assign values to the three new elements.

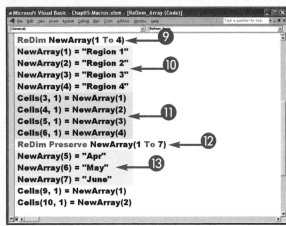

⑭ Place the values for all of the elements in the worksheet.

⑮ Press Alt+F11 to switch from the VBE to Excel, and run the macro.

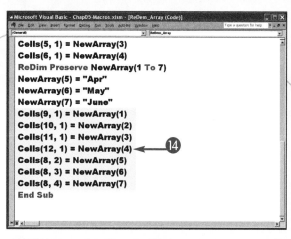

The values in the array appear in cells in your worksheet.

● These values were preserved.

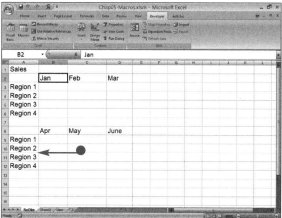

Extra

To find the upper and lower bounds of an array, VBA provides the UBound and LBound functions. The sample code finds the upper and lower bounds and assigns them to variables.

Example:
```
UpperBound = UBound(NewArray)

LowerBound = LBound(NewArray)
```

Each of these functions returns a Long data type indicating the upper or lower bounds of the specified array. If the array is multidimensional, you must specify the dimension for which you want the bounds.

Example:
```
UpperBounds = UBound(MultiArray, 2)
```

Create a User-Defined Data Type

U ser-defined data types enable you to create a single variable that records multiple pieces of information. User-defined data types resemble multidimensional arrays in that you can store related values by using one variable name. However, while all elements in the array must contain the same data type, you can create a user-defined data type that contains multiple data types.

You declare user-defined data types at the top of your module in the declarations area. You specify a user-defined data type with the `Type` and `End Type` statements. The `Type` statement indicates the start of the user-defined data type definition, and the `End Type` statement specifies the end. After the `Type` statement, you indicate the name of the new data type; for example, `Type ItemInfo` creates a data type called ItemInfo. To create a user-defined data type to store an item price and

description, you can specify a user-defined data type with two components.

After you create the data type, you can declare variables that use the specified data type. You can use a user-defined data type as the data type for an array. For example, to create an array of the ItemInfo data type, you enter `Dim NewItems(1 To 10) As ItemInfo`.

To assign values to a user-defined array, you not only specify the array element, but you also indicate the component you want to change. For example, this code changes the value of the first component in the array:
`NewItems(1).ItemDescription = "15 inch Monitor"`.

Similarly, you can copy the entire contents of one element to another by simply referring to the array element. The following code copies ItemDescription and ItemPrice of the first element of the array to the second array element:
`NewItems(2) = NewItems(1)`.

Create a User-Defined Data Type

① Create your user-defined data type in the declarations area.

② Add the Type and End Type statements.

③ Declare the components.

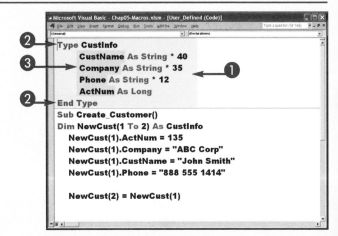

④ Create a new procedure.

⑤ Declare your user-defined data type.

⑥ Assign values to your user-defined data type.

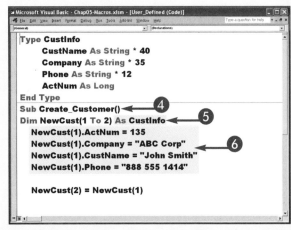

84

7 Copy the contents of one element to another element.

8 Place the contents of both elements in worksheet cells.

9 Press Alt+F11 to switch from the VBE to Excel, and run the macro.

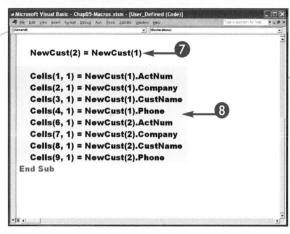

The values from the user-defined data type appear in cells in your worksheet.

● VBA copies the values from the first element to the second element.

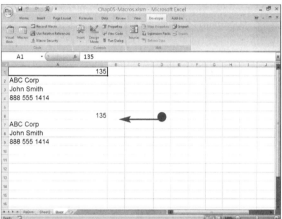

Extra

As you use VBA to develop macros, the complexity of your code may make it difficult to keep track of variables. To simplify the process, many developers use a standard naming convention where the variable name reflects the variable type. When using this type of naming convention, you preface each variable name with a standard lowercase prefix that identifies the data type of the variable. For example, you can identify an integer variable by prefixing it with *i* to create the variable name iNumVisits. The integer prefix makes it clear at any location in the code that the variable holds an integer value. The following table lists the standard variable-naming conventions for Visual Basic and VBA.

PREFIX	DATA TYPE
b	Boolean
c or cur	Currency
dt	Date/Time
d	Double
i or int	Integer
l or lng	Long
obj	Object
s or sng	Single
str	String
u	User-defined
v or var	Variant

Create
Comparisons

Comparison operators enable you to compare two expressions. Comparison expressions always return `True` or `False`. For example, the expression, `A = B`, compares the variable `A` to the variable `B`. It then returns the value `True` if the value stored in variable `A` is equal to the value stored in variable `B`, and `False` if the value stored in variable `A` is not equal to the value stored in variable `B`.

When writing a comparison expression, you use a comparison operator. You place the comparison operator between the expressions you want to compare. Use an equal (=) sign to determine if two values are equal. Use a not equal (<>) sign to determine if values are not equal. Use a greater-than (>) sign to determine if one value is greater than another value. Use a less-than (<) sign to determine if one value is less than another value. Use greater than or equal to (>=), to determine if one value is

greater than or equal to another value. Use less than or equal to (<=) to determine if one value is less than or equal to another value.

Extra

The following table is a summary of the comparison operators.

OPERATOR	FUNCTION
=	Equal to
<>	Not equal
>	Greater than
<	Less than
<=	Less than or equal to
>=	Greater than or equal to

Create Comparisons

❶ Add a comparison operator to your `Do While` loop.

In this example, If J is less than 11, VBA executes the code inside the loop.

Note: See the section, "Employ Do While Loops," in this chapter to learn more about `Do While` loops.

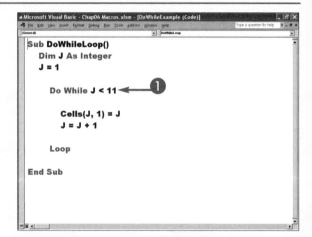

```
Sub DoWhileLoop()
    Dim J As Integer
    J = 1

    Do While J < 11 ←──❶

        Cells(J, 1) = J
        J = J + 1

    Loop

End Sub
```

❷ Add a comparison operator to your `If` and `ElseIf` statement.

Note: See the section, "Create If Then Else Statements," in this chapter to learn more about `If Then` statements.

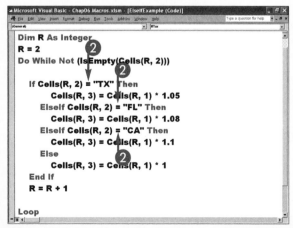

```
Dim R As Integer
R = 2
Do While Not (IsEmpty(Cells(R, 2)))

    If Cells(R, 2) = "TX" Then
        Cells(R, 3) = Cells(R, 1) * 1.05
    ElseIf Cells(R, 2) = "FL" Then
        Cells(R, 3) = Cells(R, 1) * 1.08
    ElseIf Cells(R, 2) = "CA" Then
        Cells(R, 3) = Cells(R, 1) * 1.1
    Else
        Cells(R, 3) = Cells(R, 1) * 1
    End If
    R = R + 1

Loop
```

Make Use of Logical Operators

When writing VBA code, you can use logical operators to link together comparison expressions to create complex comparison expressions. There are six logical operators: Or, And, Xor, Eqv, Imp, and Not.

Using Logical Or

The logical operator Or returns the value True if expression A is true or expression B is true.

EXPRESSION A	EXPRESSION B	RESULT
True	True	True
True	False	True
False	True	True
False	False	False

Example:
```
Sub LogicalOr()
Dim Result As Boolean
Result = 10 < 20 Or 30 < 20 'Returns True
MsgBox (Result)
End Sub
```

Using Logical AND

The logical operator And returns the value True if expression A is true and expression B is true.

EXPRESSION A	EXPRESSION B	RESULT
True	True	True
True	False	False
False	True	False
False	False	False

Using Logical XOR

The logical value Xor returns the value True if expression A is true and expression B is false, or if expression A is false and expression B is true.

EXPRESSION A	EXPRESSION B	RESULT
True	True	False
True	False	True
False	True	True
False	False	False

Using Logical Eqv

The Eqv operator returns the value True if expression A is true and expression B is true, or if expression A is false and expression B is false.

EXPRESSION A	EXPRESSION B	RESULT
True	True	True
True	False	False
False	True	False
False	False	True

Using Logical IMP

The Imp operator returns True unless expression A is true and expression B is false.

EXPRESSION A	EXPRESSION B	RESULT
True	True	True
True	False	False
False	True	True
False	False	True

Using Logical NOT

The Not logical operator negates an expression. If the expression would normally return True, using a Not operator causes it to return False and vise versa.

Example:
```
Sub LogicalNot()
Dim Result As Boolean
Result = Not (10 = 10) 'Returns False
MsgBox (Result)
End Sub
```

Employ Do While Loops

You can execute a VBA statement or a series of VBA statements as long as a condition is true by using a `Do While` loop. The following is the syntax for a `Do While` loop:

```
Do [While condition]
     [statements]
Loop
```

A condition is an expression that evaluates to either `True` or `False`. When VBA encounters a `Do While` loop, it evaluates the condition. If the condition is true, it executes the statements. After it executes all of the statements, VBA returns to the `Do While` statement and evaluates the condition again. If the condition is still true, it executes the statements again. If the condition is false, VBA executes the first statement after the `Loop` statement.

A `Do While` loop consists of four basic parts: The `Do` statement initiates the loop. The `While` statement evaluates the condition that must be met. The body of the loop contains a series of statements to perform as long as the condition is true. Finally, the `Loop` statement marks the end of the loop.

You can use the following syntax to create a `Do-Loop While` loop:

```
Do
[statements]
Loop [While condition]
```

A `Do-Loop While` loop is similar to a `Do While` loop. The primary difference is VBA evaluates the condition at the end of the block of statements so the loop always executes at least once.

Employ Do While Loops

① Name your procedure.

② Declare your variable.

③ Assign a value to your variable.

This example assigns the number 1 to the variable J and uses variable J as a counter.

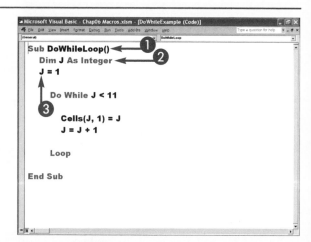

④ Use a `Do While` statement to evaluate whether a condition is true.

In this example, the code looks at the value assigned to the variable J and performs the statements inside the loop if J is less than 11.

⑤ Place the value of J in the specified cell.

In this example, the cell row is equal to the value of J and the cell column is 1.

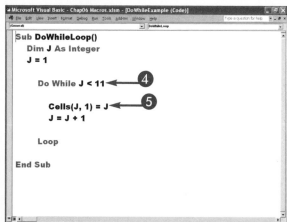

6 Increase the value of J.

In this example, VBA adds 1 to the current value of J.

7 Add the Loop statement.

VBA returns to the `Do While` statement and continues looping until your code no longer meets the condition.

8 Press Alt+F11 to switch from the VBE to Excel, and then run the macro.

Note: *See Chapter 1 to learn how to run a macro.*

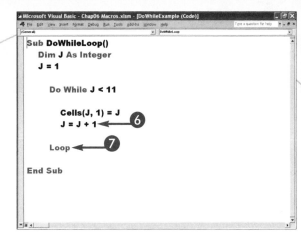

The macro places the numbers 1 to 10 in column A, rows 1 to 10.

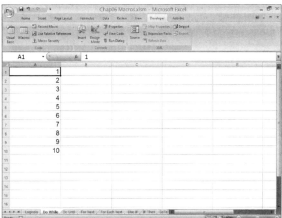

Apply It

A loop must contain a statement that changes the condition, and the condition must eventually evaluate to `False`, or the loop will continue endlessly. Programmers refer to this condition as an *infinite loop*.

To avoid an infinite loop, you can use a counter. In the following example, the procedure assigns the counter variable J an initial value of 1. The `Do While` loop verifies that it is less than 5, and then executes the loop. The loop assigns a value of 1 to the first cell on the worksheet, cell A1. The counter variable J increments by 1 and the loop retests the condition. The looping continues until the condition is false. In this example, the loop repeats four times. When J equals 5, the looping stops.

Example:
```
Dim J As Integer
J = 1
Do While J < 5
     ActiveSheet.Rows(J).Cells(1).Value = J
     J = J + 1
Loop
```

Create
Do Until Loops

I f you need to execute a statement or a series of statements until a condition is met, you can use a Do Until loop. For example, you can use a Do Until loop to apply changes to a series of cells until you encounter an empty cell.

When you use the Do Until loop, the statements you place between the Do Until and Loop statements execute until the specified condition is met. As soon as the looping structure determines that the condition is true, control moves to the next statement outside the loop.

A Do Until loop consists of four basic parts: The Do statement initiates the loop. The Until condition specifies the condition that must be met. The body of the loop contains a series of statements that execute until the

value of the statement meets the condition of the loop. Finally, the Loop statement marks the end of the loop.

When the Until condition follows the Do statement, the Do Until loop checks to see if the condition is true before executing. If the condition is not true, the loop executes. If the condition is true, the loop does not execute. When you use this structure for a Do Until loop, the code inside the loop may never execute.

You can also place the Until condition at the end of the loop. When you place the Until condition at the end of the loop, the Do Until loop always executes at least once before checking the condition. If the condition is true, the Do Until loop stops execution, and control passes to the next VBA statement in your procedure.

Loop Until a Condition Is Met

① Name your procedure.

② Declare your variable.

③ Assign a value to your variable.

In this example, the variable J is used to set the row number.

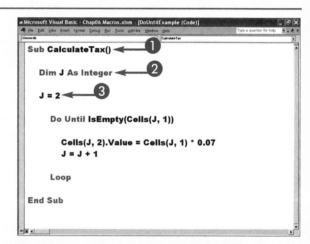

④ Add your Do Until statement.

In this example, the loop continues until it reaches an empty cell.

⑤ Type the statements you want to execute.

In this example, VBA multiplies the value in column A by 0.07 and places the result in column B.

⑥ Add the Loop statement.

VBA returns to the Do Until statement and continues looping until the condition is met.

⑦ Press Alt+F11 to switch from the VBE to Excel, and then run the macro.

Note: *See Chapter 1 to learn how to run a macro.*

The procedure places 7 percent of column A in column B.

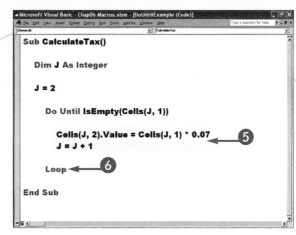

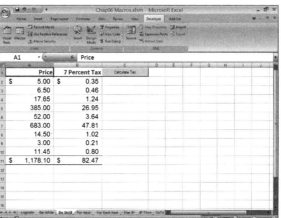

When working with loops, you may have situations where you want to jump out of a loop before executing the remaining statements in the loop. You can use an Exit Do statement. You can place an Exit Do statement anywhere within the body of your loop, and you can have multiple Exit Do statements. When VBA encounters an Exit Do statement, the control immediately transfers out of the current loop to the next statement outside the loop.

Typically, a conditional statement such as If Then appears before the Exit Do statement. The conditional statement looks for a condition to meet and then executes the Exit Do statement when your code meets the condition.

Example:
```
Do While Condition1 = True
      If Condition2 = True
            Exit Do
      End If
Loop
```

Create For Next Loops

Y ou can use a For Next loop to execute a statement or a series of statements a specific number of times. For example, by using a For Next loop, you can place text in a specified number of cells.

When you use a For Next loop, you must create a counter variable. The statements you place between the For and Next statements execute until the counter variable exceeds the maximum value. As soon as the looping structure determines that the current value of the counter is greater than the maximum value, control moves to the first statement after the loop.

For Next loops consist of three basic parts: The For statement initiates the loop. The For statement includes a counter variable with an initial and maximum value,

such as X = 1 To 5. The the body of the loop consists of a series of statements that perform until the counter exceeds the maximum value of the loop. Finally, you mark the end of the loop with the Next statement.

When the For Next loop starts, it checks to make sure the value of the counter variable does not exceed the maximum value. If the variable is less than or equal to the maximum, the loop executes. The counter variable is a numeric value that increments by default by one each time the loop executes. The loop continues to execute as long as the initial value is less than or equal to the maximum value specified for the counter variable. If the initial value starts out greater than the maximum value, the body of the loop never executes.

Create For Next Loops

① Name your procedure.

② Declare your variable.

③ Assign a value to your variable.

In this example, the variable Count is a counter.

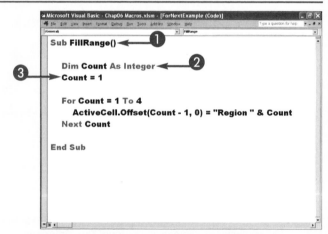

④ Add your For statement.

● Counter variable.

● Initial value.

● Maximum value.

⑤ Type the statement you want to execute.

This example places the text Region 1 through Region 4 in four consecutive cells.

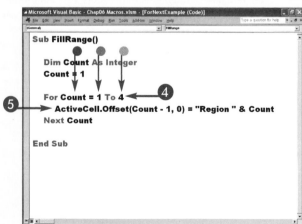

6 Add `Next`.

VBA returns to the `For` statements and if the counter exceeds the maximum value, VBA moves to the first line of code after the `Next` statement; otherwise, it executes the statements inside the loop.

7 Press Alt+F11 to switch from the VBE to Excel, and then run the macro.

Note: See Chapter 1 to learn how to run a macro.

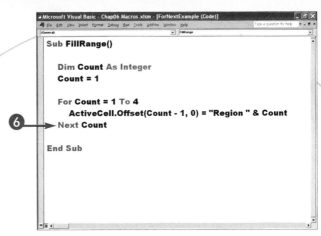

```vba
Sub FillRange()

    Dim Count As Integer
    Count = 1

    For Count = 1 To 4
        ActiveCell.Offset(Count - 1, 0) = "Region " & Count
    Next Count

End Sub
```

The procedure places the text Region 1 through Region 4 in a column in four consecutive cells.

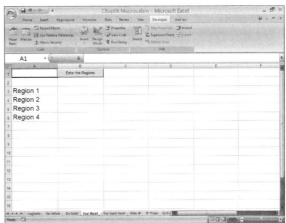

Execute For Each In Loops

You can use a For Each In loop to execute a series of statements for each element in an array or each object in a collection. When you use a For Each In loop, the statements you place between the For and Next statements execute for each element in the array or collection. After the statements execute for the last element, control moves to the next statement outside the loop. The following is the syntax for a For Each In loop:

```
For Each element In group

[Statements]

Next [element]
```

A For Each In loop consists of three parts. The For Each element In group statement initiates the loop. An element is a variable used to hold an array or collection element as you cycle through the For Each Next loop. Group is the name of the array or collection you want to cycle through. The body of the loop contains a series of statements to perform for each element. Finally, the Next statement marks the end of the loop.

If you are looping through an array, the variable you use as the element in the For Each element In group statement must be defined as a variant data type. If you are working with a collection, you can define the variable as a variant, generic object, or specific object.

Execute For Each In Loops

1. Name your procedure.

2. Declare your array.

Note: See Chapter 5 to learn more about arrays.

3. Declare your variables.

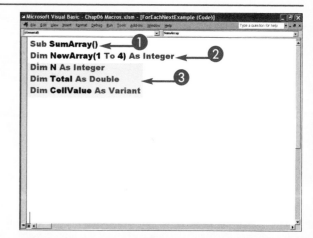

4. Assign values to your array.

In this example, the value in the active cell and three subsequent cells in the same column are assigned to the array.

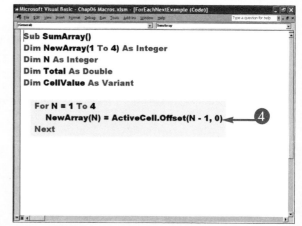

5 Add your `For Each In` statements.

● Variable that holds each element.

● Array or collection name.

● Statements to execute.

6 Add the `Next` statement.

This example totals the elements in the array.

7 Type any statements you want to execute after the `For Each In` loop executes.

8 Press Alt+F11 to switch from the VBE to Excel, and then run the macro.

Note: *See Chapter 1 to learn how to run a macro.*

● In this example, VBA totals the elements in the array and places the total in the cell that follows the array.

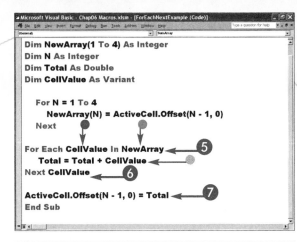

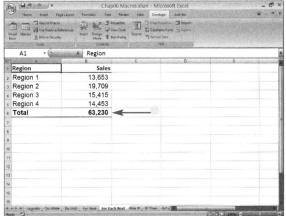

Apply It

You can nest loops to populate a multidimensional array. When you nest loops, you place one loop inside another loop. To work with a multidimensional array, you create a separate loop for each dimension of the array. The following code uses two nested `For Next` loops to access elements of the array. Notice that the inside loop, with the `L` counter variable, completely cycles each time the loop with `K` runs once. Each `Next` statement has a variable following it. You must exit the inside loop before you can exit outside loops.

TYPE THIS:

```
Sub BuildArray()
Dim NewArray(1 To 3, 1 To 3) As Integer
Dim K As Integer
Dim L As Integer
X = 1
For K = 1 To 3
     For L = 1 To 3
         NewArray(K, L) = X
         X = X + 1
     Next L
 Next K
End Sub
```

RESULT:

The code creates a two-dimensional array with the values shown in the following table:

1	2	3
4	5	6
7	8	9

Create If Then Else Statements

You can conditionally execute a group of statements by using an `If Then Else` statement. For example, you can calculate a bonus of five percent of sales if an employee's sales are greater than $50,000, or enter the text "No Bonus" if an employee's sales are less than or equal to $50,000. The following is the syntax for an `If Then Else` statement:

```
IF condition Then
      [statements]

Else
      [statements]
End If
```

An `If Then Else` statement evaluates a condition. A condition is any expression that evaluates to either `True` or `False`. For example: the expression `If Sales >` 50000 `Then` evaluates the variable Sales. If the variable Sales is greater than 50,000, the expression returns `True`; otherwise, it returns `False`. If the condition is true, the statements that follow the `Then` statement execute. If the condition is false, the statements that follow the `Else` statement execute. A null condition evaluates to false. An `End If` statement marks the end of an `If Then Else` statement.

If you have multiple conditions that you want to evaluate, you can use `ElseIf`. For example, you can use `ElseIf` when you want to calculate tax at a rate of 5 percent if the state is Texas, 8 percent if the state is Florida, and no tax for all other states. When using `ElseIf`, a single `If Then` statement is followed by several `ElseIf` statements and a final `Else` statement.

Create If Then Else Statements

IF THEN ELSE

① Add your `If Then` statement.

● Condition.

● Statement to execute.

② Add your `Else` statement.

● Statement to execute.

③ Type **End If**.

④ Press Alt+F11 to switch from the VBE to Excel, and then run the macro.

Note: *See Chapter 1 to learn how to run a macro.*

In this example, if the Sales column is over 50,000, VBA calculates a bonus of 4 percent of sales; otherwise, it prints the words "No Bonus."

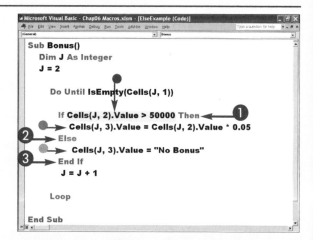

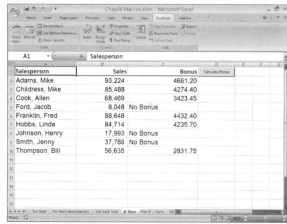

ELSEIF

1. Add your `If Then` statement.

- Condition.

- Statement to execute.

2. Add your `ElseIf` statements.

- Statement to execute.

3. Add your `Else` statement.

- Statement to execute.

4. Type **End If**.

5. Press Alt+F11 to switch from the VBE to Excel, and then run the macro.

Note: See Chapter 1 to learn how to run a macro.

In this example, the procedure calculates the sales price plus tax, based on the state tax amount.

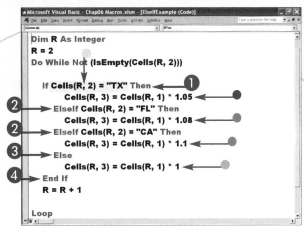

Extra

Although VBA does not require you to indent your code, you can use indentation to improve readability. Indenting enables you to analyze the structure of the code without reading each line. When working with conditional statements, such as `If Then` statements and looping statements, most programmers indent the statements that execute. The following example shows how you can indent the code for a `For Next` loop so you can easily locate the loop's beginning and end. The example also indents an `If Then` statement.

Example:
```
For I = 1 To 5
    If J < 10 Then
        J = J + 1
    End If
Next
```

If you have an `If Then` statement that consists of only one statement, you can combine the `If` statement with the `Then` statement and eliminate the `End If` statement.

Example:
```
If Sum < 10 Then Sum = Sum + 1
'This is equivalent to typing the following:
If Sum < 10 Then
    Sum = Sum + 1
End If
```

Construct Select Case Statements

You can execute a specific block of code based on a value by using a Select Case statement. Using a Select Case statement is similar to using ElseIf. You can use Select Case when you have different statements to execute and the statements that execute depend upon the value of a cell, variable, number, or string. For example, you can base the calculation of sales tax on the state. You can calculate a tax rate of 5 percent if the state is Texas, 8 percent if the state is Florida, and no tax for all other states. The following is the syntax for Select Case statements.

```
Select Case testexpression
[Case expressionlist -n
      [statements-n]]
[Case Else
      [elsestatements]]
End Select
```

The Select Case statement identifies the expression against which you want to test each case statement. Each Case statement contains a value to test and the statements to execute if the case statement is true, for example:

```
Select Case UserVal
    Case 4
            Statements
...
End Select
```

The example determines whether UserVal = 4 is True. Under each Case statement are statements that execute if the expression evaluates to true. The End Select statement marks the end of the Select Case statement.

You can also add a Case Else statement that supplies the statement to run if none of the Case statements evaluate to true.

Construct Select Case Statements

① Name your procedure.

② Declare your variable.

③ Initialize your variable.

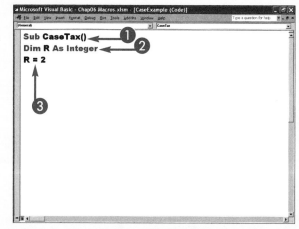

④ Create a Do While Loop.

Note: See the section, "Employ Do While Loops," in this chapter to learn how to create a Do While Loop.

⑤ Type your Select Case statement.

● Each Case statement value is compared to this value.

⑥ Type your Case statements.

● If the value in the Select Case statement is equal to the value in the Case statement, the statements that follow the Case statement execute.

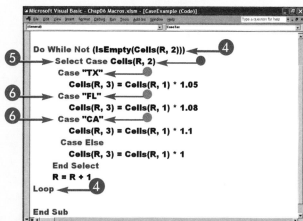

7 Add your `Case Else` statement.

The statements after the `Case Else` statement execute if none of the other Case statements match the `Select Case` value.

8 Add an `End Select` statement.

9 Press Alt+F11 to switch from the VBE to Excel, and then run the macro.

Note: See Chapter 1 to learn how to run a macro.

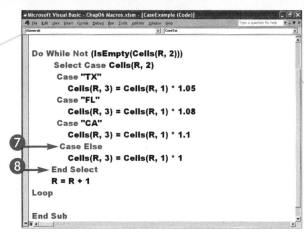

```
Do While Not (IsEmpty(Cells(R, 2)))
    Select Case Cells(R, 2)
    Case "TX"
        Cells(R, 3) = Cells(R, 1) * 1.05
    Case "FL"
        Cells(R, 3) = Cells(R, 1) * 1.08
    Case "CA"
        Cells(R, 3) = Cells(R, 1) * 1.1
    Case Else
        Cells(R, 3) = Cells(R, 1) * 1
    End Select
    R = R + 1
Loop

End Sub
```

In this example, the procedure calculates the sales price plus tax, based on the state tax amount.

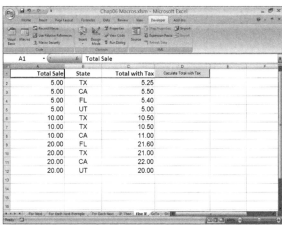

Total Sale	State	Total with Tax	Caculate Total with Tax
5.00	TX	5.25	
5.00	CA	5.50	
5.00	FL	5.40	
5.00	UT	5.00	
10.00	TX	10.50	
10.00	TX	10.50	
10.00	CA	11.00	
20.00	FL	21.60	
20.00	TX	21.00	
20.00	CA	22.00	
20.00	UT	20.00	

Apply It

With the `Select Case` statement, you can use comparison statements to compare a range of values, or multiple values.

TYPE THIS:

```
Select Case NumSales
    Case 1 To 5
        Commission = Total * .05
    Case 6 To 15
        Commission = Total * .1
End Select
```

RESULT:

The Select Case statement checks the value of NumSales to see whether it falls into one of the two specified ranges.

TYPE THIS:

```
Select Case NumStudents
    Case Is < 10
        MsgBox("Not enough students enrolled")
End Select
```

RESULT:

The Select Case statement displays the message box if the value of NumStudents is less than 10.

TYPE THIS:

```
Select Case State
    Case "TX", "CA"
        Total = Total * 1.085
End Select
```

RESULT:

If the value of State equals TX or CA, the total is calculated using 8.5 percent for the sales tax.

GoTo a Named Location

You can jump to a named location within your macro by using a GoTo statement. However, before you can use a GoTo statement, you must label the line in your procedure to which you want to move. A label is a text string followed by a colon. The GoTo command moves to the label, thereby passing control from the current location in the procedure to the label. The following is the syntax for the GoTo command:

```
Goto label
```

As you can see, there are two parts to a GoTo command: the GoTo statement and the label. You can place a label anywhere in your procedure. The GoTo command can only jump to labels within the same procedure. They

cannot jump to a label in another procedure, even if both procedures are in the same module. You can add multiple GoTo commands to the same procedure, and each GoTo command can jump to the same or different labels.

You should only use GoTo commands in situations where you cannot obtain the desired results using conditional statements or looping structures. GoTo commands date back to when each line of code had a specific line number and GoTo commands jumped to the specified line of code. While GoTo commands are often used for trapping errors in VBA, many programmers consider it bad programming to use GoTo commands too frequently. See Chapter 8 for more information on using a GoTo statement when debugging your code.

GoTo a Named Location

① Create a new procedure.

② Add your code.

```
Sub CalculateShipping()
Select Case Cells(2, 2)
        Case "TX"
            Cells(2, 3) = Cells(2, 1) * 1.075
            If Cells(2, 1) > 50 Then GoTo NoShipping
            GoTo Shipping
        Case "FL"
            Cells(2, 3) = Cells(2, 1) * 1.085
            If Cells(2, 1) > 50 Then GoTo NoShipping
            GoTo Shipping
        Case Else
            Cells(2, 3) = Cells(2, 1) * 1.09
            If Cells(2, 1) > 50 Then GoTo NoShipping
            GoTo Shipping
    End Select
```

③ Add your GoTo statements.

```
Sub CalculateShipping()
Select Case Cells(2, 2)
        Case "TX"
            Cells(2, 3) = Cells(2, 1) * 1.075
            If Cells(2, 1) > 50 Then GoTo NoShipping
            GoTo Shipping
        Case "FL"
            Cells(2, 3) = Cells(2, 1) * 1.085
            If Cells(2, 1) > 50 Then GoTo NoShipping
            GoTo Shipping
        Case Else
            Cells(2, 3) = Cells(2, 1) * 1.09
            If Cells(2, 1) > 50 Then GoTo NoShipping
            GoTo Shipping
    End Select
```

④ Add your GoTo label.

● Label names are followed by a colon.

⑤ Add any additional code.

⑥ Press Alt+F11 to switch from the VBE to Excel, and then run the macro.

Note: See Chapter 1 to learn how to run a macro.

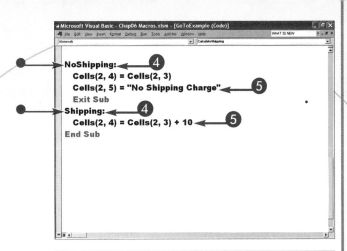

In this example, the procedure calculates a shipping charge if the cost with tax is less than $50.00.

Extra

You place labels in a procedure to mark the location of code. Labeling code does not change how it executes. Code within a loop or conditional statement executes only when the condition is met. Labeled code executes when a GoTo statement jump's to it, or when the program reaches that line of code.

If you have multiple areas of labeled code, you may not want it all to execute. To avoid execution of code that follows a labeled section, you can use another GoTo statement or an Exit Sub statement to terminate the current procedure.

The following example uses the Exit Sub command before the label procedure to avoid execution of the T =50 statement. The GoTo command jumps to the IncreaseValue label, and the T = T * 5 statement does not execute.

Example:
```
Sub TestGoTo()
Dim T As Integer
T = Cells(1,1)
If T < 5 Then GoTo IncreaseValue
     T = T * 5
Exit Sub
IncreaseValue:
     T = 50
End Sub
```

Call a Procedure

I f you are in one procedure and you want to execute another procedure, you can use a `Call` statement. You simply type the word `Call` followed by the name of the procedure you want to call, as well as any arguments the procedure requires, in parentheses and separated by commas. When you call a procedure, VBA moves to the first line of code in the called procedure and begins processing. After the called procedure completes processing, VBA returns to the next line of code after the call and continues processing the original procedure.

You can conditionally call a procedure by using a conditional VBA statement, such as an `If Then` statement with a `Call` statement. When you combine the `Call` statement with a conditional statement, VBA executes the called procedure only if the specified

condition is met. The `If Then` statement checks the specified condition. If the value of the condition is true, the control passes to the called procedure or function and then, upon the called procedure's completion, returns to the original procedure. If you do not want to continue processing the first procedure after calling the second, you can use an `Exit Sub` statement to exit the procedure.

The keyword `Call` is optional when executing a `Call` statement. You can call a procedure simply by typing the procedure name. If you omit the `Call` keyword, do not place your arguments in parentheses. Simply type the procedure name followed by its arguments, separated by commas. You can call Sub procedures, Function procedures, or Dynamic-Link Library (DLL) procedures.

Call a Procedure

① Name your procedure.

② Declare and initialize any variables.

You may need to make your variable public.

Note: See Chapter 3 to learn more about public variables.

③ Create an `If Then` condition.

④ Call another procedure.

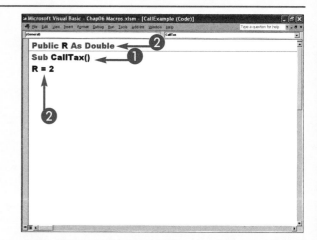

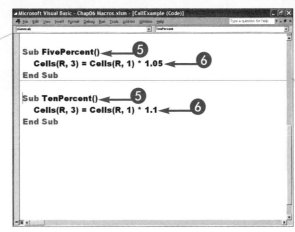

⑤ Create called procedures.

⑥ Type code to run when the procedure is called.

⑦ Press Alt+F11 to switch from the VBE to Excel, and then run the macro.

Note: *See Chapter 1 to learn how to run a macro.*

When the condition is met, the `If Then` statement calls the procedure.

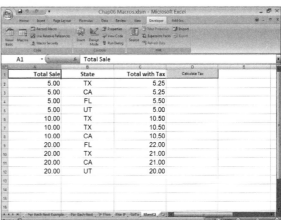

Apply It

You do not need to use the `Call` keyword when you call another procedure or function. However, using the `Call` keyword eliminates confusion by clearly indicating that you are calling a function or `Sub` procedure. When you use the `Call` keyword, you must enclose any arguments passed in parentheses. If you call a procedure without the `Call` keyword, you must omit the parentheses around the argument list, as follows:

THIS CODE:	IS EQUIVALENT TO:
`Call NewProc(Var1, Var2).`	`NewProc Var1, Var2.`

Work with Excel Worksheet Functions

A *function* is a block of code that performs a task and returns a single value. There are three types of functions: VBA functions, Excel worksheet functions, and custom functions. A VBA function is a function supplied by VBA. An Excel worksheet function is a formula that Excel has predefined. You can use them to do things such as add numbers, find an average, or find the highest number in a list. Excel provides you with more than 300 worksheet functions. Custom functions work like worksheet function; however, you define the formula the function uses.

Use the `WorksheetFunction` property to place an Excel worksheet function in your VBA procedure. The `WorksheetFunction` property is available through the `Application` object. To access a function in the `WorksheetFunction` object, you type `Application.WorksheetFunction.` followed by the

function you want to use and the function arguments enclosed in parentheses. If you want, you can omit `Application.` from the expression. For example, if you want to sum a range of cells and store the result to a variable, both of these expressions are valid:

```
SumVal = Application.WorksheetFunction_
.Sum(Range("A1:A4"))
```

```
SumVal = WorksheetFunction.Sum_
(Range("A1:A4"))
```

Generally, you cannot use an Excel worksheet function that has an equivalent VBA function. For example, both VBA and Excel have a `Cos` function that returns a numeric value that represents the cosine of an angle. If you try to use the Excel worksheet function `Cos` in your VBA procedure, you receive an error message.

Work with Excel Worksheet Functions

① Name your procedure.

② Declare the variables you want to use to store the results of your worksheet functions.

③ Declare any other variables you will use.

④ Activate the worksheet that uses this procedure by typing `.Activate` after the worksheet reference.

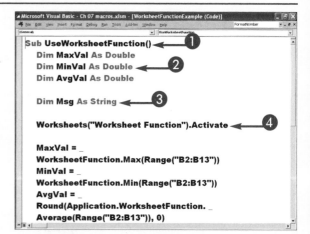

⑤ Create your worksheet functions.

● The underscore indicates that the statement is continued on the next line.

● The name of the function.

● Arguments.

● A VBA function.

⑥ Store the result to a variable.

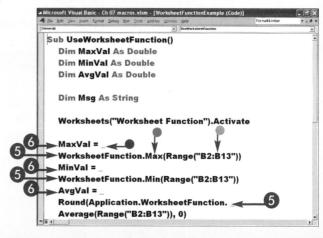

⑦ Use a message box to display the result.

Note: *See the section, "Work with the MsgBox Function," to learn more about message boxes.*

● The variable.

● This codes creates a blank line.

⑧ Press Alt+F11 to switch from the VBE to Excel, and then run the macro.

Note: *See Chapter 1 to learn how to run a macro.*

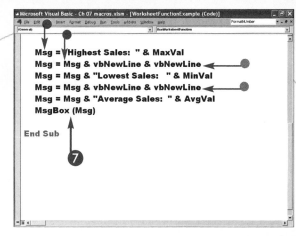

```
Msg = "Highest Sales:  " & MaxVal
Msg = Msg & vbNewLine & vbNewLine
Msg = Msg & "Lowest Sales:   " & MinVal
Msg = Msg & vbNewLine & vbNewLine
Msg = Msg & "Average Sales:  " & AvgVal
MsgBox (Msg)

End Sub
```

● The results of the worksheet functions appear in the message box.

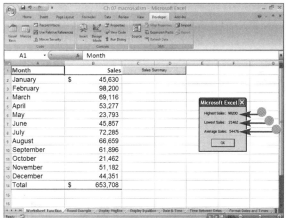

Extra

The Object Browser lists the functions that are part of the `WorksheetFunction` object. You can view this list using `WorksheetFunction` as the search criterion in the Object Browser. Press F2 to open the Object Browser. See Chapter 4 for more information on the Object Browser.

If a VBA statement does not fit on a single line, you can use the underscore (_) character to tell Excel you want to continue the statement on another line. The example in this section uses the underscore character as a continue statement indicator.

The remainder of this chapter discusses and illustrates VBA functions. The `Round` function used in the following example is a VBA function. The `Round` function takes two arguments: an expression and the number of decimal places to which you want to round the number. If you do not specify the number of decimal places, the `Round` function rounds to an integer.

Example:
```
Result = Round(124.4589, 2) returns 124.46
```

You can also use the Excel worksheet function `ROUND` when writing a VBA procedure.

Work with a MsgBox Function

The MsgBox function is a VBA function that makes writing code easier. See Chapter 3 to learn more about functions. You can use the MsgBox function to display a dialog box that provides information to the user and, if you want, returns a value to VBA that represents the user's response. The MsgBox function has a preset list of values it can return. For example, you can use the MsgBox function to prompt the user for a Yes or No response; VBA returns 6 if the user clicks Yes and 7 if the user clicks No.

When using the MsgBox function, you use arguments to designate the prompts, buttons, and title that appear in your message box. The Button and Title arguments are optional. Use the Prompt argument to specify the text

that displays in the message box. You can use a text string enclosed in quotes or you can use a variable. You can combine strings and variables by using the concatenation operator (&), as in this example: MsgBox("Total Sum: " & TotalSum).

Use the Buttons argument to specify a constant that indicates the buttons and icons that display in the message box. If you do not specify a button constant, the MsgBox function uses the default vbOKOnly and only displays the OK button. Use the Title argument to display the title that appears on the title bar of the message box. If you omit this argument, Excel displays the default title, Microsoft Excel.

Work with a MsgBox Function

① Name your procedure.

② Declare the variables you want to use as arguments in the MsgBox function.

Alternatively, you can type the arguments directly into the MsgBox function.

③ Declare the variable you want to use to store the value returned by the MsgBox function.

④ Activate the worksheet that uses this procedure by typing .Activate after the worksheet reference.

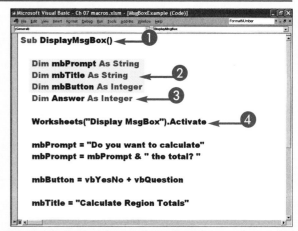

⑤ Store your message to a variable.

● This line of code concatenates the text stored in the mbPrompt variable with additional text.

⑥ Store the values that represent the buttons you want to use to a variable.

Place a plus sign between each button you want represented.

⑦ Store the title you want your message box to have to a variable.

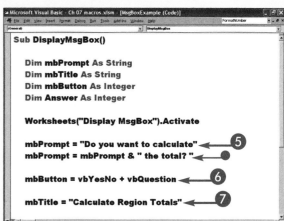

8 Create the `MsgBox` function.

● Your message.

● The buttons you want to display.

◉ The title.

9 Assign the value returned by the message box to a variable.

10 Write code to execute an action based on the value returned by the message box.

11 Press Alt+F11 to switch from the VBE to Excel, and then run the macro.

Note: *See Chapter 1 to learn how to run a macro.*

The message box displays when you run the macro.

● The title.

● The prompt.

◉ The vbYesNo buttons.

◉ The vbQuestion button.

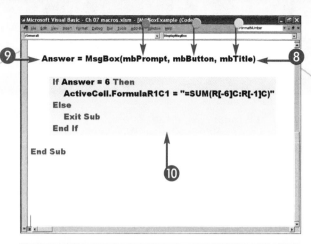

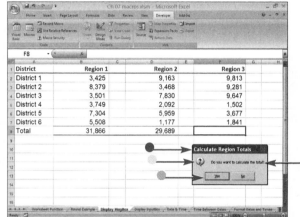

Extra

You can use 20 different constant values as the `Buttons` value for the `MsgBox` function. You can use these values separately, or combine them by placing a plus (+) sign between each constant value. The following code creates a message box containing Yes, No, and Cancel buttons, as well as the Question icon.

Example:
```
Response = MsgBox("Select button.", vbYesNoCancel + vbQuestion)
```

The `MsgBox` function returns an integer value between 1 and 7, which represents the button the user clicked. You can interpret the value the `MsgBox` function returns by looking at the integer value. The following table shows the integer values returned by the `MsgBox` function and their associated constant values.

MSGBOX RETURN	VALUE	CONSTANT	DESCRIPTION
1	vbOK	OK button clicked	
2	vbCancel	Cancel button clicked	
3	vbAbort	Abort button clicked	
4	vbRetry	Retry button clicked	
5	vbIgnore	Ignore button clicked	
6	vbYes	Yes button clicked	
7	vbNo	No button clicked	

Like `MsgBox`, the `InputBox` function is a VBA function. You can use the `InputBox` function to prompt the user for information during the execution of a procedure. The `InputBox` function displays a dialog box that requests information from the user and returns the user response to your procedure. You capture the user response by assigning the results of the `InputBox` function to a variable. The following is the syntax for the `InputBox` function:

`InputBox(Prompt[,Title][,Default] [,xPos] [,yPos])`

Use the prompt argument to specify the text that displays in the input box. You can combine strings and variables by using the concatenation operator (&). The `Title` argument is optional. You can use it to specify the title of

your input dialog box. You can use either a text string enclosed in quotes or a variable. If you omit the `Title` argument, Excel displays the default title, Microsoft Excel.

The `Default` argument is optional. You can use it to specify the default value that displays when your text box appears. You can specify the display position of the dialog box by using the optional `xPos` and `yPos` arguments. If you omit these arguments, the dialog box displays in the center of the screen. These arguments use units of measurement called *twips*. One twip equals 1/20 of a point, or 1/1,440 of an inch. The `xPos` argument indicates the distance from the left side of the screen to the left side of the dialog box. The `yPos` argument indicates the position from the top of the screen to the top of the dialog box.

Using the InputBox Function

① Name your procedure.

② Declare the variables you want to use as arguments in the `InputBox` function.

Alternatively, you can type the arguments directly into the `InputBox` function.

③ Declare the variable you want to use to store the value returned by the `InputBox` function.

④ Declare any other variables you will need.

⑤ Activate the worksheet that uses this procedure by typing `.Activate` after the workbook reference.

⑥ Store your prompt to a variable.

⑦ Store the title you want your message box to have to a variable.

⑧ Store the default value you want your input box to display to a variable.

⑨ Create your `InputBox` function.

⑩ Assign the value returned by the `InputBox` function to a variable.

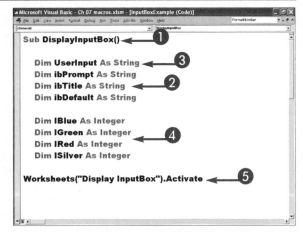

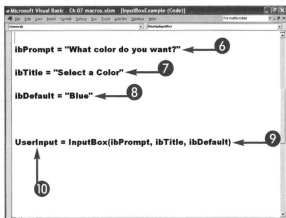

⑪ Write code that executes based on the value returned by the input box.

Note: See Chapter 6 to learn more about If Then Else statements.

⑫ Press Alt+F11 to switch from the VBE to Excel, and then run the macro.

Note: See Chapter 1 to learn how to run a macro.

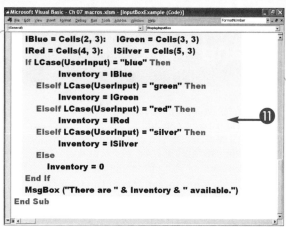

The input box displays when you run the macro.

● The title.

● The prompt.

● The default value.

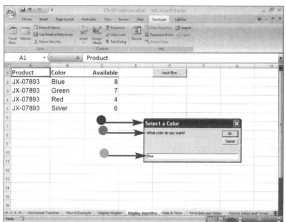

Extra

You can use named arguments to simplify your functions. Many VBA functions have optional arguments. For example, although the `InputBox` function has several arguments, only the first one is required. If you want to include additional arguments, you specify the argument values in order, leaving a space between two commas as a placeholder for any arguments you do not want to use.

Example:

```
UserInput = InputBox("Type a value:", ,"5")
```

Instead of specifying a placeholder for each value, you can use named arguments with the VBA functions. When using a named argument, you specify the name of the argument along with the corresponding value. You type the name of the argument followed by a colon, an equal sign, and the value of that particular argument. You can place named arguments in any order, and you do not have to specify a value for every argument.

Example:

```
UserInput = InputBox(Prompt:="Type a value:", Default:="5")
```

Retrieve the Current Date and Time

VBA includes several date-related, built-in functions that you can add to the procedures and functions you create. You can use these functions to return a system date and/or time, perform date calculations, set a date, or even time a process.

If you want to display the current date or time, you can select from three different functions. The DATE VBA function returns the current system date, the TIME VBA function returns the current system time, and the NOW VBA function returns both the date and time. VBA formats the date and time information in your system's short date format. You can modify the date and time formats by using the Control Panel.

When working with dates, you can avoid displaying a date outside of range by remembering the date range that

Excel accepts. VBA accommodates a much larger date range than Excel. It accepts dates between January 1, 0100, and December 31, 9999. Excel accepts dates between January 1, 1900, and December 31, 9999. If you use Excel on a Macintosh, the date range is even smaller. The acceptable date range is January 2, 1904 to December 31, 9999. If you need to display a date outside the range, you can do so by placing the date in a string variable.

You can assign the results of the Date or Time function to a variable, a worksheet cell, or another function. The following example stores the Now function to a message box:

```
MsgBox("Current Date and Time: " & Now())
```

Retrieve the Current Date and Time

RETRIEVE THE CURRENT DATE

① Name your procedure.

② Type the Date function.

In this example, the Date function is part of the prompt argument for the MsgBox function.

Note: See the section, "Work with a MsgBox Function," in this chapter to learn more about the MsgBox function.

③ Press Alt+F11 to switch from the VBE to Excel, and then run the macro.

Note: See Chapter 1 to learn how to run a macro.

The current system date displays in the message box.

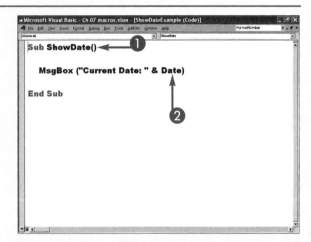

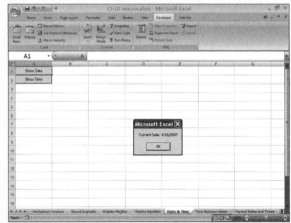

RETRIEVE THE CURRENT TIME

1 Name your procedure.

2 Type the `Time` function.

In this example, the `Time` function is part of the prompt argument for the `MsgBox` function.

Note: *See the section, "Work with a MsgBox Function," in this chapter to learn more about the* `MsgBox` *function.*

3 Press Alt+F11 to switch from the VBE to Excel, and then run the macro.

Note: *See Chapter 1 to learn how to run a macro.*

The current system time displays in the message box.

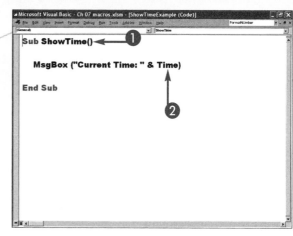

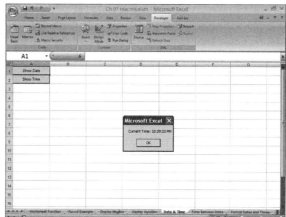

Extra

In Excel, you can convert dates and times into a serial value that Excel can add or subtract and then convert back into a recognizable date or time. Excel calculates a date's serial value as the number of days after January 1, 1900, and represents each date with a whole number. Excel calculates a time's serial value in units of 1/60 of a second. Each time can be represented as a serial value between 0 and 1. A date and time, such as January 1, 2000, at noon, consists of the date to the left of the decimal and a time to the right. In the example August 25, 2005, 5:46 p.m., the date and time serial value is 38589.74028.

VBA uses the same serial number system for dates and times as Excel. Each date and time is stored as a numeric value. Because VBA stores dates and times as numeric values, you can add and substract to perform date calculations.

Perform Date and Time Calculations

You can determine the amount of time between two dates by using the DateDiff VBA function. With this function, you can obtain time intervals between two date values, such as the number of months, days, hours, minutes, or seconds.

The DateDiff function takes five arguments: Interval, Date1, Date2, Firstdayofweek, and Firstweekofyear. The first three arguments are required. Use the Interval argument to specify the unit of time to use when returning the difference between the two dates. Use a constant value to specify the interval.

Use the Date1 and Date2 arguments to specify the dates you want to compare. You can use a date string, a value returned by a function, or the contents of a cell, as long as you use a valid date. To ensure the date is valid, you

can use the IsDate VBA function, which returns the value True if an expression is a date.

You can use the optional Firstdayofweek argument if you want to use a day other than Sunday as the first day of the week. To create the constant value you use as this argument, type vb before the appropriate day of the week. For example, to use Monday as the first day of the week, type vbMonday as the argument value.

You can use the optional Firstweekofyear argument to indicate what you want to treat as the first week of the year. If you omit this argument, VBA considers the week that contains the date January 1 as the first week of the year. If you want to have the first week contain at least the first four days, specify a value of vbFirstFourDays. See Appendix A for a list of Firstweekofyear constant values.

Perform Date and Time Calculations

① Name your procedure.

② Declare the variables you want to use to store your dates.

③ Declare any other variables you need.

This example uses a Do While loop and an If Then Else statement.

Note: See Chapter 6 to learn more about loops and If Then Else statements.

● This example evaluates two columns of cells, starting at row two.

④ Store the cell values to variables.

⑤ Use the IsDate VBA function to make sure the cells contain valid dates.

⑥ Use the MsgBox function to display an error message if the dates are not valid.

⑦ Use the `DateDiff` function to determine the amount of time between two dates.

● The Interval.

● Date1.

● Date2.

⑧ Place the results in a cell.

⑨ Press Alt+F11 to switch from the VBE to Excel, and then run the macro.

Note: *See Chapter 1 to learn how to run a macro.*

The procedure calculates the difference between two times.

You can use the `DateDiff` function to find the difference between two times.

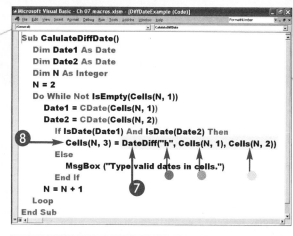

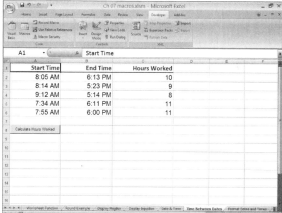

Extra

You can use one of ten constant values to specify the Interval argument and the type of date interval to return.

INTERVAL	VALUE	DESCRIPTION
yyyy	Year	Only compares the year portion of both dates. The dates 12/31/1999 and 1/1/2000 return a value of 1 year.
q	Quarter	Divides the year into four quarters and returns the number of quarters between dates.
m	Month	Only compares the month portion of both dates. The dates 12/31/1999 and 1/1/2000 return a value of 1 month.
d	Day	The number of days between two dates.
y	Day of Year	The same results as using d.
w	Weekday	Determines the day of the week of the first date — for example, Wednesday — and then counts the number of Wednesdays between the dates.
ww	Week	Relies on the value specified as the Firstdayofweek argument to determine the number of weeks between two dates.
h	Hour	The number of hours between to times. If a time is not specified, it uses midnight or 00:00:00.
n	Minute	The number of minutes between two times.
s	Second	The number of seconds between two times.

Format a Date Expression

You can format an expression that uses a date or time by using the `FormatDateTime` VBA function. The `FormatDateTime` function takes two arguments: `Date` and `NamedFormat`. The `Date` argument is required. It identifies the date expression that you want to format and accepts cell references, variable references, string expressions, or numeric values. You can reference a cell using any of the cell range reference options discussed in Chapter 11. For example, if the date you want to format is located in cell A1, you can use the following code to reference that cell:

```
X = FormatDateTime(Range("A1"))
```

You use the `NamedFormat` argument to specify the formatting you want to use. You can use any of the predefined formatting constants. If you omit the

`NamedFormat` argument, the `FormatDateTime` function uses the `vbGeneralDate` constant.

The `vbGeneralDate` constant instructs Excel to format the date portion of the expression in the system short date format and to format the time portion of the date in the system long time format. Windows maintains your default date and time settings in the Regional and Languages Options dialog box, which you can access through the Control panel. When you use a constant as the `NamedFormat` argument, you specify which of these settings you want to use to format your date and time values. By changing the values in the Regional and Languages Options dialog box, you affect how the dates and times display when you use the `FormatDateTime` function.

Format a Date Expression

① Name your procedure.

② Declare the variables you want to use to store your unformatted dates.

③ Store the contents of the cells with unformatted dates to variables.

④ Use the `FormatDateTime` function to format the variables in which you stored the dates.

● The variable containing the date.

● The format you want to apply.

⑤ Assign the results to cells.

⑥ Press Alt+F11 to switch from the VBE to Excel, and then run the macro.

Note: See Chapter 1 to learn how to run a macro.

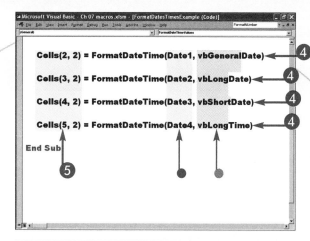

The procedure formats the dates in column A and places the results in column B.

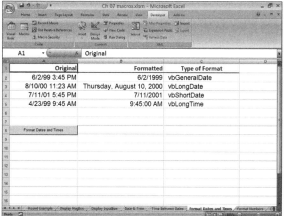

Extra

You can specify the formatting for a date and time by using the `NamedFormat` argument. If it is omitted, Excel uses the `vbGeneralDate` constant. When you use the `NamedFormat` argument, you can pass it a constant value or the numeric value that corresponds to the constant, as outlined in the following table. The actual formats used as a result of specifying these constant values are based upon the system date and time settings in the Regional and Language Options dialog box.

CONSTANT	VALUE	DESCRIPTION
vbGeneralDate	0	The default value if the `NamedFormat` argument is omitted. This value displays the date using the short date format and the time using the long time format.
vbLongDate	1	Displays the date using the system long date format.
vbShortDate	2	Displays the date using the system short date format.
vbLongTime	3	Displays the time using the system long time format.

Format a Numeric Expression

You can format a numeric expression by using the FormatNumber, FormatCurrency, or FormatPercentage function. These functions all take a numeric value and return the value formatted in the format you specify. The FormatNumber function returns a formatted number, the FormatCurrency function returns a formatted number preceded by a currency symbol, and the FormatPercentage function returns a number followed by a percentage sign.

Each function takes the same five arguments: Expression, NumDigitsAfterDecimal, Include LeadingDigit, UseParensForNegativeNumbers, and GroupDigits. The Expression argument is required.

The Expression argument specifies the numeric value to format. The NumDigitsAfterDecimal argument indicates the number of decimal places to display on the right side of the decimal. The IncludeLeadingDigit argument determines whether a zero displays before fractional values. The UseParensForNegativeNumbers argument specifies whether to place parentheses around negative numbers. Finally, the GroupDigits argument determines whether Excel groups numbers to make them more readable. With this argument, you can specify whether to display fifty thousand as 50,000 or 50000.

The last three arguments, IncludeLeadingDigit, UseParensForNegativeNumbers, and GroupDigits, all use the same three constant values. Use vbTrue as the as the argument to use the formatting, and vbFalse if you do not want to use the formatting. If you do not specify a value, or if you specify vbUseDefault, the function uses your computer's regional settings.

Format a Numeric Expression

① Name your procedure.

② Declare the variables you want to use to store your formatted numbers.

③ Declare any other variable you need.

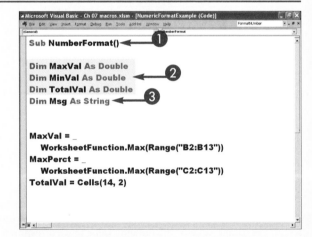

④ Store the numeric values you want to format to variables.

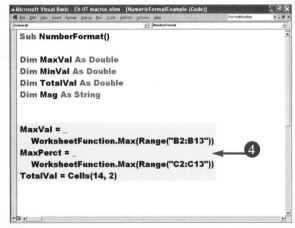

⑤ Apply a format to the variables.

In this example, the formatted numbers are part of the message box prompt.

⑥ Press Alt+F11 to switch from the VBE to Excel, and then run the macro.

Note: See Chapter 1 to learn how to run a macro.

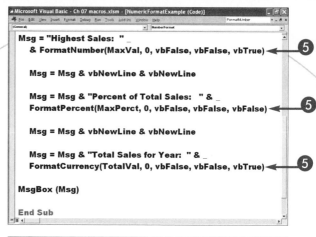

```
Msg = "Highest Sales:  " _
    & FormatNumber(MaxVal, 0, vbFalse, vbFalse, vbTrue)

Msg = Msg & vbNewLine & vbNewLine

Msg = Msg & "Percent of Total Sales:  " & _
    FormatPercent(MaxPerct, 0, vbFalse, vbFalse, vbFalse)

Msg = Msg & vbNewLine & vbNewLine

Msg = Msg & "Total Sales for Year:  " & _
    FormatCurrency(TotalVal, 0, vbFalse, vbFalse, vbTrue)

MsgBox (Msg)

End Sub
```

In this example, the procedure formats the numbers and displays the results in a message box.

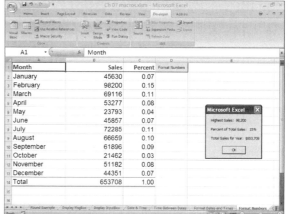

Extra

If you want to customize the way a number displays, you can also use the Format function. You can create your own number formats by combining specific characters along with symbols that represent the numbers, as in the following example: Format(NumVal, "##.##").

NUMERIC CHARACTERS	DISPLAYS
0	A numeric digit or a zero if the number does not have a digit in that place. Use this character to ensure that a digit appears in a specific place. For example, 0000 always displays a four-digit number. If there are fewer digits, a zero displays for the non-specified digits.
#	A numeric digit if the number has a digit in that place. If there is no digit, a value does not display in that place.
.	A decimal-point placeholder.
%	An expression as a percentage by multiplying by 100 and adding a percent sign.
,	A thousands separator.
E-, E+, e-, e+	A numeric expression in scientific format. The number of digits on the right side of the symbol indicates the number of digits in the exponent.
\	The character that follows a backslash or is enclosed in quotes. For example, to place a plus sign (+) in the number string, you would type \+ in the desired location.

117

Change the Case of a String

You can use the LCase and UCase VBA functions to change the case of your text. This is useful when you are formatting output or when you want to compare strings without regard to case. The LCase function changes all characters that are not already lowercase, to lowercase. The UCase function changes all characters that are not already uppercase, to uppercase.

To use the LCase function, simply type **LCase** followed by the expression you want to convert to lowercase in parentheses.

Example:
```
MyVariable = "HELLO"
SampleText = LCase(MyVariable)
```
Result:
```
hello
```

The syntax for the UCase function is similar to the syntax for the LCase function. To use the UCase function, you type UCase followed by the expression you want to convert to uppercase in parentheses.

Example:
```
MyVariable = "hello"
SampleText = UCase(MyVariable)
```
Result:
```
HELLO
```

Both the LCase and the UCase functions ignore numbers and symbols. The expression can be an actual string enclosed in quotes, or a reference to a string such as a cell or variable name. If the string contains no data, both functions return Null.

Change the Case of a String

1. Name your procedure.

2. Declare your variable.

3. Use an InputBox function to retrieve a user entry.

4. Use the UCase function to change the entry to uppercase.

   Alternatively, you can use the LCase function to change the entry to lowercase.

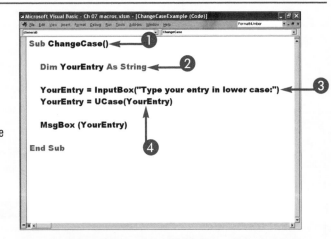

5. Use a message box to display the entry.

6. Press Alt+F11 to switch from the VBE to Excel, and then run the macro.

Note: See Chapter 1 to learn how to run a macro.

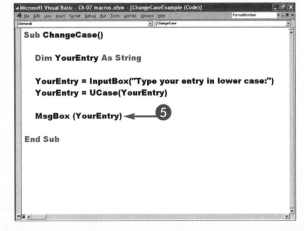

7 Make an entry using lowercase text.

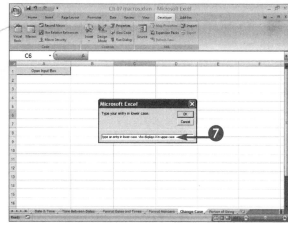

● The message box displays the text in uppercase.

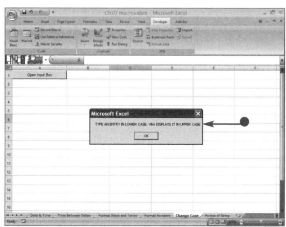

Apply It

The example used in the section, "Using the InputBox Function," earlier in this chapter, converts the user's entry to lowercase and then compares the entry to a string. Converting the entry to lowercase allows you to make a comparison without regard to case. For example, if the user types **GREEN**, **green**, or **GrEen**, the procedure returns the value `True` when it compares the user input to green.

Example:

```
If LCase(UserInput) = "blue" Then
     Inventory = IBlue
ElseIf LCase(UserInput) = "green" Then
     Inventory = IGreen
ElseIf LCase(UserInput) = "red" Then
     Inventory = IRed
ElseIf LCase(UserInput) = "silver" Then
     Inventory = ISilver
Else
     Inventory = 0
End If
```

To see this function in action, refer to the example file for Chapter 7, which is on the Web site for this book.

Return a Portion of a String

nstead of an entire string, you can use the built-in functions available in VBA to return a portion of a string. You can use three different functions: Left, Right, and Mid. The Left function returns the specified number of characters starting at the left side, or beginning, of the string. The Right function returns the specified number of characters starting at the right side, or end, of the string. These functions use similar syntax: Left(String, Length) and Right(String, Length).

The String argument specifies the string from which you want to return the specified number of characters. You can make the argument an actual string enclosed in quotes, a variable that contains a string, or a cell reference. The Length argument indicates the number of characters to return from the string.

The third built-in function for returning a portion of a string is the Mid function. Use this function to retrieve characters from the center of a string. When you use this function, you indicate the character with which to start and how many characters to return. There are three Mid function arguments: Mid(String, Start, Length).

Similar to the Left and Right functions, the Mid function String argument specifies the string to use with the function. The Start argument indicates the position of the first character in the string to return. The Length argument is the only optional argument when using the Mid function. If you omit the length argument, the function returns the remaining portion of the string. Otherwise, the Length argument indicates the number of characters to return.

Return a Portion of a String

1 Name your procedure.

2 Declare your variables.

3 Use an InputBox function to capture a user entry.

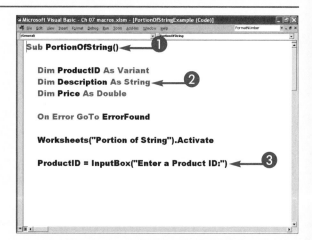

4 Use the Left function to retrieve the left portion of a user entry.

● The variable that you want to examine.

● The number of characters from the left you want to retrieve.

In this example, if the first two characters of the user entry are not "OS", then the user receives an error message.

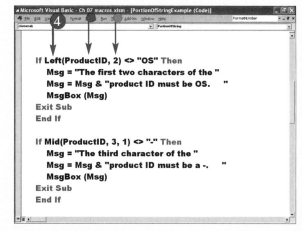

⑤ Use the Mid function to retrieve a portion of a string.

● The variable you want to examine.

● The position of the first character you want to return.

● The number of characters you want to return.

In this example, if the third character of the user entry is not a "-", then the user receives an error message.

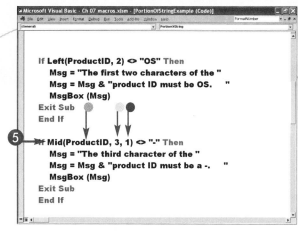

```
If Left(ProductID, 2) <> "OS" Then
    Msg = "The first two characters of the "
    Msg = Msg & "product ID must be OS.    "
    MsgBox (Msg)
Exit Sub
End If
If Mid(ProductID, 3, 1) <> "-" Then
    Msg = "The third character of the "
    Msg = Msg & "product ID must be a -.    "
    MsgBox (Msg)
Exit Sub
End If
```

⑥ Use the Right function to retrieve the right portion of the user entry.

● The variable that you want to examine.

● The number of characters from the right you want to retrieve.

● This example uses the IsNumeric function.

In this example, if the last four characters of the user entry are not numbers, then the user receives an error message.

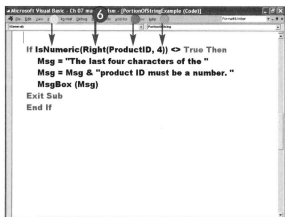

```
If IsNumeric(Right(ProductID, 4)) <> True Then
    Msg = "The last four characters of the "
    Msg = Msg & "product ID must be a number. "
    MsgBox (Msg)
Exit Sub
End If
```

Apply It

You can use the IsNumeric VBA function to determine if a value is a number. The IsNumeric function takes one argument, the value you want to examine. The IsNumeric function returns True when the value is a number, and False when the value is not a number.

You can determine the length of a string with the Len function, Len(String), which takes one argument, String. You can make the string argument an actual string, or the name of a variable that contains a string. The following example checks to see if the length of the string is not equal to 7. If the length of the string is not equal to 7, the procedure displays an error message.

Example:
```
Dim ProductID As String
ProductID = InputBox("Enter a ProductID:")
If Len(ProductID) <> 7 Then
    MsgBox("The Product ID must be 7
    characters long.")
Exit Sub
End If
```

Debug a Procedure with Inserted Break Points

Correcting errors, often referred to as *debugging,* is a normal part of writing a program. VBA has several tools you can use to help debug your procedures. For example, you can insert break points in your procedures. Break points suspend the execution of your procedure at the points you specify. Once the program stops, you can examine the results and then continue the execution of the program.

You set a break point by clicking the margin of the Code window next to the line at which you want to insert the break point. The VBE places a circle in the margin and highlights the line of code using the display options you set for the Code window. See Chapter 2 for more information on setting the display options for the Code window. While in the Break mode, if you move your cursor over a variable name, the value of the variable appears.

The VBE has a Locals window, which displays the expressions in your procedure, their current value, and their type. When you are debugging your code, you should dock the Locals window at the button of the VBE. You can then use the Locals window to view the value of expressions and variables at each break point. See Chapter 2 for more information on using the VBE windows.

When your procedure stops at a specified break point, VBA places you in break mode and stops the current procedure from running. You can continue running your procedure until it encounters another break point or the procedure ends. Each time VBA encounters a break point, the current values of the local variables appear in the Locals window.

Debug a Procedure with Inserted Break Points

① In Project Explorer, open the module containing the procedure you want to debug.

To open a module, double-click the module name.

② Click View ➪ Locals Window.

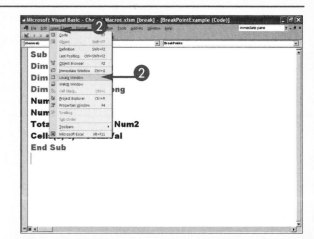

● The Locals window appears.

③ Click in the margin where you want to add a break point.

● You can add additional break points as needed.

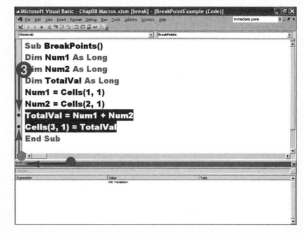

④ Click Run ➪ Run Sub/UserForm.

Alternatively, press F5.

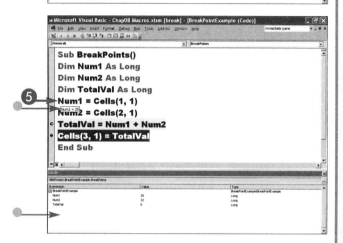

The values of the locally declared variables display in the Locals window.

⑤ Move you cursor over a variable name to see the current value.

● The value of the variable appears.

⑥ Press F5 to run the procedure.

Click Run ➪ Reset to stop.

Click Debug ➪ Clear All Breakpoints to clear all break points.

Extra

The VBE has three different modes: Design, Run, and Break. You use the Design mode to create new VBA procedures. You use the Run mode to execute a procedure. To activate the Run mode, click Run ➪ Run Sub/UserForm, or press F5. The VBE runs your procedure.

The VBE places you in the break mode whenever a procedure stops running due to a break point, a Stop statement, or a Watch statement, or when it encounters an error during execution. When the VBE places you in the break mode, the VBE highlights the line of code that caused the error and places the word *break* in the caption of the title bar. To exit the break mode, click Run ➪ Reset.

If you select a line of code, you can toggle a break point on and off by pressing F9 or by clicking Debug ➪ Toggle Breakpoint. You can remove a break point by clicking it with your mouse. You can clear all break points from your code by pressing Ctrl+Shift+F9 or by clicking Debug ➪ Clear All Breakpoints. Remember to clear all break points after you finish debugging your code.

Using the Watches Window to Debug a Procedure

If you suspect an error occurs at a particular break point, when a variable or expression reaches a certain value, or when the value of a variable or expression changes, the Watches window can be of use to you.

You can use the Add Watch dialog box to set up a watch. You start by entering an expression in the Expression field. For example, if you suspect that an error occurs when the variable K is equal to two, you can enter the expression K = 2 to have your procedure break when the variable K is equal to two. In the Procedure field of the Add Watch dialog box, select the proper procedure. In the Module field, select the proper module. If you have multiple procedures or modules that call one another and you are not sure which procedure is causing the error, you can opt to monitor all procedures and/or all modules.

The Add Watch dialog box offers three watch types: Watch Expression, Break When Value Is True, and Break When Value Changes. You can set a break point and select Watch Expression to display the expression you are evaluating and its current value in the Watches window when your procedure breaks. You can select Break When Value Is True to have your procedure break when an expression evaluates to True. For example, by using this option, you can break when the variable K is equal to two. You can select Break When Value Changes to have you procedure break when the value of an expression changes. For example, if you are using a counter, you can break every time the variable you are using to count changes.

Using the Watches Window to Debug a Procedure

① In the Project Explorer, open the module containing the procedure you want to debug.

To open a module, double-click the module name.

② Click View ➪ Watch Window.

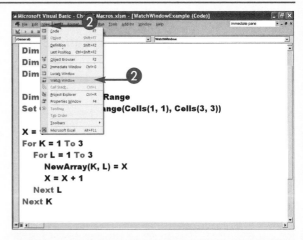

● The Watches window appears.

③ Click Debug ➪ Add Watch.

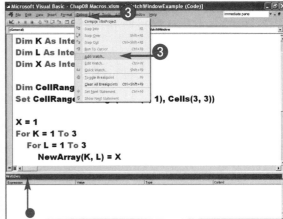

- The Add Watch dialog box appears.

④ Type the expression to watch in the Expression field.

⑤ Click here and select a procedure.

⑥ Click here and select a module.

⑦ Click to select a watch type (○ changes to ◉).

⑧ Click OK.

- The Watches window lists each watch.

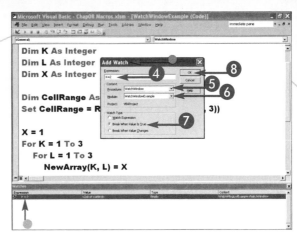

⑨ Press F5 to run your procedure.

- The procedure breaks when the expression you entered evaluates to True.

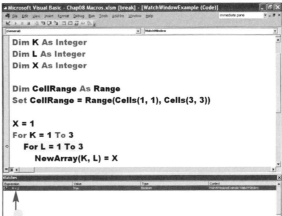

Extra

When you are in the Break mode, you can find the current value of a variable or expression by using VBA's Quick Watch feature. Select the variable or expression for which you want to find the value. Click Debug ➪ Quick Watch or press Shift+F9. The current value of the expression appears in the Quick Watch dialog box. If you want to continue to monitor the variable or expression value, click Add to add the item to the Watches window.

To delete a watch, right-click in the Watches window and then click Delete Watch in the context menu that appears. To edit a watch, right-click the watch you want to edit and then click Edit Watch in the context menu. The Edit Watch dialog box appears. Use it to edit your watch.

When evaluating an expression, such as X > 5, the value in the Watches window is either True or False, indicating whether the expression is valid. For example, if the current value of X is 6, the expression X > 5 has a value of True because 6 is greater than 5.

Step through a Procedure

Programmers call the process of stepping through code one line at a time *tracing*. With break points, VBA executes the code until it encounters a break point. With tracing, VBA executes one line of code and waits for you to indicate that you want to execute the next line of code. Tracing is an excellent way to debug your code when you do not know where your error is located.

As you step through your code, you can use the Watches and Locals windows to monitor the value of variables and expressions. See the section, "Using the Watches Window to Debug a Procedure," to learn more about the Watches window. See the section, "Debug a Procedure with Inserted Break Points," to learn more about the Locals window.

You start tracing by executing the Step Into command on the Debug menu, or by pressing the F8 key to begin the tracing process. When you are ready to move to the next statement, you execute the Step Into command or press the F8 key again. You can continue executing the Step Into command or pressing F8 for each line of code you want to execute.

Each time you execute the Step Into command or press F8, the VBE highlights the next line of code. The Locals window updates the value of the local variables and the Watches window monitors the values of any watch expressions created for the procedure.

As you step through a procedure, if a code statement calls another procedure, the VBE also steps through the called procedure. After that procedure runs, the control returns to the original procedure.

Step through a Procedure

① In the Project Explorer, open the module containing the procedure you want to debug.

    To open a module, double-click the module name.

② Click View ➪ Watch Window.

③ Click View ➪ Locals Window.

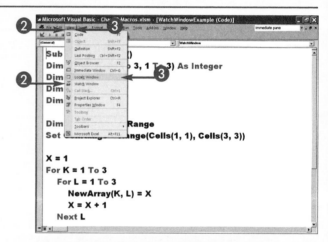

● The Watches and Locals windows appear.

④ Press F8.

    Alternatively, click Debug ➪ Step Into.

● As you begin stepping into the code, VBA highlights the first line of code.

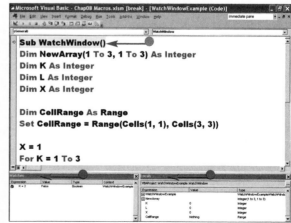

⑤ Continue pressing F8 to step through the entire procedure.

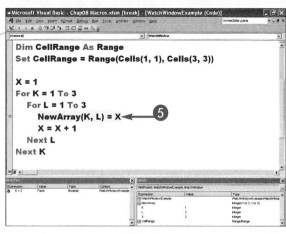

● As you step through the code, local variable values appear in the Locals window, and any watches that are set appear in the Watches window.

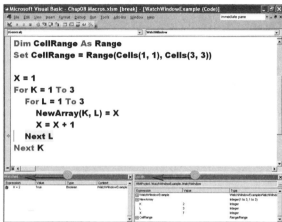

Extra

You step into procedures by pressing F8 or by clicking Debug ⇨ Step Into. If your procedure contains calls to other procedures, you can step through those procedures by using the Step Into command. If you do not want to step through called procedures, you can step over them. To step over a called procedure, click Debug ⇨ Step Over or press Shift+F8. VBA executes the entire called procedure without stopping and then returns control to the next line in the original procedure.

If you decide to step through the called procedure, you still have the option of stepping out of it at any time. To step out of a called procedure, click Debug ⇨ Step Out or press Ctrl+Shift+F8. The remainder of the called procedure runs, and then control returns to the next line of code after the called procedure in the original procedure.

If your code is running and you need to break, press Ctrl+Break. This feature is useful when you find yourself in an infinite loop.

Use the
Immediate Window

The Immediate window is useful when you want to evaluate expressions, find out the value of a variable, or quickly test a procedure. You can open the Immediate window by pressing Ctrl+G.

You can print values to the Immediate window by placing a `Debug.Print` command in your code. When VBA executes the `Debug.Print` command, it prints the value you indicate to the Immediate window. For example, if you place `Debug.Print X` in your code, and then you step through your code, when VBA executes the `Debug.Print X` command, the value of the variable X appears in the Immediate window.

You can use the Immediate window to return a value. Use the `Print` statement or a question mark (?) to return the

value of a variable or expression. For example, if you want to display the value of the variable X, you can go to the Immediate window and type:

```
Print X
```

or

```
? X
```

You can also use the Immediate window to execute commands. Type the command in the Immediate window. As soon as you press Enter, VBA executes the command. When using the Immediate window, control statements must appear on a single line. For example, you would use the following code for a `For Next` loop:

```
For J = 1 to 4: Print J: Next J
```

Use the Immediate Window

USE DEBUG PRINT

① Add the `Debug Print` command to your code.

② Click View ⇨ Immediate Window, or press Ctrl+G.

● The Immediate window appears.

③ Press F8 to step through your code.

As you step through your code, the values you requested with the `Debug Print` command appear in the Immediate window.

● The X value.

● The Y value.

● The TotalVal value.

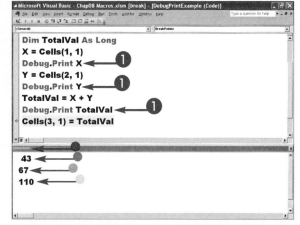

USE PRINT

① Create a break point.

② Press F5 to run your code.

③ Type **Print** followed by the variable you want to retrieve.

④ Press Enter.

● The Immediate window retrieves the value.

⑤ Type **?** followed by the value you want to retrieve.

● The Immediate window retrieves the value.

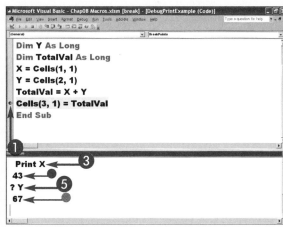

EVALUATE AN EXPRESSION

1 Type your expressions.

● The Immediate window evaluates the expressions.

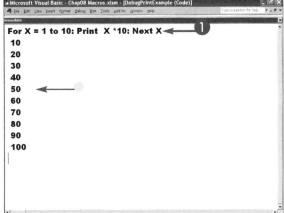

```
X = Cells(1,1)     ──1
? X
 43
Y = Cells(2,1)     ──1
? Y
 67
Z = X + Y + 200    ──1
? Z
 310
A = X > Y          ──1
? A
False
B = IsEmpty(Cells(1,1))  ──1
?B
False
```

EVALUATE A FOR NEXT LOOP

1 Type your For Next loop.

All of the statements must be on one line.

● The results appear in the Immediate window.

```
For X = 1 to 10: Print  X *10: Next X  ──1
 10
 20
 30
 40
 50     ←
 60
 70
 80
 90
 100
```

Extra

The VBE has a toolbar you can use when debugging your code. To view the toolbar, click View ⇨ Toolbars ⇨ Debug. The toolbar appears below the menu. The following table lists the functions the buttons on the toolbar perform.

BUTTON	FUNCTION
▶	RunSub/Userform
❚❚	Break
◼	Reset
●	Toggle Breakpoint
▣	Step Into
▣	Step Over
▣	Step Out
▣	Open Locals Window
▣	Open Immediate Window
▣	Open Watches Window
▣	Open Quick Watch

Resume Execution When an Error Is Encountered

A *run-time error* is an error that occurs when your code attempts to perform an invalid operation, such as trying to access a value that does not exist. If you do not provide a way for VBA to handle run-time errors, when VBA encounters them, it stops running your code and displays an error message to the user, or it acts in an unpredictable way.

VBA has special code you can use to handle run-time errors. You can instruct VBA to continue the execution of a procedure when it encounters an error by using the On Error GoTo statement. The following is the syntax for the On Error GoTo command:

```
On Error GoTo label
```

When you use this command, control jumps to a labeled section of code whenever VBA encounters a run-time error. A label is a text string followed by a colon. The On Error GoTo command moves to the label, thereby passing control from the current location in the procedure to the label. Usually, you place your labeled code at the end of your procedure. For example, you can use ErrorFound: as a label for the code you want to run if VBA encounters an error.

An Exit Sub or Exit Function statement causes VBA to end the execution of your procedure. You can place an Exit Sub or Exit Function statement prior to the labeled section of your code to keep the procedure from executing the labeled code when VBA does not encounter an error.

Resume Execution When an Error Is Encountered

① Name your procedure.

② Type your On Error GoTo command.

● This is the label.

③ Type the VBA code for the procedure.

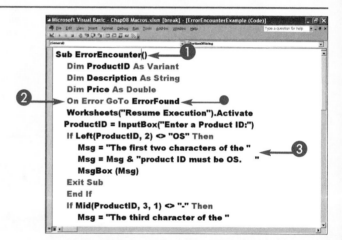

④ Type **Exit Sub** at the end of the main procedure code.

The Exit Sub statement causes the procedure to exit without running the error code.

⑤ Create a label.

VBA moves to the label when a run-time error occurs.

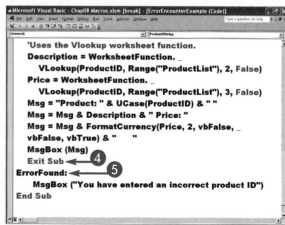

⑥ Type the VBA code to execute when an error occurs.

⑦ Press Alt+F11 to switch from the VBE to Excel, and then run the macro.

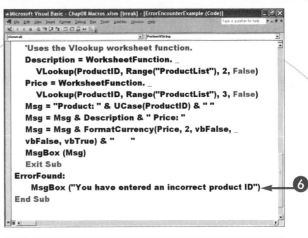

```
'Uses the Vlookup worksheet function.
Description = WorksheetFunction. _
    VLookup(ProductID, Range("ProductList"), 2, False)
Price = WorksheetFunction. _
    VLookup(ProductID, Range("ProductList"), 3, False)
Msg = "Product: " & UCase(ProductID) & " "
Msg = Msg & Description & " Price: "
Msg = Msg & FormatCurrency(Price, 2, vbFalse, _
vbFalse, vbTrue) & "    "
MsgBox (Msg)
Exit Sub
ErrorFound:
    MsgBox ("You have entered an incorrect product ID")    ◄—⑥
End Sub
```

If a run-time error occurs, the appropriate VBA code executes.

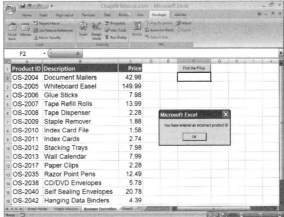

Extra

If you place a Resume statement at the end of your labeled code, control returns to the line of code that caused the run-time error, and the line of code executes again. If the code produces an error, the error-handling code executes again. This option enables you to recheck for the error.

If you place a Resume Next statement at the end of your labeled code, control returns to the next line of code in the procedure after the location that produced the run-time error. Your code continues execution without the line of code that produced the error. This option enables you to complete the procedure.

If you place a Resume Label statement followed by a label name at the end of your block of code, you can transfer control to the labeled line of code.

Process a Run-Time Error

Whenever VBA encounters a run-time error, it places the error information, which includes an error code and description, in the `Err` object. You can use this information to correct the error.

To capture the error without halting the execution of your code, you can place the `On Error Resume Next` statement immediately after the `Sub` statement for your procedure. This statement instructs VBA to capture the error and continue processing.

The `Err.Number` property contains the most recent run-time error code. The error codes for run-time error are always numbers. Essentially, if the `Err.Number` property has a value greater than zero, then an error has occurred. You can quickly check to see if an error exists by checking the `Number` property of the `Err` object. If an error exists, you can use `If Then` statements or `Case`

statements to respond to the error, as in the following code: `If Err.Number = 13 Then`.

You can design your error-processing code to react to the specific run-time error encountered. For example, if the `Err.Number` property has a value of 13, the value passed to a variable is not the correct data type; the user may have entered a string for a variable that requires a number. You can write code that examines the run-time error and prompts the user for the correct data type.

If you want to see the error description, use the `Err.Description` property. The following code creates a Division by Zero error and then displays the error number and code in a message box:

```
On Error Resume Next
X = 1/0

MsgBox (Err.Number & " " & Err.Description)
```

Process a Run-Time Error

1. Name your procedure.

2. Type the `On Error GoTo` command.

- This is the label.

3. Type **Exit Sub** at the end of the main body of code.

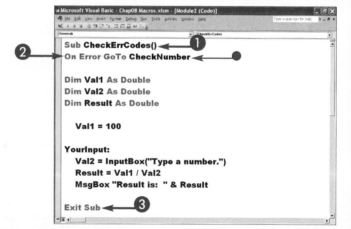

4. Create a label.

5. Create a conditional statement to check the value of the `Err.Number` object property.

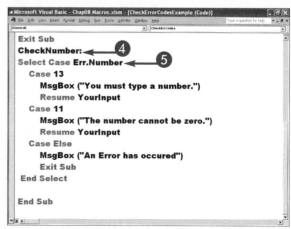

⑥ Type the code to execute if a specific error occurs.

⑦ Press Alt+F11 to switch from the VBE to Excel, and then run the macro.

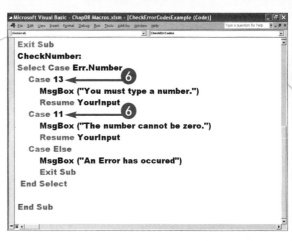

If a run-time error occurs, the appropriate VBA code executes.

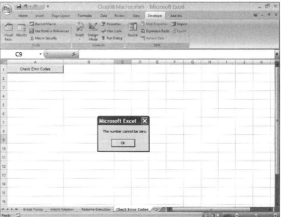

Extra

The following table lists some of the most common errors that VBA returns when it encounters a run-time error. Each error code has a description message you can display using the `Err.Description` property. You can also capture the code and display your own custom messages.

CODE	ERROR	REASON
3	Return without GoSub	The Return statement exists without a corresponding GoSub statement.
5	Invalid procedure call	The call to another procedure or function cannot be made. This is usually due to a problem with the arguments; either not calling with a valid number of arguments, or the value of an argument is not valid for the procedure.
9	Subscript out of range	An attempt was made to access an array element that does not exist.
10	The array is fixed or temporarily locked	This occurs when you try to redimension a fixed length array.
11	Division by zero	This occurs when the divisor is zero.
13	Type mismatch	The value passed to a variable is not the correct data type.
35	Sub, Function, or Property not defined	This occurs when you attempt to call a procedure, function, or property that does not exist.

Open a Workbook

You can use the Open method with the WorkBooks object to open a workbook. This is similar to clicking the Office button and using the menu to open a workbook. Each time you open a new workbook, Excel adds the workbook to the Workbooks collection.

The Open method has 16 parameters. This section discusses the FileName, WriteResPassword, Password, ReadOnly, IgnoreReadOnlyRecommended, and AddToMru parameters. Refer to VBA help for a discussion of the remaining parameters.

Use the FileName parameter to tell VBA the workbook you want to open. You can use the name of the workbook if the workbook is located in the current folder. If the workbook is located in another folder, enter the path to the workbook. You must enclose the workbook name or path in quotes.

If you want the user to enter a password before they can modify the workbook, set the WriteResPassword parameter to the password you want them to enter. If you want the user to enter a password before they can open a protected workbook, set the Password parameter to the password you want them to enter.

Set the ReadOnly parameter to True to make a workbook Read-Only. If the workbook is Read-Only Recommended, Excel prompts users to open the file as Read-Only each time the workbook opens. To eliminate the prompt, set the IgnoreReadOnlyRecommended parameter to True.

Set the AddToMru parameter to True to add the workbook to the Recent Documents list.

Open a Workbook

① Name your procedure.

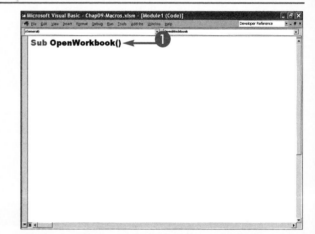

② Create your Open command.

● The workbook you want to open.

● Adds the file to the Recent Documents list.

● Sets the file to Read-Only.

③ Press Alt+F11 to switch from the VBE to Excel, and run the macro.

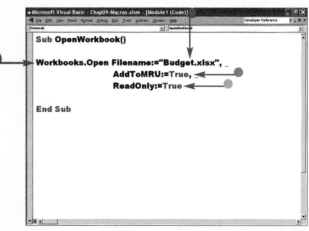

The macro opens the file and adds the filename to the Recent Documents list.

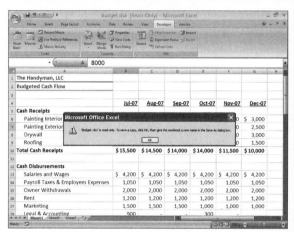

If users try to make a change and save the file, Excel warns that the file is Read-Only.

Extra

When working in Excel, use the Save As dialog box to set a password for your file, set your file to Read-Only Recommended, or set your file to Read-Only. To open the Save As dialog box, click the Office button, click Save As, and then click any Save As option. The Save As dialog box appears. In the lower-left corner of the Save As dialog box, click the Tools button. The Tools menu appears. Click General Options. The General Options dialog box appears. Enter a password in the Password to Open or Password to Modify field to password-protect your file. Select the Read-Only Recommended option to set your file to Read-Only Recommended. Click OK to close the dialog box. To make your file Read-Only, click Properties on the Tools menu. The Properties dialog box appears. Click the General tab and then select the Read-Only attribute.

Open a Text File as a Workbook

Many software applications have an option for exporting the application's data to a text file. You can use VBA's OpenText method with the Workbooks object to import a text file. You can then use all of Excel's data-analysis capabilities to analyze the file. With the OpenText method, Excel opens the text file as a single worksheet in a new workbook. The file remains a text file. Users can modify it and save it as a text file or as an Excel worksheet.

The list of parameters for the OpenText method is extensive. Only the FileName parameter is required. You use the FileName parameter to tell VBA the name of the file to open. You can enter the name of a file as the parameter if the workbook is located in the current folder. If the file is located in another folder, enter the path to

the file. Make sure you enclose the path statement in quotes.

The OpenText method can handle any delimited or fixed-width file. A delimited file uses a comma, space, semicolon, tab, or other character to mark the end of each column. A fixed-width file aligns the columns and gives each column a defined width. Use the DataType parameter to tell VBA whether your file is a delimited file or a fixed-width file. Use the constant xlDelimited for delimited files, and the constant xlFixedWidth for fixed-width files.

If your file is delimited, you can tell VBA what the delimiter is. For example, if the delimiter is a comma, then you set the Comma parameter to True.

Open a Text File as a Workbook

① Name your procedure.

② Create your OpenText command.

● The file you want to open.

● The file type.

● The delimiter.

③ Press Alt+F11 to switch from the VBE to Excel, and run the macro.

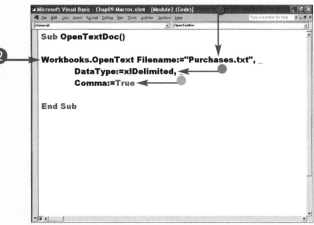

The text file appears.

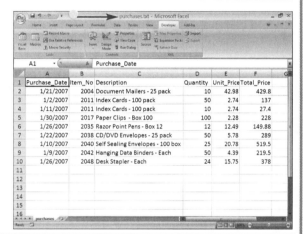

You can open the file in Excel.

● The macro opens the text file as a worksheet in Excel.

The file remains a text file.

Extra

Use the following parameters with the `OpenText` method to open a text file in a workbook.

PARAMETERS	DESCRIPTION
FileName	The name and location of the text file.
Origin	Indicates the original file platform: xlMacintosh or xlWindows
StartRow	The first row to import.
DataType	The format of the text file, either xlFixedWidth or xlDelimited.
TextQualifier	The character that identifies text.
ConsecutiveDelimiter	Type **True** to treat consecutive delimiters as one delimiter.
Tab, Semicolon, Comma, Space	Set each of these parameters to True if they are a delimiter.
Other	Set to True to specify the delimiter.
OtherChar	If Other is set to True, use this parameter to specify the character to use as a delimiter.
FieldInfo	The column number followed by an XlColumnDataType constant.
DecimalSeparator	The character VBA recognizes as a decimal separator.
ThousandsSeparator	The character VBA recognizes as a thousands separator.
TrailingMinusNumbers	Set to True to designate trailing minus signs as negative numbers.
Local	Set to True to use the computer's regional settings.

Open a File Requested by the User

You can retrieve the name of the file a user wants to open by prompting the user with an Open dialog box and then using a method to open the file.

To display an Open dialog box from an Excel procedure, use the `GetOpenFilename` method. This method does not open the file when the user clicks OK. Instead, the method passes the name of the file the user selects to a variable you assign to the statement. If you want to open the selected file, you must use a method. If the user does not select a file, the statement returns `False`.

The `GetOpenFilename` has several optional parameters. The `FileFilter` parameter lets users select the type of file they want to open. You can create a list of values for the Files of Type drop-down menu in the Open dialog box. For example, `"XML Files (*.xml), *.xml"` tells

VBA that Excel should only open XML files. You can specify multiple file types if you separate the file types with commas. Users can then select the file type they want to use.

Use the `FilterIndex` parameter to indicate the default `FileFilter` option. You specify a filter value between 1 and the number of filters you selected. If you omit this parameter, VBA uses the first filter specified as the default value.

Use the `Title` parameter to place a title on your dialog box. For example, for a dialog box that opens text files, you can change the title of the dialog box to "Open Text Files".

To enable users to select and open multiple files at once, set the `MultiSelect` parameter to `True`.

Open a File Requested by the User

① Name your procedure.

② Create a variable to store the filename returned by the `GetOpenFilename` method.

③ Create your `GetOpenFilename` command.

● Types of files the user can open.

● The title of the Open dialog box.

④ Create a command to open the workbook.

⑤ Press Alt+F11 to switch from the VBE to Excel, and run the macro.

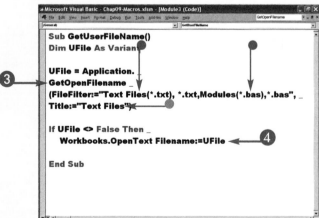

The macro opens the Open dialog box.

● The list of file types the user can open.

● The title of the dialog box.

6 Double-click the file you want to open.

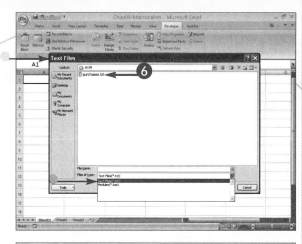

The macro opens the file.

Extra

The `FileFilter` parameter enables you to create a list of files users can select in the `Open` dialog box. You describe the file and follow the description with a comma and a wildcard file specification. If you do not set this parameter, VBA lists all of the file types Excel can open.

Example:
```
Text Files (*.text), *.txt
```

An asterisk (*) is a wildcard character that represents any string of characters, and a question mark (?) is a wildcard character that represents a single character. The notation *.txt means any filename that ends with .txt.

FILE TYPE	DESCRIPTION
*.txt, *.prn, *.csv	Text files
*.xls, *.xlm, *.xl, *.xlc, *.xlsx, *.xlsm	Microsoft Excel files
*.htm	Web pages
*.xml	XML files
*.odc, *.udl, *.dsn	Data sources
*.mdb, *.mde	Access databases
*.wk?	Lotus files
*.wks	Microsoft Works 2.0 files
*.dbf	dBase files

Save a Workbook

To save an Excel workbook, you can use the Save or SaveAs method of the Workbook object. VBA creates a workbook object for each workbook you open. You can reference a specific workbook object by name. For example, Workbooks("Sample.xlsx") refers to the Sample.xlsx workbook.

If you do not know the name of the workbook you want to save, you can make the workbook you want to save the active workbook, and then use the ActiveWorkbook property to save the workbook. For example, the code ActiveWorkbook.Save saves the active workbook.

If the workbook you want to save contains the macro that is currently running, you can use the ThisWorkbook property. For example, the code ThisWorkbook.Save saves the workbook in which the macro is located. The workbook that contains the macro is often the active workbook. However, if you open a new workbook during the execution of a macro, the new workbook can become the active workbook.

To set save specifications for a workbook, use the Workbook.SaveAs method, which has the following parameters: FileName, FileFormat, Password, WriteResPassword, ReadOnlyRecommended, CreateBackup, AccessMode, ConflictResolution, AddToMru, and Local.

Use the FileName parameter to specify the filename and the folder in which to save the workbook. If you do not set this parameter, Excel uses the workbook's filename.

Use the FileFormat parameter to specify the file format for saving the file. You can use any of the file formats that Excel supports by entering one of the XlFileFormat constant values. See Appendix A for a list of the XlFileFormat constant values. Set the AddToMru parameter to True if you want to add the workbook to the Recent Documents list.

Save a Workbook

① Name your procedure.

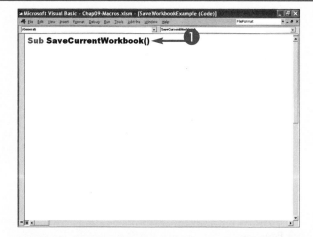

② Create your SaveAs command.

● The name you want to give the saved file.

● The file format.

● Adds the file to the Recent Documents list.

③ Press Alt+F11 to switch from the VBE to Excel, and run the macro.

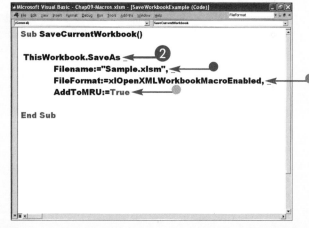

○ The macro saves your file.

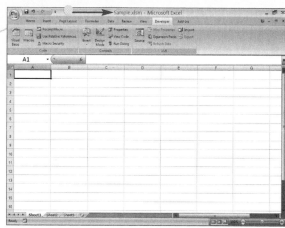

● The macro adds your file to the Recent Documents list.

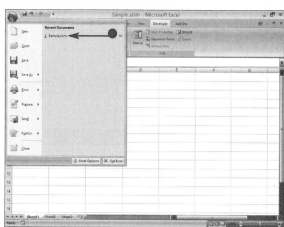

Extra

The `SaveAs` method has several optional parameters that determine how the file is saved. Remember to use the named parameter option to specify parameter values for the method.

SAVEAS PARAMETER	DESCRIPTION
FileName	Indicates the name and location to save the file.
FileFormat	Contains an `XlFileFormat` constant that indicates the format for saving the file. See Appendix A for a list of `XlFileFormat` constant values.
Password	Contains up to a 15-character password that is required to open the file.
WriteResPassword	Contains the password for write-restricting the file.
ReadOnlyRecommended	Set to `True` to display a message that recommends that the user open the file as Read-Only.
CreateBackup	Set to `True` to create a backup file.
AccessMode	Contains a constant value of xlExclusive, xlNoChange, or xlShared to indicate access mode.
ConflictResolution	Contains a constant indicating how to resolve conflicts. A value of xlUserResolution displays a Conflict Resolution box, xlLocalSessionChanges accepts a local user's changes, and xlOtherSessionChanges accepts changes from other users.
AddToMru	Set to `True` to add a workbook to the Recent Documents list.
Local	Set to `True` to save files in the language used by Excel; set to `False` to save files in the language used by VBA.

Save a Workbook in a Format Specified by the User

You can use the GetSaveAsFilename method to request the name, location, and format to use when saving a workbook file. This method displays the Save As dialog box from which the user selects the file they want to save. The GetSaveAsFilename method does not save the file; instead, VBA returns the user's information to the variable you assign to the GetSaveAsFilename statement. If the user does not make an entry, the variable returns False. To save the file, use the SaveAs method. See the section, "Save a Workbook," for more information. The GetSaveAsFilename method has the following optional parameters: InitialFilename, FileFilter, FilterIndex, and Title.

Use the InitialFilename parameter to suggest a name for the file. If you do not suggest a name, Excel uses the name of the active workbook. Use the FileFilter

parameter to create a list of file formats users can use to save the file. If you do not include this parameter, Excel lists all available formats. To create the list, describe the file type, place a comma after the description, and then place a wildcard specification after the comma, for example:

Text Files (*.text), *.txt

An asterisk (*) is a wildcard character that means any string of characters. The notation *.txt means any file that ends with .txt.

Use the FilterIndex parameter to select a default file-filtering option from the FileFilter parameter options. You can use a filter value between 1 and the total number of filters. If you omit this parameter, VBA uses the first filter as the default value. Use the Title parameter to place a title on the dialog box.

Save a Workbook in a Format Specified by the User

1. Name your procedure.

2. Declare your variables.

3. Create a GetSaveAsFilename command.

- The filter list.

- The dialog box title.

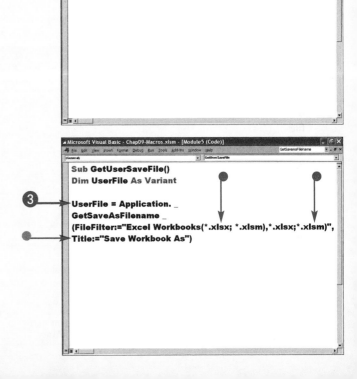

④ Create a command to save the file.

⑤ Press Alt+F11 to switch from the VBE to Excel, and run the macro.

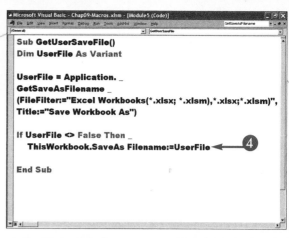

```
Sub GetUserSaveFile()
Dim UserFile As Variant

UserFile = Application. _
GetSaveAsFilename _
(FileFilter:="Excel Workbooks(*.xlsx; *.xlsm),*.xlsx;*.xlsm)",
Title:="Save Workbook As")

If UserFile <> False Then _
    ThisWorkbook.SaveAs Filename:=UserFile   ④

End Sub
```

The macro opens the Save Workbook As dialog box and then saves the file you specify.

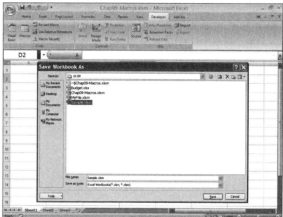

Extra

Instead of saving an individual workbook, you can save the entire workspace. Saving workspaces enables you to save all open workbooks as a group. When you open a workspace, all of the workbooks open. Workspace files have an .xlw filename extension.

To save a workspace, use the `SaveWorkspace` method of the `Application` object. The `SaveWorkspace` method has one parameter: `FileName`. To save your file in the current folder, enter the name of the file as the `FileName` parameter. To save to another folder, enter the path and the filename as the filename parameter.

Examples:
```
Application.SaveWorkspace("Sample")
Application.SaveWorkspace("C:\Workbooks\Sample")
```

Determine if a Workbook Is Open

The Workbooks collection contains all of the workbooks that are open in Excel. You can determine if a workbook is open by examining the workbooks in the `Workbooks` collection. As a new workbook opens, it becomes a Workbook object and Excel adds it to the `Workbooks` collection. Excel stores workbooks in the Workbooks collection sequentially and assigns each workbook an index value based on its sequence. For example, the first workbook opened is the first workbook in the collection, and VBA assigns it an index value of 1; the next workbook opened is the second workbook, and VBA assigns it an index value of 2. If you know the order in which a workbook opened, you can access the workbook by using the associated index value.

The code `MyWorkbook = Workbook(1).Name` uses the `Name` property to return the name of the first workbook in the collection to the `MyWorkbook` variable. The `Name` property is a read-only property. You can use it to return the name of a workbook, but you cannot use it to change the name of a workbook. To learn how to change the name of a workbook, see the section, "Save a Workbook."

To locate a workbook, look at each workbook in the `Workbooks` collection. With a `For Each Next` loop statement, you can cycle through all open workbooks. See Chapter 6 for more information about using a `For Each Next` loop statement.

Within a looping structure, you can compare the name of each workbook with the name of the desired workbook. With an `If Then` statement, you can check the name of each workbook and then execute a series of statements when the workbook you want is found. See Chapter 6 for more information about using an `If Then` statement.

Determine if a Workbook Is Open

① Name your procedure.

② Declare your variables.

③ Assign `False` to a Boolean variable.

You set this variable to `True` if the active workbook is the workbook that you want to activate.

④ Assign the file you are looking for to a variable.

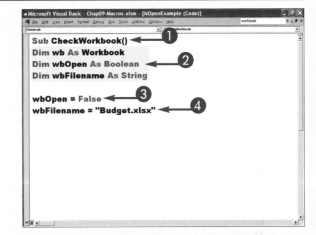

⑤ Create a `For Each In` loop.

This statement allows you to review every open workbook.

⑥ Create an `If Then` statement.

The code looks at every open workbook; if it finds the workbook you requested, it activates the workbook and displays a message.

● If the macro does not find the workbook, it looks in the current directory and opens the workbook.

⑦ Press Alt+F11 to switch from the VBE to Excel, and run the macro.

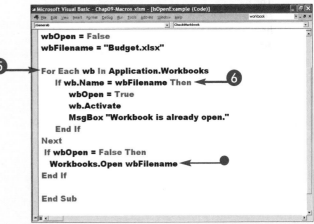

The macro opens the file you specified and activates it.

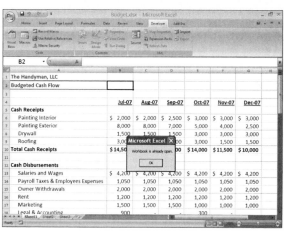

If the file is already open, the macro displays the message, "Workbook is already open."

Extra

If a workbook is open, you can activate it by using the Activate method of the Workbook object. The activated workbook becomes the currently selected workbook in Excel. The Activate method has no parameters. Specify the workbook to activate, followed by the method.

Example:
Workbooks("Budget.xlsx").Activate

Using Application.Workbooks returns all workbooks, including hidden workbooks, but it does not return any open add-ins. To return a specific add-in, reference the add-in by name.

Example
Workbooks("OpenAddin.xla").

The Open method opens the specified add-in file. If you do not specify the path, Excel looks for the workbook in the current folder. See Chapter 16 for more information on add-ins.

Close a Workbook

You can close a workbook by using the `Close` method and referencing the `Workbook` object that contains the workbook you want to close. When you open a workbook, VBA assigns the workbook an index value. For example, VBA assigns the first workbook you open an index value of 1, and the next workbook you open an index value of 2. The Workbooks collection contains all open workbooks as individual Workbook objects. You can reference a workbook by using an index value, the name of the workbook, the `ActiveWorkbook` property, or the `ThisWorkbook` property. If you close a workbook that is running the macro and you have code after the `Close` statement, Excel may ignore the code. The following examples close a workbook:

```
Workbooks(1).Close
Workbooks("Budget.xlsx").Close
ActiveWorkbook.Close
ThisWorkbook.Close
```

The `Close` method has three optional parameters: `SaveChanges`, `Filename`, and `RouteWorkbook`. Set the `SaveChanges` parameter to `True` to save changes to a workbook as it closes. A `SaveChanges` value of `False` closes the workbook without saving, and you lose any changes you have made since your last save. Use the `FileName` parameter to tell VBA the name you want to give your file when you save it.

If you set up the workbook to route, you can use the `RouteWorkbook` parameter to route the workbook to the next recipient on the routing list. You specify a value of `True` to route the workbook; you specify a value of `False` if you do not want the workbook to be sent to the next recipient.

Close a Workbook

① Name your procedure.

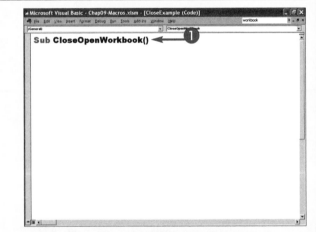

② Create your `Close` command.

● The workbook that you want to close.

● Saves any changes.

● The new filename.

146

③ Create a message for the user.

④ Press Alt+F11 to switch from the VBE to Excel, and run the macro.

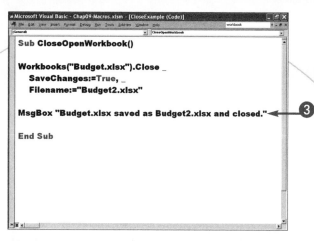

The macro closes the file specified in the macro, saves it under the name specified in the macro, and then displays a message to the user.

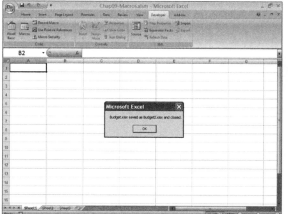

Extra

By using the Close method with the Workbooks object, you can close all workbooks that you have open in Excel. If the SaveChanges parameter does not have a value specified, Excel checks to ensure that you have saved each workbook since its last modification. If a workbook contains modifications, Excel prompts you to save the workbook. The following example closes all open workbooks.

Example:
```
Workbooks.Close
```

When you close all workbooks, Excel remains open. If you want Excel to close, use the Quit method with the Application object.

Example:
```
Application.Quit
```

Before closing Excel, the Quit method first closes the open workbooks. If any of the workbooks contain changes, Excel prompts you to save the changes. If you do not want to save modified worksheets and you do not want the dialog box to ask you to save changes, set the DisplayAlerts property to False. This property determines whether the alert message displays when Excel performs a task.

Example:
```
Application.DisplayAlerts = False
```

Create a New Workbook

To create a new Excel workbook, use the `Add` method with the `Workbooks` collection. The `Add` method has one optional parameter: `Template`. The following is the syntax for the `Add` method:

`Workbooks.Add(Template)`.

To tell VBA how to create a workbook, use the Template parameter. You can use another workbook or one of the four `XlWBATemplate` constant values as the template parameter.

When you use a workbook as the template, Excel copies the workbook into a new workbook. You can use the name of the workbook as the parameter if the workbook is located in the current folder. If the workbook is located in another folder, use the path to the workbook.

The `XlWBATemplate` constant has four values. You can use `xlWBATWorksheet` to create a workbook containing one worksheet; `xlWBATChart` to create a workbook containing one chart sheet; `xlWBATExcel4MacroSheet` to create an Excel 4.0 macro sheet; and `xlWBATExcel4IntMacroSheet` to create an international macro sheet.

When you use the `Add` method without the template parameter, Excel creates a new workbook with the name Book1.xlsx. If a workbook already exists with that name, Excel assigns the name Book2.xlsx. You can use the `Title` property to specify the title of the workbook. To name and save the new workbook, you can use the `SaveAs` method. See the section, "Save a Workbook," for more information on the `SaveAs` method.

Create a New Workbook

1. Name your procedure.

2. Declare a new Workbook object.

3. Create your `Add` command.

● The workbook that you want to use as a template.

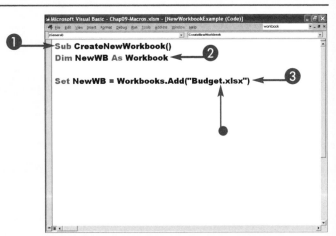

4. Assign a title to your workbook.

5. Name and save your workbook.

6. Press Alt+F11 to switch from the VBE to Excel, and run the macro.

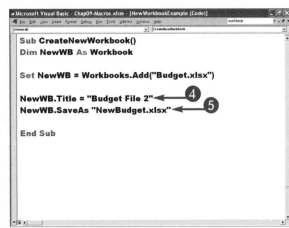

- The macro creates and saves the new workbook.

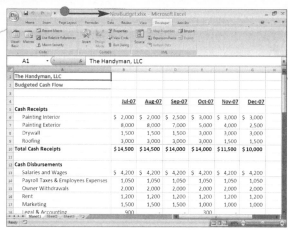

- The macro adds the title to the Document Properties pane.

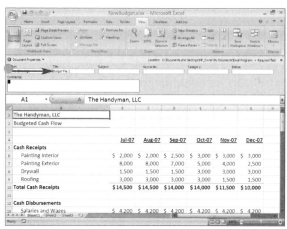

You can use the following properties with the Workbook object.

PROPERTY	DESCRIPTION
ActiveSheet	The string indicating the name of the active sheet in the workbook.
FileFormat	The Read-Only value indicating the format of the workbook. This value returns an XlFileFormat constant; see Appendix A for more information.
FullName	The Read-Only string indicating the name and complete path to the workbook.
HasPassword	The Read-Only Boolean value indicating whether the workbook is password-protected.
Name	A string indicating the name of the workbook.
Password	Returns or sets the password string for the workbook.
Path	Returns the complete Excel application path.
ProtectStructure	The Read-Only Boolean value indicating whether the order of the sheets in the workbook is protected. If True, you cannot move, delete, or add worksheets.
ReadOnly	The Read-Only Boolean value indicating whether the workbook was opened as Read-Only.
ReadOnlyRecommended	The Read-Only Boolean value indicating whether the workbook was saved as Read-Only.
Saved	Contains a Boolean value indicating whether changes were made since the workbook was saved.

Delete a File

The VBA `Kill` statement deletes a workbook or file. You can use this statement to delete any file that the user has permission to delete. The following is the syntax for the `Kill` statement:

`Kill(Pathname)`

The `Kill` statement requires one argument: `Pathname`. The `Pathname` argument is a string referencing the files you want to delete. You can use the name of a workbook as the parameter if the workbook is located in the current folder. If the workbook is located in another folder, use the path to the workbook. Make sure you enclose the path in quotes.

You can specify the name of a single file by typing the complete filename, including the extension. You can

remove multiple files at once by using wildcard symbols to specify multiple characters. An asterisk (`*`) represents multiple characters, and a question mark (`?`) represents a single character. For example, you can remove the entire contents of a folder by using the `*.*` specification. The statement `Kill "C:\Excel Files\*.*"` deletes every file in the Excel Files folder. If you only want to remove the Excel workbooks, you can use `Kill "C:\Excel Files\*.xls?"`.

You cannot delete open files. If you attempt to do so, a Permission Denied error appears. You also cannot delete files that are Read-Only. If you attempt to delete a Read-Only file, Excel displays a Path/File access error message.

Delete a File

① Name your procedure.

② Declare your variables.

This example uses the `DeleteWb` variable to store the name of the file you want the user to delete.

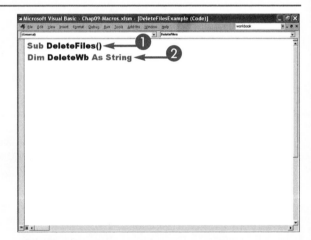

③ Use the `GetSaveAsFilename` method to request from the user the file that the user wants to delete.

Note: See the section, "Save a Workbook in a Format Specified by the User," to learn more about the `GetSaveAsFilename` method.

④ Delete the file.

⑤ Press Alt+F11 to switch from the VBE to Excel, and run the macro.

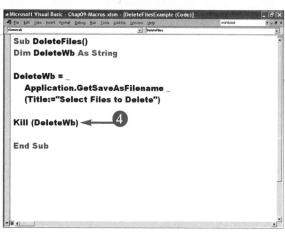

```
Sub DeleteFiles()
Dim DeleteWb As String

DeleteWb = _
    Application.GetSaveAsFilename _
    (Title:="Select Files to Delete")

Kill (DeleteWb)    ◄── ④

End Sub
```

The macro requests a filename and then deletes the file.

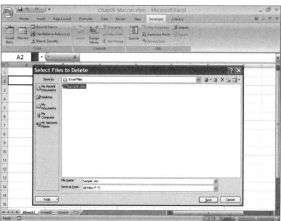

Extra

The `Kill` statement only removes files; it does not remove folders. To delete a folder, use the `RmDir` statement. The `RmDir` statement takes one argument: `Path`. If you omit the argument, VBA tries to delete the current folder. For the path argument, specify the location of the folder that you want to remove. For example, the code `RmDir("Excel Files")` removes the Excel Files folder. The `RmDir` statement only removes folders; it does not remove any files. If the folder you are deleting contains any files, an error appears telling you that Excel cannot remove the folder.

When working with folders, you may need to know the current path. To determine the path to the current folder, use the `CurDir` function. The `CurDir` function returns a string containing the path to the current folder. You can assign the value returned by the function to a variable, as shown in following example.

Example:
```
CurrentFolder= CurDir
```

Add a Sheet

To add a new sheet to a workbook, you can use the Add method with the Sheets object. You can use this method to add a worksheet, chart sheet, or macro sheet. The Add method has four optional parameters that specify where in the workbook to place the sheet, the number of sheets to add, and the type of sheet to create. The following is the syntax for the Add method when used with the Sheets object:

expression.Add(Before, After, Count, Type)

Use the expression to identify the workbook to which you want to add a worksheet. Use the Before parameter to tell VBA the worksheet before which you want to place the new worksheet, or use the After parameter to tell VBA the worksheet after which you want to place the new worksheet. Excel references sheets in a Worksheets collection based on the order of the sheets in the workbook from left to right. The first worksheet on the left has an index value of 1 and is referred to as Worksheet(1). To reference a sheet, you can use the sheet name or the Worksheets collection with an index value, as in this example: ThisWorkbook.Sheets.Add Before:=Worksheets(1).

You can use the Count parameter to add multiple sheets to a workbook. If you do not specify a value for the Count parameter, Excel adds one sheet.

By default, the Add method creates a worksheet. You can also use this method to create chart or macro sheets. You specify the type of sheet you want to create by using one of the four XlSheetType constant values: You use xlWorksheet to add a new worksheet, xlChart to add a chart sheet, xlExcel4MacroSheet to add a macro sheet, and xlExcel4IntMacroSheet to add an international macro sheet.

Add a Sheet

① Name your procedure.

② Create your Add command.

● The sheet before which you want to add the new sheets.

● The number of sheets you want to add.

● The type of sheet you want to add.

③ Press Alt+F11 to switch from the VBE to Excel, and run the macro.

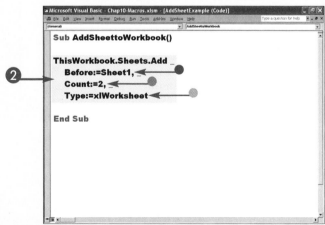

● The workbook before you run the macro.

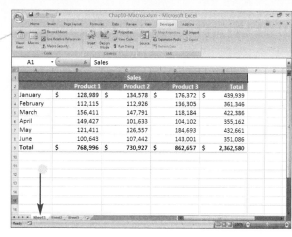

● The workbook after you run the macro.

The macro adds two worksheets before the first worksheet in the workbook.

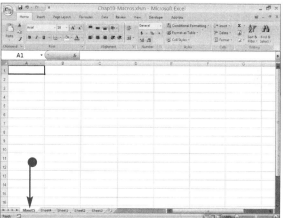

Extra

If you know that you want Excel to add new sheets before the first sheet in the workbook or after the last sheet, reference an element of the Worksheets collection. Excel always makes the first sheet in the workbook the first element in the Worksheets collection. You can refer to it as Worksheets(1). You can use the Count method with the Worksheets object to determine the last sheet in the workbook. The expression Worksheets.Count returns the total number of worksheets in the Worksheets collection. The following example places a worksheet after the last sheet in the workbook.

Example:
```
ThisWorkbook.Sheets.Add _
     After:=Worksheets(Worksheets.Count)
```

You can also reference a sheet by name. For example, by default, Excel names worksheets Sheet1, Sheet2, and so on. If you want to place new sheets before Sheet1, use the following as the Before parameter:
```
Before:=Worksheets("Sheet1").
```

Delete a Sheet

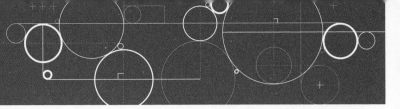

You can delete or remove from a workbook any sheet you can modify. If you open the workbook in Read-Only mode or if someone has protected the worksheet, you may not be able to remove the sheet.

To delete worksheets, use the `Delete` method with the `Sheets` object. You can remove any sheet from the workbook, including sheets, chart sheets, and macro sheets. To use the `Delete` method, you simply identify the sheet you want to remove. The following example removes the first sheet in a workbook:

`Sheets(1).Delete`

Every sheet has an index value. This example deletes the sheet with the index value of 1. Excel numbers sheets and charts as you add them to the workbook as follows: Sheet1, Sheet2, and so on (or Chart1, Chart2, and so on).

However, the VBA index number does not always correspond with the number given to the sheet by Excel. VBA assigns index values numerically, starting with the first sheet on the left. If you move sheets within your workbook, Excel reorders them in the `Sheets` object. The first sheet on the left always has an index value of 1.

You can also use the sheet name to reference the sheet you want to delete. You must enclose the name of the sheet in quotes, as in the following example:

`Sheets("Sheet3").Delete`

Whenever you perform a deletion, Excel displays a message box to verify that you really want to remove the sheet. Click Yes to remove the specified sheet from the workbook. Remember that if the sheet contains any data, Excel permanently removes the data.

Delete a Sheet

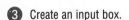

① Name your procedure.

② Declare your variables.

③ Create an input box.

The users enter the name of the sheet they want to delete into the input box, and VBA stores the name to a variable.

④ Create a Delete command.

● The variable containing the worksheet that the user wants to delete.

⑤ Press Alt+F11 to switch from the VBE to Excel and then run the macro.

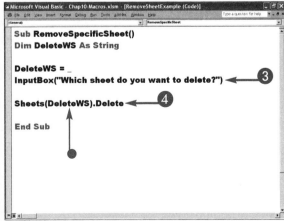

- The macro displays the message box requesting the sheet the user wants to delete.

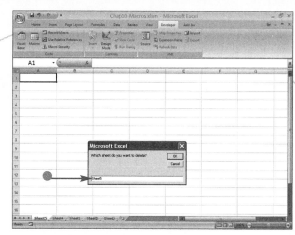

- The macro deletes the sheet.

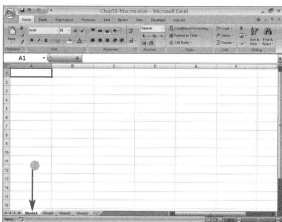

Extra

If you want to create a procedure that removes only worksheets from the workbook, you can use the `Delete` method with a `Worksheets` object instead of the `Sheets` object. The `Sheets` object contains all worksheets, chart sheets, and macro sheets that are open in a workbook, whereas the `Worksheets` object only keeps track of the open worksheets. If you use the `Worksheets` object to remove the first worksheet in the workbook, Excel ignores any chart sheets before the first worksheet. The following statement deletes the first worksheet in the workbook and ignores any other sheet types.

Example:
```
Worksheets(1).Delete
```

If you want to create a procedure that removes only chart sheets from a workbook, you can use the `Delete` method with the `Charts` object. The `Charts` object contains all of the chart sheets that are contained in the workbook. This method works only with chart sheets, not charts embedded in worksheets. When you use the `Charts` object with the `Delete` method, Excel only considers actual chart sheets and ignores any worksheets, even if they exist before the specified chart sheet. The following statement deletes the first chart sheet in the workbook and ignores any other sheet types.

Example:
```
Charts(1).Delete
```

Move a Sheet

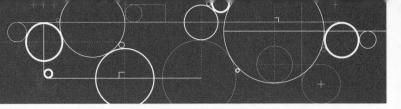

You can use the Move method with the Sheets object to rearrange sheets within a workbook. When you move a sheet, you indicate the new location by specifying the name of the sheet before or after which you want to place the sheet you are moving.

The Move method has two optional parameters: Before and After. Although both parameters are optional, you can use only one of them at a time. Use the Before parameter to specify the sheet in front of which you want to place a sheet, and the After parameter to specify the sheet after which you want to place a sheet. For example, the following statement moves the first sheet in a workbook and places it after the third sheet:

```
Sheets(1).Move After:=Sheets(3)
```

If you do not specify a Before or After parameter value, Excel creates a new workbook and places the worksheet in that workbook. The worksheet becomes the only worksheet in the new workbook.

The Sheets object references all sheets in the workbook, including all worksheets, chart sheets, and macro sheets. As shown in the example, you can use index values to reference specific sheets based on their order in the workbook. You can also reference a sheet by using the name on the sheet tab.

Moving a sheet before or after a nonexistent sheet causes VBA to display a "Subscript out of range" error. To avoid this error, you can use the Count method to determine the number of sheets in the workbook before you attempt to move the sheets.

Move a Sheet

① Name your procedure.

② Declare your variables.

③ Count the number of sheets in your workbook.

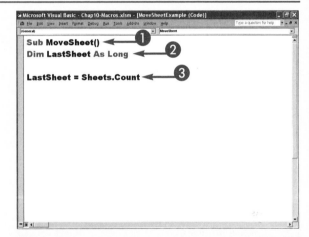

④ Create your Move command.

● The sheet you want to move.

● The location where you want to move your sheet.

⑤ Press Alt+F11 to switch from the VBE to Excel, and run the macro.

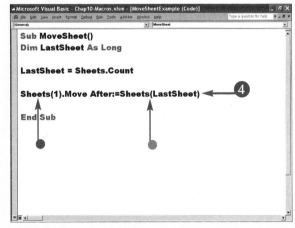

● The worksheet before the move.

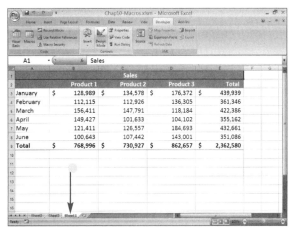

● The worksheet after the move.

Apply It

As you work with Excel objects in VBA, especially collection objects that contain several objects, you frequently must determine the number of objects in the collection. Because the number of objects in a collection varies, you may need to determine the number of objects as your code runs. The best way to do this is by using the Count property, which works with virtually all VBA collection objects and returns the number of items in the collection.

Example:
```
NumSheets = Worksheets.Count
```

The Count property is Read-Only, meaning you can use it to count, but not change, the number of sheets in a workbook.

Copy and Paste a Sheet

If you want to copy and paste sheets in a workbook, you can use the Copy method with the Sheets object. When you copy a sheet, you indicate where you want to place the copy by specifying the name of the sheet before or after which you want the copy to appear.

The Copy method has two optional parameters: Before and After. Although both parameters are optional, you can only use one of them at a time. Use the Before parameter to specify the sheet in front of which you want to place the copy of the sheet, or use the After parameter to specify the sheet after which you want to place the copy of the sheet. The following statement copies the first sheet in a workbook and places the copy after the third sheet: Sheets(1).Copy After:=Sheets(3). If you do not specify a Before or After value, Excel creates a new workbook and places the copy in the new workbook.

When you use the Sheets object, you can reference all sheets within a workbook, including chart sheets and macro sheets. You can use index values to reference sheets based on their order in the workbook, or you can reference sheets by using their sheet names.

Be careful with the sheet references you use. If you try to place a copy of a sheet before or after a nonexistent sheet, VBA displays a "Subscript out of range" error. To avoid this error, consider using the Count method to determine exactly how many sheets you have in a workbook before you copy and paste.

Copy and Paste a Sheet

① Name your procedure.

② Declare your variables.

③ Count the number of sheets in your workbook.

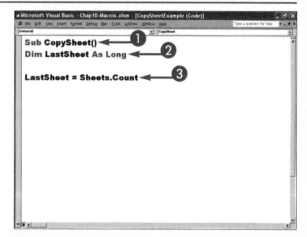

④ Create your Copy command.

● The sheet you want to copy.

● Where you want to place the copy.

⑤ Press Alt+F11 to switch from the VBE to Excel, and run the macro.

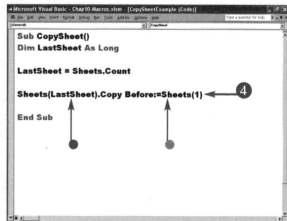

● The workbook before you run the macro.

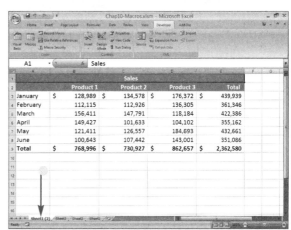

◉ The workbook after you run the macro.

Extra

The Copy method produces the same results when you use it with a Chart object, Charts collection object, Worksheet object, or Worksheets collection object instead of the Sheets object. You can use these other objects when you want to work with a specific type of sheet. For example, to make a worksheet the first worksheet in a workbook, type **Worksheet(3).Copy Before:=Worksheets(1)**. This code places a copy of the third worksheet in front of the first worksheet. If the first sheet in the workbook is a chart, the copied sheet comes after the chart but before the first worksheet. You can copy chart sheets the same way, but use the Charts collection object to specify the chart sheet to copy. You can combine your object references within a Copy statement. For example, you can place a copy of the first worksheet before the first chart sheet.

Example:
```
Worksheets(1).Copy Before:=Charts(1)
```

When you copy a sheet in a workbook, Excel indicates the sheet is a copy by placing a number in parentheses after the sheet name. For example, for Sheet3, Excel indicates the copied sheet as Sheet3 (2), with the number in parentheses indicating that the sheet is the second version. Copying the worksheet again creates Sheet3 (3).

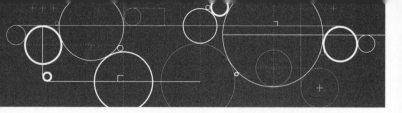

Hide a Sheet

I f you want to hide sheets in a workbook, you can use the `Visible` property with the `Sheets` object. You may want to hide sheets in a workbook to prevent users from viewing them. These sheets might contain the raw values that you use to calculate data.

Hiding a sheet does not always keep users from accessing it. Users can unhide sheets in Excel by using the Unhide option on the Format menu. If you want others to be able to unhide a sheet but not be able to change a sheet, protect the sheet. See the section, "Protect a Worksheet," for more information about protecting sheets.

Using the `Visible` property, you can determine the current state of a sheet — visible or not visible — or you can change the state of a sheet. To determine the current state of a sheet, you assign the `Visible` property to a Boolean variable as follows: `SheetProps = Sheets(1).Visible`. If you declare the `SheetProps` variable as a Boolean value, the variable receives a value of `True` if the specified sheet is visible; otherwise, it receives a value of `False`. If you do not declare the variable as Boolean, Excel assigns a numeric value of –1 if the sheet is visible and 0 if the sheet is not visible.

To change the visibility of a sheet, you can assign a Boolean value of `True` or `False` to the sheet's `Visible` property. You can hide all but one sheet in a workbook, because Excel requires that a workbook have at least one visible sheet. The following example hides a sheet:

```
Sheets(2).Visible = False
```

Hide a Sheet

① Name your procedure.

② Declare your variables.

③ Count the number of sheets in your workbook.

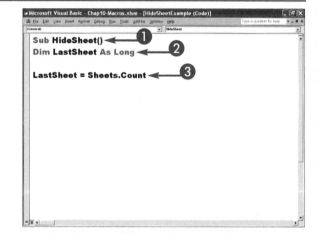

④ Set the `Visible` property to `False`.

● This example uses a `For Next` loop to hide every worksheet except for the first one.

⑤ Press Alt+F11 to switch from the VBE to Excel, and run the macro.

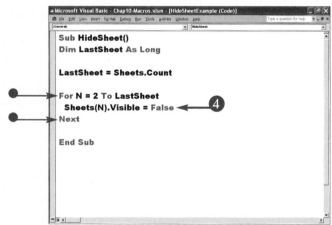

● The workbook before you execute the macro.

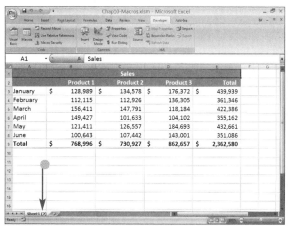

● The workbook after you execute the macro.

Sheets that you hide by setting the Visible property to False are still accessible to users from within Excel. To see which sheets are hidden in a workbook, on the Home tab, click Format →Hide & Unhide →Unhide Sheet. The Unhide dialog box appears, listing all of the sheets that you have hidden. To unhide a sheet, click the sheet and then click OK. This is equivalent to setting the Visible property for a sheet to True.

There are three XlSheetVisibility constant values. You can use them to set the visibility status of a sheet.

CONSTANT VALUE	FUNCTION
xlSheetHidden	Hides a sheet. The user can use the Ribbon to unhide the sheet.
xlSheetVeryHidden	Hides a sheet. The user cannot use the Ribbon to unhide the sheet.
xlSheetVisible	Displays a sheet.

Example:
```
Sheets("Formulas").Visible = xlSheetVeryHidden
```

Change the Name of a Sheet

If you have a number of sheets in a workbook, naming your sheets enables your users to determine which sheet they want to access. For example, if you keep your budget on a sheet named Budget and your sales figures on a sheet named Sales, when a user opens your workbook, they can quickly determine the sheet they want to access.

To change the name of a sheet in a workbook, use the `Name` property of the `Sheets` object. By default, Excel names all worksheets Sheet#, replacing # with the order in which you add the sheet to your workbook. For example, a typical workbook contains three worksheets: Sheet1, Sheet2, and Sheet3. If you add a worksheet, Excel names it Sheet4. Excel uses the name Chart# for chart sheets. Again, Excel assigns chart sheets numbers, based on the order in which you add them, with the first

chart sheet being Chart1. Macro sheets and dialog sheets have the same naming conventions. Excel names the first macro sheet you add to a workbook Macro1 and the first dialog sheet Dialog1.

You can change the name of a sheet by assigning a name to the `Name` property of the `Sheet` object. For example, the following code changes the name of Sheet1 to Budget:

```
Sheets(1).Name = "Budget"
```

You can assign a string or a variable to the `Name` property. You can determine what the current name of a sheet is by assigning the `Name` property to a variable, as in the following example:

```
StringName = Sheets(1).Name
```

This example returns the name of `Sheet(1)` to the variable `StringName`.

Change the Name of a Sheet

① Name your procedure.

② Declare your variables.

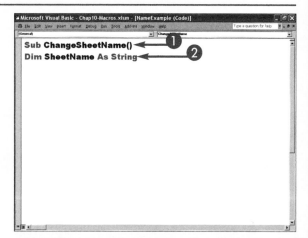

③ Create an input box.

The users enter the name they want to change the active sheet to into the input box, and VBA stores the name to a variable.

④ Create a `Name` command to rename the sheet.

● The variable containing the name the user wants to give to worksheet.

● The sheet to be renamed.

In this example, the code is renaming the active sheet.

⑤ Press Alt+F11 to switch from the VBE to Excel, and run the macro.

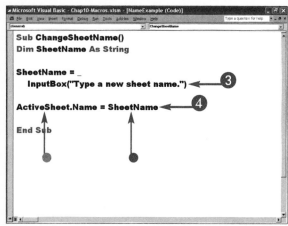

● The macro displays a message box requesting the name the user wants to give the active sheet.

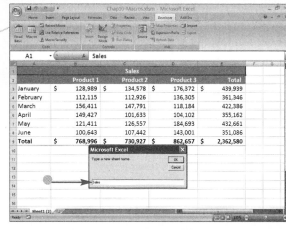

● The macro renames the sheet.

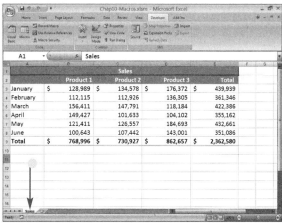

Extra

You can manually change the name of a sheet in Excel by clicking the Home tab and then selecting Format → Rename Sheet. Excel highlights the sheet's name tab. You click the tab and type the new name. After you modify the name, click elsewhere on the sheet and Excel updates the sheet name.

Because users can easily modify the name of a worksheet, be careful when referencing sheet names with your macros. If you reference the name of a sheet that has a changed name, Excel returns an error message.

No matter what the sheets are named, Excel keeps track of them based on the order in which they exist within the Sheets collection. If you use Project Explorer to view the list of sheets in the workbook, you see listings of Sheet1, Sheet2, and so on, with the corresponding sheet name in parentheses.

You can also use the Name property in conjunction with the Parent property to determine the name of the workbook that contains the current sheet. To determine the name of the corresponding workbook, use the code CurrentWB = ActiveSheet.Parent.Name.

Save a Sheet to Another File

You can save any sheet to another file by using the `SaveAs` method with a `Sheets` collection object. The `SaveAs` method has eight parameters that tell VBA how to save the sheet: `FileName`, `FileFormat`, `Password`, `WriteResPassword`, `ReadOnlyRecommended`, `CreateBackup`, `AddToMru`, and `Local`.

The `FileName` parameter is required. You use the `FileName` parameter to specify the name of the file you want to save the sheet to, and the folder in which you want to save the sheet. If you do not specify a path when you specify a filename, Excel saves the file in the current folder.

Use the `FileFormat` parameter to specify the file format in which you want to save the file. You can save in any file format supported by Excel, by using one of the `XlFileFormat` constant values. See Appendix A for a list of the `XlFileFormat` constant values. If you do not

specify a file format, Excel uses the format that was previously used to save the file if the file was previously saved or the file format used by the current version of Excel is the file has never been saved. Use the `Password` parameter to specify a password of up to 15 characters for opening the file. Use the `WriteResPassword` parameter to restrict the file to open as Read-Only, unless the user has the password.

The remaining parameters accept the Boolean values `True` or `False`. You set `ReadOnlyRecommended` to `True` to display a message to the user when the file opens, suggesting that they open the file as Read-Only. You set `CreateBackup` to `True` to create a backup file; `AddToMru` to `True` to add the file to the Recent Documents list; `Local` to `True` if you want to save the file in the language used by Excel; and `Local` to `False` if you want to save the file in the language used by VBA.

Save a Sheet to Another File

① Name your procedure.

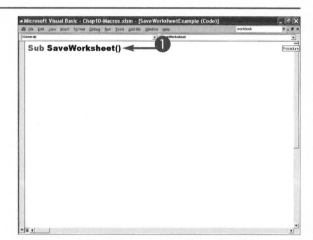

② Create your `SaveAs` command.

● The name of the new file.

● The format in which you want to save the file.

This example saves the file in HTML format.

◉ Creates a backup.

◉ Adds the file to the Recent Documents list when the file is saved.

③ Press Alt+F11 to switch from the VBE to Excel, and run the macro.

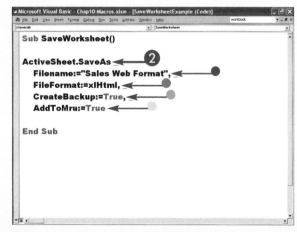

- The macro saves the file in HTML format,
adds the file to the Recent Documents list,
and creates a backup.

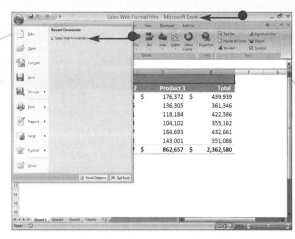

The HTML file that the macro created,
displayed in a browser.

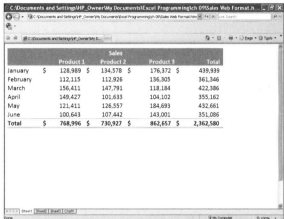

Extra

The `FileFormat` parameter accepts any of the `XlFileFormat` constant values that are listed in Appendix A. The list of available file formats is rather extensive. You can save a worksheet to another workbook by specifying the `xlWorkbookNormal` constant. This constant creates a new workbook based on the default workbook format for the current version of Excel. If you need to save the workbook in a format used by an earlier version of Excel, you need to specify the appropriate format parameter. For example, xlExcel5 saves the workbook in a format that you can open in Excel 5.0 or later. To save an Excel 2007 file in a macro-enabled format, use `xlOpenXMLWorkbookMacroEnabled`.

Protect a Worksheet

Protecting your worksheet enables users to make certain types of changes while disallowing others. For example, you can allow users to make changes to formats; insert or delete columns, rows, or hyperlinks; sort; filter; use PivotTables; and edit objects or scenarios.

You use the `Worksheet.Protect` method to protect a worksheet. The `Worksheet.Protect` method has several parameters, all of which are optional. With the exception of the `Password` parameter, you use the Boolean value `True` to activate a parameter and the Boolean value `False` to deactivate a parameter. The parameters are `Password`, `DrawingObjects`, `Contents`, `Scenarios`, `UserInterfaceOnly`, `AllowFormatting Cells`, `AllowFormattingColumns`, `AllowFormatting Rows`, `AllowInsertingColumns`, `AllowInsertingRows`, `AllowInsertingHyperlinks`, `AllowDeletingColumns`, `AllowDeletingRows`, `AllowSorting`, `AllowFiltering`, and `AllowUsingPivotTables`.

If you want to password-protect your worksheet, set the `Password` parameter to the password you want to use. You can use any string as a password, but remember passwords are case-sensitive. In other words, Excel interprets "Password" and "PASSWORD" differently.

Set the `DrawingObjects` parameter to `False` if you want the user to be able to modify shapes. The default value is `True`. By default, Excel protects locked cells, to remove this protection, set the `Contents` parameter to `False`. To unprotect scenarios, set the `Scenarios` parameter to `False`. If you set the `UserInterfaceOnly` parameter to `False`, Excel applies protection to macros and to the user interface. If you only want the user interface protected, set the `UserInterfaceOnly` parameter to `True`.

The remaining parameters are self-explanatory and they all have a default value of `False`. To allow any of these options, set the parameter to `True`.

Protect a Worksheet

① Name your procedure.

② Create your `Protect` command.

● Sets the password.

● Protects the user interface only.

● Allows format changes.

③ Press Alt+F11 to switch from the VBE to Excel, and run the macro.

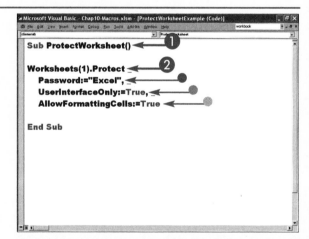

If the user tries to change a cell, Excel does not permit the change.

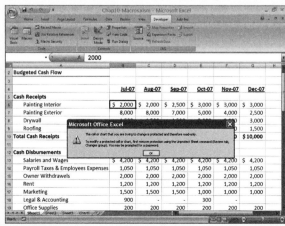

The user can make permitted changes.

● In this example, the user can change the formats.

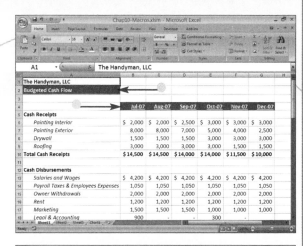

If the user knows the password, they can enter the password to unprotect the worksheet.

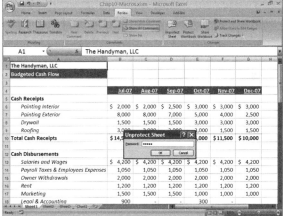

Protect a Chart

You can use the `Chart.Protect` method to protect a chart so that a user cannot modify it. The `Chart.Protect` method takes several parameters that enable you to determine the type of protection you want to assign to the chart. All of the parameters are optional. With the exception of the `Password` parameter, you use the Boolean value `True` to activate a parameter and the Boolean value `False` to deactivate a parameter. The following is the syntax for the `Chart.Protect` method:

`expression.Protect(Password, DrawingObjects, Contents, UserInterfaceOnly)`

The `expression` parameter identifies the chart you want to protect. If you want to password-protect your chart, you can set the `Password` parameter to the password you

want to use. You can use any string as a password, but remember that passwords are case-sensitive. In other words, Excel interprets "Password" and "PASSWORD" differently.

If you set the `DrawingObjects` parameter to `False`, the user can add shapes to your chart and modify the shapes in your chart. The default value is `True`. If you set the `Contents` parameter to `False`, the user can modify the chart. If you set the `UserInterfaceOnly` parameter to `False`, Excel applies protection to macros and to the user interface. If you only want the user interface protected, set the `UserInterfaceOnly` parameter to `True`.

To unprotect a chart using a procedure, use the `Unprotect` method. You must include the password if the chart is password-protected, as follows:

`Charts(1).Unprotect Password:="Excel"`

Protect a Chart

① Name your procedure.

② Create your `Protect` command.

● Sets the password.

● Protects the user interface only.

● Allows the user to draw objects.

③ Press Alt+F11 to switch from the VBE to Excel, and run the macro.

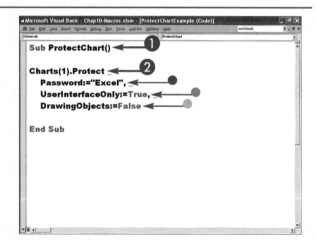

● If the user tries to make a change that your macro does not permit, Excel does not allow the user to make the change.

● Excel grays out the Ribbon options to indicate that they are not available.

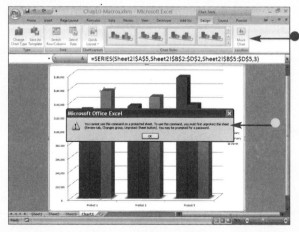

The user can make permitted changes.

● In this example, the user can add shapes.

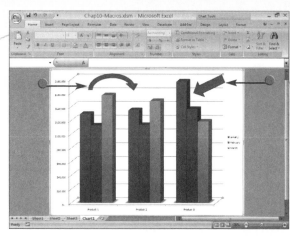

If the user knows the password, they can enter the password to unprotect the worksheet.

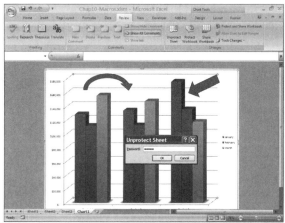

Apply It

VBA provides properties that you can use with `Worksheet` and `Chart` objects to determine if parts of a sheet are protected. This helps eliminate errors caused by attempting to modify a protected sheet. Each of these properties is Read-Only.

PROPERTY	DESCRIPTION
ProtectContents	Returns a value of True if the sheet is protected. For a chart, the property looks to see if the entire chart is protected. For a worksheet, the property looks to see if the cells are protected. To turn off this property, set the Contents parameter of the Protect method to False.
ProtectDrawingObjects	Returns a value of True if the shapes in the sheet are protected. To turn off this property, set the DrawingObjects parameter of the Protect method to False.
ProtectScenarios	Returns a value of True if the scenarios are protected. To turn off this property, set the Scenarios parameter of the Protect method to False.
ProtectionMode	Returns a value of True if the user interface is protected.

Print a Sheet

Y ou can use the PrintOut method to create a procedure to print the contents of a sheet. The PrintOut method has several parameters for specifying how Excel prints the sheet: From, To, Copies, Preview, ActivePrinter, PrintToFile, Collate, and PrToFileName.

Use the From and To parameters to indicate the range of pages within the specified sheet that you want to print. Indicate the page number of the first page to print as the value of the From parameter, and the page number of the last page as the value of the To parameter. If you omit these parameters, Excel prints the entire sheet.

By default, Excel prints one copy of the sheet. For multiple copies, use the Copies parameter to indicate the desired number. You can specify a value of True for the Collate parameter to have Excel collate the copies.

If you want the Excel preview window to show the contents of the print selection, set the value of the Preview parameter to True. The Print button on the Print Preview screen prints the copy, and the Close button cancels the print.

To specify a printer, use the ActivePrinter parameter. If you do not set the ActivePrinter parameter, VBA uses the computer's default printer.

You can send the printout to a file instead of a printer by setting the PrintToFile parameter to True, and specifying the name of the file to which you want to send the printout by using the PrToFileName parameter. If you do not specify a filename, Excel prompts you for one when your procedure runs.

Print a Sheet

1 Name your procedure.

2 Set up your page.

● Sets the orientation to landscape.

● Sets the print area.

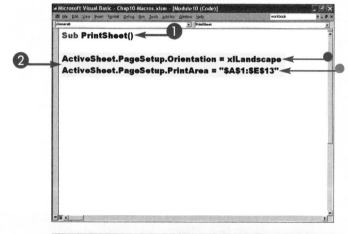

3 Create your PrintOut command.

● The number of copies to print.

● Displays the Print Preview before printing.

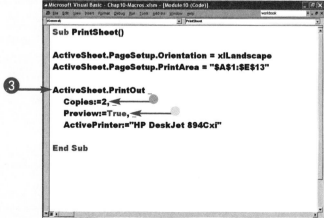

170

- The printer to which you want to send the report.

④ Press Alt+F11 to switch from the VBE to Excel, and run the macro.

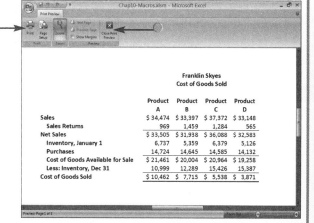

The macro displays the Print Preview screen.

- The Print button prints the file.

- The Close button cancels the printing.

Apply It

You can set a print area for a worksheet by using the `PageSetup` object with the `PrintArea` property. Assign the `PrintArea` property a range of cells as the print area. For example, `ActiveSheet.PageSetup.PrintArea = "$A$1:$E$9"` sets the range of cells in the print area from A1 to E9. If cells outside that range contain data, Excel does not print them.

When you use the `PrintArea` property to set the range of cells to print, you can omit the `From` and `To` parameters of the `PrintOut` method. To clear the print area, assign the `PrintArea` property a value of `False` or an empty string. Both of the following lines of code clear the print area:

Examples:
```
ActiveSheet.PageSetup.PrintArea = False
ActiveSheet.PageSetup.PrintArea = " "
```

When printing, you can set the orientation by using the `PageSetup` object with the `Orientation` property. Use the `xlLandscape` constant value to set the orientation to landscape. Use the `xlPortrait` constant value to set the orientation to portrait.

Sort Worksheets by Name

You can use VBA to sort worksheets in a workbook based on the worksheet names. When you first create a new workbook, Excel lists the sheets in order: Sheet1, Sheet2, Sheet3. However, as you add sheets, the order of the sheets can change dramatically. For example, if your active sheet is Sheet2 and you instruct Excel to add a new sheet, Excel adds it before Sheet2 and names it Sheet4, making the order of your sheets Sheet1, Sheet4, Sheet2, Sheet3.

You can easily resolve this problem by manually renaming or moving the sheets within the workbook. Alternatively, you can create a procedure that sorts the worksheets and lists them in alphabetical order. You start by using the Count property to determine the number of sheets in the workbook. When you know the number of

sheets in a workbook, you can use a For Next loop to cycle through the sheets so that Excel can compare the names and place the sheets in order. You use nested looping, which is the process of placing one loop inside another loop. The inside loop executes completely, and then control returns to the outside loop. See Chapter 6 for more information on using For Next loops.

Within the second For Next loop, use an If Then statement to compare the name of a sheet to the sheet that is currently considered the alphabetically lowest sheet name. If the compared name is alphabetically lower, it becomes the new alphabetically lowest name. Excel does an alphabetical comparison when you are working with strings.

Sort Worksheets by Name

① Name your procedure.

② Declare your variables.

③ Count the number of sheets.

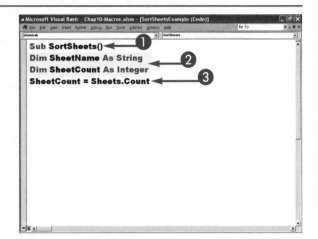

④ Create a For Next loop to loop through each index position.

⑤ Store the name of the sheet with the index value of N to the variable SheetName.

N starts at 1 and increments with each loop.

⑥ Create a For Next loop within the previous loop, assign the value of N to M, and loop through the total number of sheets, starting at the value of M.

⑦ If the name of the sheet with an index value of M is less than SheetName, store the name of the sheet with an index value of M to the variable SheetName and then keep looping; otherwise, do nothing and keep looping.

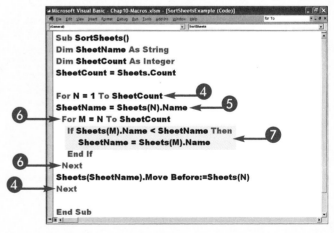

172

When the loop has finished, SheetName contains the lowest value.

(8) Move the sheet identified by the variable SheetName before the sheet with an index value of N.

(9) Move to the sheet with the next index value and perform the loop again.

(10) Press Alt+F11 to switch from the VBE to Excel, and run the macro.

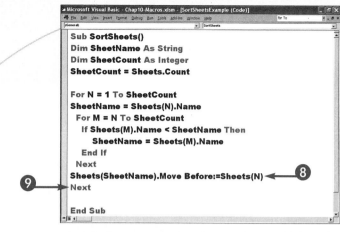

```
Sub SortSheets()
Dim SheetName As String
Dim SheetCount As Integer
SheetCount = Sheets.Count

For N = 1 To SheetCount
SheetName = Sheets(N).Name
  For M = N To SheetCount
   If Sheets(M).Name < SheetName Then
      SheetName = Sheets(M).Name
   End If
  Next
  Sheets(SheetName).Move Before:=Sheets(N)       (8)
  Next       (9)

End Sub
```

● The macro sorts the sheets.

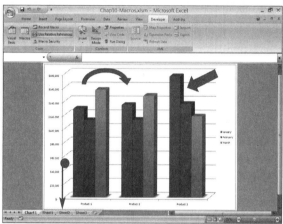

Apply It

The steps in this section determine the sheet with the lowest name in the inside loop and place that sheet before the index value that it is evaluating. Although this code works correctly, it is not the most efficient method for sorting a large list of items. The code attempts to move the sheet without first checking to see if the smallest sheet is also the current sheet. To make the execution of the code more efficient, add a conditional If Then statement that compares the two sheets and performs the move only if they are not the same sheet. The code runs more effectively because it determines that no move is required if the sheets are already in the correct order.

TYPE THIS:

```
If Sheets(SheetName) <> Sheets(N) Then
    Sheets(SheetName). Move Before:=Sheets(N)
End If
```

RESULT:

This code checks that the sheet you are moving and the sheet before which you intend to move it are not the same sheet. If the sheets are the same, Excel ignores the Move statement and continues with the looping statements.

Using the Range Property

When working in Excel, a lot of the work that you do involves ranges. You can define a range by using the Range property. Defining a range creates a Range object, which can be a single cell, an entire column, a row, or a selection of multiple cells.

You can use the Range property with the Application, Worksheet, or Range objects. The statements Application.Range and ActiveSheet.Range return the same results. If you use the Range property without an object, Excel assumes you are referencing the ActiveSheet.

You can use two syntax forms with the Range property. The first form requires two parameters: Cell1 and Cell2. This form of the Range object references the upper-left corner of the desired range with the Cell1

parameter, and the lower-right corner of the range with the Cell2 parameter. For example, to specify a range of cells between A1 and E15, you would use the code Range("A1", "E15").

The other form of the Range property requires a Name parameter. This required parameter indicates a range, using the A1-style reference. You place a colon between two cells to specify a range. For example, Range("A3:F5") refers to the range of cells from A3 to F5. You place a comma between the range definitions to refer to two or more noncontiguous ranges. For example, Range("A3, A1, B4:C10") specifies the range of cells A3, A1, and B4 to C10. You leave a space between the two range definitions to specify the location where two ranges intersect. For example, Range("A3:F3 D2:G5") specifies where the range of cells A3 to F3 intersects with the range of cells D2 to G5.

Using the Range Property

1. Name your procedure.

2. Define a range and select it.

● The range.

3. Ask the user if they want to calculate a total.

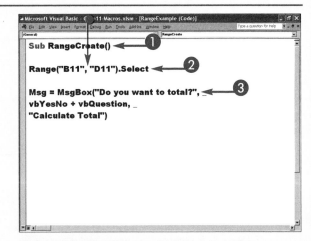

4. If the user responds, "Yes," then calculate the total.

● This same range was selected in step 1 using a different syntax.

5. Press Alt+F11 to switch from the VBE to Excel, and run the macro.

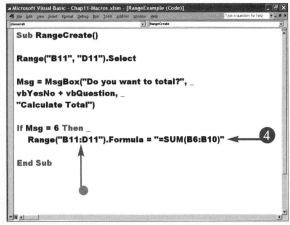

- The macro selects the range and then displays a message box.

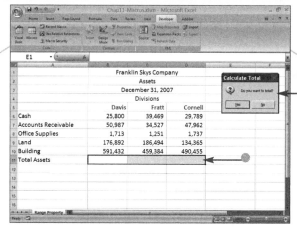

- If the user clicks the Yes button, the macro totals the columns.

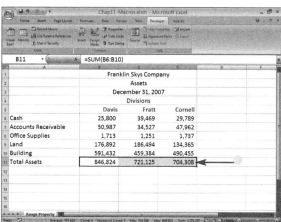

Extra

To highlight a cell or range of cells in a worksheet, use the Select method with a Range object. For example, to select the range of cells from A3 to A6, you would type **Range("A3:A6").Select**.

When you use the Select method with a Range object, the active cell becomes the first cell in the specified range. If you specify individual cells with the Select method, the active cell is the first cell specified. For example, Range("A3, A1, A5").Select makes cell A3 the active cell.

You can also use the Activate method to highlight a cell or range of cells. With the Activate method, the first cell referenced in the range is the active cell, but VBA highlights all of the other cells in the range to indicate that VBA has selected them as well. For example, the code Range("B4:C6").Activate, makes B4 the active cell and highlights cells B4 to C6. When you use the Activate method, the first cell in the range becomes the active cell. The Select method and the Activate method are interchangeable.

Using the Cells Property

You can use the `Cells` property to reference specific cells in a worksheet and make changes to the values or properties of the cells, such as the font settings. The Excel object model does not contain a `Cells` object. To reference specific cells, use either the `Cells` property or the `Range` property, each of which returns a `Range` object with the specified cells. See the section, "Using the Range Property," for more information about the `Range` property.

You can use the `Cells` property with the `Application`, `Range`, and `Worksheet` objects. Using the `Cells` property with the `Application` and `Worksheet` objects returns the same result. For example, you can type `Application.Cells`, or `ActiveSheet.Cells` to return a `Range` object containing all cells in the active worksheet.

The `Cells` property has two parameters. The first parameter, `Row`, contains a value indicating the row index. The second parameter, `Column`, contains a value indicating the column index. For example, to reference cell B5, you assign a value of 5 for the row parameter and a value of 2 for the column parameter, as shown in the code `Cells(5,2)`.

One advantage of using the `Cells` property instead of the `Range` property is that you can use variables to change the values easily. For example, you can use a variable to represent either the row or column, as shown in the code `Cells(N,1) = 5.` which sets the value of a cell in column A and a row specified by N to 5.

Using the Cells Property

1 Name your procedure.

2 Declare your variable.

3 Create a `For Next` loop.

4 Use the Cells property to indicate the cells you want to format.

5 Format the cells.

6 Press Alt+F11 to switch from the VBE to Excel, and run the macro.

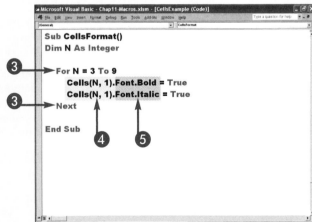

176

The worksheet before you run your macro.

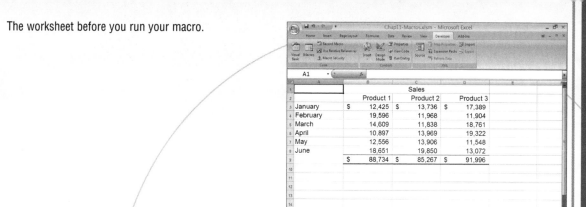

The worksheet after you run your macro.

- The macro moves down the first column and adds bold and italic formatting to each cell.

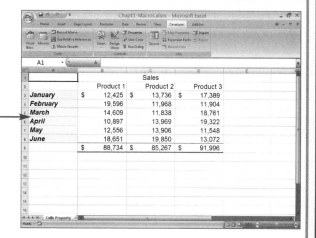

Extra

To set the font attributes for objects in Excel, use the `Font` object. You typically use the `Font` object to modify the attributes of a cell or a range of cells. The `Font` object has several properties for obtaining or modifying the attributes of a specified object. Some of these properties are listed in the following table.

FONT PROPERTY	DESCRIPTION
Bold	A Boolean value indicating whether the font for the object is bold.
Color	Indicates the color of the font. Use the RGB function to set the font color.
FontStyle	Indicates the font style. For example, to set both a bold and an underline font style, specify Font.FontStyle = "Bold Underline".
Italic	A Boolean value indicating whether the font for the object is italic.
Shadow	A Boolean value indicating whether the font is a shadow font.
Size	Indicates the size of the font.
Strikethrough	A Boolean value indicating whether to use a strikethrough font to draw a horizontal line through each character.
Subscript	A Boolean value indicating whether the font is subscript.
Superscript	A Boolean value indicating whether the font is superscript.
Underline	A Boolean value indicating whether the font is underlined.

Combine Multiple Ranges

To create a multiple area range, you can use the Union method. A multiple area range contains more than one block of cells, and the blocks of cells are noncontiguous. For example, you can use the Union method to create a Range object containing the cells A1 to B5 and D1 to E5.

When you use the Range property in conjunction with the Union method, you can specify up to 30 ranges, and you must specify at least two ranges. You assign the ranges by using any option that returns a valid Range object, such as the Range property or the Cells property. See the sections, "Using the Range Property" and "Using the Cells Property," for more information. The following example specifies two ranges:

```
Dim RangeVar As Range
```

```
Set RangeVar = Union (Range("A1:A3"),
Range("A5:A15"))
```

The code `Set RangeVar = Union (Range("A1:A3"), Range("A5:A15"))` uses the Union method to combine two Range objects created with the Range property and assigns the result to a range object variable. With this sample code, the new range contains the cells A1 to A3 and A5 to A15. Notice that the two blocks of cells are noncontiguous.

Because you must declare the variable to which you assign the multi-area range as a Range object, you use the Set statement when creating the assignment statement. You must use the Set statement whenever you assign an object to an object variable. See Chapter 4 for more information on assigning objects to variables.

Combine Multiple Ranges

① Name your procedure.

② Declare the Range object variables that you will use to store your ranges.

③ Store each range to a variable.

④ Use the Union method to create a single range object that contains multiple ranges.

⑤ Apply formats to multiple ranges using one Range object.

⑥ Press Alt+F11 to switch from the VBE to Excel, and run the macro.

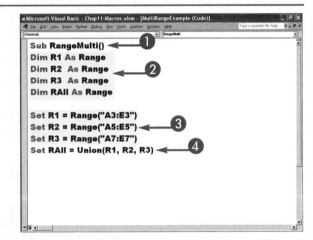

The worksheet before you run your macro.

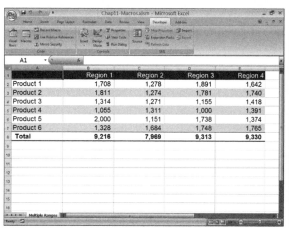

The worksheet after you run your macro.

The macro uses a Union range to apply a format to multiple ranges.

Extra

When you use the Union method, you combine multiple ranges. Each range is a Range object and is part of the Areas collection. Each member of the Areas collection represents a contiguous block of cells, with one Range object representing each contiguous block of cells.

You cannot apply some VBA operations to ranges that contain multiple areas; therefore you may need to determine the number of areas in a range. To do this, use the Count property. The Count property counts the number of areas in the range; if the Count property returns a value greater than 1, the range contains more than one area. The following example uses the Count property to determine the number of areas in a range:

Example:
```
NewRange = Selection.Areas.Count
```

Each range in an Areas collection has an index value. The first range added to the collection has an index value of 1, the next 2, and so forth. You can reference an area by its index value.

Using the Offset Property

U sing the `Offset` property is another way to specify a range of cells. The `Offset` property defines a range as an offset from another range, with the offset being the distance in rows and columns between the new range and the existing range.

The `Offset` property has two parameters. Although both are optional, if you do not specify at least one of the parameters, the `Offset` property returns the current range. Use the `RowOffset` parameter to indicate the number of rows to offset the new range from the current range. A positive number offsets the range downward. A negative number offsets the range upward. The `Offset` property bases the offset on the upper-left cell in the active range. For example, if the active range is cells A1 to B4, the Offset property bases the offset values on the

number of rows and columns from cell A1. Use the `ColumnOffset` parameter to specify the number of columns to offset the range from the current range. A positive number offsets the range to the right. A negative number offsets the range to the left. The default value for both parameters is zero.

If you only assign a value to one of the parameters, Excel gives the other parameter a value of zero. For example, with a value of 5 for the `RowOffset` and no `ColumnOffset` parameter value, the property returns the range that is five rows from the current range selection.

If you specify a value outside the valid number of rows and columns in a worksheet (for example, if you specify Offset(-1, -1) and the current cell is A1, VBA returns an error.

Using the Offset Property

① Name your procedure.

② Declare the Range object variables that you will use to store your ranges.

③ Store your range to an object variable.

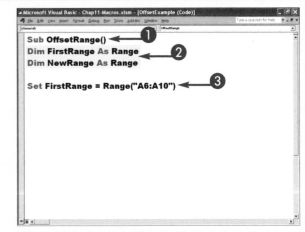

④ Use the Offset property to define the range.

● The same row.

● Four columns to the right.

⑤ Place a formula in the offset range.

⑥ Press Alt+F11 to switch from the VBE to Excel, and run the macro.

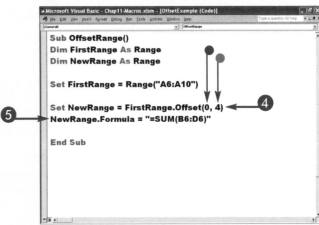

The worksheet before you run the macro.

The worksheet after you run the macro.

● The macro uses the offset property to create the values under the Total column.

Extra

You can use the `Offset` property in a `For Next` loop to cycle through a range of cells.

Example:
```
Dim Count As Integer
Count = 1
For Count = 1 To 4
     ActiveCell.Offset(Count -1, 0) = "Region" & Count
Next Count
```

The initial value of Count is 1. Count -1 is equal to zero. The code offsets from the ActiveCell. As a result, the code starts executing from the active cell, ActiveCell.Offset(Count -1, 0), which resolves to ActiveCell.Offset(0,0). With each loop, the value of Count increases by 1, and so VBA stays in the same column, but moves down one row. See Chapter 6 to learn more about using a For Next loop and to see this code in action.

Delete a Range of Cells

To remove a range of cells from a worksheet, use the `Delete` method. Excel completely removes the cells and adjusts the remaining values in the worksheet to fill the gap left by the deletion. For example, if you remove column B, Excel shifts the values in column C to the left to become the new column B values, and all remaining column values shift to the left as well. Conversely, if you delete a row, Excel shifts all values up one row. You can reference an entire column by using the syntax `Columns(ColumnNumber)`. You can reference an entire row by using the syntax `Rows(RowNumber)`. The following examples delete column 2 and row 3, respectively:

```
Columns(2).Delete
```

```
Rows(3).Delete
```

Excel easily determines how to shift the cells when you remove entire rows and columns, but if you remove a block of cells, you must specify how the remaining values fill by using the `Shift` parameter with the `Delete` method. When you use the `Shift` parameter, you assign it one of the `XlDeleteShiftDirection` constant values. The value, `xlShiftToLeft`, tells Excel to shift values to the left to fill the gap created by the deletion. The `xlShiftUp` constant value tells Excel to shift values up to fill the gap. For best results, specify how to shift the cells.

Excel ignores the `Shift` parameter value if it is not a valid shift direction for the deleted range. For example, the code `Column(2).Delete Shift:=xlShiftUp` deletes a column, but Excel shifts the cells to the left because there are no cells to shift up.

Delete a Range of Cells

1. Name your procedure.

2. Declare a Range object variable.

3. Store your range to an object variable.

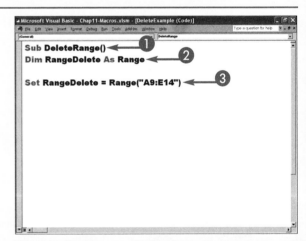

4. Delete your range.

   ● The range you want to delete.

   ● The instruction to shift up.

5. Press Alt+F11 to switch from the VBE to Excel, and run the macro.

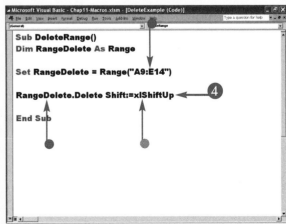

The worksheet before you run your macro.

● The rows that the macro will delete.

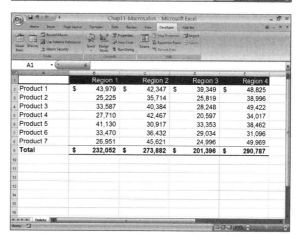

The worksheet after you run your macro.

Extra

You may not be able to remove cells from or add cells to a protected worksheet. You can use the AllowEdit property to determine if you can modify a range. The AllowEdit property returns a Boolean value of True if you can modify the specified range. In the example code, the AllowEdit property checks a range to make sure you can modify the range before it calls the Delete method.

Example:
```
If RangeDelete.AllowEdit Then
    RangeDelete.Delete Shift:=xlShiftUp
End If
```

The code checks the AllowEdit property for the specified Range object. The If Then statement ensures that the code attempts to delete the specified range of cells only if you can modify the range. Otherwise, Excel ignores the Delete statement.

To protect worksheets, use the Protect method. See Chapter 10 for more information on using the Protect method to protect a worksheet.

Hide a Range of Cells

You can use the `Hidden` property with the `Range` object to hide a range of cells. You commonly hide portions of a worksheet so that you can focus in on other data. For example, a worksheet may contain monthly data and quarterly summaries. You can hide the monthly data so you can focus on the quarterly summaries.

With the `Hidden` property, the range of cells you hide must consist of an entire row or column. You hide a range by assigning a value of `True` to the `Hidden` property for the specified range. You make the range visible again by assigning the value `False` to the Hidden property. When you hide a range of cells, Excel sets either the width of the columns or the height of the rows to zero, as in the following example:

`Rows(2).Hidden`

You can use the `Hidden` property either to determine if a range is hidden. You can find out if a range of cells is hidden by checking the `Hidden` property. For example, you can check to see if column A is hidden by typing `HiddenRange = Columns(1).Hidden`. If you declare the `HiddenRange` variable as a Boolean value, the variable receives a value of `True` if the specified range is hidden; otherwise, it receives a value of `False`. If you do not declare the variable as Boolean, Excel assigns a numeric value of –1 if the range is hidden and zero if the range is visible.

Hide a Range of Cells

① Name your procedure.

② Create `For Next` loops.

In this example, the `For Next` loop enables you to hide multiple columns — columns 2 to 4 in the first loop and columns 6 to 8 in the second loop.

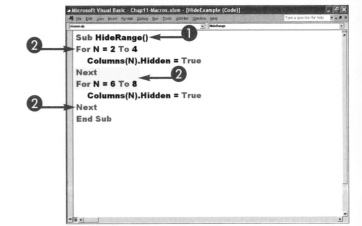

③ Set the `Hidden` property to `True` to hide the columns.

You can set the `Hidden` property to `False` to unhide the columns.

④ Press Alt+F11 to switch from the VBE to Excel, and run the macro.

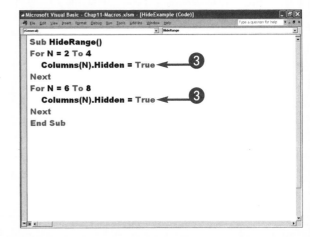

The worksheet before you run the macro.

The worksheet after you run the macro.

The macro hides the columns you specified.

Apply It

When you hide a row or column in Excel, you can still access the values contained in the cells by referencing them in functions and macros. Excel indicates the existence of hidden rows and columns by skipping over the hidden rows and columns in the row and column headings. For example, if you hide columns C and D, you see the column labels for columns A, B, E, F, and so on.

To unhide rows or columns in a worksheet, set the Hidden property to `False`. The following code unhides all columns in a worksheet.

Example:
```
Columns.Hidden = False
```

This statement is useful for ensuring that all cells in a worksheet are visible. You can use the Rows property to unhide all hidden rows.

Example:
```
Rows.Hidden = False
```

Create a Range Name

In Excel, you can name ranges. Range names are easier to remember than cell addresses. When you name a range, you can refer to the range using the range name when creating formulas or performing other tasks. When you move a range to a new location, Excel automatically updates any formulas that refer to it.

When you use a named range in a procedure, you do not need to know the location of the cells that contain the desired values. For example, if cell B3 contains the sales tax rate, assign the name *Tax_Rate* to the cell so you can reference the cell by name when you want to use it.

In VBA, you use the Name property to assign a name to a range of cells, as follows:

```
Columns(3).Name = "May_Sales"
```

This example assigns the name May_Sales to Column C in the active worksheet. To view the assigned name in Excel, you select the range, and the name appears in the Name box on the Formula bar.

Whenever you need to reference a range in your procedure, you can use its range name. You can reference range names created by your procedure and range names created manually in Excel. You can modify and delete the range names you define in a VBA procedure in Excel.

To delete a range name using a procedure, use the Delete method. The following example deletes the range name *May_Sales*:

```
ActiveWorkbook.Names("May_Sales").Delete
```

Create a Range Name

① Name your procedure.

② Declare your variable.

③ Assign a name to a range.

● The range to which you want to assign a name.

● The name that you want to assign the range.

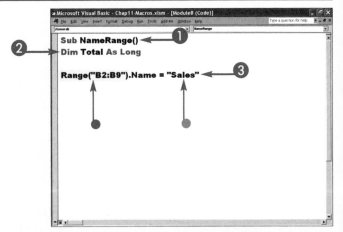

④ Use the range name.

In this example, the worksheet function Sum totals the range.

⑤ Assign the result of the worksheet function to a cell.

⑥ Press Alt+F11 to switch from the VBE to Excel, and run the macro.

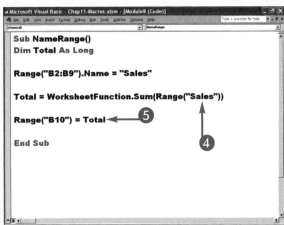

The worksheet before you run your macro.

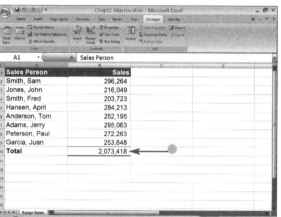

The worksheet after you run your macro.

● The macro uses the named range to sum a range of cells.

Extra

To create a named range in Excel, select the range, click the Formulas tab on the Ribbon, and then click Define Name in the Defined Names group. The New Name dialog box appears. Type a name in the Name field, and then click OK.

Click Name Manger on the Formulas tab to open the Name Manger. The Name Manager contains a list of all named ranges. To see which cells a named range includes, select the range name in the Name Manager; the corresponding range displays in the Refers To field. If you want to delete a named range, highlight the range name and then click Delete. If you delete a named range, any macros that reference the named range will not work.

You can also use the Name Manager to modify a named range. In the Name Manager, click the Edit button. The Edit Name dialog box appears. Use the Refers To field to define the range of cells to which the range name refers.

Resize a Range

Y ou can use the `Resize` property to change the size of a range. When you resize a range, you change the number of rows and columns. You can specify either more or fewer rows or columns.

The `Resize` property has two optional parameters; however, you should set at least one of the two parameters. If you do not use either parameter, Excel returns the original range. The first parameter, `RowSize`, sets the number of rows in the new range. The second parameter, `ColumnSize`, sets the number of columns in the new range.

When you resize the range, the upper-left corner of the original range remains the same. For example, if the original range is B1 to C4 and you resize the range to contain only two rows and two columns, then B1 remains

the upper-left cell value. VBA adjusts the range based on that cell, creating a new range of cells from B1 to C2.

You may need to know how many rows and columns currently exist in a range before you can determine how to resize it. If you are working with a range that is defined elsewhere, such as a named range, use the `Count` property to determine the number of rows and columns in the range, as shown in the following code: `NumberOfRows = Range("Named_Range").Rows.Count`. The `Count` property counts the number of rows in Named_Range and assigns that result to the `NumberOfRows` variable. You use the same syntax with the `Columns` property to count the number of columns in a range. Once you know the size of the range, you can use the `Resize` property to modify the number of rows and columns.

Resize a Range

① Name your procedure.

② Declare your variables.

③ Count the number of rows in a range and assign the result to a variable.

④ Count the number of columns in a range and assign the result to a variable.

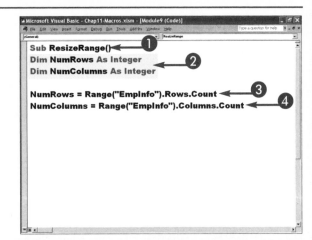

⑤ Add 3 to the values stored in your variables.

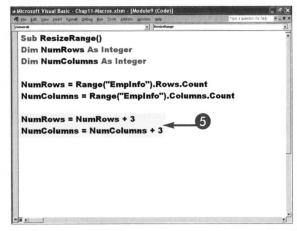

⑥ Resize your range.

● The range you want to resize.

● Sets the number of rows to the value in your NumRow variable.

● Sets the number of columns to the value in your NumCol variable.

⑦ Press Alt+F11 to switch from the VBE to Excel, and run the macro.

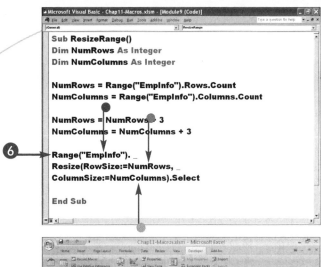

The macro resizes the range.

● The original size of the range.

● The current size of the range.

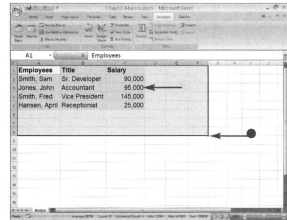

Extra

Besides determining the number of rows and columns in a range, you may need to know the exact row or column in which the range begins. To do this, use either the Row property or the Column property. The following code determines the number of the first row in a range:

Example:
```
FirstRowNum = Range("EmpInfo").Row
```

This code assigns the integer value representing the first row in the specified range to the FirstRowNum variable. You can also determine the first column in the range by using the Column property, as shown in this code:

Example:
```
FirstColNum = Range("EmpInfo").Column
```

Insert a Range

You can use the `Insert` method to insert a range of cells into a worksheet. When you insert a range of cells, VBA adjusts the values in the existing cells by moving them either down or to the right so that it can insert the new cells into the specified location. For example, if you insert a new row of cells in row 3, VBA shifts the existing values in row 3 down to row 4 and shifts all of the values in cells below row 3 down as well. If you add a new column, Excel shifts all existing values to the right. The following examples insert a column and a row, respectively:

```
Columns(2).Insert
```

```
Rows(3).Insert
```

How the cell values in the worksheet should shift when you add an entire row or column is obvious. With a

smaller block of cells, you must use the `InsertShift` parameter to tell VBA how the cells shift. To make sure the cells shift correctly, assign the shift parameter one of the `XlInsertShiftDirection` constant values. You can use the `xlShiftToRight` constant value to shift the cell values to the right. You can use the `xlShiftDown` constant value to shift the cell values down. The following example shifts cells to the right:

```
Range("B5:B7").Insert:=xlShiftToRight
```

You use the `Cut` and `Copy` methods to paste data to the Office Clipboard. You can insert data that is on the Office Clipboard into your worksheet by placing a `Cut` or `Copy` command before the `Insert` command in your procedure. See Chapter 12 to learn more about the `Cut` and `Copy` methods.

Insert a Range

① Name your procedure.

② Copy a range.

③ Insert the range.

● The point at which to begin the insertion.

● The shift direction.

④ Press Alt+F11 to switch from the VBE to Excel, and run the macro.

The worksheet before you run the macro.

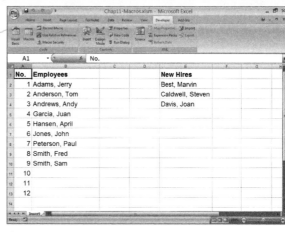

The worksheet after you run the macro.

- The macro places the copied data in the insert location.

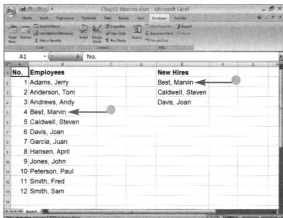

Extra

You can also use the Insert method to add a value to a cell. To insert a value in a cell, use the Insert method with the Characters object. You can insert a string of characters at the beginning of a cell or at any location in the cell. For example, to insert the string "New String" in cell B1 and replace the contents, type the following code:

Example:
```
Range("B1").Characters.Insert("New String")
```

To place the new string within the existing string of characters, indicate the location to place the new string and the number of characters to replace at that location. For example, in the string "Excel 2008 Worksheet," you can replace the "2008" with "2009" by using the Insert method. The following code illustrates how to make the replacement when the string is located in cell A1.

Example:
```
Range("A1").Characters(7,4).Insert("2009")
```

The Characters object has two parameters, Start and Length. The Start parameter indicates the number of the character at which to start the insert — in this case, character 7. The Length parameter indicates the number of characters to replace.

Set the Width of Columns in a Range

To set the width of a column, use the `ColumnWidth` property. By default, Excel assigns a width of 8.43 characters to each column. Excel bases this width size on the number of zeros it can place in the cell using the Normal style. One unit is equal to one character. In the following example Excel sets column 1 to 15 characters in the Normal style:

```
Columns(1).ColumnWidth = 15
```

You can also use the `ColumnWidth` property to determine the width of the columns in a range. If all columns in the range have the same width, the `ColumnWidth` property returns the number of characters that can display in each column using the Normal style. If the column widths in the selected range vary, the `ColumnWidth` property returns Null. The following example,

```
ColWidth = Columns(1).ColumnWidth
```

returns the width of column 1.

Every worksheet has a default width, commonly referred to as the standard width. You can use the `StandardWidth` property to set the columns in a worksheet to the standard width. The following example sets every column in a worksheet to the standard width:

```
Columns.ColumnWidth = _
    ActiveSheet.StandardWidth
```

Set the Width of Columns in a Range

SET A COLUMN WIDTH

1. Name your procedure.

2. Create a `For Next` loop.

3. Create a `ColumnWidth` command.

- The column for which you want to set the column width.

- The amount to which you want to set the column width.

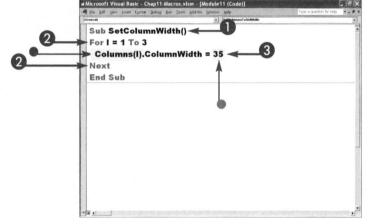

SET COLUMNS TO A STANDARD WIDTH

1. Name your procedure.

2. Create a `For Next` loop.

3. Create a ColumnWidth command.

- The column for which you want to set the column width.

- The amount to which you want to set the column width.

4. Press Alt+F11 to switch from the VBE to Excel, and run the macros.

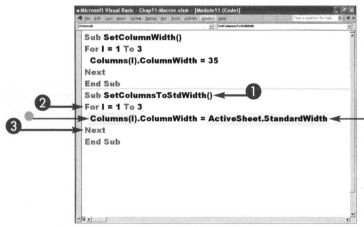

When you run the `SetColumnWidth` macro, the macro sets columns 1, 2, and 3 to 35.

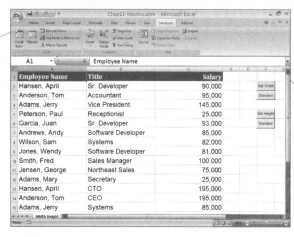

When you run the `SetColumnstoStdWidth` macro, the macro sets columns 1, 2, and 3 to the standard width.

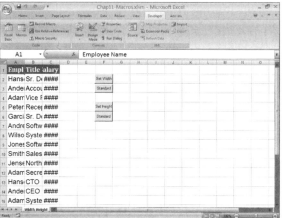

Extra

You can also use the `Width` property to obtain the width of a particular column. The `Width` property returns the measurement of the column width in points, unlike the `ColumnWidth` property, which returns characters. You typically use points to reference font sizes (1 point is equivalent to 1/72 of an inch).

The `Width` property is Read-Only, meaning that you can only use it to return the width of a column. To return the `Width` property of a column, assign the value to a variable, as shown in the following code.

Example:
```
ColWidth = Column(4).Width
```

The `Width` property is useful when you want to compare a column width to a row height, because Excel stores row heights in points.

Set the Height of Rows in a Range

To modify the height of rows in a range, you can use the RowHeight property. By default, Excel assigns a height of 12.75 points to each row. Excel measures font sizes in points, with each point being approximately 1/72 of an inch. Because the default font size in Excel is 10 points, the default row size of 12.75 points is usually adequate for displaying text in cells. For a larger font size or text that wraps in a cell, you can specify a larger row size by using the RowHeight property.

You can set the height of the row by assigning a numeric value to the RowHeight property. For example, to change the height of row 2 to 25 points, use the code Rows(2).RowHeight=25. When you use the Rows property without referencing a Range object, Excel automatically uses the active sheet. If the row height you specify is not high enough to display the entire font, the text appears cut off in the row when you view it in Excel.

You can also use the RowHeight property to obtain the height of the rows in a range. If all rows in the range have the same height, the height is returned as the number of points. If the rows in the selected range do not have the same height, the RowHeight property returns Null. The following example demonstrates how to use the RowHeight property to obtain the height of a row:

```
RowHeight = Rows(1).RowHeight
```

Every worksheet has a default height, commonly referred to as the standard height. You can use the StandardHeight property to set the standard height for a worksheet and to set rows in a worksheet to the standard height. The following example sets every row in a worksheet to the standard height:

```
Rows.RowHeight = ActiveSheet.StandardHeight
```

Set the Height of Rows in a Range

SET THE ROW HEIGHT

1. Name your procedure.

2. Create a For Next loop.

3. Create a RowHeight command.

- The rows for which you want to set the height.

- The amount to which you want to set the row height.

SET ROWS TO THE STANDARD HEIGHT

1. Name your procedure.

2. Create a For Next loop.

3. Create a RowHeight command.

- The row for which you want to set the height.

- The amount to which you want to set the row height.

4. Press Alt+F11 to switch from the VBE to Excel, and run the macros.

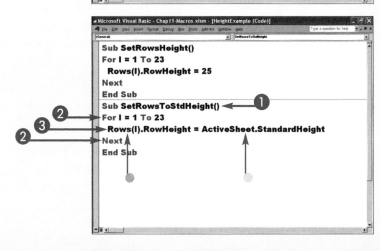

When you run the `SetRowsHeight` macro, the macro sets rows 1 to 23 to 25.

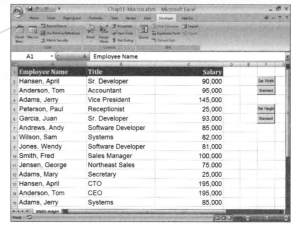

When you run the `SetRowstoStdHeight` macro, the macro sets rows 1 to 23 to the standard height.

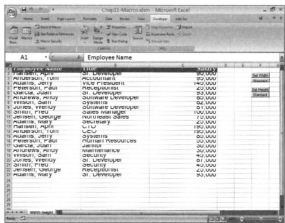

Apply It

You can also use the `UseStandardHeight` property to set a row to the standard height. The following example sets row 1 of the active sheet to the standard height.

Example:
```
ActiveSheet.Rows(1).UseStandardHeight = True
```

You can use the `Height` property to determine the total height of a range of cells. Excel returns the height of the range in points. The `Height` property is Read-Only. You can obtain the range height by assigning the height value to a variable, as shown in this code.

TYPE THIS:
```
HeightofRange = Range("A1:A10").Height
```

RESULT:

The code assigns the total height of the rows specified by the Range object to the `HeightofRange` variable.

Convert a Column of
Text into Multiple Columns

When you need to break a column of text into multiple columns, you can use the TextToColumns method. For example, if a list contains both first and last names in one column, you can use TextToColumns to break that list into two columns — one for the first name and one for the last name.

You use the TextToColumns method with the Range object. The Range object should contain the columns that you want to parse into multiple columns. The TextToColumns method provides several optional parameters you can use to specify how to separate the text.

You use the Destination parameter to specify the range into which VBA should place the results. For the DataType parameter, you specify a constant value of xlDelimited to break the text based on a delimiter value. You use xlFixedWidth if the text is a fixed width.

You use one of the XlTextQualifier constants, xlTextQualifierDoubleQuote, xlTextQualifierNone,

or xlTextQualifierSingleQuote, to indicate the text qualifier character.

A delimiter is a character, such as a comma or space, which indicates a separation between strings. Specify a value of True for the ConsecutiveDelimiter parameter to have consecutive delimiters treated as one. For the Tab, Semicolon, Comma, Space, and Other parameters, specify a value of True for each delimiter that is used in the selected range. If you specify Other as the delimiter, set value for the OtherChar parameter to the delimiter character.

The FileInfo parameter contains information for parsing individual columns in the range, with the first element being the column number, and the second element being one of the xlColumnDataType constants.

Specify the character used to separate decimals with the DecimalSeparator parameter, and the character used to thousands with the ThousandsSeparator parameter value.

Convert a Column of Text into Multiple Columns

① Name your procedure.

② Declare a Range object variable.

③ Store column 1 to the Range object variable.

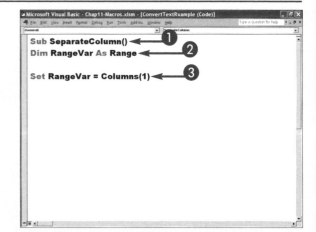

④ Create your TextToColumns command.

● Where you want to place the separated text.

● The type of data.

● The delimiter.

⑤ Press Alt+F11 to switch from the VBE to Excel, and run the macro.

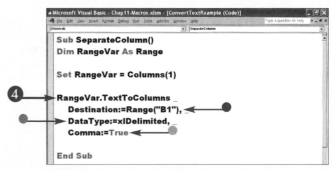

The worksheet before you run your macro.

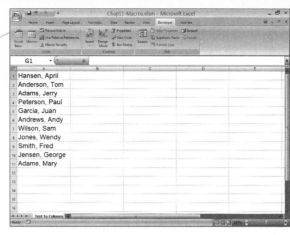

The worksheet after you run your macro.

The macro separates one column of data into two columns of data.

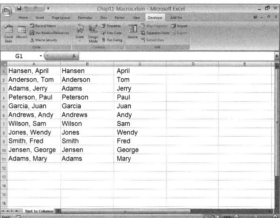

Extra

You can use the Parse method to separate data values in one column into multiple columns. This method works well for string data that is the same length, such as phone numbers. When using the Parse method, you specify how the strings in each cell should break, and VBA applies that format to each cell.

There are two optional parameters for the Parse method. The first parameter, ParseLine, is a string containing left and right brackets, indicating where the cells should split. For example, [xxxx][xxxx] breaks each string so that the first four characters are placed in the first column and the second four characters are placed in the second column. Any characters outside those eight characters are ignored. For example, for the string "alphabetical", Excel would place the first four characters (alph) in the first column and the second four characters (abet) in the second column. Excel would ignore the remaining characters in the string. The second parameter, Destination, specifies the range where the Parse method places the data. If the range has more than one cell, Excel uses the upper-left corner of the range as the first cell.

Find the Intersection of Two Ranges

You can use the `Intersect` method to determine where multiple ranges intersect on a worksheet. A multiple-area range contains more than one block of cells that may or may not be connected. Use the Intersect method to create a Range object containing the cells that are common between two ranges. For example, for the ranges A1 to C5 and C1 to E5, the `Intersect` method returns the range C1:C5 because those cells are common to both ranges. If the specified ranges have no cells in common, the `Intersect` method returns an empty range.

With the `Intersect` method, you can assign up to 30 parameter values and you must specify at least two. Each parameter value must be a range of cells. You specify the ranges for the `Intersect` method by using any option that returns a valid `Range` object, such as the `Range` property or the `Cells` property. See the sections, "Using

the Range Property" and "Using the Cells Property," for more information on the `Range` and `Cells` properties.

The following example uses the Intersect method:

```
Dim NewRange As Range

Set NewRange = _
    Intersect(Range("A1:C5"),Range("C1:E5"))
```

This example assigns the intersection of A1:C5 and C1:E5, which is C1:C5, to the object variable `NewRange`.

Because you must declare the variable to which you assign the multiple-area range as a `Range` object, use the `Set` statement as part of the assignment statement. You must use the `Set` statement whenever you assign an object to a variable. When you assign an intersecting range to a range object variable, the `Intersect` method only assigns the cells in the intersection of the range to the variable. See Chapter 4 for more information on assigning objects.

Find the Intersection of Two Ranges

① Name your procedure.

② Declare your `Range` objects.

③ Assign your ranges to your object variables.

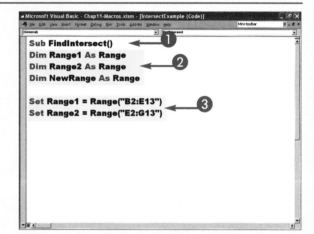

④ Create a range from the intersection of the two ranges.

⑤ Clear the intersection range.

⑥ Press Alt+F11 to switch from the VBE to Excel, and run the macro.

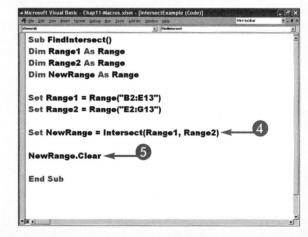

The worksheet before you run your macro.

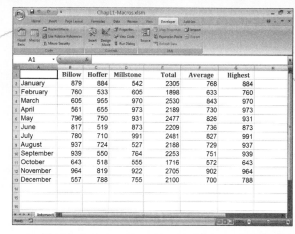

The worksheet after you run your macro.

● The macro clears the intersection range.

Extra

You can use one of the `Clear` methods to clear the contents of a cell or range of cells in your worksheet. The `Clear` method clears the entire contents, including cell values, formatting, and formulas, from the specified cells. The following is an example of the `Clear` method:

Example:
```
RangeVar.Clear
```

Use the `ClearFormats` method to clear all formatting from the specified range. All cell values and formulas remain in the cells. With this method, the contents of the specified range use default-formatting options. The following is an example of the `ClearFormats` method:

Example:
```
RangeVar.ClearFormats
```

You can clear the cell values and formulas from a range of cells by using the `ClearContents` method. This method clears everything except the formatting that you applied to the cells. When you add new values to the cells in the range after you have cleared the range, Excel uses the applied formatting. The following is an example of the `ClearContents` method:

Example:
```
RangeVar.ClearContents
```

Cut and Paste Ranges of Cells

Cut, Copy, and Paste are among the most commonly used commands, and you can find them in almost every application. When writing VBA code, you can use the Cut and Copy methods to cut, copy, and paste a range of cells. The following is the syntax for the Cut method (see "Copy and Paste Ranges of Cells" for an explanation of the Copy method):

expression.Cut([Destination])

The Cut method enables you to cut a range of cells and paste them either to the Windows Clipboard or to another range of cells. The *expression* identifies the range you want to cut. You can use the Cut method's optional Destination parameter to tell VBA where you want to

paste. If you do not include a destination, VBA pastes to the Windows Clipboard.

If you include a destination, you can use a Range object to specify the location to which you want to paste. The following example uses the Cut method to cut and paste a range of cells:

Range("A1:A5").Cut Range("C1:C5")

When using this syntax, you must make the cut range and the destination range the same size or VBA returns an error. Alternatively, you can specify a single cell as the destination range. VBA makes the cell you specify the upper-left corner of the paste range.

Cut and Paste Ranges of Cells

CUT AND PASTE A SINGLE CELL

1 Create your Cut statement.

- The range you are cutting.

- The upper-left corner of the range to which you are pasting.

- This code resizes columns to ensure that the contents display in the cells.

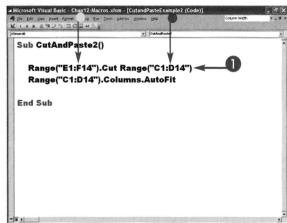

CUT AND PASTE A RANGE OF CELLS

1 Create your Cut statement.

- The range you are cutting.

- The range to which you are pasting.

Note: *The range from which you cut must be the same size as the range to which you paste.*

2 Press Alt+F11 to switch from the VBE to Excel, and run the macro.

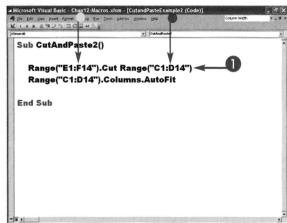

The original worksheet.

● The macro cuts and pastes this information.

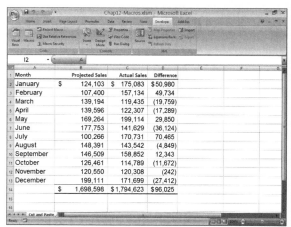

The worksheet after the cut-and-paste macro has executed.

Both of the macros shown in this example yield the same result.

Apply It

When you paste values in cells, the cells may not be able to hold the new content. If the values you paste are numeric and the cells are not wide enough for the numbers, Excel displays pound signs (####) in the cells. When you write a VBA procedure, VBA provides formatting options you can use to resize cells so that your values fit into the cells to which you paste them. For example, you can use the AutoFit method to resize the rows and columns. The AutoFit method uses the following syntax:

Example:
```
Range("C1:D14").Columns.AutoFit
```

You can use the ShrinkToFit property to reduce the font size of the text so the entire contents of the cell display. You set the ShrinkToFit property by assigning the Range property the value of True, as shown in the following example:

Example:
```
Range("C1:D14").ShrinkToFit=True
```

You can also use the WrapText property to ensure text displays properly. Assigning a value of True to the WrapText property causes text to wrap within the cell.

Example:
```
Range("C1:D14").WrapText=True
```

Copy and Paste Ranges of Cells

I n this section, you learn how to *copy* and *paste* a range of cells. You can copy and paste cell ranges by using the Copy method. The Copy method is essentially the same as the Copy and Paste commands within Excel. The following is the syntax for the Copy method:

expression.Copy([Destination])

The Copy method enables you to copy a range of cells and paste them either to the Windows Clipboard or to another range of cells. The Copy method enables you to copy a range of cells and paste them either to the Windows Clipboard or to another range of cells. The expression identifies the range you want to copy. You can use the Copy method's optional Destination parameter to tell VBA where you want to paste the cells. If you do not include a destination, VBA pastes the cells to the Windows Clipboard.

If you include a destination, you can use a Range object to specify the location to which you want to paste. The following code illustrates using the Copy method to cut and paste a range of cells:

```
Range("A1:A5").Copy Range("C1:C5")
```

When using this syntax, you must make the copy range and the destination range the same size or VBA returns an error. Alternatively, you can specify a single cell as the destination range. VBA makes the cell you specify the upper-left corner of the paste range.

A block of cells surrounded by blank cells is called the *current region*. You can use the CurrentRegion property to copy and paste or to cut and paste when using VBA. When entering the range, you specify any cell within the block of cells you want to cut or copy as the range, and then follow the range specification with .CurrentRegion.

Copy and Paste a Range of Cells

COPY AND PASTE BY USING A SINGLE CELL

1 Create your Copy statement.

● The range from which you are copying.

This example uses CurrentRegion.

The CurrentRegion property enables you to manipulate a range of cells without specifying the entire range.

● The upper-left corner of the range to which you are pasting.

2 Press Alt+F11 to switch from the VBE to Excel, and run the macro.

The macro copies and pastes the information.

● The range you copied.

● The pasted data.

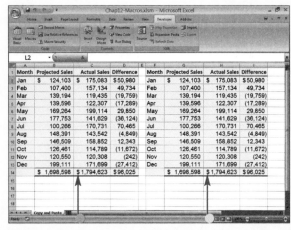

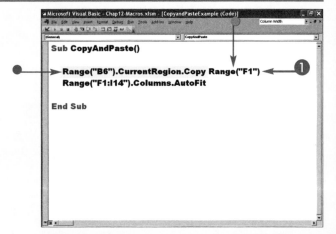

COPY AND PASTE BY USING A RANGE OF CELLS

1 Create your `Copy` statement.

● The range from which you are copying.

● The range to which you are copying.

The range to which you copy must be the same size as the range from which you copy.

● Formats the copy to range.

Changes the color of the interior of cells, the border that surrounds cells, and the font

2 Press Alt+F11 to switch from the VBE to Excel, and run the macro.

The macro copies and pastes the information.

● The range you copied.

● The pasted information.

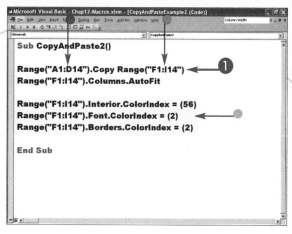

```
Sub CopyAndPaste2()

Range("A1:D14").Copy Range("F1:I14")    1
Range("F1:I14").Columns.AutoFit

Range("F1:I14").Interior.ColorIndex = (56)
Range("F1:I14").Font.ColorIndex = (2)
Range("F1:I14").Borders.ColorIndex = (2)

End Sub
```

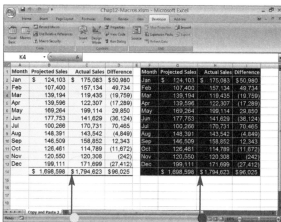

Extra

You can use the `ColorIndex` property with the `Interior`, `Borders`, and `Font` objects to change the color of the interior of cells, the border that surrounds cells, and the font. You can assign an index value of 1 to 56 to the `ColorIndex` property to assign the color you want. The following example demonstrates the `ColorIndex` property.

Examples:
```
Range("F1:I14").Interior.ColorIndex = (1)
Range("F1:I14").Borders.ColorIndex = (2)
Range("F1:I14").Font.ColorIndex = (2)
```

The following table lists 16 of the possible colors you can use with the `ColorIndex` property. Refer to VBA help for a complete list.

INDEX	COLOR
1	Black
2	White
3	Red
4	Green
5	Blue
6	Yellow
7	Fuchsia
8	Light Blue
9	Brown
10	Forest Green
11	Navy Blue
12	Yellow-Brown
13	Maroon
14	Blue-Green
15	Light Gray
16	Gray

Using Paste Special Options When Pasting

Cells can contain a lot of information. When you use the PasteSpecial method, you decide exactly what information you want to paste. You can choose to paste everything or you can choose to paste just one element of the cell's contents, such as the formula, value, or column width. You can also use the PasteSpecial method to perform simple arithmetic operations on each cell in a range. For example, in a list of salaries, you may want to increase every salary by five percent. You can use the PasteSpecial method to make the change quickly. Just copy the value by which you want to multiply to the Clipboard and then use xlPasteSpecialOperationMultiply when you paste with the PasteSpecial method.

You can use the PasteSpecial method with values you have added to the Windows Clipboard using the Cut or Copy methods. The following is the syntax for the PasteSpecial method:

```
expression.PasteSpecial(Paste, Operation,
SkipBlanks, Transpose)
```

Use the Paste parameter to indicate how you want to paste the information into the new range. By default, Excel uses the xlPasteAll constant value for this parameter, which pastes the entire contents of the copied or cut cells into the new range.

Use the Operation parameter to perform a mathematical operation, such as multiplying the current value of a cell by the pasted value. The default constant value used by Excel is xlPasteSpecialOperationNone, which does not perform any mathematical operations.

Set the SkipBlanks parameter to True if you do not want to overwrite a destination cell with a blank cell if the destination cell contains data in it and the copied cell does not.. If you want to transpose the data values from rows to columns or vice versa, set the Transpose parameter to True.

Using Paste Special Options When Pasting

PASTE PARAMETER

1️⃣ Copy a range of cells to the Clipboard.

Do not include the Destination parameter.

2️⃣ Type your PasteSpecial command.

● The range to which you are pasting.

● This statement pastes the column widths, thereby making sure that the source column widths match the destination column widths.

● This statement pastes the data.

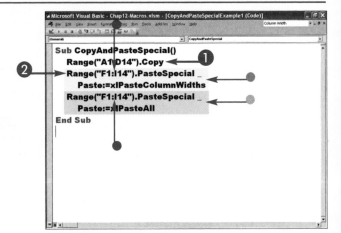

OPERATION PARAMETER

1️⃣ Copy a cell to the Clipboard.

In this example, cell B1 contains the number needed to calculate an annual salary increase.

2️⃣ Type your PasteSpecial command.

● The range to which you are pasting.

In this example, range B5 to B10 contains the salaries you want to increase.

● The Operation parameter.

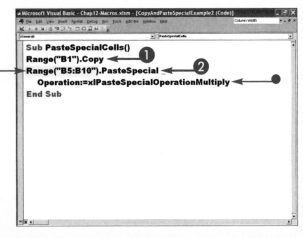

③ Press Alt+F11 to switch from the VBE to Excel, and run the macro.

The worksheet before you run the macro.

● The cell you copied.

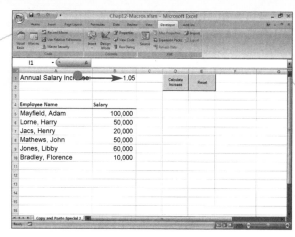

The worksheet after you run the macro.

● The PasteSpecial range.

The macro multiplies each cell in the PasteSpecial range by the value in the cell you copied.

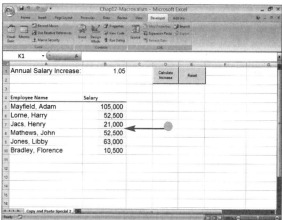

Extra

The Paste parameter requires one of the following constant values.

NAME	DESCRIPTION
xlPasteAll	The default value, which pastes the entire contents of the cells.
xlPasteAllExceptBorders	Pastes everything except border settings.
xlPasteAllUsingSourceTheme	Pastes everything using the source theme.
xlPasteColumnWidths	Pastes the column widths.
xlPasteComments	Pastes the cell comments only.
xlPasteFormats	Pastes the formats only.
xlPasteFormulas	Pastes the formulas only.
xlPasteFormulasAndNumberFormats	Pastes the formulas and number formats.
xlPasteValidation	Pastes the cell validation only.
xlPasteValues	Pastes the cell values only.
xlPasteValuesAndNumberFormats	Pastes the cell values and number formats.

You can use the following values with the Operation parameter:

xlPasteSpecialOperationAdd, xlPasteSpecialOperationSubtract, xlPasteSpecialOperationMultiply, xlPasteSpecialOperationDivide, and xlPasteSpecialOperationNone.

Add Comments to a Cell

When several people work on a single workbook, comments can provide useful information. Excel associates a comment with an individual cell and indicates its presence with a small, red triangle in the cell's upper-right corner. You can view a comment by clicking in the cell or by moving your cursor over the cell. In VBA, by using the AddComment method with the Range object, you can add a comment to any cell in your worksheet.

When the user creates a comment in Excel, Excel adds the user's name to the comment. When you create a comment by using the AddComment method, VBA does not automatically include a username. The following is the syntax for the AddComment method:

expression.AddComment(Text)

The expression is the variable or range object that represents the cell to which you want to add a comment. The following code adds a comment to cell A1:

```
Cells(1,1).AddComment "Sample Comment Text"
```

If you want to add the same comment to multiple cells, you can use a looping statement, such as a Do Until loop, to cycle through the range of cells. See Chapter 6 to learn more about loops.

If you attempt to add a comment to a cell that already contains a comment, Excel returns an error message. To avoid errors, you can use the ClearComments method to clear an existing comment from a cell. The following is an example of the ClearComments method:

```
Cells(1,1).ClearComments
```

Add Comments to a Cell

① Add a loop, if you are going to loop through a series of cells.

② Add Case statements, if you are going to add comments selectively.

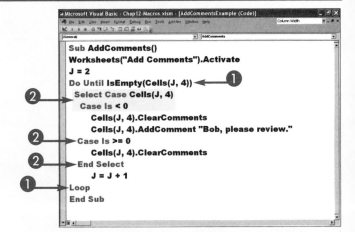

③ Add a ClearComments statement.

● The range.

The ClearComments statement clears any comments that are already in the cell.

④ Add an AddComment statement.

● The range.

● The comment.

The AddComment statement adds comments to your worksheet.

⑤ Press Alt+F11 to switch from the VBE to Excel, and run the macro.

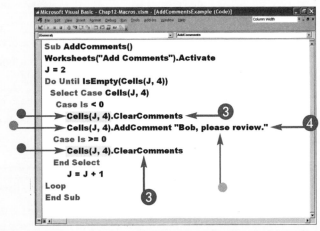

The worksheet before you run the macro.

The worksheet after you run the macro.

The macro adds the comments to your worksheet.

Apply It

When you add a comment to a cell, Excel creates a `Comment` object for that cell. The `Comment` object is part of the `Comments` collection, which contains all comments within a particular range of cells. You can reference particular comments in a worksheet using the `Comments` collection and an index value. For example, to access the second comment in a worksheet, you would type the following:

Example:

```
SecondComment=ActiveSheet.Comments(2).Text
```

You can also use the properties of the `Comment` object. If you want comments to automatically display on the worksheet, you can set the `Visible` property to `True` as shown below.

Example:

```
Cells(1,1).Comment.Visible = True
```

You may want to delete comments that a particular author created. The `Comment` object provides an `Author` property that you can use to return the author of a comment. Excel adds the author when it creates a comment. The following example deletes a comment by a particular author:

Example:

```
CountComments = ActiveSheet.Comments.Count
For N = 1 To CountComments
     If Comment(N).Author = "John Smith" Then
          Comment(N).Delete
     End If
Next
```

Automatically Fill a Range of Cells

In Excel, AutoFill helps you quickly enter data when a data series has an intrinsic order such as days of the week, months of the year, or numeric increments. You can use the AutoFill method to create an AutoFill using VBA. The following is the syntax for the AutoFill method:

`expression.AutoFill(Destination, Type)`

The `expression` is the variable or range object that represents the cell or cells you want to use when you create an AutoFill. VBA uses the values in this source range to determine the type of values to add to the cells in the destination range. For example, if the source range is cells A1 and A2 and the cells contain the values January and February, respectively, then Excel fills the cells in the destination range with the months of the year starting with March.

The AutoFill method has two parameters, `Destination` and `Type`. The `Destination` parameter, which is required, must contain a range indicating which cells to fill. The `Destination` range must encompass the source range. For example, if the source range is A1 and A2, these cells must be included in the destination range, as shown in the following example:

```
Range("A1:A2").AutoFill _
    Destination:=Range("A1:A12").
```

VBA uses the values in the source range to determine the pattern you want to use when adding values to the cells in the destination. If you want to tell VBA the pattern to use to add values to the destination, you must include the `Type` parameter. The `Type` parameter accepts an `xlAutoFillType` constant, which specifies the type of fill.

Automatically Fill a Range of Cells

FILL A RANGE

① Type your AutoFill command.

● The range you want to use as the source.

● The cells you want to fill.

● The fill type.

This example uses months.

② Press Alt+F11 to switch from the VBE to Excel, and run the macro.

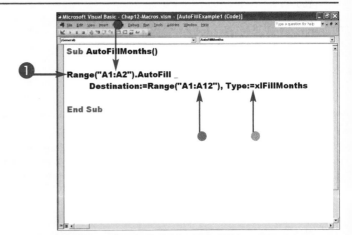

The worksheet after you run the macro.

● The source cells.

● The destination cells.

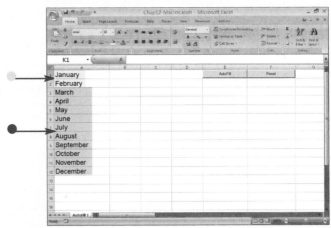

CREATE AN AUTOFILL

1 Create your AutoFill command.

● The range you want to use as the source.

This example uses the active cell, which is the first cell in your selection.

● The cells you want to fill.

This example uses your selection.

No fill type is given, as VBA bases the fill type on the cell you use as the source.

2 Press Alt+F11 to switch from the VBE to Excel, and run the macro.

The worksheet after you run the macro.

The macro fills the cells.

● The source cell.

● The fill.

You must type the first value in the range, select the cells you want to fill, and then press Enter.

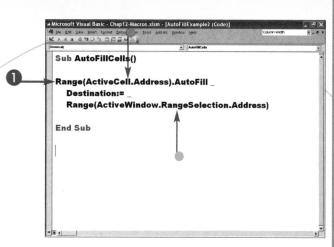

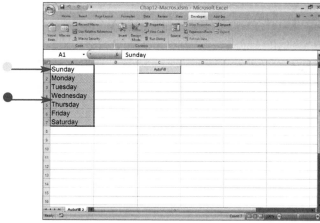

Extra

The XlAutoFillType constant values specify how Excel fills the range of cells for the Destination parameter. The following table describes each of the XlAutoFillType constant values.

CONSTANT	DESCRIPTION
xlFillDays	Increments the values by days. If only one date is specified for the source, it increments by one day. If multiple dates are specified, it uses those dates to determine the increment value.
xlFillFormats	Applies the formats of the source cells to the destination cells.
xlFillSeries	Creates a series based upon the contents of the source range.
xlFillWeekdays	Increments based on weekdays, omitting dates that fall on Saturday or Sunday.
xlGrowthTrend	Fills cells based on a growth trend.
xlFillCopy	Copies the formatting and values, and increments based on source values.
xlFillDefault	The default value. Excel determines the fill type based upon values in the source cells.
xlFillMonths	Increments by month.
xlFillValues	Copies the values in the source cells.
xlFillYears	Increments the year portion of the date.
xlLinearTrend	Fills cells based on a linear trend.

Copy a Range to Multiple Sheets

Y ou can copy a range of cells and place the contents in the same location on multiple sheets with the `FillAcrossSheets` method. When you use this method, Excel copies the cells you specify to each worksheet you specify. You can copy everything in the range of cells, just the values in the cells, or just the formatting. The following is the syntax for the `FillAcrossSheets` method:

expression.FillAcrossSheets(Range, Type)

The `expression` is the variable or object that represents the list of worksheets to which VBA copies the range of cells. The worksheets must exist within the current workbook and you must include the worksheet that you are copying from in the list.

The `FillAcrossSheets` method has two parameters: `Range` and `Type`. The `Range` parameter, which is required, specifies the range of cells you want to copy to the other worksheets. You can specify the range of cells using any valid range statement. See Chapter 11 for more information on specifying ranges.

The `Type` parameter is optional. Use this parameter to tell VBA what you want to copy. The `Type` parameter accepts one of the three `XlFillWith` constant values. If you do not specify a `Type` parameter, VBA uses the default value of `XlFillWithAll`, which copies the entire contents of the range of cells, including the formatting. If you only want to copy the cell values, use the `XlFillWithContents` constant value. This constant value instructs Excel to copy everything but the cell formatting. If you only want to copy the formatting, use the `XlFillWithFormats` constant value. When you use `XlFillWithFormats`, Excel ignores the values and applies the formatting only.

Copy a Range to Multiple Sheets

① Declare a variable to store your array.

You use an array to store the list of worksheets to which you want to copy.

② Create your array and store it to the variable you created.

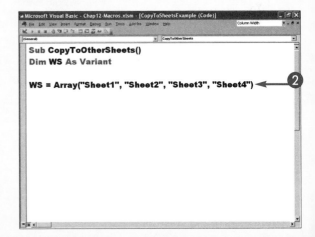

③ Add your `FillAcrossSheets` command.

● The sheets to which you want to copy.

● The range you want to copy.

● What you want to copy.

Use `XlFillWithAll` to copy everything.

Use `XlFillWithContents` to copy the contents only.

Use `XlFillWithFormats` to copy the formats only.

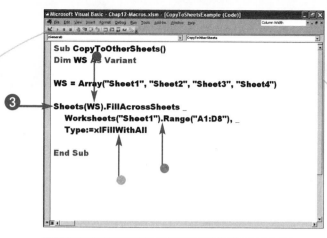

④ Press Alt+F11 to switch from the VBE to Excel, and run the macro.

● Your macro copies the range you specified to the worksheets you specified.

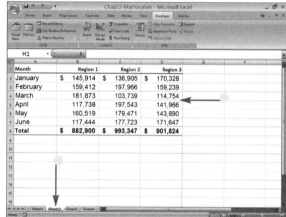

Apply It

You can fill a range of cells in a specific direction within a worksheet using one of the fill methods. For example, you may want to fill across a worksheet with the first value in the left corner of the range. VBA offers four Range object methods for filling in a specific direction: `FillUp`, `FillDown`, `FillRight`, and `FillLeft`.

You can use the `FillUp` method to fill a range of cells with the value specified in the last cell of the range. For example, if you have the range A1:A10 and you apply the `FillUp` method, as shown here, the value in cell A10 copies and pastes in cells A1:A9.

Example:
```
Range("A1:A10").FillUp
```

The `FillDown` method works opposite to the `FillUp` method. This method takes the value in the top of the range and copies it to all the other cells.

You can use the `FillRight` method to fill across rows. For example, if you use this method with the range A1:G1, Excel takes the value in cell A1 and pastes it into cells B1 to G1. The `FillLeft` method works opposite to the `FillRight` method. This method takes the value in the last cell on the right and copies it to all cells to the left.

Place a Border Around a Range of Cells

When creating an Excel worksheet, you can highlight important information by adding a border. A border adds color to the lines that surround a range of cells. In VBA, you can add borders to a range of cells using the BorderAround method. When you use this method, the border outlines the range, not each individual cell. The BorderAround method uses the following syntax:

expression.BorderAround(LineStyle, Weight, ColorIndex, Color)

The expression identifies the range you want to place the border around. Use an XlLineStyle constant value to set the style of the line. If you do not set an XlLineStyle, VBA uses the default value, XlContinuous, to draw a continuous line around the range of cells. Use an

XlBorderWeight constant value to set the Weight of the line. If you do not set a Weight, VBA uses the default value xlThin, which draws a thin line around the range of cells. VBA sets either the line style or the line weight, not both.

You can use either a ColorIndex or the RGB function to set the color of a border; however, you cannot use both. Use a ColorIndex value between 1 and 64. See the section, "Copy and Paste Ranges," for a partial list of ColorIndex values. Set the ColorIndex to xlColorIndexAutomatic to use the default line color.

If you want to use an RGB color value to assign a color, use the Color parameter and assign it an RGB color with the RGB function. When you use the RGB function, you specify three values from 0 to 255 indicating the red, green, and blue component values.

Place a Border Around a Range of Cells

COLOR INDEX BORDER

1 Create your BorderAround command.

● The range that the border surrounds.

● The color index.

● The line style.

2 Press Alt+F11 to switch from the VBE to Excel, and run the macro.

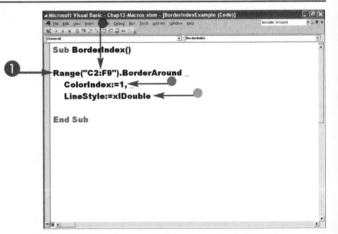

The worksheet after you run your macro.

VBA places a border around the range you specified.

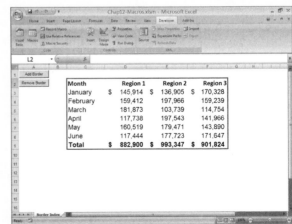

RGB COLOR BORDER

① Create your `BorderAround` command.

○ The range that the border surrounds.

● The RGB color.

○ The weight.

② Press Alt+F11 to switch from the VBE to Excel, and run the macro.

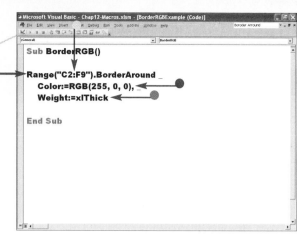

```
Sub BorderRGB()

Range("C2:F9").BorderAround _
    Color:=RGB(255, 0, 0),
    Weight:=xlThick

End Sub
```

○ The worksheet after you run your macro.

VBA places a border around the range you specified.

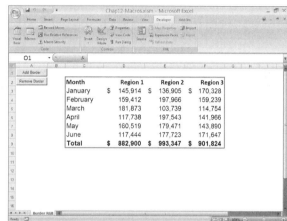

Extra

You use the `XlBorderWeight` constant values, `xlHairline`, `xlMedium`, `xlThick`, and `xlThin`, to specify the width of the line used to draw a border around a range of cells.

VBA bases the style of line that it draws upon the `xlLineStyle` parameter. You use the `xlLineStyle` constant values, outlined in this table, to specify the line style.

CONSTANT	DESCRIPTION
xlContinuous	The default value, which draws a continuous line around the range of cells.
xlDash	Draws a dashed line around the range of cells.
xlDashDot	Draws a broken line using a dash-dot pattern.
xlDashDotDot	Draws a broken line using a dash-dot-dot pattern.
xlDot	Draws a dotted line around the range of cells.
xlDouble	Draws a double continuous line around the range of cells.
xlLineStyleNone	Does not modify the line style.
xlSlantDashDot	Draws a broken line in a dash-dot pattern using a slanted line.

Find Specific Cell Values

You can use the `Find` method to search for a value within a range of cells. This method is similar to the Find command in Excel. The following is the syntax for the `Find` method:

expression.Find(What, After, LookIn, LookAt, SearchOrder, SearchDirection, MatchCase)

The expression identifies the range you want to search. The `What` parameter is the only required parameter. You can use the `What` parameter to tell VBA what you want to find. You can use the `After` parameter to tell VBA the cell before which you want to start searching. If you omit this parameter, Excel starts the search with the top-left cell in the range. The `LookIn` parameter tells VBA what you want to search. You can assign one of the `xlFindLookIn` constants: `xlValues` searches cell values,

`xlComments` searches comments, and `xlFormulas` searches formulas.

The `LookAt` parameter tells VBA how to match your search criteria. Assign the `LookAt` parameter `xlWhole` if you want your search criteria to match the contents of the cell exactly; assign `xlPart` if you want VBA to return a match if your search criteria is found anywhere in the cell.

The `xlSearchOrder` parameter tells VBA the order in which you want to search. Assign the value `xlByRows` if you want to search by rows, or assign the value `xlByColumns` if you want to search by columns.

Use the `SearchDirection` parameter to indicate the direction you want to search. A value of `xlNext` finds the next matching value. A value of `xlPrevious` finds the previous matching value. Assign `True` to the `MatchCase` parameter if you want your search to be case-sensitive.

Find Specific Cell Values

In this example, the user enters a value in a cell and VBA searches a range for the value.

1️⃣ Declare the variable VBA uses to store the search criteria.

2️⃣ Type **On Error Resume Next**.

This statement tells VBA to continue processing if an error occurs.

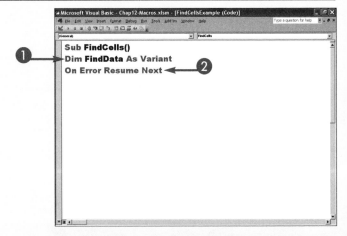

3️⃣ Activate the relevant worksheet.

If a procedure only works with a particular worksheet, activate the worksheet.

4️⃣ Store the contents of the cell in which the user enters the search criteria to a variable.

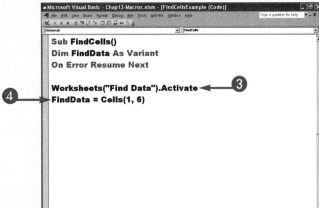

⑤ Type your Find command.

● The range you want to search.

● The data for which you are searching.

  In this example, the data is stored in the FindData variable.

● What you want to search.

● How you want to match your search criteria.

● The search order.

● Your instruction as to what VBA should do when it finds the item for which you are searching.

⑥ Press Alt+F11 to switch from the VBE to Excel, and run the macro.

● The cell in which the user places the search criteria.

● When you execute the macro, if VBA finds the item, Excel moves to the first instance of the item for which you are looking.

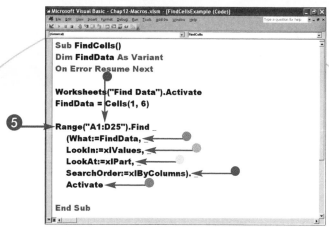

Extra

The introduction to this task does not mention two Find method parameters: MatchByte and SearchFormat. If you have installed double-byte language support on your computer, assign the value True to the MatchByte parameter.

The SearchFormat parameter enables you to match formats. If you assign the value True to this parameter, you must specify the format for the Application .FindFormat object.

VBA remembers the values specified for the What, LookIn, LookAt, SearchOrder, and MatchByte parameters. If you run a search again without setting these parameter values, Excel uses the settings from the previous Find or Replace method execution. These values are also set when you run a Find or Replace from within Excel. To avoid running searches that have unexpected results, you should set these parameters each time you run the Find method.

You can continue a search and find the next match using the FindNext or FindPrevious methods. When using these methods, you must specify an After parameter. The After parameter tells Excel the cell after which you want to execute the next search.

Example:

```
SearchRange.FindNext(After)
SearchRange.FindPrevious
(After)
```

Y ou can use the `Replace` method to search for and replace values within a range of cells. This method is similar to the Find and Replace command in Excel. The following is the syntax for the `Replace` method:

```
expression.Replace(What, Replacement,
LookAt, SearchOrder, MatchCase,
SearchFormat, ReplaceFormat)
```

The expression identifies the range you want to search. The `Replace` method has two required parameters: `What` and `Replacement`. The `What` parameter tells VBA what you want to find. The `Replacement` parameter tells VBA with what you want to replace the data you find.

The `LookAt` parameter tells VBA how to match your search criteria. You can assign the `LookAt` parameter `xlWhole` if you want your search criteria to match the contents of the cell exactly. You can assign `xlPart` if you want VBA to return a match if your search criteria is found anywhere in the cell.

The `xlSearchOrder` parameter tells VBA the order in which you want to search. You can assign the value `xlByRows` if you want to search by rows, or assign the value `xlByColumns` if you want to search by columns.

You can assign `True` to the `MatchCase` parameter if you want your search to be case-sensitive.

The `SearchFormat` and the `ReplaceFormat` parameters tell VBA the format you want to search for or replace. If you want to search for or replace a format, then you must set the appropriate parameter to `True` and specify the format properties for the `Application.FindFormat` object or the `ReplaceFormat` object, or both. For example, to replace text with a bold format, you can use the following code:

```
Application.ReplaceFormat.Font.FontStyle =
"Bold"
```

Find and Replace Values in Cells

① Type **On Error Resume Next**.

This statement tells VBA to continue processing if an error occurs.

② Activate the relevant worksheet.

③ Type your `ReplaceFormat` or `FindFormat` command.

In this example, you make the replacement text bold and italic.

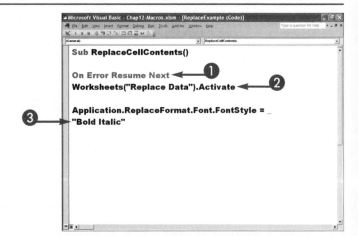

④ Type your Replace command.

● The range you want to search.

● The data for which you are searching.

● Your replacement.

Your `ReplaceFormat` object is set to `True`.

VBA will use your `ReplaceFormat` command.

● How you want to match your search criteria.

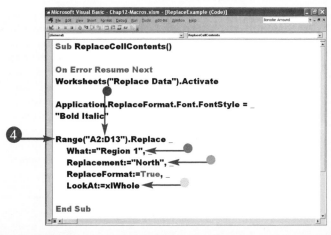

5 Press Alt+F11 to switch from the VBE to Excel, and run the macro.

Your worksheet before you execute your macro.

Your worksheet after you execute your macro.

The macro replaces the Region 1 text with North and applies bold and italics.

Extra

When you specify a value of `True` for the `SearchFormat` parameter or for the `ReplaceFormat` parameter, VBA looks for the search or replacement format settings. If you want to use formatting as part of the search criteria, you need to specify the format settings by using the `FindFormat` property of the Application object. With the `ReplaceFormat` parameter, you need to specify the replacement format settings by using the `ReplaceFormat` property. Set these properties at the top of the procedure, before the code that sets the associated parameter. You can use these properties to set the `Font` object properties for searching and replacing text. You can use the `With` statement to set the property values. For example, to set replacement text properties, you can type code similar to the following:

Example:
```
With Application.ReplaceFormat.Font
        .Name = "Arial"
        .FontStyle = "Bold"
        .Size = 12
End With
```

UserForm Basics

Every Windows application uses dialog boxes to gather information from the user, and Excel is no exception. For example, you can use the Open dialog box in Excel to select a file to open. VBA has two ready-made dialog boxes, MsgBox and InputBox, that you can use with your code. In addition, you can create you own custom dialog boxes. See Chapter 7 for more information on the MsgBox and InputBox dialog boxes.

Parts of the Visual Basic Editor

By using the VBE, you can create custom dialog boxes to use with your Excel procedures. The VBE refers to these custom dialog boxes as UserForms. When you create a UserForm, you design it by using the various controls available in the Toolbox.

Arrow Button

Label Button

Textbox Button

Combobox Button

Listbox Button

Checkbox Button

Option Button

Toggle Button

Frame Button

Command Button

Tabstrip Button

Multipage Button

Scrollbar Button

Spin Button

Image Button

Refedit Button

The VBE Toolbox appears only when you select a UserForm in the VBE. The Toolbox contains controls that you can add to your custom UserForm. See the section, "Create a Custom Dialog Box," for more information about adding Toolbox controls.

The Toolbox contains several standard controls that you can add to a UserForm. You can also create custom controls and add them to the Toolbox. See the section, "Create Custom UserForm Controls," for more information on adding custom controls.

Label

For adding text to a UserForm. This control is not designed to interact with the UserForm; you add labels for informational purposes only.

TextBox

Enables the user to type in text.

ComboBox

A user can either click an item from the list or type the appropriate value.

ListBox

Presents a list of items from which a user can select the desired item.

CheckBox

A user can select or deselect options. Typically, a CheckBox control returns a value of True if it is selected, and False if it is not selected.

OptionButton

A user can select from a list of items. You place Option Button controls in a group. When the user selects a control, the other controls are automatically deselected.

ToggleButton

The button appears to be either pressed or unpressed. When pressed, the button returns a value of True; when unpressed the button returns a value of False.

Frame

This control is a container for grouped controls.

TabStrip

A multiple-page area for a section of your UserForm.

CommandButton

A user clicks a button to perform a specific action. When you create a CommandButton control, you specify the text that displays on the button as part of the control property.

MultiPage

Tabbed dialog boxes with which a user can switch between pages of options in the dialog box.

By default, when you add the MultiPage control to your UserForm, it creates two pages. To add additional pages, right-click one of the Page tabs and select the New Page option.

ScrollBar

A user can scroll through information that is not on the screen, or indicate a position on a scale.

SpinButton

A user can specify a value by clicking one of the arrow buttons to increment or decrement the value.

Image

Use this control to add a graphic to the UserForm. Excel stores the graphic in the worksheet. If you distribute the worksheet, Excel includes the graphic. You can use a graphic that is in any of the following file formats: BMP, CUR, GIF, ICO, JPEG, and WMF.

RefEdit

A text field and a button with which a user can select a range of cells from a worksheet. When the user clicks a button, the corresponding dialog box minimizes so that the user can drag the pointer across the worksheet to select the desired range of cells.

Create a Custom Dialog Box

You can create custom dialog boxes to use with any of your macros. Dialog boxes are a user interface that enable users to click buttons to indicate a desired selection or type appropriate values in a field. You can use VBA to create custom dialog boxes. VBA refers to these dialog boxes as Forms or UserForms.

To create a custom dialog box in the VBE, select the UserForm option on the View menu. The VBE creates a new UserForm called UserForm# and creates a Forms folder in the Project Explorer window. The Forms folder displays only if you have created UserForms. See Chapter 2 for more information about the Project Explorer window.

You can change the name of a UserForm to make it easier to identify when you look at the UserForms list in the Project Explorer window by changing the Name property

in the Properties window. To open the Properties window press F4.

After you create a UserForm, you can custom design it by using the Toolbox controls, which only appear when you select the UserForm window. You add controls to the UserForm by dragging them from the Toolbox to the appropriate location on the UserForm. For example, to request a text value from the user, you drag the TextBox control onto the UserForm. After you add a control, you can resize it as needed. The VBE assigns default values to the control's properties. You can change the assigned values in the Properties window. You must select the control on the UserForm before you can set the properties.

Create a Custom Dialog Box

① In the Project Explorer window, click the project to which you want to add a UserForm.

② Click Insert → UserForm.

● The VBE creates a blank UserForm with a default name of UserForm1, and the Toolbox appears.

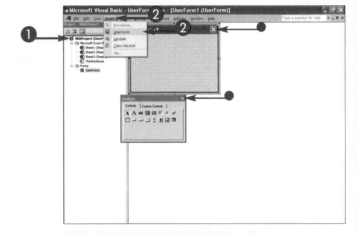

③ Press F4.

● The Properties window appears.

④ Type a form name in the Name field of the Properties window.

⑤ Click the UserForm.

● The Toolbox reappears.

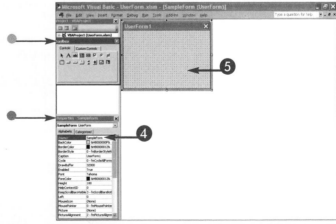

6 Click and drag a control from the Toolbox to the UserForm.

Continue adding controls as needed.

7 Type captions in the caption field.

Use the Properties window to change any properties you want to change.

8 Press F5.

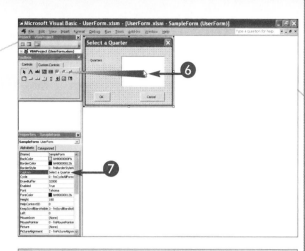

The VBE moves you to Excel and provides you with a preview of the dialog box.

9 To return to the VBE, click the Close button in the dialog box.

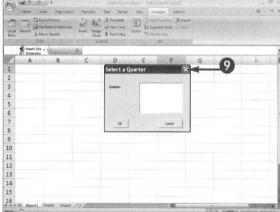

Extra

You can specify several properties for each control you add to a UserForm. Although each control type has unique properties, most of the properties are common to all controls. To change the value of a control, either type a new value or click a value from the drop-down list. The following table describes some common control properties.

CONTROL PROPERTY	DESCRIPTION
(Name)	The name of the control.
BackColor	The background color of the control.
Caption	The text that displays on the control, such as the button text.
Font	The font used to display all values on the control.
Height	The height of the control in pixels.
Text	The default text value of the control.
TextAlign	The way text aligns on the control.
Width	The width of the control in pixels.

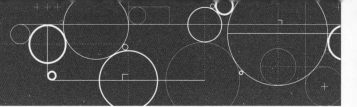

Call a Custom Dialog Box from a Procedure

You can call and display custom dialog boxes. Moreover, you can use custom dialog boxes to obtain user input. For example, you can use a dialog box to request the values you need from the user to perform a calculation.

To display a custom dialog box, use the Show method of the UserForm object. The Show method instructs Excel to display the specified UserForm. The Show method has one optional parameter, modal. The following is the syntax for the Show method:

UserForm.Show *modal*

The Modal parameter determines whether the UserForm displays as a modal or modeless dialog box in Excel. The default value of vbModal makes the dialog box modal,

which means that users must either close or hide the dialog box before selecting any other options in Excel. When Excel opens a modal dialog box, Excel passes control to the dialog box, and the user can only interact with the dialog box. A value of vbModeless means that although the dialog box remains open until a user closes it, the user can perform other functions.

Dialog boxes contain a Close or Cancel button a user can click to close the dialog box. In a procedure, you can also close a dialog box by using the Unload method. You must use a Click event with CommandButton controls to create a procedure that calls the Unload method. See the section, "Capture Input from a Custom Dialog Box," for more information about specifying the code to run when a user clicks a button.

Call a Custom Dialog Box from a Procedure

① Create a UserForm.

Note: *See the section, "Create a Custom Dialog Box," to learn how to create a UserForm.*

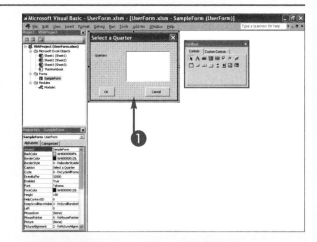

② Create a new Sub procedure.

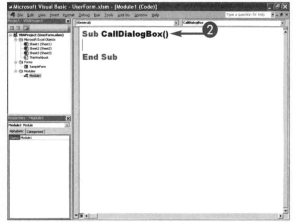

③ Create a Show command.

④ Press Alt+F11 to switch from the VBE to Excel, and run the macro.

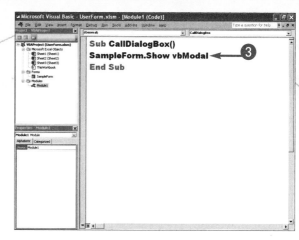

```
Sub CallDialogBox()
    SampleForm.Show vbModal ◄─── ③
End Sub
```

Excel displays the dialog box.

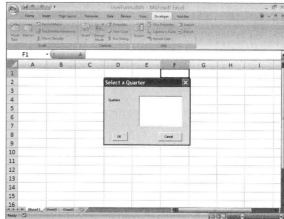

Extra

You can use the Unload statement to remove a UserForm from memory. When you call the statement, all controls on the UserForm are reset to their default values; as a result, you cannot access the options specified by the user after the UserForm unloads from memory. To maintain access to the necessary values, you can either store the values in global variables or hide the UserForm until your procedure terminates. To unload a UserForm, specify the Unload statement followed by the name of the UserForm that you want to unload, or use the following shorter code:

THIS CODE:		IS EQUIVALENT TO:
Unload UserForm1		Unload Me

You can hide a UserForm so that it is no longer visible. To hide a UserForm, use the Hide method. When you hide a UserForm, you can still access it from your procedure.

TYPE THIS:		RESULT:
UserForm1.Hide		Excel hides the form.

After hiding a form, Excel may appear to freeze as your code continues to access the UserForm. This condition clears as soon as the code that accesses the UserForm finishes processing.

Capture Input from a Custom Dialog Box

Dialog boxes in Excel gather input from the user. The input can be anything, from which button the user clicks to text the user types into a field. You can capture user input by using UserForm events. For example, when the user clicks an OK CommandButton control, you can use a CommandButton_Click Sub procedure to tell Excel what to do next.

Excel considers every user interaction that occurs in a dialog box to be an event. For example, scrolling through a list of items, clicking an OK button, and typing text in a text box are all events. Each UserForm control has several events that you can capture. The most common event is the `Click` event, which occurs each time a user clicks a control. To make `UserForms` interactive, you can create procedures that execute when specific events occur.

Each `UserForm` has two views: a graphical layout window and a code window. The graphical layout window is where you add controls that display in the dialog box. See the section, "Create a Custom Dialog Box," for more information on designing custom dialog boxes. The code window contains the code associated with the UserForm. You can use the code window to create event procedures for each control. To create event code, you double-click the control. By default, the VBE creates a private click event for a control when you double-click it. If a Click event already exists, the VBE simply displays the code window. Users cannot execute private click event procedures by using the Macro dialog box. The only way execute a private click event procedure is to click the appropriate control.

Capture Input from a Custom Dialog Box

① Create a UserForm.

Note: See the section, "Create a Custom Dialog Box," for information on creating UserForms.

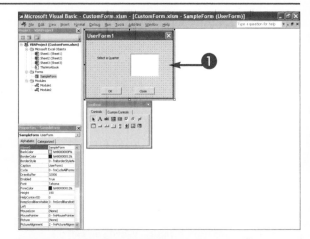

② Double-click a Command button.

In this example, you write code for the OK button, and so you double-click OK.

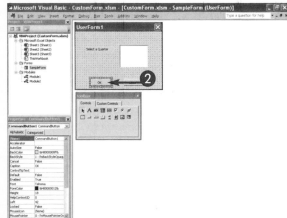

● VBA creates a Sub procedure.

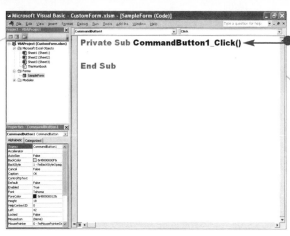

③ Assign the user selection to a variable.

④ Close the dialog box.

Extra

A Click event occurs when the user clicks a control or a value in a control. For most controls, you can write a procedure to handle the Click event by simply placing _Click after the control name.

Example:
```
Sub CommandButton1_Click()
```

A Click event also occurs when the user presses Enter while a control has focus, when the user presses the accelerator key that corresponds to the control, or when the user presses the Spacebar while a CommandButton has focus.

If you need to capture the Click event to determine the page or tab selected with a MultiPage or TabStrip control, the procedure also includes an index parameter value that specifies the index to the page or tab.

Example:
```
Sub MultiPage1_Click(1)
```

With the MultiPage and TabStrip controls, create a separate procedure to handle the selection of each page or tab by using the corresponding index value.

continued ➡

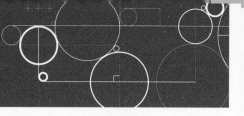

Y ou can create code to monitor events and determine when specific code should execute. Each control has its own events, and the VBE lists them for you in the procedure list box. You can quickly create an event procedure in the code window by selecting the appropriate control name in the Object list box and then selecting the corresponding event from the Procedure list box. When you select an event, the VBE creates a procedure with the name of the control followed by the event name.

The dialog box displays and returns. Control values on a UserForm are only active as long as the dialog box is open. If you close the dialog box prior to saving user input values, you lose the user input. To avoid potential problems relating to lost data, consider saving user responses to global variables that can pass into other procedures. For example, you can call a UserForm from

another procedure to capture user responses and then pass the values back to the main procedure.

You declare public variables at the top of your module, before any procedure code, by using the Public statement. Declaring public variables enables you to declare variables that all procedures in a project can access. See Chapter 3 for more information on declaring variables.

When working with a single-column list box or combo box, you can use the AddItem method to create the list of choices that appears in the box. The following is the syntax for the AddItem method:

object.AddItem *Item*

You can use the With statement to shorten the code required to create the list. See Chapter 4 for more information on using the With statement.

Capture Input from a Custom Dialog Box *(continued)*

⑤ Create a new module.

Note: *See Chapter 2 to learn how to create a new module.*

⑥ Declare a public variable to hold the user selection.

⑦ Create a Sub procedure.

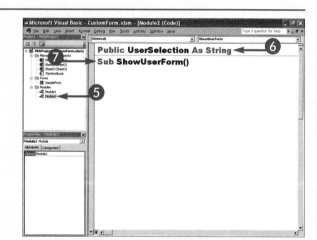

⑧ Add items to the list box.

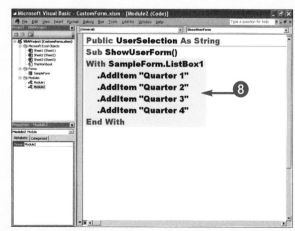

9 Show the dialog box.

10 Press Alt+F11 to switch from the VBE to Excel, and run the macro.

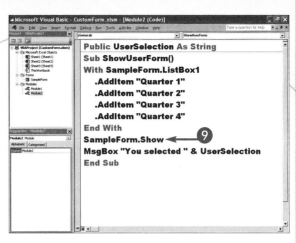

The dialog box displays and then a message box returns.

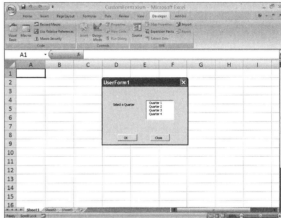

Apply It

You use control events to determine when to execute specific code. The following list identifies the most common events that occur with the various controls placed on UserForms. Not all events are available for each control. In the code window, check the Procedure list box to see the events that are associated with the selected control.

CONTROL EVENT	OCCURRENCE
BeforeDragOver	The user is dragging-and-dropping data onto a control.
BeforeUpdate	Before data on a control is changed.
Change	The Value property of the control changes.
Click	The user clicks the control.
DblClick	The user clicks the control twice.
Enter	Before a control receives focus.
KeyDown	The user presses a key.
MouseDown	The user presses the left mouse button.

Validate Input from a Dialog Box

Y ou can validate the values returned by controls in a dialog box before passing them to your procedure. You validate the data values for two reasons: First to ensure the user specifies a value for a control. Second, and probably more important, to ensure errors do not occur in your code as a result of wrong data passing to a procedure.

You can create code that validates the user input for any event that occurs in a UserForm. The best time to validate is prior to closing the dialog box. For example, if a CommandButton control, such as an OK button, passes values to variables and closes the dialog box, the OK button is the ideal place to validate your data. When you create the validation code, you can use a conditional statement, such as an `If Then` statement, to check the properties of each control. For example, to make sure the user typed a string in the Name text field of a dialog box,

you can add the following `If Then` statement to your procedure: `If TextBox1.Text = " " Then`.

The `If Then` statement checks the `Text` property for the specified TextBox control to ensure that it contains a value. If the TextBox control does not contain a value, your VBA code can call the MsgBox function and display a message telling the user that a value must be entered.

In addition to checking for values, you can also use the VBA validation functions to verify that the control contains the appropriate data type. For example, you can use the statement `If Not IsNumeric(TextBox1.Value) Then` to ensure that the user typed a number in a TextBox control.

When working with a list box, you can use the `ListIndex` property to find out if the user typed in a value. The `ListIndex` property returns –1 if the user did not type in a value, 0 if the user selected the first value in the list, 1 if the user selected the second value in the list, and so on.

Validate Input from a Dialog Box

① Double-click the control to which you want to add validation.

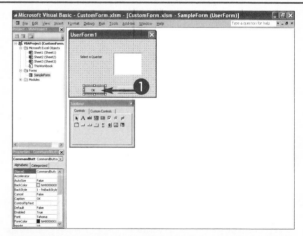

● The code window opens.

② Add the validation code.

In this example, if the user does not make a selection, a message box appears.

③ Press Alt+F11 to switch from the VBE to Excel, and run the macro.

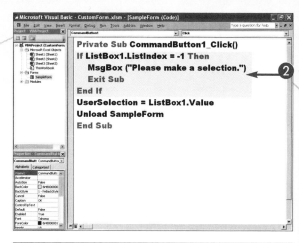

```
Private Sub CommandButton1_Click()
If ListBox1.ListIndex = -1 Then
    MsgBox ("Please make a selection.")
    Exit Sub
End If
UserSelection = ListBox1.Value
Unload SampleForm
End Sub
```

If you do not make a selection, a message box appears.

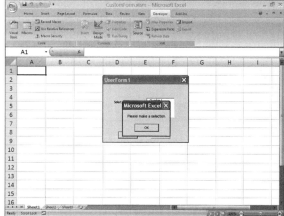

Extra

You can use the UserForm events to launch validation code, as shown in the following example. The code captures the `QueryClose` event to ensure that the user selected a ListBox control prior to the dialog box closing. A `QueryClose` event occurs before a UserForm closes.

Example:
```
Private Sub
UserForm_QueryClose(Cancel As
Integer, CloseMode As Integer)
If Not IsNumeric(TextBox1.Value)
Then
    MsgBox "Must be a number"
    Cancel = 1
End If
```

The `QueryClose` event has two arguments, `Cancel` and `CloseMode`. The `Cancel` argument accepts an integer value. If the value of the argument is anything other than zero, the `QueryClose` event stops and the associated dialog box remains open. The `CloseMode` argument contains a constant value indicating the cause of the `QueryClose` event, as shown in the following table.

CONSTANT	VALUE	DESCRIPTION
vbFormControlMenu	0	The user selected the Close button in the dialog box.
vbFormCode	1	The code initiated an Unload statement.
vbAppWindows	2	The Windows operating session is ending.
vbAppTaskManager	3	The Windows Task Manager is closing Excel.

Create Custom UserForm Controls

You can customize the Toolbox to suit your needs. The Toolbox that displays when you select a UserForm in the Visual Basic Editor contains all of the standard controls you can add to a UserForm. These controls display on a single tabbed page called Controls. By using the Properties window, you can change the tip text that displays when a user drags across the icon, the color of the control and many other features. You can also create new controls and add them to the Toolbox.

To create new controls, you customize and combine the existing controls. For example, if you add an OK button to all of your UserForms, you can create a custom button and set the appropriate properties, such as Caption, Width, Height, and Default. If you place the button in the Toolbox, the VBE adds it as a new control. Alternatively, you can create new controls by combining multiple controls. For example, you can create a new control that consists of an OK and a Cancel button.

To keep your custom controls separate from the existing controls in the Toolbox, you can add a new page to the Toolbox. You create a new page in the Toolbox by using the New Page option. You can assign a name to the new page by using the Rename option.

When you create a custom control by dragging a control from a form to the Toolbox, you only transfer the properties. Code that you have added to the control does not transfer. Each time you use a custom control you must add the necessary code.

Create Custom UserForm Controls

① In the Toolbox, click the control you want to customize.

② Drag the control to the UserForm.

③ In the Properties window, type the control name in the Name field.

④ Type the text you want to appear on the control in the Caption field.

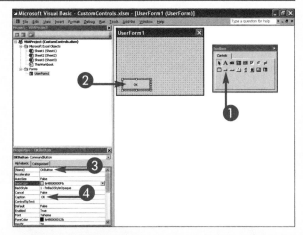

⑤ In the Toolbox, right-click the Controls tab.

⑥ Click New Page.

The VBE adds a new page to the Toolbox.

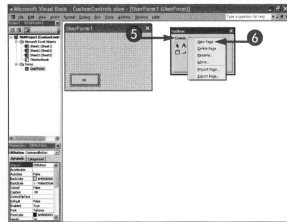

230

⑦ Click the control on the UserForm and drag the control to the Toolbox.

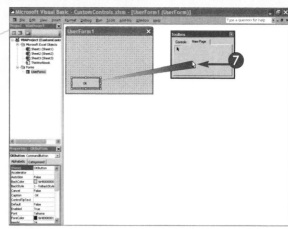

The control appears on the new page of the Toolbox.

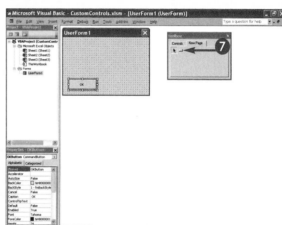

Extra

You can add multiple pages to the Toolbox. To change the order of the pages, right-click the page tab and then click the Move option on the menu to display the Move dialog box. Click the desired page to select it, and then click the Move Up or Move Down buttons to reorder your pages.

If you want to rename a tab, right-click the tab, and then click Rename. The Rename dialog box appears. Type the name you want to give the tab in the Caption field.

Creating a separate page in the Toolbox to store your custom controls gives you the ability to export the page for loading on another computer. To export a page, right-click the page tab and then click the Export Page option. In the Export Page dialog box, specify the name and location for the page file. The VBE assigns the page file an extension of .pag.

To import a page file into the Toolbox, right-click a tab menu and then click the Import Page option. In the Import Page dialog box, specify the name and location of the page file to import.

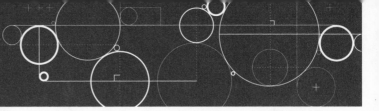

Create a UserForm Template

If you find that you create the same basic UserForm repeatedly, you can create a UserForm template file to save you time and effort. When you create UserForms, the Visual Basic Editor attaches them to the project in which you create them. Each time you create a new project, you must re-create the UserForm or copy it from another project by using the Project Explorer window. See Chapter 2 for more information on working with the Project Explorer window.

When you create a UserForm template, you design a basic UserForm and save it to a file. You can then add the UserForm to any other project you create. You can save a UserForm to a file by using the Export File command on the File menu. In the Export File dialog box, you specify the name and location for saving the UserForm file. You

may want to create a folder in which to save Excel project files.

When you create a UserForm for use as a template, you should keep it generic so you can customize it for each new project. For example, if you frequently create a UserForm that contains a TextBox control for gathering user input, as well as two CommandButton controls, OK and Cancel, you can create a generic version with the three controls. However, if you do not place the Label control for the text box in the template version, you can import the form and customize it for the type of data you want to gather from the user.

To add a UserForm template to a project, you can use the Import option. The VBE creates a new UserForm and assigns it the next sequential name.

Create a UserForm Template

CREATE A TEMPLATE

① Create a UserForm.

Note: *See the section, "Create a Custom Dialog Box," for information on how to create a UserForm.*

② Click File ➔ Export File.

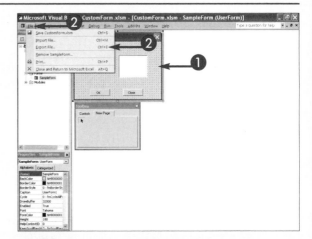

③ Locate the folder in which you want to save the file.

④ Type the filename.

⑤ Click Save.

VBA exports the file.

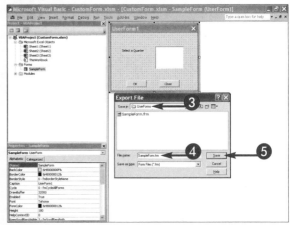

232

IMPORT A TEMPLATE

① Click the project to which you want to add a UserForm.

② Click File → Import File.

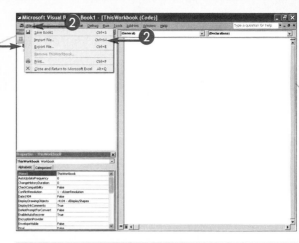

The Import File dialog box appears.

③ Locate the folder in which you saved the form.

④ Click the file containing the UserForm.

⑤ Click Open.

The VBE adds the UserForm to the project.

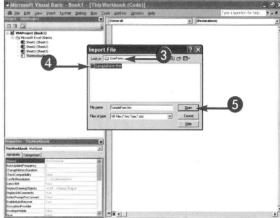

Extra

You can specify the order that Excel uses to move between controls on the UserForm by setting the controls' tab order. Tab order is the order in which the VBE selects the control to move to when a user presses the Tab key. By default, the tab order is the order in which you add controls to a UserForm.

Each control has two properties that relate to tab order. You can use the Properties window to set these properties. The first property, TabStop, determines whether focus stops on the control when the user presses the Tab key. If you set the TabStop property for a control to False, then when the user tabs through the controls, Excel skips the control. The second property, TabIndex, is a value between zero and the number of controls, it sets the order in which Excel moves from control to control when the user presses the Tab key. You can use the Tab Order dialog box to set the tab order. This dialog box appears when you right-click the UserForm and then click Tab Order.

Create a
CustomUI.xml File

With Office 2007, Microsoft introduced a new user interface for Excel. Earlier versions used toolbars and menus to provide access to Excel commands. Office 2007 uses the Ribbon. Using XML, you can customize the Excel Ribbon. Microsoft refers to the markup system you use as RibbonX. You create and use a file named customUI.xml to modify the Ribbon. Because you write XML in plain text, you can use any text editor to create a customUI.xml file.

Creating a basic Ribbon modification requires that you use control markups. The `ribbon` control markup represents the Ribbon.

The `tab` control markups represent the tabs on the Ribbon. All `tab` markups are contained within the `tabs` control markup. The tabs control markup does not have any attributes. You can set an `id` attribute and a `label`

attribute for a `tab` control. You define `id` attributes. They uniquely identify controls. `Label` attributes assign a label to a control. You can assign many attributes to elements.

The `group` control markup identifies a group on a tab. You can set an `id` attribute and a `label` attribute with the `group` markup.

The `button` control markup creates a button on a tab. You can set `id`, `label`, `imageMso`, `size`, `onAction`, and `screenTip` attributes for a button control. The `imageMso` attribute identifies the built-in image you want to use as the button. The `size` attribute determines the size of the button. You can set the `size` attribute to either normal or large. The customUI.xml file can call the `onAction` attribute when the user clicks a control. The `screenTip` attribute specifies the screen tip that displays when the user rolls the mouse pointer over the button.

Create a CustomUI.xml File

1 Create a file named customUI.xml.

You can use Notepad or another text editor to create the file.

2 Type **<customUI xmlns="http:// schemas.microsoft.com/office/ 2006/01/customui">**.

You start every customUI.xml file with this code.

3 Create a ribbon markup control.

4 Create a tabs markup control.

5 Create a tab markup control.

⑥ Create a group.

⑦ Create buttons.

⑧ Save your file with the filename customUI.xml.

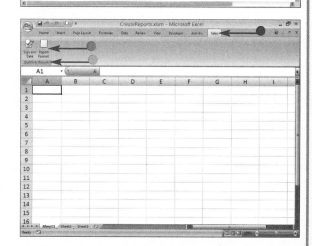

```
customUI.xml - Notepad
File Edit Format View Help
<customUI
xmlns="http://schemas.microsoft.com/office/2006/01/customui">
<ribbon>
 <tabs>
  <tab id="CustomTab"
      label="Sales">          ⑥
   <group id="Group1"
      label="  Quarterly Reports  ">
⑦  <button id="Button1"
      imageMso="ReviewAcceptChange"
      size="large"
      label="Sign and Date"
      onAction="ThisWorkbook.SignAndDate"
      screentip = "Sign and Date Report" />
⑦  <button id="Button2"
      imageMso="CreateReportBlankReport"
      size="large"
      label="Report Format"
      onAction="ThisWorkbook.ReportFormat"
      screentip = "Create a Report Format" />
⑥  </group>
  </tab>
 </tabs>
</ribbon>
</customUI>
```

After you add your file to a workbook, your Ribbon should look like the one shown here.

● XML adds a new tab.

● Two buttons.

● A group.

Extra

You use the `imageMso` attributes to identify the built-in image you want to appear on the Ribbon by using the following syntax:

`imageMso = "ImageName"`

To obtain the name of the image, click the Office button and then click Excel Options. The Excel Options dialog box appears. Click Customize. In the Choose Commands From field, select All commands. Move the mouse pointer over the command with the button that you want to use. A screen tip appears. The name of the image appears at the end of the screen tip in parentheses.

You can also download 2007OfficeIconsGallery from the Microsoft Web site. The 2007OfficeIconsGallery is an Excel workbook. When you open the workbook, galleries containing built-in images appear on the Developer tab. When you place your mouse pointer over an image or click an image, the name of the image appears. You can specify the size if the image by using the `size` attribute. Set the `size` attribute to `large` to display a large button. Set the `size` attribute to `normal` to display a normal size button.

Customize the Ribbon

To seamlessly integrate the procedures that you create with the Microsoft Excel user interface, you can place buttons on the Ribbon that will execute your macro when the user clicks the button. You modify the Excel Ribbon by placing a customUI.xml file in your workbook file, and then creating a relationship between the workbook and the customization file. See the section, "Create a CustomUI.xml File," to learn more about creating a customization file.

You can open an Excel workbook file by changing the filename extension to .zip and then double-clicking the file. When the file opens, you will see several files and folders. You refer to this ZIP file as a package, and the files in the ZIP file as parts. To modify the Ribbon, you place your customUI.xml file in a folder named customUI and then place the folder and file in the package.

Relationships define how the parts of a document come together to form the document. Relationships are stored in the /_rels folders in .rels files in the root and in subdirectories of the file. To modify the Ribbon, you must create a relationship between the workbook and the customization file by adding a relationship to the .rels file under _rels in the root directory. You create the relationship by placing the following code between the last Relationship tag and the Relationships tag.

```
<Relationship Id="someID" Type="http://
schemas.microsoft.com/office/2006/relations
hips/ui/extensibility" Target=customUI/
customUI.xml" />
```

When your procedures are going to be executed through Ribbon buttons, you place your procedures in the ThisWorkbook module and place `ByVal control As IRibbonControl` between the parentheses if you are using an `onAction` attribute with a button, as follows:

```
Sub SubName (ByVal control As
IRibbonControl)
```

Customize the Ribbon

1. Create a folder on your desktop named customUI.

2. Place your customUI.xml file in the folder.

Note: See the section, "Create a CustomUI.xml File," to learn how to create a custom UI file.

3. Open the file that will contain the macros you want to execute.

4. In the VBE, double-click ThisWorkbook.

   The workbook module opens.

5. Name your Sub procedure and place `ByVal control As IRibbonControl` in parentheses.

   You add this code because you are going to use an `onAction` attribute.

6. Type your procedure.

7. Save and close your file.

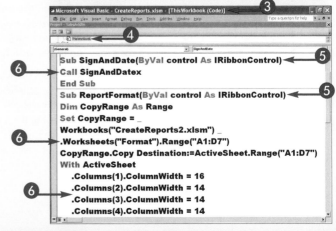

8 Locate your file in Windows Explorer.

9 Change the extension on the filename to .zip.

10 Double-click the file to open it.

11 Drag the customUI folder from the desktop to the ZIP file.

12 Drag the _rels folder from the ZIP file to the desktop.

13 Double-click the rels folder to open it.

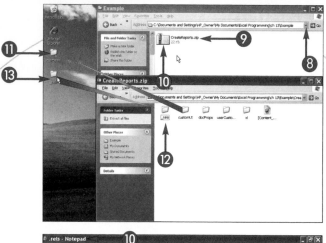

The RELS file appears.

14 Open the RELS file in Notepad or another text editor.

15 Create a Relationship.

16 Save and close the file.

17 Delete the RELS file in the ZIP file and replace it with the new RELS file.

18 Rename the ZIP file back to its original name.

A new tab appears in the file.

Extra

The procedure outlined in the steps modifies the Ribbon for an individual workbook. If you want to modify the Ribbon for multiple workbooks by using VBA, you can use an add-in. You create an add-in by saving a workbook in the add-in format. Add-ins enable you to integrate additional functionality into Microsoft Excel. You can create an add-in and distribute it to others. See Chapter 16 to learn more about add-ins.

If you are planning to convert a workbook with a modified Ribbon to an add-in, do not place your code in ThisWorkbook. Create your Sub procedures in ThisWorkbook as you normally would. Place your code in standard modules and then call the standard Sub procedure from the code in ThisWorkbook.

Example:
```
Sub SignAndDate(ByVal control As IRibbonControl)
Call SignAndDateX
End Sub
```

Add Additional Options to the Ribbon

You can create a customUI.xml file, and use that file to create a new Ribbon tab, add buttons to the tab, and use the buttons to execute your procedures. You can also add control markups to your customUI.xml file that will create launchers, combo boxes, toggle buttons, check boxes, and edit boxes.

When creating your XML code, you use callbacks to run procedures based on the information returned when the user interacts with a control. For example, check boxes return a Boolean value of either True or False when you use the onAction callback. Your procedure can perform one action if the value returned is True, and another action if the value returned is False.

Excel uses dialog boxes to enable users to access advanced features. The user is able to open the dialog box

by clicking a launcher located in the lower-right corner of the group. You can create launchers to open the dialog boxes you create for your custom applications. Dialog boxes are useful when you want to obtain information from the user. Use the dialogBoxLauncher element to create a launcher. Each group can have one launcher. The launcher element must be the last element in the group and must contain a button control. You can use the onAction callback with a dialog box to tell VBA what procedure to execute when the user clicks the launcher.

Use the comboBox element to present the user with a menu of options. When you present the user with a menu, the procedure that executes depends on the option the user selects. You typically use conditional statements with a combo box.

Add Additional Options to the Ribbon

ADD A LAUNCHER

1. Add code to your customUI.xml file.

● The dialogBoxLauncher tag.

● The required button tag.

2. Open the VBE.

3. Add the code that will execute to ThisWorkbook.

○ Opens an input box.

○ Inserts a title in your worksheet.

ADD A COMBO BOX

① Add a tag to end the previous group.

② Add tags for the new group.

This label will appear at bottom of the group.

③ Create your combo box tags.

Ids can be anything you want, but they must be unique.

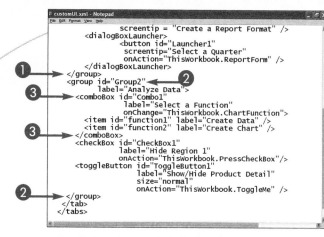

```
                    screenip = "Create a Report Format" />
            <dialogBoxLauncher>
                <button id="Launcher1"
                    screenip="Select a Quarter"
                    onAction="ThisWorkbook.ReportForm" />
            </dialogBoxLauncher>
①       </group>
        <group id="Group2"                    ②
            label="Analyze Data">
③       <comboBox id="Combo1"
                    label="Select a Function"
                    onChange="ThisWorkbook.ChartFunction">
            <item id="function1" label="Create Data" />
③           <item id="function2" label="Create Chart" />
        </comboBox>
        <checkBox id="CheckBox1"
                label="Hide Region 1"
                onAction="ThisWorkbook.PressCheckBox"/>
        <toggleButton id="ToggleButton1"
                    label="Show/Hide Product Detail"
                    size="normal"
                    onAction="ThisWorkbook.ToggleMe" />
②       </group>
        </tab>
        </tabs>
```

④ Open the VBE.

⑤ Add the code that will execute to ThisWorkbook.

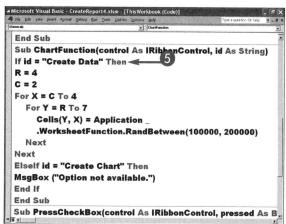

```vb
End Sub
Sub ChartFunction(control As IRibbonControl, id As String)
If id = "Create Data" Then              ⑤
R = 4
C = 2
For X = C To 4
   For Y = R To 7
      Cells(Y, X) = Application _
      .WorksheetFunction.RandBetween(100000, 200000)
   Next
Next
ElseIf id = "Create Chart" Then
MsgBox ("Option not available.")
End If
End Sub
Sub PressCheckBox(control As IRibbonControl, pressed As B
```

Extra

Prior to Office 2007, developers used command bars to modify the user interface. In most cases, this code will work in Office 2007 without any modification. The changes appear on the Add-ins tab. If the developer added an item to a menu in Office 2003, then Office 2007 creates a Menu Commands group and places the information there. If the information was assigned to a toolbar, then Office 2007 places the information in a Toolbar Commands group.

You can use XML markup and any Microsoft .NET framework-base language to make modifications to the user interface.

A check box returns either the Boolean value True or the Boolean value False. You can use a checkbox to set a property to True or False. For example, you can use a check box to set the Hidden property for a worksheet column. If the Hidden property is False the column is visible. If the Hidden property is set to True the column is not visible.

continued →

You can use the `toggleButton` element to add a toggle button to the Ribbon. Toggle buttons are useful when you want to enable the user to turn an option on and off with a single mouse click. For example, if you have a worksheet in your workbook that contains values on which you base calculations and those values seldom change, you may want to hide the worksheet. The example for this section has a Workbook_Open command that hides the worksheet from which VBA copies the report format that VBA places in the active worksheet when the user presses the Report Format button. You could add a toggle button to the Ribbon to show and hide this worksheet by using an `onAction` callback and adding the following code to ThisWorkbook:

```
Sub HideSheets(control As IRibbon, _
pressed As Boolean)
```

```
Sheets("Format").Visible = pressed
End Sub
```

When used with a toggle button, the `onAction` callback returns `True` when a toggle button is pressed, and `False` when it is not. The values are returned to the variable `pressed`. The code unhides the worksheet when the button is in a pressed state, and hides the worksheet when the button is in an unpressed state. Toggle buttons are always in one of two states, pressed or unpressed. In Excel, bold is an example of a toggle button.

You can use the `checkBox` element to add check boxes. For example, if your data consists of three columns with data for Region 1, Region 2, and Region 3, then you can create a check box that hides and unhides the information for each of the regions.

Add Additional Options to the Ribbon (continued)

VIEW CHANGES TO THE RIBBON

① Click the launcher to open a dialog box.

The dialog box appears.

- Notice that there are two groups.

- Notice the custom tab.

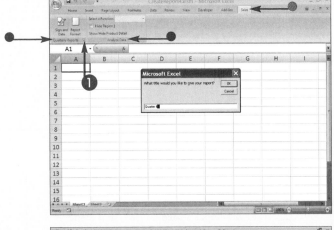

- The dialog box adds a title to your worksheet.

② Click this button to add a format to your worksheet.

Note: To add this button, see the section, "Customize the Ribbon".

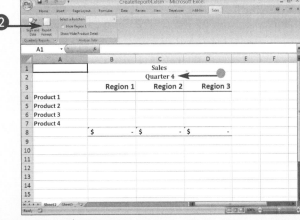

③ Click the combo box to see a list of options.

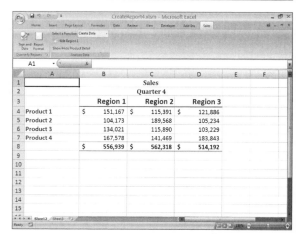

The Create Data option fills your worksheet with numbers.

Extra

The following XML script creates a check box and a toggle button.

```
<checkBox id="CheckBox1" label="Hide Region 1" onAction="ThisWorkbook.PressCheckBox"/>
<toggleButton id="ToggleButton1" label="Show/Hide Product Detail" size="normal"
onAction="ThisWorkbook.ToggleMe"/>
```

The following code hides or unhides a column when the user clicks the check box. When the user checks the check box the Boolean value True is returned to the variable pressed; when the user unchecks the checkbox the Boolean value False is returned to the variable pressed.

```
Sub PressCheckBox(control As IRibbonControl, pressed as Boolean)
Columns(2).Hidden = pressed
End Sub
```

The following code hides or unhides rows four through seven when a toggle button is pressed.

```
Sub ToggleMe(control As IRibbonControl, pressed As Boolean)
R = 4
For X = R to 7
    Rows(X).Hidden = pressed
Next
End Sub
```

Create a Chart Sheet

You can use VBA to add a new chart sheet to your workbook. When you create a chart, VBA creates a new Chart object. Each Chart object contains several objects that represent the settings for the chart. For example, the ChartTitle object contains the chart title, its font and border properties, and other associated attributes.

When you create a chart, you can create a new chart sheet or embed a chart in a worksheet. When creating a new chart sheet, you use the Chart object directly, whereas when you create an embedded chart, you use a ChartObjects object. See the section, "Embed a Chart in a Worksheet," for more information on creating embedded charts.

To create a new chart sheet, you use the Add method with the Charts object. After you create your chart, you can use a With statement to set chart properties such as chart type, the name you want to place on the chart's tab, the title of the chart, and the chart style. You select a chart type by assigning an XlChartType constant value to the ChartType property. You use the Name property to assign a name to the chart tab. If you want to place a title on the chart, set the HasTitle property to True and then use the ChartTitle property to assign the title. If you want to apply a style, assign a style number between 1 and 48 to the ChartStyle property. Every style in the Excel style gallery has a number, and you can run your mouse pointer over the style to find out what the number is. Use the SetSourceData method to tell VBA where your data is located.

Create a Chart Sheet

① Create a Chart object variable.

② Set the Chart object variable.

● Use the Add method to add the new chart.

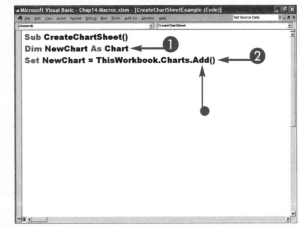

③ Create a With statement.

④ Use the ChartType property to specify a chart type.

⑤ Name the chart sheet tab.

⑥ Place a title on the chart.

⑦ Assign a chart style.

⑧ Specify your data source.

● The worksheet tab name.

⑨ Press Alt+F11 to switch from the VBE to Excel, and run your macro.

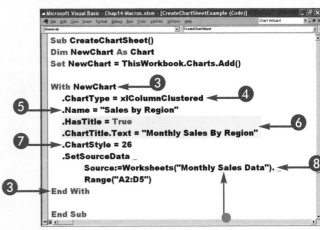

- Your source data.

- The worksheet tab name.

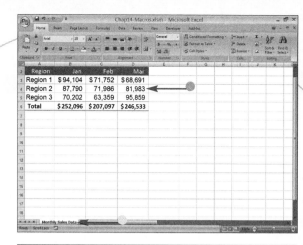

The macro creates a chart.

- The tab name.

- The title.

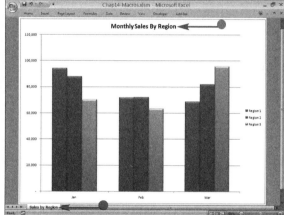

Apply It

When creating a chart, you must specify the chart's data source. If you omit the data source information, your chart appears blank. You use the `SetSourceData` method to specify the data source for your chart. The following is the syntax for `SetSourceData`:

Example:
```
NewChart.SetSourceData(Source.Range, PlotBy)
```

Use the `Source` parameter to specify the actual data range your chart will use. The `Source` parameter can reference any valid data range. See Chapter 11 for more information on defining a range of values. When working with a chart sheet, you must indicate the name of the worksheet containing the data as part of the range reference. For example, the following code references the range of cells contained in Sheet1 in the same workbook.

Example:
```
NewChart.SetSourceData Source:=Worksheets("Sheet1").Range("A1:B15")
```

With the `SetSourceData` method, you can use the `PlotBy` parameter to tell VBA how to plot the data in the specified range. You assign `PlotBy` one of the `XlRowCol` constant values.

Embed a Chart in a Worksheet

You can use VBA to embed a new chart in a worksheet within a workbook. When you embed a chart, Excel creates a new Chart object. Each Chart object contains several objects that represent the settings for the chart, such as the ChartTitle object, which contains the chart title, its font, border properties, and other associated attributes.

When you embed a chart in a worksheet, the corresponding Chart object that Excel creates becomes a part of the Worksheet object. Because you can embed multiple charts in one worksheet, the Worksheet object contains a ChartObjects collection object that contains all Chart objects on the worksheet. When you add or remove embedded charts, you must use the ChartObjects collection object.

To add a chart to a worksheet, you must use the Add method with the ChartObjects object. The Add method has four parameters you can use to set the location and size of the chart in points: Left, Top, Width, and Height. Use the Left parameter to specify the location of the chart in relation to the left edge of column A. Use the Top parameter to specify the location of the chart in relation to the top edge of row A. Use the Width and Height parameters to specify the initial width and the height of the Chart object.

You specify the type of chart that Excel creates by using the ChartType property with one of the XlChartType constant values. For example, to create a line chart, you use the constant xlLine. See Appendix A for a list of the XlChartType constants.

Embed a Chart within a Worksheet

① Create a Chart object variable.

② Set the Chart object variable to the new chart.

● The name of the worksheet in which you want to place the chart.

● Sets the chart position and size.

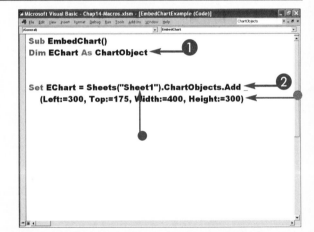

③ Create a With statement.

④ Use the ChartType property to specify a chart type.

⑤ Place a title on the chart.

⑥ Assign a chart style.

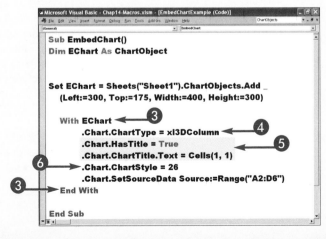

7 Specify your data source.

8 Press Alt+F11 to switch from the VBE to Excel, and run your macro.

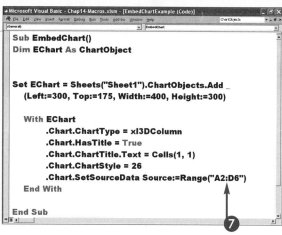

```vb
Sub EmbedChart()
Dim EChart As ChartObject


Set EChart = Sheets("Sheet1").ChartObjects.Add _
    (Left:=300, Top:=175, Width:=400, Height:=300)

    With EChart
        .Chart.ChartType = xl3DColumn
        .Chart.HasTitle = True
        .Chart.ChartTitle.Text = Cells(1, 1)
        .Chart.ChartStyle = 26
        .Chart.SetSourceData Source:=Range("A2:D6")
    End With

End Sub
```

The macro creates your chart.

- Your source data.

- The tab name.

- The title.

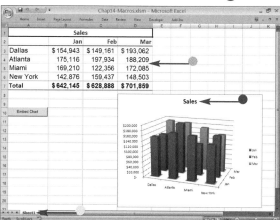

Extra

The only real difference between embedded charts and chart sheets is the Chart object for an embedded chart is part of the ChartObjects collection for the worksheet, whereas the Chart object for a chart sheet is part of the Workbook object. If you compare the code that creates an embedded chart to the code that adds a new chart sheet, you will notice that with an embedded chart, specifying chart methods and properties requires reference to the Chart object. This is because when you create a new chart sheet, you create a new Chart object, but when you create an embedded chart, you add a Chart object to the ChartObjects collection for the worksheet; therefore the Chart object becomes a child of the ChartObjects collection object. To set the chart type of an embedded chart, you can use the following code:

Example:
```
Worksheets("Sheet1").ChartObject(1).Chart.ChartType = xlColumnStacked
```

This code sets the chart type of the first chart object in the worksheet named Sheet1 to a stacked column chart. If you compare this code to the code required for changing the chart type of a chart sheet, you can see the similarities.

Example:
```
Sheets("Chart1").ChartType = xlColumnStacked
```

Apply Chart Wizard Settings to a Chart

When writing VBA code, you can use the `ChartWizard` method to format or reformat a chart quickly. You use the `ChartWizard` method with a `Chart` object. This method has 11 optional parameters that enable you to set chart properties. The following is the syntax for the `ChartWizard` method:

expression.ChartWizard(Source, Gallery, Format, PlotBy, CategoryLabels, SeriesLabels, HasLegend, Title, CategoryTitle, ValueTitle, ExtraTitle)

Use the Source parameter to specify or modify the chart's data source. When you are working with a chart sheet, you must specify the name of the worksheet that contains the data source. Use the `Gallery` parameter to specify the chart type. Assign one of the `XlChartType` constant values to indicate the desired chart type. See Appendix A for a list of `XlChartType` constants.

Specify a value of 1 to 10 for the `Format` parameter. The `Format` parameter applies one of VBA's built-in formats. The format that it uses depends on the chart type you select. The `PlotBy` parameter tells VBA whether the data series is in rows or columns. Assign the `PlotBy` parameter `xlRows` if the data series is in rows. Assign it `xlColumns` if the data series is in columns.

Assign an integer value to the `CategoryLabels` and `SeriesLabels` parameters to indicate the number of rows or columns in the category or series that have labels. Assign the `HasLegend` parameter the value `True` if you want your chart to have a legend.

Use the `Title` parameter to assign a title to your chart, the `CategoryTitle` parameter to assign a title to your horizontal axis, and the `ValueTitle` parameters to assign a title to your left vertical axis. For a 3-D chart, you use the `ExtraTitle` parameter to assign a title to your depth axis. You must set any additional properties individually.

Apply Chart Wizard Settings to a Chart

① Create a `Chart` object variable.

② Set the `Chart` object variable to the chart you want to modify.

● The name of the chart sheet.

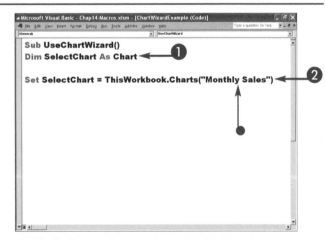

③ Create your `ChartWizard` command.

④ Set your parameters.

⑤ Press Alt+F11 to switch from the VBE to Excel, and run the macro.

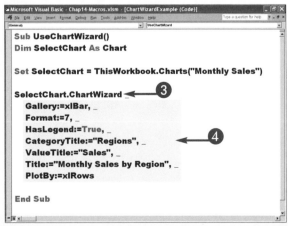

Your chart before you apply the macro.

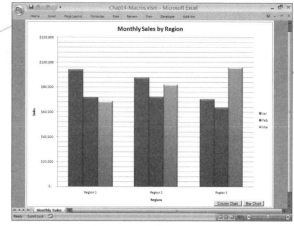

Your chart after you apply the macro.

Your macro changes the format of your chart.

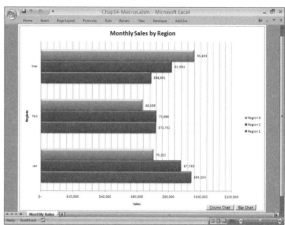

Extra

When working in Excel, once you have your chart designed exactly the way you want it, you can save your design as a template. You can also use VBA to save your chart as a template.

Example:
```
Sub CreateTemplate()
Dim SelectChart as Chart
Set SelectChart = ThisWorkbook.Charts("Monthly Sales")
SelectChart. _
     SaveChartTemplate("My Template")
End Sub
```

To apply your template to an existing chart, in Excel, click your chart. The Chart tools become available. Click the Design tab. Click Change Chart Type in the Type group. The Change Chart Type dialog box appears. Click Templates, click your template, and then click OK. Excel applies your template to your chart.

Add a New Data Series to a Chart

A data series is a group of data values that Excel displays in your chart. Each data series appears as a legend item. After you create a chart, you can redefine the range of data Excel uses to display values in your chart by adding a new data series. For example, if you have a bar chart showing the sales in Regions 1, 2, and 3 for January, February, and March, you can add another data series that contains the sales data for April.

The SeriesCollection collection object contains all of the data series that Excel plots on a specific chart, with each data series representing a Series object. To define a new data series, create a new Series object and add it to the SeriesCollection collection object by using the Add method.

When used with the SeriesCollection object, the Add method has five parameters: Source, Rowcol,

SeriesLabels, CategoryLabels, and Replace. Use the Source parameter to specify the data series you want to add to the chart. Use the Rowcol parameter to tell VBA whether the new series is in a row or a column. Use xlRows if the data series is in a row, or use xlColumns if the data series is in a column.

Set the SeriesLabels to True if the first row or column of the data series contains a label. Set the CategoryLabels to True if the first row or column of the data series contains a category label. Category labels display on the horizontal axis of your chart. If you specify a value of True for the CategoryLabels parameter and for the Replace parameter, Excel replaces the current category labels with the labels from the new range.

Add a New Data Series to a Chart

① Create your SeriesCollection Add statement.

● The worksheet name.

● Identifies the chart.

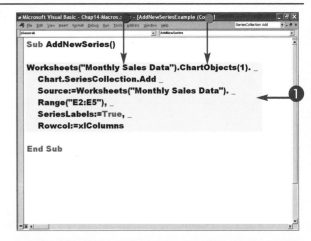

● The data series you want to add.

● Tells VBA that the series has labels.

● Tells VBA the data is organized in columns.

② Press Alt+F11 to switch from the VBE to Excel, and run the macro.

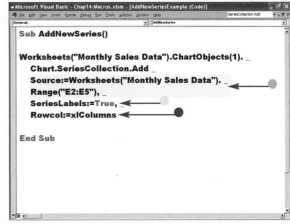

Your chart before you apply the macro.

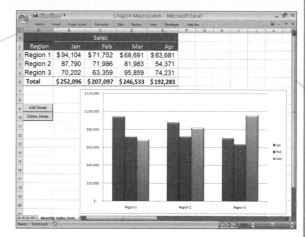

Your chart after you apply the macro.

● The macro adds a new data series.

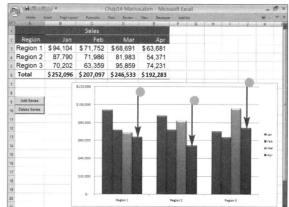

Extra

Each chart embedded in a worksheet is a member of the worksheet's `ChartObjects` collection. Each chart in the worksheet's `ChartObjects` collection has an index number. The first chart is `ChartObjects(1)`, the second chart is `ChartObjects(2)`, and so on. You can refer to a chart by its index number. You can also refer to a chart by its name. To find what a chart's name, in Excel, click your chart. The Chart tools become available. Click the Layout tab, and then click Properties. The chart name appears.

Each chart sheet in a workbook is part of the `Charts` collection. Each member of the `Charts` collection has an index number. The leftmost chart is `Chart(1)`, the next chart is `Chart(2)`, and so on. You can refer to Chart objects by their index number.

You can remove a series from a chart using the `Delete` method. The following code removes the series that was added in the example.

Example:
```
Worksheets("Monthly Sales Data")._
ChartObjects(1)._
Chart.SeriesCollection("Apr") _
.Delete
```

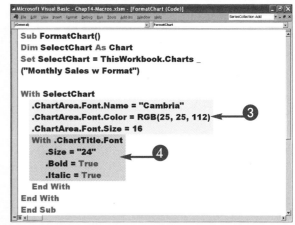

Format Chart Text

As with all text elements in a workbook, you can format the text that displays in your chart by changing the Font properties. When Excel adds text to a chart, such as a chart title, axis label, or even data label, it applies default formatting. You can reformat the text by using the Font object properties. By setting the Font properties, you can make your chart easier to read.

The chart area encompasses everything in your chart. By applying Font object properties to the ChartArea object, you can set the font attributes for all of the text in the chart. For example, if you want to change the font color for the entire chart, you apply the Font object Color property to the ChartArea object.

Excel also enables you to format individual elements of text that display in your chart. For example, if you use the Font object properties with the ChartTitle object, you can modify the chart title. To change how Excel displays legend text, use the Font object properties with the Legend object.

You can use the ChartArea object to set the font settings for the entire chart and then use the individual objects to customize various portions of the chart. You can set the properties for any of the following objects by using the Font object: ChartTitle, DataTable, Legend, Characters, AxisTitle, DataLabel, and TickLabels. See Chapter 11, "Using the Cells Property" to see a partial list of the Font properties you can set.

Format Chart Text

① Create a Chart object variable.

② Set the Chart object variable to the chart you want to format.

● The name of the chart sheet tab.

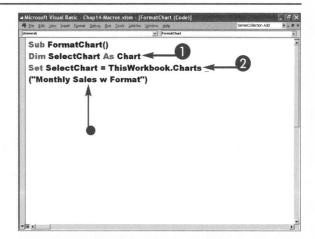

③ Format the text in the chart area.

④ Format the chart title.

⑤ Press Alt+F11 to switch from the VBE to Excel, and run the macro.

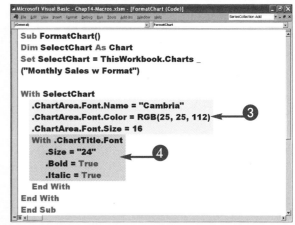

The chart without formatting.

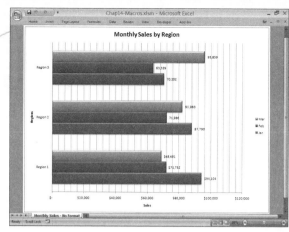

The macro formats the data.

The chart with formatting.

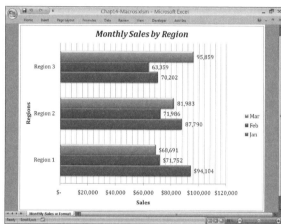

Apply It

You may not want to apply the same font settings to an entire `Chart` object. For example, you may want to underline the first character in the chart title. With the `AxisTitle`, `ChartTitle`, and `DataLabel` objects, you can use the `Characters` object to specify the character within the text string where formatting should start, as well as the number of characters to format. For example, to underline the first two characters in a chart title, type code similar to that shown in the example. The `Characters` object has two parameters: `Start` and `Length`. Use the `Start` parameter to indicate the character in the text string at which VBA should begin applying the format. Use the `Length` parameter to indicate the number of characters to which VBA should apply the format.

TYPE THIS:

```
ThisWorkbook.Charts(1).ChartTitle.
Characters(1,2).Font.Underline = True
```

RESULT:

Excel underlines the first and second characters in the chart title, but all remaining characters maintain their original font settings.

Create Charts with Multiple Chart Types

If you show more than one type of data in your chart, you may want to create a chart that uses a different chart type for each data series. For example, if your chart displays the population of various cities and the average income in those cities, you may want to create a column chart to display population, and a line chart to display average income. A chart that uses more than one chart type is called a *combination chart*.

To set the chart type for a data series, use the SeriesCollection object. The SeriesCollection collection object contains each of the data series in the range of data shown in your chart as an individual SeriesCollection object. You reference an individual object by using an index value. VBA numbers each data

series. The first data series is SeriesCollection(1), the second is SeriesCollection(2), and so on.

To set the chart type for a data series, you set the ChartType property for the specific SeriesCollection object. When you initially create your chart, you can use this method to set the chart type for each individual data series, or you can set the chart type for the entire chart, and then modify the ChartType property for the individual data series you want to change.

When you use the ChartType property, you assign it an XlChartType constant value that represents the chart type you want to use for the data series. See Appendix A for a list of the XlChartType constant values that you can assign to the ChartType property.

Create Charts with Multiple Chart Types

① Create a Chart object variable.

② Set the Chart object variable.

● Use the Add method to add a new chart.

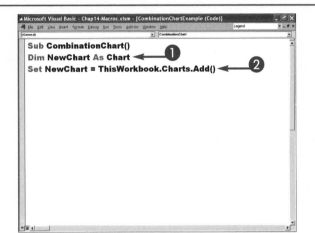

③ Set your data source.

④ Assign a chart type to your chart.

⑤ Assign a chart style to your chart.

⑥ Tell VBA whether your data is in columns or rows.

⑦ Assign a new chart type to a data series.

In this example, you assign a new chart type to series 1.

⑧ Format your chart.

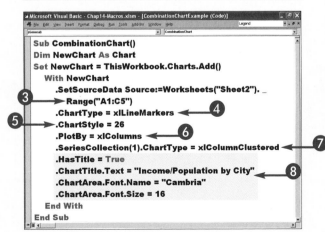

9 Press Alt+F11 to switch from the VBE to Excel, and run the macro.

Your data source.

● Series 1.

● Series 2.

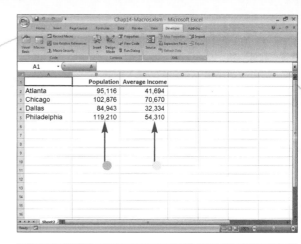

The macro creates a combination chart.

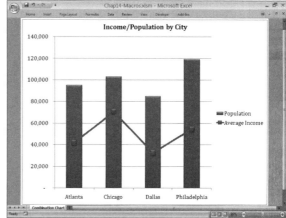

Extra

You can use a different chart type for each data series. Excel keeps track of the data series chart types, and groups the common types together as ChartGroup objects. Each ChartGroup object contains one or more data series with the same chart type. Excel stores all ChartGroup objects within the ChartGroups collection object, which you can access through the ChartGroup property.

The ChartGroups object provides methods for returning the collection of the ChartGroup objects that correspond to a particular type. For example, if you want to access the line chart type ChartGroup objects, you can use the LineGroups method. The example that follows illustrates how to count the number of column chart types in a chart. You can use the methods shown in the table with the ChartGroup objects.

Example:
```
DataSeriesCount = ThisWorkbook.Charts(1).ColumnGroups.Count
```

METHOD	DESCRIPTION
AreaGroups	Determines the number of series with an area data type.
BarGroups	Determines the number of series with a bar chart data type.
ColumnGroups	Determines the number of series with a column chart data type.
DoughnutGroups	Determines the number of series with a doughnut chart data type.
LineGroups	Determines the number of series with a line chart data type.
PieGroups	Determines the number of series with a pie chart data type.

Add a Data Table to the Chart

A data table displays the values in your chart. You can add data tables to any chart you create. VBA stores the data table associated with a chart in the `DataTable` object. Use the `HasDataTable` property to tell VBA whether you want to include a data table in your chart. This property accepts the Boolean values of `True` and `False`. If you want to display a data table, set this property to `True`. Conversely, if you do not want to display a data table, set this property to `False`.

After you set the `HasDataTable` property, you can format your data table by using the methods and properties associated with the `DataTable` object. You specify the font by using the `Font` properties. For example, `DataTable.Font.Name = "Arial"` tells VBA to use an Arial font in the data table. See the section,

"Format Chart Text," for more information on working with the `Font` object in a chart.

You can choose to display or not display borders in and around your data table by using the `HasBorderHorizontal`, `HasBorderOutline`, and `HasBorderVertical` properties. By default, Excel displays all borders on a data table. If you do not want to display one or more of these borders, set their value to `False`. For example, the following code removes the horizontal border from a data table:

`.DataTable.HasBorderHorizontal = False`

A legend key tells the user what each data series represents. You can use the `ShowLegendKey` property to tell VBA whether you want to show a legend key in your data table.

Add a Data Table to the Chart

① Create a `Chart` object variable.

② Set the `Chart` object variable to the chart to which you want to add a data table.

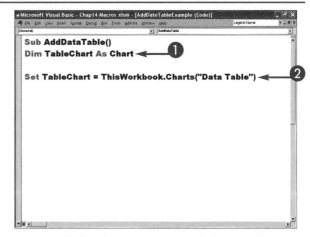

③ Create a `With` statement.

④ Set the `HasDataTable` property to `True`.

⑤ Assign a font to your data table.

⑥ Assign a border color.

⑦ Set the `ShowLegendKey` property for the data table to `True`.

This code shows a legend in the data table.

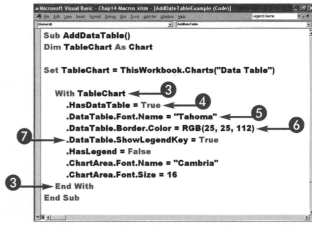

254

8 Set the `HasLegend` property for the chart to `False`.

This code suppresses the chart legend.

9 Set the chart area properties.

10 Press Alt+F11 to switch from the VBE to Excel, and run the macro.

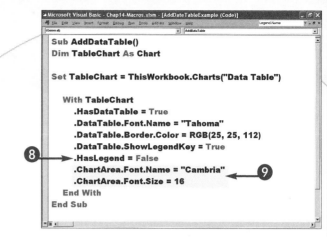

```vba
Sub AddDataTable()
Dim TableChart As Chart

Set TableChart = ThisWorkbook.Charts("Data Table")

    With TableChart
        .HasDataTable = True
        .DataTable.Font.Name = "Tahoma"
        .DataTable.Border.Color = RGB(25, 25, 112)
        .DataTable.ShowLegendKey = True
        .HasLegend = False
        .ChartArea.Font.Name = "Cambria"
        .ChartArea.Font.Size = 16
    End With
End Sub
```

The macro creates a chart with a data table.

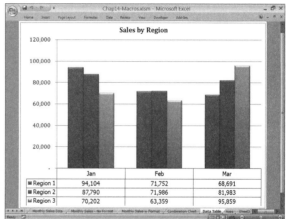

Extra

When you add a data table to a chart, you can include the chart legend with the data table. To create a data table that contains a chart legend, set the `ShowLegendKey` property to `True` for the `DataTable` object. The following example sets the value of the `ShowLegendKey` property.

Example:
```vba
ThisWorkbook.Charts(1).DataTable _
.ShowLegendKey = True
```

If you display the legend as part of your data table, you typically do not want the legend to display separately on your chart. To hide the chart legend, set the `HasLegend` property for the Chart object to `False`.

Example:
```vba
ThisWorkbook.Charts(1).HasLegend = False
```

Customize a Chart Axis

You can customize each axis on your chart with the Axis object methods and properties. Most charts that you create have two axes, a category axis and a values axis. For example, if you look at a column chart, the category axis runs horizontally across the bottom, while the values axis runs vertically along the left side of the chart. When working with 3-D charts, there is also a series axis, which shows the depth.

Each chart axis is a separate Axis object. The Axes collection object contains all of the Axis objects for a chart. You can use the Axes method to access an individual chart's Axis objects. When using the Axes method, use one of the XlAxisType constants to indicate the axis type. Use xlValue for the value axis, xlCategory for the category axis, or xlSeriesAxis for the depth axis on a 3-D chart.

You can modify each axis by using the AxisTitle, Border, Gridlines, DisplayUnitLabel, and TickLabels child objects. Each of these objects has child objects and corresponding methods and properties. The AxisTitle object represents the title that Excel adds to the axis. You can modify the appearance of the axis title by using the Font object properties. See the section, "Format Chart Text" for more information on working with the Font object in a chart. If you set the HasTitle property to True, you can assign an axis title. You can also modify other objects. For example, the Border object refers to the axis border. The following code changes the color of your border to blue.

```
.Border.Color = RGB(0,0,255)
```

Customize the Chart Axis

① Create a Chart object variable.

② Set the Chart object variable to the chart for which you want to modify an axis.

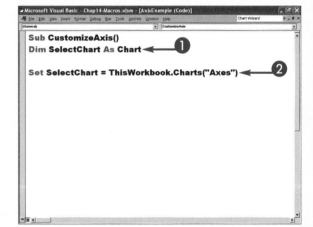

③ Create a With statement.

④ Tell VBA which axis you want to modify.

⑤ Assign a title to the axis.

● Sets the HasTitle property to True.

● Assigns the title.

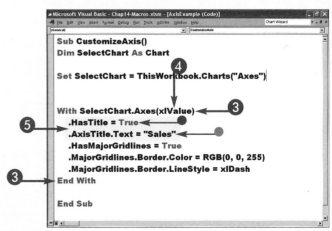

6 Place major gridlines on the chart.

7 Assign a major gridline border color.

8 Assign a major gridline borderline style.

9 Press Alt+F11 to switch from the VBE to Excel, and run the macro.

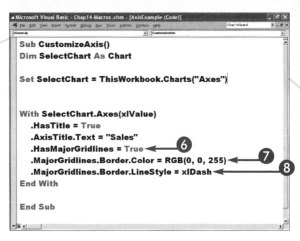

The macro creates a chart with an axis label and gridlines.

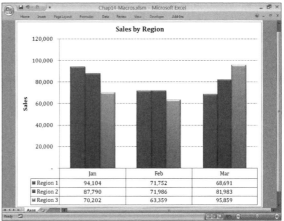

Extra

Gridlines mark major and minor intervals in your chart. For example, if your axis values run from 0 to 200,000, then major gridlines might appear at 20,000, 40,000, 60,000, and so on. Minor gridlines might appear at 2,000, 4,000, 6,000, and so on. Gridlines run either horizontally or vertically from the corresponding axis. You can use the Gridlines object to add both major and minor gridlines. The following code illustrates how to use the `HasMajorGridlines` property to turn on the gridlines, and how to customize the appearance of the gridlines with the `MajorGridlines` properties. Notice that the code customizes the appearance of the gridlines for the specified axis by using the `Border` object. You can use the following properties with the `Border` object: `Color`, `ColorIndex`, `LineStyle`, `Parent`, and `Weight`.

Example:
```
With Charts(1).Axes(xlValue)
        .HasMajorGridlines = True
        .MajorGridlines.Border.Color = RGB(0,255,0)
        .MajorGridlines.Border.LineStyle = xlDot
        .MajorGridlines.Border.Weight = xlThin
End With
```

Understanding Excel Events

An event occurs in Excel whenever the user performs any type of action. For example, the user closes the workbook. You can use events to trigger the execution of a procedure by creating an event-handling procedure. Event-handling procedures are procedures that execute when a particular event occurs.

There are five categories of events: workbook, worksheet, chart, UserForm, and application events. To trap or capture an event with an event-handling procedure, you must place the procedure code in the correct type of module. For example, workbook-related events must be in the `ThisWorkbook` object standard module.

Each event category has a set of events associated with it. For example, the `BeforeClose` event is a workbook event that is activated when the user chooses to close a workbook, before the workbook closes.

Workbook Events

Excel associates workbook-level events with the workbook in which they reside. You place workbook-level event procedures in the `ThisWorkbook` object module. You create workbook event procedures by naming them `Workbook_event` *Name*. The following table lists the workbook events.

EVENT	WHEN THE EVENT OCCURS
`Activate`	Occurs when Excel activates a workbook.
`AddinInstall`	Occurs when a workbook is installed as an add-in.
`AddinUninstall`	Occurs when a workbook is uninstalled as an add-in.
`AfterXmlExport`	Occurs after XML data saves or the export of XML data.
`AfterXMLImport`	Occurs after XML data is refreshed or imported.
`BeforeClose`	Occurs before a workbook closes. See the section "Run a Procedure before Closing a Workbook."
`BeforePrint`	Occurs before Excel prints a portion of a workbook.
`BeforeSave`	Occurs before Excel saves a workbook. See the section "Run a Procedure before Saving a Workbook."
`BeforeXmlExport`	Occurs before XML data saves or the export of XML data.
`BeforeXMLImport`	Occurs before XML data is refreshed or imported.
`Deactivate`	Occurs when Excel deactivates a workbook.
`NewSheet`	Occurs when Excel adds a new sheet to a workbook.
`Open`	Occurs when Excel opens a workbook. See the section "Run a Procedure as a Workbook Opens."
`PivotTableCloseConnection`	Occurs after a Pivot table report closes the data source connection.
`PivotTableOpenConnection`	Occurs after a Pivot table report opens the data source connection.
`Rowset Complete`	Occurs when a user drills through a recordset.
`SheetActivate`	Occurs when Excel activates a sheet in the workbook.
`SheetBeforeDoubleClick`	Occurs when a user double-clicks a sheet.
`SheetBeforeRightClick`	Occurs when a user right-clicks.
`SheetCalculate`	Occurs after Excel calculates a sheet.
`SheetChange`	Occurs when cells in a worksheet change.

Workbook Events *(continued)*

EVENT	WHEN THE EVENT OCCURS
SheetDeactivate	Occurs when Excel deactivates a sheet.
SheetFollowHyperlink	Occurs when a user clicks a hyperlink on a sheet.
SheetPivotTableUpdate	Occurs after Excel updates a sheet of a Pivot table report.
SheetSelectionChange	The selection changes in a worksheet.
Sync	Occurs when a local copy of a worksheet is synchronized with a copy on the server.
WindowActivate	Occurs when Excel activates a workbook window.
WindowDeactivate	Occurs when Excel deactivates a workbook window.
WindowResize	Occurs when Excel resizes a workbook window.

UserForm Events

Excel associates UserForm events not only with the form but also with the controls that exist on the form. Event-handling procedures related to a UserForm should be in the standard module for the UserForm object. The following table lists the UserForm events.

EVENT	WHEN THE EVENT OCCURS
Activate	Occurs when Excel activates a UserForm.
AddControl	Occurs when Excel adds a run-time control to a UserForm.
BeforeDragOver	Occurs when the user performs a drag-and-drop operation.
BeforeDropOrPaste	Occurs when the user is about to paste the data from the drag-and-drop operation.
BeforeUpdate	Occurs before a data control is changed.
Change	Occurs when the value property changes.
Click	Occurs when the user clicks on a UserForm object.
DblClick	Occurs when the user double-clicks a UserForm object.
Deactivate	Occurs when the user deactivates the UserForm.
Error	Occurs when Excel detects a UserForm control error.
KeyDown	Occurs when the user presses a key.
KeyPress	Occurs when the user presses an ANSI key. ANSI keys produce visible characters.
KeyUp	Occurs when the user releases a key.
MouseDown	Occurs when the user presses a mouse button.
MouseMove	Occurs when the user moves the pointer on the UserForm.
MouseUp	Occurs when the user releases the pointer.
QueryClose	Occurs when Excel closes the UserForm.
RemoveControl	Occurs when Excel removes a control from the UserForm at runtime.
Scroll	Occurs when the user repositions a scroll box on a control.
Terminate	Occurs when Excel terminates the UserForm.
Zoom	Occurs when the user zooms the UserForm.

continued ➡

Chart Events

Excel associates chart-level events with the currently selected chart sheet. Event-handling procedures related to a chart should be in the standard module for the `chart` object. The following table lists the chart events for which you can create event-handling procedures.

EVENT	WHEN THE EVENT OCCURS
Activate	Occurs when Excel activates a chart sheet.
BeforeDoubleClick	Occurs when the user double-clicks a chart sheet.
BeforeRightClick	Occurs when the user right-clicks a chart sheet. See the section "Run a Procedure When Right-Clicking a Chart."
Calculate	Occurs after Excel plots a chart.
Deactivate	Occurs when Excel deactivates a chart sheet.
DragOver	Occurs when the user drags a range of cells over a chart.
DragPlot	Occurs when the user drags and drops a range of cells onto a chart.
MouseDown	Occurs when the user presses a mouse button while over a chart.
MouseMove	Occurs when the position of the pointer changes over a chart.
MouseUp	Occurs when the user releases the mouse button over a chart.
Resize	Occurs when the user resizes a chart.
Select	Occurs when the user selects a chart element.
SeriesChange	Occurs when the user changes the value of a chart data point.

Worksheet Events

Excel associates worksheet-level events with the currently selected worksheet. Event-handling procedures related to a worksheet should be in the standard module for the worksheet object. The following table lists the worksheet events.

EVENT	WHEN THE EVENT OCCURS
Activate	Occurs when Excel activates a worksheet.
BeforeDoubleClick	Occurs when the user double-clicks a worksheet.
BeforeRightClick	Occurs when the user right-clicks a worksheet.
Calculate	Occurs after Excel calculates a worksheet.
Change	Occurs when a user or external link modifies cells on a worksheet. See the section "Monitor a Range of Cells for Changes."
Deactivate	Occurs when Excel deactivates a worksheet.
FollowHyperlink	Occurs when a user clicks a hyperlink on a worksheet.
PivotTableUpdate	Occurs after a PivotTable report is updated on a worksheet.
SelectionChange	Occurs when a selection changes on a worksheet.

Application Events

Application events include all events recognized by the Application object. To access an application event, create a class module to contain your application event-handling procedure code. See the section "Run a Procedure When Excel Creates a Workbook" for more information on placing event-handling code in a class module. The following table lists the application-level events that occur in Excel.

EVENT TYPE	DESCRIPTION
Application	An event that occurs for the application. For example, Excel triggers the NewWorkbook event when it creates a new workbook.
NewWorkbook	Occurs when Excel creates a new workbook. See the section "Run a Procedure When Excel Creates a Workbook."
SheetActivate	Occurs when Excel activates any sheet in any workbook.
SheetBeforeDoubleClick	Occurs when the user double-clicks any sheet.
SheetBeforeRightClick	Occurs when the user right-clicks any sheet.
SheetCalculate	Occurs when Excel calculates any worksheet.
SheetChange	Occurs when cells on a worksheet are changed by a user or an external link.
SheetFollowHyperlink	Occurs when a user clicks a hyperlink on a sheet.
SheetPivotTableUpdate	Occurs when Excel updates a worksheet of a PivotTable report.
SheetSelectionChange	Occurs when the selection changes on any worksheet.
WindowActivate	Occurs when Excel activates a worksheet window.
WindowDeactivate	Occurs when Excel deactivates a worksheet window.
WindowResize	Occurs when the user resizes a worksheet window.
WorkbookActivate	Occurs when the user activates a workbook.
WorkbookAddInInstall	Occurs when an add-in installs a workbook.
WorkbookAddInUninstall	Occurs when an add-in uninstalls a workbook.
WorkbookBeforePrint	Occurs when Excel prints an open workbook.
WorkbookBeforeSave	Occurs when Excel saves an open workbook.
WorkbookDeactivate	Occurs when Excel deactivates a workbook.
WorkbookNewSheet	Occurs when Excel adds a new sheet to an open workbook.
WorkbookOpen	Occurs when Excel opens a workbook.
WorkbookPivotTableClose Connection	Occurs after a PivotTable report closes the data source connection.
WorkbookPivotTableOpen Connection	Occurs after a PivotTable report opens the data source connection.

Run a Procedure as a Workbook Opens

Y ou can create a procedure that runs automatically each time a particular workbook opens. Because this type of procedure executes only when the workbook opens, it works well for opening other workbooks, determining if specific conditions are met, and displaying welcome messages. The procedure executes when the workbook opens by using the Workbook_Open event, which is triggered by the opening workbook.

To create a procedure that executes when a workbook opens, create a new procedure and add it to the ThisWorkbook object standard module for the workbook. All event-handling procedures for monitoring workbook events must reside in the ThisWorkbook object if you want Excel to execute them automatically. To create a procedure that executes when a workbook opens, name the procedure Workbook_Open.

Although the procedure resides in the ThisWorkbook object standard module, it can access other procedures in the same workbook. Therefore, you can create a Workbook_Open procedure that calls procedures in other modules.

If you want a procedure to execute whenever Excel opens, place the procedure in the ThisWorkbook object for the Personal Macro Workbook – Personal.xlsb. Because the Personal Macro Workbook always loads as a hidden workbook in Excel, any procedures in this workbook execute when Excel opens. Keep in mind, however, that Excel associates the Personal Macro Workbook with an individual user.

You can keep a Workbook_Open procedure from executing for a particular workbook by holding down the Shift key as the workbook opens. Because workbooks open quickly, make sure you press and hold the Shift key as you select the workbook.

Run a Procedure as a Workbook Opens

① Open Project Explorer.

② Double-click the ThisWorkbook node under the workbook to which you want to add a Workbook_Open event.

● The standard module for the ThisWorkbook object opens.

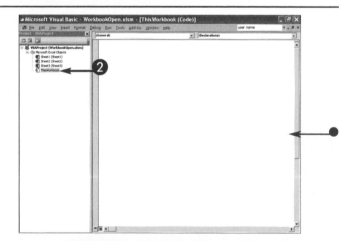

③ Click here and select the Workbook option.

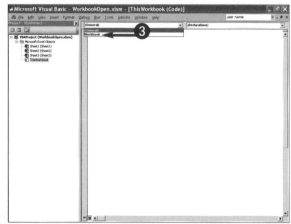

- The Visual Basic Editor creates a Private sub procedure and names it Workbook_Open.

4 Type the VBA code to run when the workbook opens.

- Displays the user's name.

5 Press Ctrl+S to save your workbook.

6 Close your workbook.

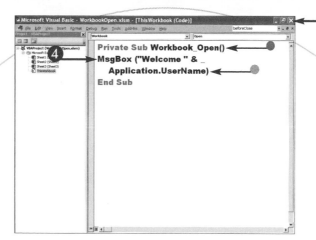

```
Private Sub Workbook_Open()
MsgBox ("Welcome " & _
       Application.UserName)
End Sub
```

7 Open the workbook you just closed.

The Workbook_Open procedure executes.

In this example, a welcome message appears.

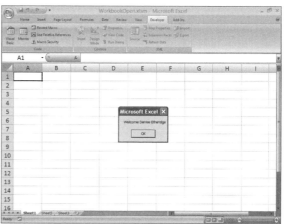

You can use the Workbooks collection object Open method of to specify the workbook that Excel should open along with the current workbook. For example, if your workbook relies on data values in another workbook, you can open the workbook your workbook relies on, whenever your workbook opens. See Chapter 9 for more information on using the Open method.

You can use the Object drop-down list in the Code window to create your Workbook_Open sub procedure. The Object drop-down list contains the objects for which you can create sub procedures in the current standard module. If you access the ThisWorkbook standard module, the only available object is Workbook.

When you select the Workbook object from the Objects drop-down list, the VBE automatically creates a private Sub procedure called Workbook_Open because the default event for the Workbook object is the Open event.

Run a Procedure before Closing a Workbook

You can create a `BeforeClose` event procedure that runs automatically before a particular workbook closes. If the user has made changes to the workbook, the event executes before Excel asks users if they want to save their changes. Because this type of procedure executes only as the workbook closes, it works well for recalculating, resetting the workbook back to default values, and even automatically saving the workbook.

To produce a procedure that executes when a workbook closes, create a new procedure and add it to the `ThisWorkbook` object standard module for the particular workbook. All event-handling procedures that you create for monitoring workbook events must reside in the `ThisWorkbook` object for Excel to execute them automatically. To create a procedure that executes

when a workbook closes, name the procedure `Workbook_BeforeClose`.

Although the procedure resides in the `ThisWorkbook` object standard module, it can access other procedures in the same workbook. Therefore, you can create a `Workbook_BeforeClose` procedure that calls procedures in another module.

The `BeforeClose` event has one parameter, `Cancel`. You can use the Cancel parameter to change what Excel does after the `BeforeClose` event completes. If the `Cancel` parameter has a value of `False`, which is the default, the workbook closes normally. If your procedure sets the value of the `Cancel` parameter to `True`, Excel cancels the closing process and does not close the workbook. You can set the `Cancel` parameter to `True` and then prompt the user for additional information before closing.

Run a Procedure before Closing a Workbook

① Open Project Explorer.

② Double-click the `ThisWorkbook` node under the workbook to which you want to add a `Workbook_Open` event.

● The standard module for the `ThisWorkbook` object opens.

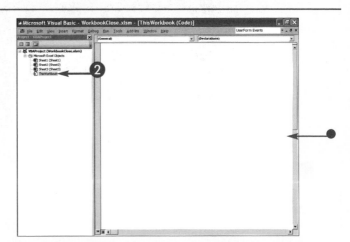

③ Click here and select Workbook.

④ Click here and select BeforeClose

● The Visual Basic Editor creates a new Private Sub procedure named Workbook_BeforeClose.

Delete the `Workbook_Open` Sub procedure if it appears.

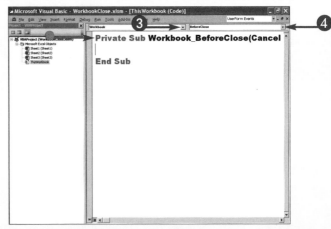

5 Type the VBA code that will run before the workbook closes.

6 Close the workbook.

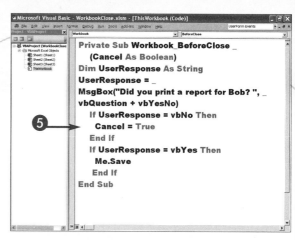

```
Private Sub Workbook_BeforeClose _
    (Cancel As Boolean)
Dim UserResponse As String
UserResponse = _
MsgBox("Did you print a report for Bob? ", _
vbQuestion + vbYesNo)
    If UserResponse = vbNo Then
        Cancel = True
    End If
    If UserResponse = vbYes Then
        Me.Save
    End If
End Sub
```

The `Workbook_BeforeClose` procedure executes.

In this example, Excel asks if you printed a report.

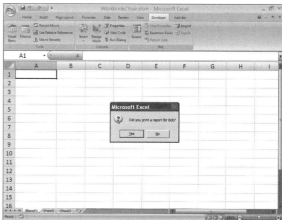

Extra

You can use the `Me` operator in standard modules for Excel objects. The `Me` operator references the object associated with the module. For example, code created in the `ThisWorkbook` object module links to the actual workbook object. When you use the `Me` operator, you reference the workbook object. Therefore, when you add the code `Me.Close` to a module, Excel closes the workbook. The code `Me.Close` is equivalent to using the `ThisWorkbook` object reference. You cannot use `Me` in a standard module. You can use the `Me` operator when working with UserForm modules. When used with a user form, the `Me` operator references the corresponding UserForm and not the controls that you have added to the UserForm.

If your procedure has made a change that affects all workbooks, you can use a `BeforeClose` event procedure to undo the change before the workbook closes. For example, if you have a procedure that loads an add-in, you can use the `BeforeClose` event procedure to unload the add-in before the workbook closes.

Run a Procedure before Saving a Workbook

You can create a BeforeSave event procedure that runs automatically before Excel saves a workbook. By creating a BeforeSave procedure, you can customize the save process. For example, when users select the Save or SaveAs option, you may want to ask if they have performed all required tasks.

To create a procedure that executes before saving a workbook, create a new procedure using the BeforeSave event and add it to the ThisWorkbook object standard module for the particular workbook. All event-handling procedures that you create for monitoring workbook events must reside in the ThisWorkbook object to have Excel execute them automatically. To create a procedure that executes before Excel saves the workbook, you name the procedure Workbook_BeforeSave.

Although the procedure resides in the ThisWorkbook object standard module, it can access other procedures in the same workbook. Therefore, you can create a Workbook_BeforeSave procedure that calls procedures in another module in the same workbook.

The BeforeSave event has two parameters that VBA passes to your procedure when the event triggers — SaveAsUI and Cancel. Use the SaveAsUI parameter to indicate whether the Save As dialog box displays during the Save command. Set the value of the SaveUI parameter to True to always display the Save As dialog box. Use the Cancel parameter to indicate whether the workbook saves. If the Cancel parameter has a value of False, Excel saves the workbook. The default value is False. If you set the value of the Cancel parameter to True, Excel does not save the workbook. From within the Workbook_BeforeSave procedure, you can set the value of the Cancel parameter to specify whether the workbook actually saves.

Run a Procedure before Saving a Workbook

1 Open Project Explorer.

2 Double-click the ThisWorkbook node under the workbook to which you want to add a Workbook_Open event.

The module for the ThisWorkbook object opens.

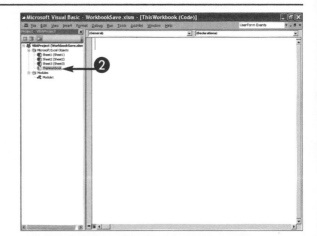

3 Create a Private Workbook_BerforeSave Sub procedure.

4 Click the Close button to close Project Explorer.

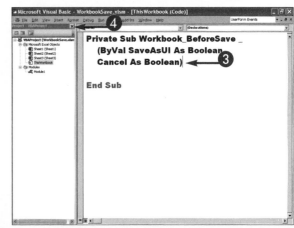

```
Private Sub Workbook_BeforeSave _
    (ByVal SaveAsUI As Boolean
    Cancel As Boolean)

End Sub
```

⑤ Type the VBA code that will run when the workbook saves.

⑥ Press Alt+F11 to switch from the VBE to Excel.

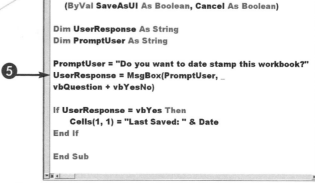

```
Private Sub Workbook_BeforeSave _
    (ByVal SaveAsUI As Boolean, Cancel As Boolean)

Dim UserResponse As String
Dim PromptUser As String

PromptUser = "Do you want to date stamp this workbook?"
UserResponse = MsgBox(PromptUser, _
vbQuestion + vbYesNo)

If UserResponse = vbYes Then
    Cells(1, 1) = "Last Saved: " & Date
End If

End Sub
```

⑦ Click the Save button to save the workbook.

The Workbook_BeforeSave procedure executes.

● In this example, the procedure prompts you, "Do you want to date stamp this workbook?"

● Click Yes if you want to date stamp your file.

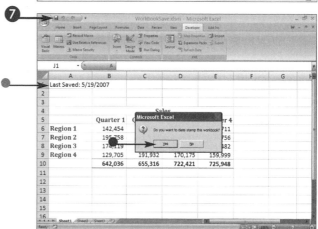

Extra

When you want to make sure that a variable in a procedure does not change the value of variables in other procedures, use the ByVal keyword. VBA uses the ByVal keyword. For example, the Workbook_BeforeSave Sub procedure includes a ByVal, SaveAsUI parameter. To aid in your understanding of ByVal, consider the following example, where the message box displays a value 10 because the value of TestVal in the Test2 Sub procedure is ByVal. Any changes to TestVal in the Test2 Sub procedure do not pass back to Test1.

Example:
```
Sub Test1()
    Dim TestVal As Integer
    TestVal = 10
    Call Test2(TestVal)
    MsgBox TestVal
End Sub


Sub Test2(ByVal TestVal)
    TestVal = 2598
End Sub
```

Run a Procedure When Excel Creates a Workbook

I f you have settings you apply to every workbook, you can use the NewWorkbook application event to set those setting every time you open a workbook. For example, when you open an Excel workbook, by default it contains three worksheets. If you always need five worksheets, you can create a NewWorkbook application event to create two additional worksheets.

The NewWorkbook application event executes a procedure whenever Excel opens a new workbook. The application triggers the NewWorkbook event. Because the event comes from the application and not from an individual object such as a workbook or chart, the process of creating an application event is a little more complex.

When working with application events, first create a class module. Excel only makes code in a standard module available to other modules in the same project or workbook. When you create a procedure for an application

event, you want all open projects to be able to access the code; therefore, you need to use a class module.

Because Excel does not recognize your application event code until the workbook containing the code opens, open the workbook containing the code first. You may want to consider adding the code to the Personal.xlsb workbook. The Personal.xlsb workbook opens whenever you open Excel, so the application event code activates as the workbook opens. See Chapter 1 for more information about the Personal Macro workbook.

In the class module, declare an event custom object by using the WithEvents keyword. The WithEvents keyword instructs Excel to notify you whenever the Application object triggers a NewWorkbook event. Use the Public keyword because you want all open projects to access this object variable. See Chapter 3 for more information on using the Public keyword.

Run a Procedure When Excel Creates a Workbook

① Click the workbook in which you want to add a NewWorkbook event.

② Click Insert → Class Module.

VBA creates a blank class module.

③ Press F4.

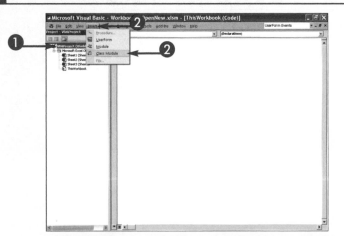

The Properties window opens.

④ Type a Name for your class module in the Name field.

⑤ Declare a public Application object using the WithEvents keyword.

6 Click here and select the name you typed in step 5.

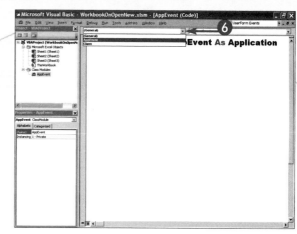

- VBA creates a Private `AppEvent_NewWorkbook` Sub procedure.

7 Type the code you want to execute when a new workbook opens.

8 In Project Explorer, double-click the `ThisWorkbook` node.

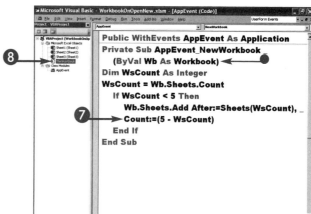

Extra

When you use the `WithEvents` keyword to declare a public Application object, the VBE creates a new object and adds it to the Object drop-down list. When you select this object, the Procedure box contains a list of all corresponding application events. To create a new event procedure, select the object from the Object drop-down list and the appropriate event from the Procedure drop-down list. The VBE creates a new Sub procedure with the appropriate arguments. For example, if your object is `AppEvent` and you select the `WindowActivate` event, the Editor adds the following code to the class module:

Example:
```
Private Sub AppEvent_WindowActivate(ByVal Wb As Workbook, ByVal Wn As Window)
```

You can use the Object Browser to find out more about a particular event by pressing F2 while in the VBE. Type the event you want to know about and click Search. The Object Browser displays a list of matching items. Excel indicates the Events with a small lightning bolt. If you click an event, the event syntax displays at the bottom of the Object Browser window.

continued

After you declare an event custom object by using the WithEvents keyword, use the NewWorkbook event to specify that the event executes when Excel creates a new workbook. The NewWorkbook event has one parameter, Wb, which passes into the Sub procedure. The Wb parameter contains the newly created workbook. You can access any of the methods and properties of the new workbook by using the Wb parameter. For example, you can use the Name property to return the name of the new workbook. See Chapter 9 for more information on working with the Workbook object.

Creating the NewWorkbook Sub procedure in the class module defines the code to run for the event but does not activate the code. To activate the Sub procedure, add code to a Workbook_Open procedure that activates the Application event procedure. Because the

Application event code is meant to work with all events generated by the application, you want to add a class module and the activation code in a workbook you open frequently, such as the Personal Macro workbook. See Chapter 1 to learn more about the personal macro workbook.

To activate the class module code, the module containing the activation procedure must contain a Dim statement, which declares an object of the type defined in the class module. Place the Dim statement at the top of the standard module. For example, Dim NewSheets As New AppEvent creates a new object variable of the type created in the class module. In a procedure, a Set statement actually activates the event. To make the Set statement execute automatically, place the Set statement in the Workbook_Open procedure.

The standard module opens for the ThisWorkbook object.

⑨ Declare an object variable using the Application object you created.

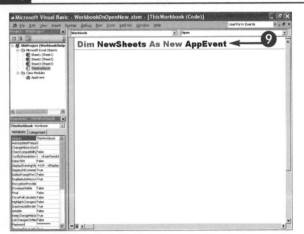

⑩ Create a private Workbook_Open Sub procedure.

⑪ Use a Set statement to activate your event.

⑫ Close and reopen Excel.

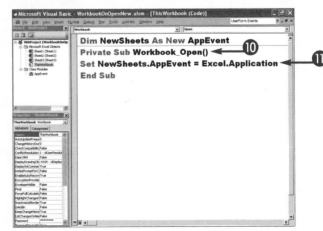

⑬ Open the workbook containing the `Workbook_open` Sub procedure.

⑭ Click the Office button and then click New.

⑮ Click Create.

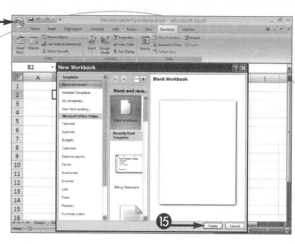

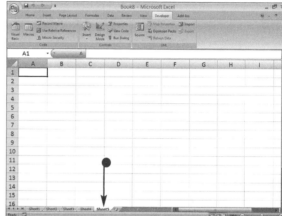

The event-handling procedure executes the code.

● In this example, the procedure adds two sheets to the new workbook.

Apply It

When you open the workbook containing the code that activates the application event, the code executes each time you trigger the event. You may find circumstances where you need to deactivate an event so that it no longer triggers. You can create a separate Sub procedure that you can call from within Excel at any point to cancel an event. Essentially, you set the property of the application object to `Nothing`, as shown in the following example:

TYPE THIS:

```
Sub CancelEvent()
Set OpenAppEvent.AppEvent = Nothing
End Sub
```

⬇

RESULT:

The code cancels the event for the current session of Excel. The next time you start Excel, the event is reactivated. Creating this type of Sub procedure so you can disable an event-handling procedure at any time is a good idea. You can also set the `EnableEvents` property to `False` for the `Application` object, as shown in this code:

TYPE THIS:

```
Sub CancelEvents()
Application.EnableEvents = False
End Sub
```

⬇

RESULT:

This code disables all event-handling procedures for the current session of Excel. The next time you start Excel, the event-handling procedures are reactivated.

Execute a Procedure at a Specific Time

You can create a procedure that executes at a specific time by using the OnTime event. For example, you can create a MsgBox, which reminds the user of an event 5 minutes before the event starts. Unlike most other events, the OnTime event is not associated with a specific object. You must access this event by using the OnTime method with the Application object.

The OnTime method has four parameters; only the first two are required: EarliestTime, Procedure, LatestTime, and Schedule. Use the EarliestTime parameter to specify the time at which the procedure executes. Use the Excel time-numbering system. Use the Procedure parameter to indicate the procedure to execute at the specified time. Enclose the procedure name in quotes.

Use the optional LatestTime parameter to indicate the latest time when the procedure can run. If the procedure has not run by the time specified by this parameter, it

will not run. The other optional parameter, Schedule, has a default value of True to schedule the OnTime procedure to run again at the specified time or False to clear a previously set procedure.

Because the OnTime event is not associated with a specific object, you can place a procedure containing the method for accessing the event in any standard module. If you place the OnTime method procedure in a standard module, you must run that module to activate the OnTime event code. You can also place the OnTime method in the Workbook_Open procedure so that the event code loads as the workbook opens. See the section "Run a Procedure as a Workbook Opens" for more information.

When using the OnTime event, you can use Excel's time-numbering system or you can use VBA's TimeValue function. Using VBA's TimeValue function simplifies the process.

Execute a Procedure at a Specific Time

CREATE AN ONTIME EVENT USING EXCEL'S TIME-NUMBERING SYSTEM

1. Name your procedure.

2. Create an OnTime event.

● This is the time the procedure will execute.

This will execute a procedure at 11:25 AM.

CREATE AN ONTIME EVENT USING VBA'S TIMEVALUE FUNCTION

1. Name your procedure.

2. Create an OnTime event.

● This is the time the procedure will execute.

This will execute a procedure at 11:25 AM.

● This is the procedure that will execute.

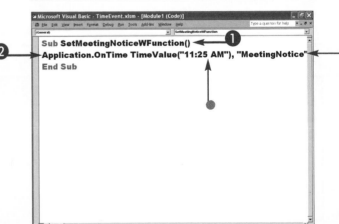

CREATE A PROCEDURE

1 Name your procedure.

2 Type the code that you want to execute.

○ This causes the computer to beep.

● This displays a message box.

3 Press Alt+F11 to switch from the VBE to Excel and run the macro.

Excel executes the procedure at the designated time.

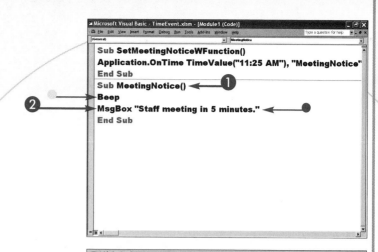

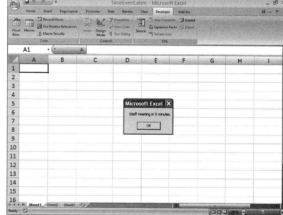

Extra

The `EarliestTime` and `LatestTime` parameters expect time values based on Excel's time-numbering system, which stores all times as decimal values ranging from 0.0 to 0.99999999. For example, Excel stores 12:00 noon as 0.5 and 6:00 PM as 0.75. Because fractional times can be overwhelming, VBA provides the `TimeValue` function with which you can convert a standard time into the decimal equivalent required. To use the `TimeValue` function, enclose the time you want to convert in quotes. For example, `TimeValue("5:45 PM")` converts 5:45 PM to the appropriate decimal value.

Another useful VBA time function is the `Now` function, which returns the current date and time. When you use the `Now` function in combination with a `TimeValue` function, you can specify how long before an event occurs. For example, to have an event take place in 30 minutes, express the time as follows:

Example:
```
Now + TimeValue("00:30:00")
```

Execute a Procedure When You Press Keys

You can use the OnKey event to create a procedure that executes when you press a specific key or combination of keys. For example, you can press Alt+S to sign and date a worksheet. To do this, you define the keys you want to use to execute an event. If you specify a key combination that Excel already uses, your new definition overrides the Excel combination.

Unlike most other events, the OnKey event is not associated with a specific object. For that reason, you access this event by using the OnKey method with the Application object.

The OnKey method has two parameters, Key and Procedure. Use the Key parameter to specify the key combination, which you express as a string consisting of the combined keys you capture. Represent standard keys, such as *a* and *5*, by simply typing the character for the

key. Specify nonstandard keys, such as Delete and Insert, by placing the key name in curly braces: {DELETE} or {INSERT}.

Use the Procedure parameter to indicate the name of the procedure to execute. Enclose the procedure name in quotes.

Because the OnKey event is not associated with a specific object, you can place your procedure containing the method for accessing the event in any standard module. However, if you place the OnKey method procedure in a standard module, you need to run the macro to activate the code. You can place the OnKey method in the Workbook_Open procedure so that it loads as the workbook opens. See the section "Run a Procedure as a Workbook Opens" for more information.

Execute a Procedure When You Press Keys

1 Double-click the ThisWorkbook node under the workbook to which you want to add a Workbook_Open event.

● The module for the ThisWorkbook object opens.

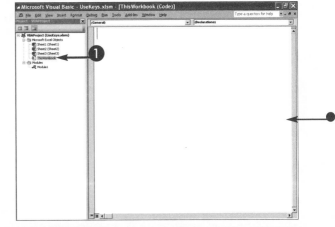

2 Click here and select the Workbook option.

● The Visual Basic Editor creates a Private Sub procedure and names it Workbook_Open.

Note: *See the section "Run a Procedure as a Workbook Opens" for information on the* Workbook_Open *procedure.*

3 Create your OnKey command.

● This is the Alt key.

See the Extra section of this task for more information.

● This is the name of the procedure you want to run.

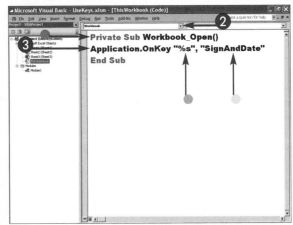

④ Create a Sub procedure with the same name you specified in step 3.

⑤ Type the code that you want to execute.

⑥ Press Alt+F11 to switch from the VBE to Excel and run the macro.

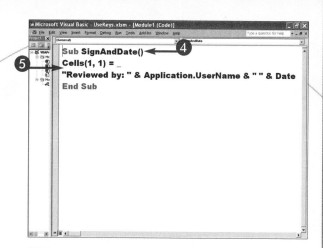

```
Sub SignAndDate()
    Cells(1, 1) = _
    "Reviewed by: " & Application.UserName & " " & Date
End Sub
```

When you press the designated keys. Excel executes the macro.

In this example, Excel places the user name and the date in cell A1.

Extra

When specifying keys that do not create a character, such as Delete or Down Arrow, enclose the name of the key in curly braces: {Delete} or {Down}. For some keys, Excel provides special characters to represent the key when you combine it with other characters:

CHARACTER	REPRESENTS
+	SHIFT
^	CTRL
%	ALT
~	ENTER

To reassign a particular key combination to its original meaning, omit the `Procedure` parameter:

TYPE THIS:

```
Application.OnKey._ "+^{LEFT}"
```

RESULT:

The custom key combination assignment is removed, and Excel executes the default command for that key combination, if one exists.

To use one of the special characters in your key combination, enclose the character in braces. For example, to specify a procedure to execute when you press the percent sign, type the following code:

TYPE THIS:

```
Application.OnKey "{%}", _
    "ExecutePercent"
```

RESULT:

Whenever the user presses %, the `ExecutePercent` procedure executes.

Create an Add-In

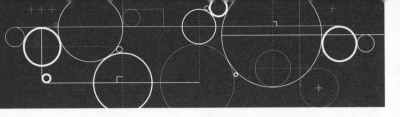

With add-ins, you can seamlessly integrate additional functionality into Microsoft Excel. You can create an add-in and distribute it to others. An add-in can contain user-defined functions, custom dialog boxes, Sub procedures, and a custom Ribbon. When you open the Insert Function dialog box, add-in functions appear in the User Defined category. You can select and use them just as you would any other functions. See Chapter 3 to learn more about functions. When you install an add-in, any key combinations you assign to a Sub procedure become available to the user.

You create an add-in by saving a workbook in the add-in format. When you attempt to save a workbook in add-in format, Excel suggests the AddIns folder in your user directory; for example, C:\Documents and Settings*user*\Application Data\Microsoft\AddIns. Saving

the file to this folder makes the add-in available to only the current user. To make the add-in available to others, save the file under the Office program in the Library folder. Excel gives Office 2007 add-ins an .xlam extension. After you save a workbook in add-in format, the worksheets in the workbook are no longer visible and users cannot make them visible by using the Unhide command. You can copy and paste information from the add-in workbook to other workbooks, but users cannot see or edit the sheets in the add-in workbook. In addition, the add-in workbook does not become a part of the Workbooks collection.

Before you convert a workbook to add-in format, you should thoroughly test it. Simulate how the macro will function by opening another workbook and executing the macros.

Create an Add-in

① Create the workbook you want to use as an add-in.

Make sure it is completely debugged.

② Click the Office button.

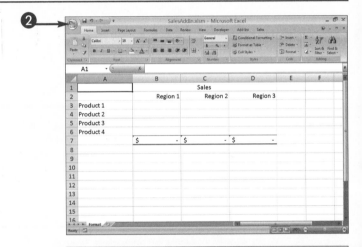

③ Click Save As.

④ Click Other Formats.

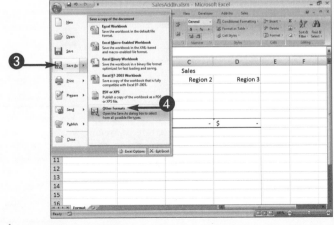

The Save As dialog box appears.

⑤ Click here and select Excel Add-In
(*.xlam).

Excel moves to the AddIns directory
for the user.

⑥ Type a name for your file.

⑦ Click Save.

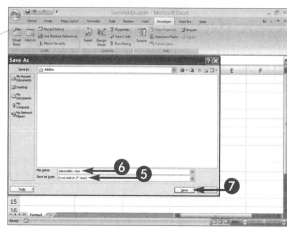

Excel creates your add-in.

Note that no worksheets appear
in the window.

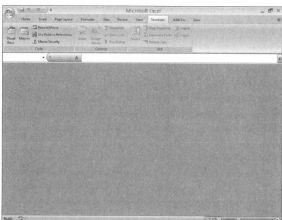

Extra

To distribute your add-in to others, give them
a copy of your XLAM file and tell them the
proper directory in which to install it. You should
password-protect your file. See the task "Set Add-In
Properties" to learn how to password-protect an
add-in file. You do not need to distribute copies of
your XLSM file.

You can open an add-in file by clicking the Office
button, clicking Open, locating the add-in, and then
clicking Open. The add-in opens; however, the name
of the macro does not appear on the title bar and
no worksheet appears. You can open another
worksheet and use the add-in. This is a great way to
test your macro before making it available to the
Add-Ins manager. When you save your add-in to the
office library or to a user's AddIns directory, the
add-in becomes available in the Add-ins section of
the Excel Option dialog box for you to load.

Set Add-in Properties

When you create an add-in, the sheets included in the add-in file are not visible to users; however, if users press F11 or click the Visual Basic button on the Developer tab of the Ribbon, they move to the VBE where they can view and modify your code. If you do not want users to modify your code, you must use the Project Properties dialog box to password-protect your code. Although password protecting provides some level of security, you should be aware that there are products on the market that can recover your password.

Use the General tab of the Project Properties dialog box to name and describe your add-in. The Project Name and description appear at the bottom of the View and Manage Microsoft Office add-ins pane and provide the user with brief introduction to your add-in before installing.

The sheets associated with an add-in workbook are not visible. If you want to view the sheets, open the Properties window in the VBE by pressing F4. If you then click `ThisWorkbook` in the Project Explorer, the properties for the workbook become available. If you set the `IsAddin` property to `False`, the sheets in your workbook become available.

All functions you create in an add-in file are normally available to users through the Insert Function dialog box whenever the add-in is available. If you create functions you intend to only be available to other functions or procedures, use the `Private` keyword when you create them. To learn more about the `Private` keyword, see Chapter 3.

Set Add-in Properties

NAME AND PASSWORD PROTECT

1 Click *Tools* → *Filename Properties*.

The Project Properties dialog box appears.

2 Click the General tab.

3 Type a project name.

4 Type a project description.

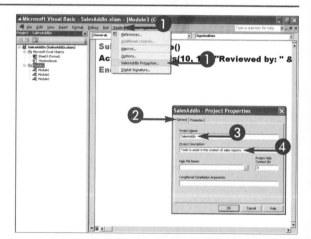

5 Click the Protection tab.

6 Select the Lock project for viewing option (☐ changes to ☑).

7 Type a password.

8 Type the password again.

9 Click OK.

VBA password-protects and adds a name and description to your project.

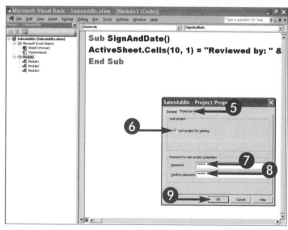

SET ISADDIN TO FALSE

1 Press F4.

Alternatively, click View → Properties Window.

The Properties window appears.

2 Click ThisWorkbook.

The workbook properties appear.

3 Set IsAddin to False.

The worksheets appear in the add-in.

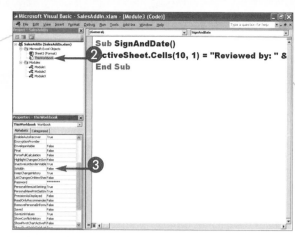

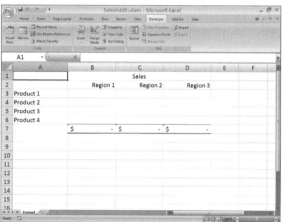

Extra

Before creating your add-in, a good idea is to add information to the Properties pane. Click the Office button, click Prepare, and then click Properties. The Properties pane appears. Type a title in the Title field, type a description in the Comments field, and then close the Properties pane.

In addition to the add-ins you create, you can obtain add-ins from third parties. To learn about special-purpose Excel add-ins in your field, perform a Google search by going to www.google. com. Your search terms should include Excel; the field of knowledge — for example, chemistry; and other information you might have, such as vendor name. Third-party vendors are responsible for supporting their own products.

As with macros, add-ins can spread viruses. For Excel to consider an add-in safe, the add-in must have a current valid digital signature issued by a certificate authority, and the developer of the add-in must be a trusted publisher. If the Excel Trust Center considers an add-in unsafe, it disables the add-in and displays a message bar to alert you to the potentially unsafe add-in. You can click the Options button on the message bar to enable the add-ins.

Install
Add-Ins

B undled add-in software is included with Excel, but Excel does not automatically install the software when you install Excel. The following are among the add-ins that come standard with Excel:

- The Conditional Sum Wizard enables you to create a formula that sums only the values that meet the criteria you specify.

- The Euro Currency Tools add-in enables you to calculate exchange rates between the Euro and other currencies.

- The Data Analysis Toolpak provides a number of tools you can use for statistical analysis.

- Solver enables you to produce the formula result you want by directly or indirectly adjusting cells related to the cell that contains the formula.

You install bundled add-ins and the add-ins you create by using the Excel Options dialog box. You can find all add-ins in the Add-Ins section. When you save an add-in to a user's AddIns folder or to the Library folder under the Office program, it becomes available for installation in the Excel Options dialog box. Once installed, the add-in is available right away.

You can download additional Excel add-ins from the Microsoft download site. For example, for Excel 2007, Microsoft has an add-in that adds a Get Started tab to the Excel 2007 Ribbon. The commands on this tab give you quick access to free online content to help you learn Excel 2007 quickly.

You can take advantage of third-party add-ins. Consult the developer of these programs for documentation.

Install Add-Ins

① Click the Office button.

A menu appears.

② Click Excel Options.

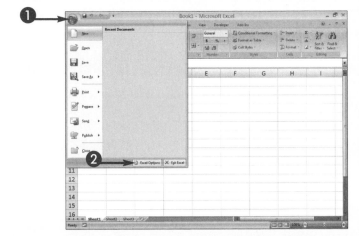

The Excel Options dialog box appears.

③ Click Add-Ins.

- The View and Manage Microsoft Office Add-Ins screen appears.

④ Click an add-in.

The example uses the Sales Report Helper add-in created earlier in this chapter.

⑤ Click Go.

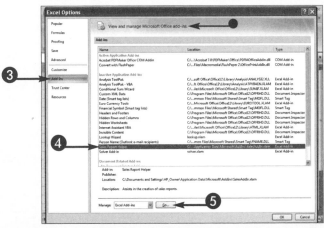

The Add-Ins dialog box appears and provides access to several options.

6 Click to select the add-in you want to install (☐ changes to ☑).

7 Click OK.

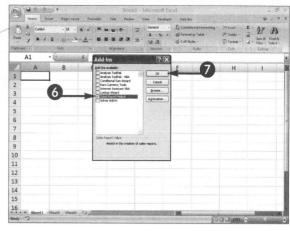

Excel installs the add-in.

● In this example, you know Excel installed the add-in because you can see the custom Ribbon tab.

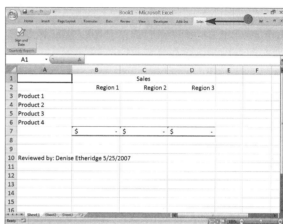

Extra

Removing an add-in from Excel is easy. Click the Office button, click Excel Options, click Add-ins, click the add-in you want to remove, and then click Go. The Add-Ins dialog box appears. Click to deselect the add-in you want to remove and then click OK. Excel removes the add-in.

The only way to remove an add-in from the Add-Ins section of the Excel Options dialog box is to delete the file from the folder in which it is stored. Then try to use the add-in. Excel realizes it is not there and deletes it from the Excel Options dialog box.

Microsoft has a set of SQL Server 2005 Data Mining add-ins for Office 2007 with which you to take advantage of SQL Server 2005's predictive analytics in Excel 2007. The add-ins are named Table Analysis. You can download these add-ins from the Microsoft Web site.

Using VBA to Load Add-Ins

If you want to add an add-in by using a procedure, use the Add method with an AddIn object. The Add method adds an add-in to the Excel Options dialog box. The Add method does not install an add-in. The following is the syntax for the Add method:

`expression.Add(Filename, Open)`

Use the expression to identify the add-in or a variable that represents the add-in. Use the Filename parameter to identify the add-in you want to add. If the file is located in the current folder, type the file name, enclosed in quotes. If the file is located in another folder, type the path to the file enclosed in quotes. If your add-in is located on a removable disk such as a floppy disk or a compact disc and you want to move the file from the

removable disk to the Library folder under the Office program, set the Open parameter to True. If you want the file to remain on the removable disk, set the Open parameter to False. If you do not include this parameter and your add-in is located on a removable disk, Excel displays a prompt asking the user if he or she wants to move the file to the hard drive. If your add-in is not located on a removable disk, VBA ignores the Open parameter.

As stated earlier, the Add method does not install an add-in. To install an add-in, you must set the Install property to True. You can add an add-in and install it in a single step by using the following syntax:

`AddIns.Add("Sample.xlam").Installed = True`

Using VBA to Load Add-Ins

① Name your procedure.

② Declare a variable as an AddIn object.

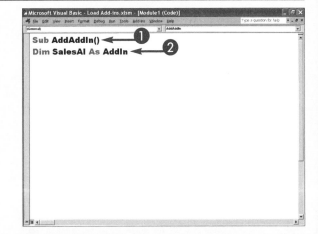

③ Add the add-in.

● This is the add-in file you want to add.

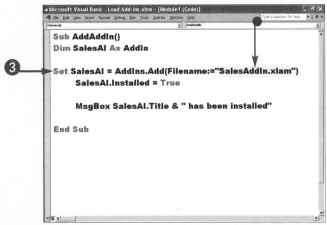

④ Display a `MsgBox` letting you know the add-in has been installed.

⑤ Press Alt+F11 to switch from the VBE to Excel, and run the macro.

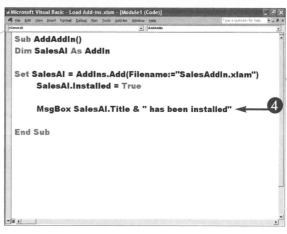

```
Sub AddAddIn()
Dim SalesAI As AddIn

Set SalesAI = AddIns.Add(Filename:="SalesAddIn.xlam")
    SalesAI.Installed = True

    MsgBox SalesAI.Title & " has been installed"   ◄── ④

End Sub
```

The macro installs the add-in and displays a message box.

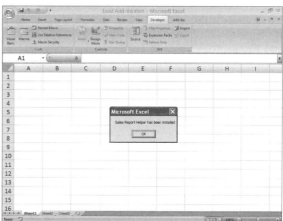

Extra

The Add-Ins dialog box tells you a lot about add-ins. To open the Add-Ins dialog box, click the Office button, click Excel Options, click Add-Ins, and then click Go. The Add-Ins dialog box appears. All of the add-ins available in Excel appear in the Add-Ins dialog box. Each add-in listed is part of the `AddIns` collection. You can reference Add-ins in the `AddIns` collection by their title or by their index value. You determine the index value by the order in which Excel lists the add-ins in the Add-Ins dialog box. The first add-in has an index value of 1, the second 2, and so on. The title of an add-in is the name listed in the Add-Ins dialog box.

You can reference the index value of an add-in or its title to uninstall the add-in. To uninstall an add-in, set the `Installed` property to `False`. The following example uninstalls an add-in.

Example:
```
Addins.("sample").Installed = False
```

Introducing XML

The default file format for Office 2007 is EXtensible Markup Language (XML). For this reason, as a VBA programmer, you should have a basic understanding of XML. The appeal of XML is that it makes exchanging data between different software applications and different computer systems easier. When you markup up your data using XML, it is then available to be processed by a variety of different systems, without regard to hardware or operating system. You can use the same XML data in Word, Excel, Access, and other programs. Prior to Office 2007, Office files were in a proprietary format. Manipulating and sharing the data with other applications and systems was difficult.

XML is similar to HyperText Markup Language (HTML), the language used to format data displayed in a Web page. If you are familiar with HTML, learning XML will be easy. Both HTML and XML are markup languages and, as such, they both use tags. In HTML, the tags are predefined; in XML, you define the tags.

XML and HTML have different purposes. You use HTML to format data so you can display your data in a Web page. You use XML to describe your data. Your XML tags can be anything you want them to be, but they should describe your data. Each XML tag describes the data contained in the tag.

You do not need to purchase any software to create an XML file; you can create XML in any text editor. For example, you can use Notepad to create an XML file. However, you must give your XML files an .xml file extension.

A complete explanation of XML is beyond the scope of this book. However, the brief overview of XML that follows provides a basic understanding of the examples provided in this book.

Declaration Statement

You start each XML file with a declaration. The declaration lets the program processing your file know that your file is an XML file. The following is an example of a declaration statement:

```
<?xml version="1.0" encoding="UTF-8 "standalone="yes" ?>
```

`Xml` identifies the file as an XML file, 1.0 is the version of XML used, `UFT-8` is the character set used to encode the data, and `standalone` tells the processing program whether the document contains references to other documents.

Tags

In XML, you call a unit of data an element. You use tags to describe each element. Angle brackets surround tags: < and >. In this example, `<CustomerName>Royal Flyers </CustomerName>`, `<CustomerName>`, and `</CustomerName>` are the opening and closing tags for the element. They tell you that Royal Flyers is the name of the customer. The opening tag marks the beginning of the element. The closing tag marks the end of the element. The closing tag always includes a forward slash. In addition, be aware that XML is case-sensitive. The tag `<UnitPrice>` is not the same as `<unitprice>`. Your opening tag and closing tag must be in the same case. You place your data between the opening tag and the closing tag. Every tag must include a closing tag or be an empty tag.

Attributes

You can include attributes within an XML tag. Attributes provide information to the program that is manipulating the data. The following is an example of a tag that includes a `FileType` attribute.

```
<CustomerName FileType ="J5793" > Royal Flyers
</CustomerName>
```

You must enclose attributes in quotes. You can use single quotes or double quotes. An element can have multiple attributes.

Empty Tags

Empty tags are tags that do not have any content. Empty tags do not require a closing tag. However, empty tags must include a forward slash as part of the tag. The following is an example of an empty tag.

Example:
```
<button id="Button1" imageMso="AccessFormWizard"
size="large" label = "Report Format"
onAction= "ThisWorkbook.SignAndDate" />
```

In the example, the element has attributes but no content. You use the element to pass information to the reading program.

Structure

You structure XML hierarchically. Consider the following example:

```
<CustomerInfo>

    <CustId>C001</CustId>

    <CustomerName>Royal Flyers</CustomerName>

    <TransDate>2007-06-01</TransDate>

        <PurchaseInfo>

            <Quantity>12</Quantity>

            <ItemNo>OS-001</ItemNo>

            <Description>Pencils</Description>

            <UnitPrice>3.99</UnitPrice>

        </PurchaseInfo>

        <PurchaseInfo>

            <Quantity>6</Quantity>

            <ItemNo>OS-004</ItemNo>

            <Description>Paper</Description>

            <UnitPrice>25.98</UnitPrice>

        </PurchaseInfo>

</CustomerInfo>
```

The data between the CustomerInfo tags contains information about a single customer. The file can contain multiple customers. The information between the PurchaseInfo tags contains information about an individual purchase. In the example, a single customer made two purchases, so the PurchaseInfo tags are inside the CustomerInfo tags. Shown graphically, you can structure data as follows:

```
CustInfo

    Customer 1

        Purchase 1

        Purchase 2

    Customer 2

        Purchase 1

CustInfo
```

Every XML file must have a set of root tags. The root tags describe the document and surround the child tags. Every document ends with a root tag. In the example, <CustomerInfo> and </CustomerInfo> are root tags. All of the tags between the <CustomerInfo> tags are child tags.

When structuring your XML file, you must properly nest your tags. In the example, you must close each purchase before you start a new purchase.

If you want to exchange your data with other systems, your XML file must be well formed. If your data is not well formed, your XML file will not work. Well-formed XML files comply with the following rules:

- They begin with a declaration.
- They contain a root tag.
- Every tag either has a closing tag or is an empty tag.
- Opening and closing tags use the same case.
- Tags are properly nested.
- Attributes are enclosed in either single or double quotes.

Element Names

You can name elements anything you want; however, element names should describe your data. Element names must also conform to the following rules:

- Names can contain letters, numbers, and other characters.
- Names cannot contain spaces.
- Names cannot start with the letters XML, a number, or a punctuation character.
- You can use an underscore to separate the words in a name, as in Customer_Information.

You should try to keep your element names short and, although it is allowed, avoid using the "—" and the "." in your element names. If you create an element name such as Customer-Info, the reading program may try to subtract Customer from Info; if you create a name such as Customer.Info, the reading program may think Info is a property of customer.

Schemas

Schemas are another important component of XML. Schemas contain the rules that help the processing program validate your data. For example, a schema tells the processing program whether a tag should contain text or a number. In that way, the schema prevents the entry of invalid data. For example, if data between your LastName tags should always be a string, a schema prevents the entry of numbers.

If you are importing an XML file into Excel, and your XML file does not have a schema, Excel creates one. Excel maps the items in cells to the items in the schema. Mapping allows you to display in your worksheet only the data you want to see. It also allows you to refresh your data and save your data in XML format.

Understanding Excel XML Files

Prior to Office 2007, by default, Office files were saved as binary files in a proprietary format. You can still save your files in the binary format by saving them as Excel 97-2003 files if you need to share files with users who do not have Office 2007. However, the binary file type is no longer the default. Moreover, when you save your file as an Excel 97-2003 file, Office 2007 features that are not supported in earlier versions are lost.

In Office 2007, the default file type is based on XML. The XML file format has several advantages.

- XML files are smaller. The XML file format uses Zip technology, which compresses the files. As a result, when you compare XML files to binary files, the XML files can be up to 75 percent smaller. This

means they take up less space and are easier to transfer via mechanisms such as e-mail.

- XML files are more secure. In the default XLSX format, you cannot include macros. This gives you assurance that your XLSX files do not include any malicious macro viruses. If you want to save macros in your Excel file, you must save the file with an .xlsm extension. Excel places the macros in a separate part of the file that is more secure.

- Data is easier to recover in XML files. XML files are human-readable. You can open the files and read the contents by using a text editor such as Notepad. If part of the file becomes corrupted, you can open the file and recover the part that is not corrupted.

Understanding Excel XML Files

CREATE AND SAVE AN EXCEL FILE

1 Create an Excel file.

- Include an Image.

- Include a comment.

- Include data.

- Include properties.

2 Click the Save button to save the file.

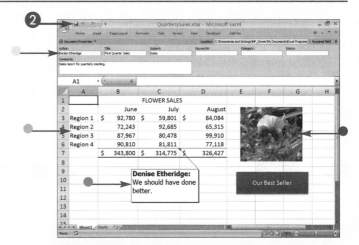

OPEN AN EXCEL FILE

1 In Windows Explorer, move to the folder where you saved your file.

2 Right-click the file name.

3 Click Rename.

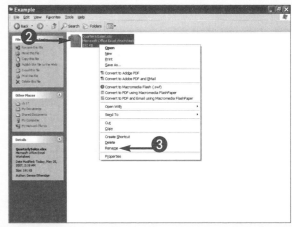

④ Change the file extension to .zip.

Windows asks if you are sure you want to change the file extension. Click Yes.

⑤ Double-click the file.

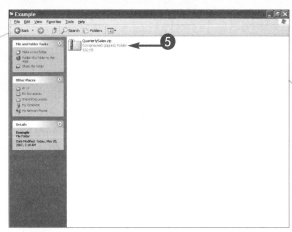

The file opens.

● The _rels folder stores information about relationships.

● The [Content_Types].xml part stores information about what is in the package.

● The xl folder stores the workbook component files.

● The docProps folder stores information about the document properties.

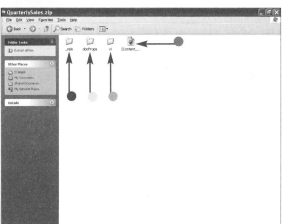

Extra

To assign properties to a file, click the Office button, click Prepare, and then click Properties. The Properties pane appears in your workbook. Enter the properties you want to enter. In the upper-right corner of the Properties pane, click Document Properties, and then click Advanced Properties. The Properties dialog box appears. You can use the Properties dialog box to review properties and to add custom properties.

If you have a computer with Excel 97-2003 installed, you can go to the Office Update Web site and download the 2007 Microsoft Office system Compatibility Pack for Excel. After you install the Compatibility Pack, you can open Excel 2007 files in Excel 97-2003. Excel features and formatting may not display in the earlier version, but they are still available when you open the file again in Excel 2007.

To view the contents of an Excel workbook file, change the file extension to .zip and then double-click the file. To use the file again, change the extension back to the extension the file originally had.

continued →

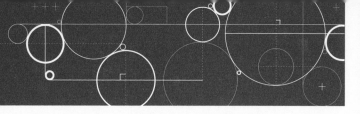

I f you want to see the XML layout for an Excel 2007 file, change the file extension on the Excel file to .zip and then double-click the file. The file opens and several folders and files appear.

Office 2007 files are in a compressed ZIP format; each ZIP file is called a package. A package has three major components: Part Items, Content Type Items, and Relationship Items.

Each file inside a package is called a part. When you open an Excel file, a workbook.xml file is in the xl folder. You may also find a styles.xml file. These files are "parts" of the package. Most parts are XML files that describe the data contained in the Excel workbook.

Excel uses content type items to describe the contents of a part. These descriptions enable you to determine the

contents of a file so you can write code that correctly processes the file.

Relationships define how the parts of a document come together to form a document. The relationships are stored in the /_rels folders in .rels files in the root and in subdirectories of the file.

Excel divides a workbook package into several parts. Some of the parts you may see in a package are charts, comments, themes, styles, and workbook drawings. You can manually modify and replace document parts, and you can write programs to modify and replace document parts.

If your document includes images, the actual images are stored in the file. For security proposes, the images are named image1, image2, and so on.

Content Type.xml

XML FILE

1 Double-click Content_Type.xml.

The file opens in Internet Explorer or your default XML Editor.

_RELS FILE

1 Double-click the _rels folder to open it.

The .rels file appears.

2 Double-click the .rels in the file.

The file opens in Internet Explorer.

The file sets relationships.

XL FILE

❶ Double-click the xl folder to open it.

A number of files and folders appear.

❷ Double-click each part and examine it.

This example opens the media folder and then opens the image file.

DOCPROPS FILE

❶ Double-click the docProps folder.

❷ Double-click the parts and examine them.

The document properties appear.

This example opens the core XML file.

Extra

For a detailed explanation of the concepts presented in this section, download "Introducing the Office (2007) Open XML File Formats" (http://msdn2.microsoft.com/en-us/library/aa338205.aspx) from the Microsoft Web site.

You can modify the contents of an Excel package. In the example, you opened the media folder and viewed the image in your Excel document. If you want to change the image, you can take out the image that is in the file and replace it with a new image manually or by using a program. You can also change the text in the document manually or by using a program. For example, if you open a comment file, you will see comments. If you change a comment, the new comment will appear when you open your workbook in Excel again.

As you can see, the XML file format gives you a great deal of flexibility by making your files easy to modify.

Open an XML File in Excel as a Table

I f your Excel data consists of columns and rows, you can convert your data to a table. In Excel, tables allow you to manipulate your data easily. Each column heading in a table contains a down arrow. Use the down arrow to sort, filter, and otherwise manipulate your data. Having your data in an Excel table greatly enhances your ability to work with your data.

If you have data that is in well-formed XML format, you can easily open the XML file in Excel as a table and then use Excel to manipulate the data. To find out more about well-formed XML format, see the section "Introducing XML".

Excel needs a schema to import your XML data. Schemas enable processing programs such as Excel to validate your data. For example, a schema tells the processing

program whether a particular element should contain text or a number. When you open an XML file, if your data does not have a schema, Excel creates one. Excel infers the schema from the data that is contained in the XML file.

When you open an XML file as a table, Excel also creates an XML map. Excel uses the map to relate the schema to the data in the worksheet. A single workbook can contain several XML maps, and several maps can refer to the same schema.

Excel creates a graphical hierarchical representation of your data in the XML Source task pane when it opens your XML file as a table. Open the Source pane to see the representation.

Open An XML File in Excel

① Click the Office button.

② Click Open.

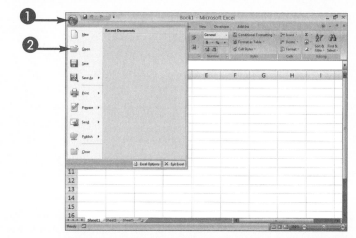

The Open dialog box appears.

③ Locate the folder that contains your XML file.

④ Click the file.

⑤ Click Open.

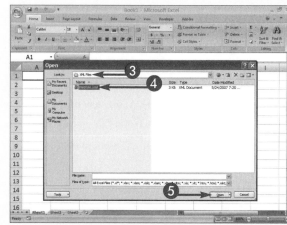

The Open XML dialog box appears.

6 Click As an XML table (○ changes to ⊙).

If Excel asks if you want to create a schema, click Yes.

7 Click OK.

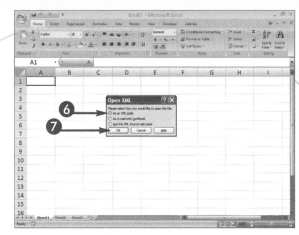

The file appears in Excel as an Excel table.

8 Click the Developer tab.

9 Click Source.

The map to your data appears.

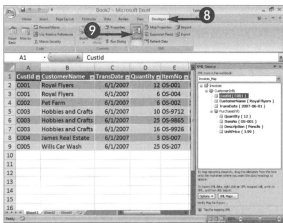

Extra

The Open XML dialog box presents three choices. You can open the file as an XML table, as a Read-Only workbook, or as a read-only file, or you can use the XML Source task pane. The As an XML table task option is explained in this section. The As a read-only workbook opens the file as read-only and does not create a map to your data. The Use the XML Source task pane option creates a map but does not place any elements in your worksheet. For details on how to work with an XML map, see the section "Create an XML Map".

When you import or open an XML file, if the file does not have a schema, Excel creates one for you. To view the schema, click the Developer tab and then click Visual Basic to open the VBE. Once in the VBE, press Ctrl+G to open the Immediate window. In the Immediate window, type Print activeworkbook.XmlMaps(1).Schemas(1).xml. VBA prints the schema to the Immediate window. You can copy and paste it into a text or XML editor.

Create an
XML Map

When you open your file as an Excel table, Excel places all of your data in your worksheet, and you can use the table features in Excel to manipulate your data. You can also create a map to map just the elements you want to use to your worksheet. You complete the process in three steps: create a map, map the elements you want to use to your worksheet, and then refresh your data.

When you use the mapping method, you choose which elements you want to appear in your worksheet. This is especially useful when your XML file has a large number of elements and you only want to work with a subset of those elements. Click on an element in the XML Source task pane and then drag the element onto your worksheet. Excel calls the list of data elements in the XML Source task pane a map, and the process of clicking and dragging elements to your worksheet is mapping. Excel creates a connection between the element in the XML Source task pane and your data. If you want to see the connection after you place an element in your worksheet, click the element in the Source task pane and Excel highlights the data in your worksheet. If you click data in your worksheet, Excel highlights the element name in the XML Source task pane.

When you create a map and then bring your data into Excel, you gain the same benefits as when you open a file in XML format. You can use all of Excel's table features to sort and filter your data.

Create an XML Map

① Click the Developer tab.

② Click Source.

The XML Source task pane appears.

③ Click XML Maps.

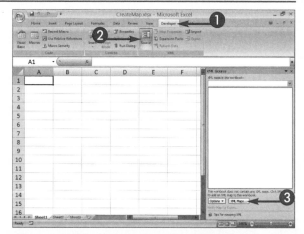

The XML Maps dialog box appears.

④ Click Add.

The Select XML Source dialog box appears.

⑤ Locate the folder that contains the file you want to map.

⑥ Click the file.

⑦ Click Open.

If Excel asks if you want to create a schema, click Yes.

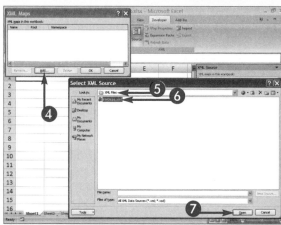

- Excel creates your map.

⑧ Click OK.

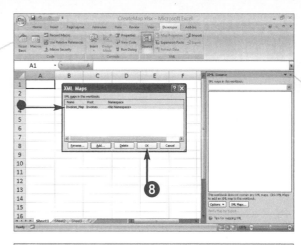

Excel adds a map to the XML Source task pane.

⑨ Click and drag elements from the XML Source task pane to your worksheet.

⑩ Click Refresh Data.

- Excel adds the data in your XML file to your worksheet.

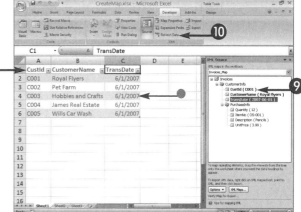

Extra

After you add an element from your XML file to your Excel worksheet, you may want to delete it. If so, right-click the field heading, click Delete, and then click Delete Columns. Excel deletes the column. If you want to remove the connection between the XML map and your worksheet, right-click the item in the XML Source task pane and then click Remove Element. If you want to restore a connection, right-click the item in the XML Source task pane and then click Map Element. The Map XML Elements dialog box appears. Type the cell address where you want to place the field heading and then click OK.

You can copy and paste your mapped table, but your copy will not have a connection to your map. However, if you move your mapped table by cutting and pasting, your table maintains its connection to the XML map.

Import and Export
XML Files Using Excel

When working with XML data, the data in the XML file may change or you may want to import the additional data. Conversely, you may make changes to the data and want to export the changes to an XML file. If you want to import and export XML data into and out of Excel, use the Import and Export features on the Developer tab. The Import feature opens the Import dialog box, where you can choose the file you want to import. The Export feature opens the Export dialog box, where you can name the file you are exporting.

Importing data enables you to either overwrite your current data or append data to your table. You can use the XML Map Properties dialog box to specify which you want to do. The default is to overwrite existing data with new data. If the system outputting the data has corrected

the data or if your old data is no longer relevant, overwriting your data is the better choice. If the system outputting the data outputs data periodically, appending data is the better choice. Appending data enables you to keep your database up-to-date.

You can export data in XML format by using the Export feature on the Developer tab. When you export data, all of the data must be from a single node in your XML map. If you want to verify that Excel can export your data, click Verify Map for Export on the XML Source task pane before exporting. Excel exports your data as a well-formed XML file. A well-formed XML file adheres to all the rules for creating XML files. For more information about well-formed files, see the section "Introducing XML".

Import and Export XML Files

IMPORT AN XML FILE

1 Click the Developer tab.

2 Click Import.

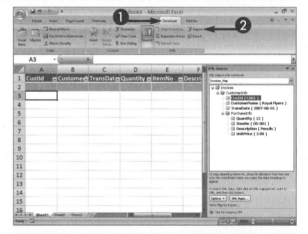

The Import XML dialog box appears.

3 Locate the folder where the file you want to import is located.

4 Click the file you want to import.

5 Click Import.

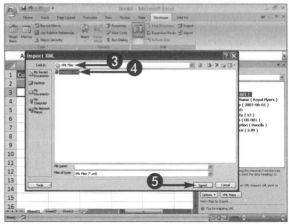

Excel imports the XML data.

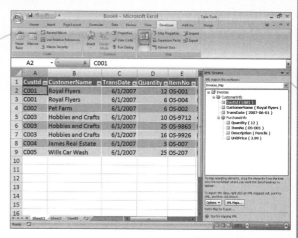

EXPORT AN XML FILE

① Click the Developer tab.

② Click Export.

The Export XML dialog box appears.

③ Locate the folder where you want to save the file.

④ Type a file name.

⑤ Click Export.

Excel exports the file.

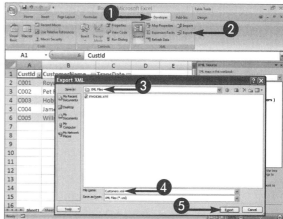

Extra

When you import or refresh data, you can either overwrite your current data or append data. Use the XML Map properties dialog box to specify which you want to do. To open the XML Map properties dialog box, click the Developer tab, and then click Map Properties in the XML group. The overwrite and append options are at the bottom of the dialog box.

The XML Source task pane has several options you can set by clicking the Options button in the lower-left corner. Select the Preview Data in Task Pane option to see a sample of the data elements in your XML file in the task pane. Select the Hide Help Text in the Task Pane to prevent Help from appearing at the bottom of the task pane. Select Automatically Merge Elements When Mapping to create a single table when you place elements side by side in a single row in the worksheet.

Load XML Files Using VBA

If you want to automate the process of loading XML data, use the OpenXML method. OpenXML is the VBA equivalent to opening an XML file as a table. When you open an XML file as a table, OpenXML provides several choices. Make your choice by specifying one of the following XlXmlLoadOption options: xlXmlLoadImportToList, xlXmlLoadMapXml, or xlXmlLoadPromptUser.

If you select the xlXmlLoadImportToList option, VBA creates a map of your data, places the map in the XML Source task pane, and then places all of your XML data in a worksheet formatted as a table.

If you select the xlXmlLoadMapXml option, VBA creates a map of your data and places the map in the XML Source task pane. Excel does not place any data in a worksheet.

If you select the xlXmlLoadPromptUser option, VBA displays the Open XML dialog box. The user can choose

to open the XML file as a table or as a read-only workbook or to use the XML Source task pane. Opening the file as a table is equivalent to the xlXmlLoadImportToList option. Using the XML Source task pane is equivalent to the xlXmlLoadMapXml option.

The following is an example of the OpenXML method:

```
Sub OpenXMLPromptUser()

    Application.Workbooks.OpenXML _

        Filename:"invoices.xml", _

        LoadOption:=xlXmlLoadPromptUser

End Sub
```

Use the FileName parameter to specify the name of the file you want to load. If the file is not located in the current folder, specify the path to the folder.

Load XML Files using VBA

① Name your procedure.

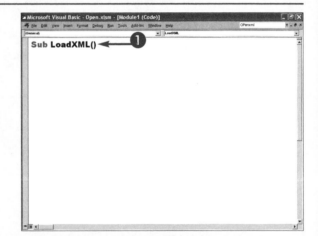

② Create your OpenXML command.

● This is the file you want to load.

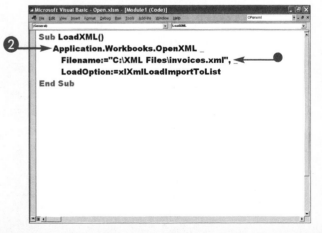

- This is the Load option you want to use.

3 Press Alt+F11 to switch from the VBE to Excel, and run the macro.

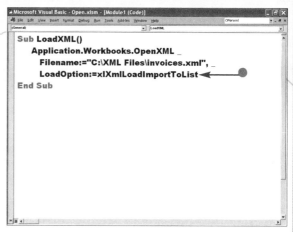

The macro loads the XML file.

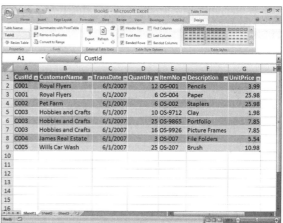

Extra

If you want to use VBA to create a document map, use code similar to the following:

```
Sub CreateMap()
'Create an XmlMap object
Dim InvMap As XmlMap
'Add a map and assign the map to the XmlMap Object
Set InvMap = Application _
     .Workbook(1) _
     .XmlMaps.Add("C:\XML Files\invoices.xml")
'Name the Map
InvMap.Name = "Invoices"
```

Import XML Files Using VBA

You can use the `XmlImport` method to load data into a map that already exists. This process is similar to clicking the Import button on the Developer tab. You can refresh your data or import new data into your worksheet. The `XmlImport` method has the following parameters: `Url`, `ImportMap`, `Overwrite`, and `Destination`.

The `Url` parameter is required. Use this parameter to target a URL as a data source. Insert the URL as a string enclosed in double quotes. You can also use this parameter to target a file on your local computer. If the file is located in the current directory, type the file name; otherwise, type the path.

The `ImportMap` parameter is also required. For this parameter, supply the schema map you want VBA to use. You can identify the map by name. When you create a

map, Excel assigns it a name. The name appears in the drop-down list at the top of the XML Source task pane. You can also view the list of XML maps in your workbook by clicking the XML Maps button in the XML Source task pane. If you want Excel to create the map, assign `Nothing` to the parameter, as in `ImportMap:=Nothing`.

Use the `Overwrite` parameter to specify whether you want to overwrite the existing data. Set the parameter to `True` if you want to overwrite the data. Set the parameter to `False` if you want to append to the existing data. `True` is the default value.

Use the `Destination` parameter to specify the top-left corner of the range where you want to create the table. If you are importing data into a map that already exists, do not set this parameter.

Import XML Files using VBA

① Create a map and place the elements in your worksheet.

Note: To learn how to create a map, see the section "Create an XML Map."

● This is the name of your map.

② Press Alt+F11.

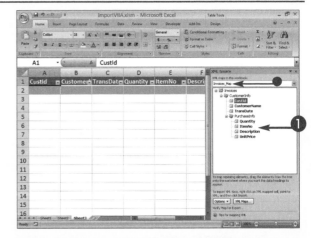

Excel moves you to the VBE.

③ Name your procedure.

④ Declare a variable as an `XmlMap` object.

⑤ Assign your map the `XmlMap` object variable.

● This is the map name.

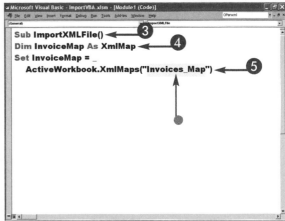

6. Create your XmlImport command.

● This is the file location.

● This is the map you want to use.

7. Press Alt+F11 to switch from the VBE to Excel, and run the macro.

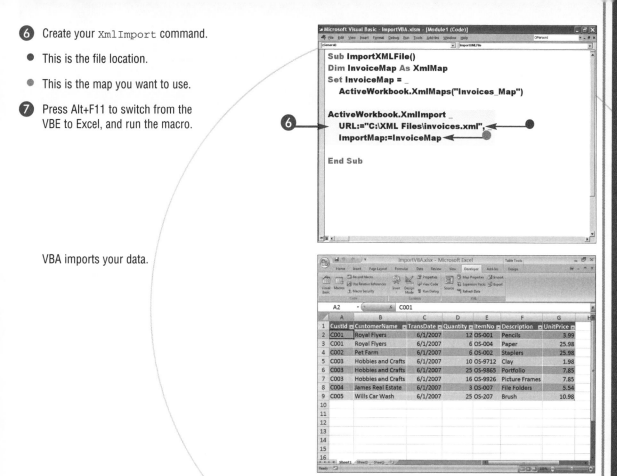

VBA imports your data.

Extra

As an alternative to the syntax in the example, you can use the following syntax to import an XML file. This syntax uses the XMLMaps Import method. The second parameter is Overwrite. Setting the Overwrite parameter to False causes the command to append instead of overwriting data.

Example:
```
Sub
     ActiveWorkbook _
     XMLMaps("Invoices_Map") _
     .Import "C:\XML Files\Invoices.xml", _
     False
End Sub
```

VBA and Excel Object Model Quick Reference

VBA Statements Quick Reference

Legend

Plain courier text = required

Italics = user-defined

[] = optional

. . . = list of items

| = or

File and Folder Handling

STATEMENT	DESCRIPTION
ChDir *path*	Changes to the specified folder location.
ChDrive *drive*	Changes to the specified drive.
Close [*filenumber*]	Closes a file opened by using an Open statement.
FileCopy *source, destination*	Copies a file from the source to the specified destination.
Kill *pathname*	Deletes files from a disk. Use wildcards * for multiple characters and ? for single characters.
Lock [#]*filenumber*[, *recordrange*]	Locks all or a portion of an open file to prevent access by other processes.
MkDir path	Creates a new directory or folder.
Open pathname For mode [Access access][lock] As [#]filenumber [Len=reclength]	Opens the specified file to allow input/output operations.
Print #*filenumber*[, *outputlist*]	Writes display-formatted data sequentially to a file.
Put [#]*filenumber,* [*recnumber,*] *varname*	Writes data contained in a variable to a disk file.
Reset	Closes all files opened using the Open statement.
RmDir *path*	Removes the specified folder.
SetAttr *pathname, attributes*	Sets the attribute information for the specified file.
Unlock [#]*filenumber*[, *recordrange*]	Unlocks a file to allow access by other processes.
Width #*filenumber, width*	Assigns the output line width for a file opened using the Open statement.
Write #*filenumber*[, outputlist]	Writes data to a sequential text file.

Interaction

STATEMENT	DESCRIPTION
AppActivate *title*[, *wait*]	Activates an application window.
DeleteSetting *appname, section*[, *key*]	Deletes a section or key setting from an application's entry in the Windows Registry
SaveSetting *appname, section, key, setting*	Saves an application entry in the application's entry in the Windows Registry.
SendKeys *string*[, *wait*]	Sends one or more keystrokes to the active window as if they were typed on the keyboard.

Program Flow

STATEMENT	DESCRIPTION
[Public | Private] Declare Sub name Lib "libname" [Alias "aliasname"] [([arglist])]	Declares a reference to an external DLL library function.
Do [{While | Until} *condition*] [*statements*] Loop	Repeats a block of statements while or until a condition is true. The condition is checked at the beginning of the loop.
Do [*statements*] Loop [{While | Until} *condition*]	Repeats a block of statements while or until a condition is true. Because the condition is checked at the end of the loop, the block of statements always executes at least once.
Exit Do | For | Function | Property | Sub	Exits the specified Do Loop, For Next, Function, Sub, or Property code.
For Each *element* In *group* [*statements*] Next [*element*]	Repeats a block of statements for each element in an array or collection.
For *counter* = *start* To *end* [Step *step*] [*statements*] Next [*counter*]	Repeats a section of code the specified number of times.

[Public | Private | Friend] [Static] Function *name* [(*arglist*)] [As *type*]
    [*statements*]
    [*name* = *expression*]
End Function
	Defines a procedure that returns a value.

If *condition* Then
[statements]
 	
[ElseIf *condition-n* Then]
[*elseifstatements*]]
 	
[Else [*elsestatements*]]
 	
End If
	Conditionally executes a block of statements based upon the value of an expression.

[Public | Private | Friend] [Static] Property Get *name* [(*arglist*)] [As *type*]
    [*statements*]
    [*name* = *expression*]
 	
End Property
	Declares the name and arguments associated with a procedure.

[Public | Private | Friend] [Static] Property Let *name* ([*arglist*,] *value*) [*statements*] End Property	Declares the name and arguments of a procedure that assigns a value to a property.
[Public | Private | Friend] [Static] Property Set *name* ([*arglist*,] *reference*) [*statements*] End Property	Declares the name and arguments of a procedure that sets a reference to an object.

continued

continued ➔

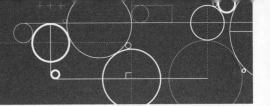

VBA Statements Quick Reference *(continued)*

Program Flow (continued)

STATEMENT	DESCRIPTION

Select Case *testexpression*
[Case *expressionlist-n*
  [*statements-n*]]
[Case Else
  [*elsestatements*]]
End Select
	Executes one block out of a series of statement blocks depending upon the value of an expression.

[Private | Public | Friend] [Static] Sub name [(*arglist*)] [*statements*] End Sub	Declares the name, arguments, and code that form a Sub procedure.
While *condition* [*statements*] Wend	Executes a block of statements as long as the specified condition is true.
With *object* [*statements*] End With	Executes a block of statements on a single object or on a user-defined data type.

Variable Declaration

STATEMENT	DESCRIPTION
[Public | Private] Const *constname* [As type] = *expression*	Declares a constant value.
Dim [WithEvents] *varname*[([*subscripts*])] [As [New] *type*]	Declares variables and allocates the appropriate storage space.
Friend [WithEvents] *varname*[([*subscripts*])] [As [New] *type*]	Declares a procedure or variable to only have scope in the project where it is defined.
Option Compare {Binary | Text | Database}	Specifies the default comparison method to use when comparing strings.
Option Explicit	Forces declaration of all variables within the module.
Option Private	Indicates that all code within the entire module is Private. This option is used by default. You can overwrite the effects of this option by declaring a specific procedure Public.
Private [WithEvents] *varname*[([*subscripts*])] [As [New] *type*]	Declares variables and procedures to only have scope within the current module.
Public [WithEvents] *varname*[([*subscripts*])] [As [New] *type*]	Declares variables and procedures to have scope within the entire project.

VBA Statements Quick Reference *(continued)*

Variable Declaration (continued)

STATEMENT	DESCRIPTION
ReDim [Preserve] *varname*(*subscripts*) [As *type*]	Changes the dimensions of a dynamic array.
[Private	Public] Type *varname* *elementname* [([*subscripts*])] As *type* [*elementname* [([*subscripts*])] As *type*] ... End Type	Defines a custom data type.

VBA Function Quick Reference

Legend

Plain courier text = required   [] = optional | = or

Italics = user-defined   . . . = list of items

Array Functions

FUNCTION	DESCRIPTION	RETURNS
Array(*arg1*,*arg2*, *arg3*, . . .)	Creates a variant array containing the specified elements.	Variant
LBound(*arrayname*[, *dimension*])	Returns the smallest subscript for the specified array.	Long
UBound(*arrayname*[, *dimension*])	Returns the largest subscript for the specified array.	Long

Data Type Conversion Functions

FUNCTION	DESCRIPTION	RETURNS
Asc(*string*)	Returns the character code of the first letter in a string.	Integer
CBool(*expression*)	Converts an expression to Boolean data type (True or False)	Boolean
CByte(*expression*)	Converts an expression to Byte data type.	Byte
CCur(*expression*)	Converts an expression to Currency data type.	Currency
CDate(*expression*)	Converts an expression to a Date data type.	Date
CDbl(*expression*)	Converts an expression to Double data type.	Double
CDec(*expression*) (Decimal)	Converts an expression to a decimal value.	Variant
Chr(*charactercode*)	Converts the character code to the corresponding character. Chr(9) returns a tab, Chr(34) returns quotation marks, etc.	Variant
CInt(*expression*)	Converts an expression to an Integer data type, rounding any fractional parts.	Integer

continued

continued →

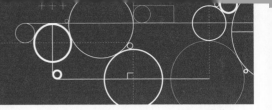

VBA Function Quick Reference *(continued)*

Data Type Conversion Functions (continued)

FUNCTION	DESCRIPTION	RETURNS
CLng(*expression*)	Converts an expression to the Long data type.	Long
CSng(*expression*)	Converts an expression to the Single data type.	Single
CStr(*expression*)	Returns a string containing the specified expression.	String
CVar(*expression*)	Converts any data type to a Variant data type. All numeric values are treated as Double data types and string expressions are treated as String data types.	Variant
Format(*expression*[, format[, firstdayofweek[, firstweekofyear]]])	Formats the expression using either predefined or user-defined formats.	Variant
FormatCurrency(*Expression*[, NumDigitsAfterDecimal [, IncludeLeadingDigit [,UseParensForNegativeNumbers [, GroupDigits]]]])	Formats the expression as a currency value using the system-defined currency symbol.	Currency
FormatDateTime(*Date*[, NamedFormat])	Formats an expression as a date and time.	Date
FormatNumber(*Expression* [, NumDigitsAfterDecimal [, IncludeLeadingDigit [, UseParensForNegativeNumbers [, GroupDigits]]]])	Formats the expression as a number.	Mixed
FormatPercent(*Expression* [,NumDigitsAfterDecimal [,IncludeLeadingDigit [,UseParensForNegativeNumbers [,GroupDigits]]]])	Returns the expression formatted as a percentage with a trailing % character.	String
Hex(*number*)	Converts a number to a hexadecimal value. Rounds numbers to nearest whole number before converting.	String
Oct(*number*)	Converts a number to an octal value. Rounds numbers to nearest whole number before converting.	Variant (String)
Str(*number*)	Converts a number to a string using the Variant data type.	Variant (String)
Val(*string*)	Returns the numeric portion of a string formatted as a number of the appropriate data type.	Mixed

VBA Function Quick Reference *(continued)*

Date and Time Functions

FUNCTION	DESCRIPTION	RETURNS
Date	Returns the current system date.	Date
DateAdd(*interval, number, date*)	Returns a date that is the specified interval of time from the original date.	Date
DateDiff(*interval, date1, date2*[, *firstdayofweek*[, *firstweekofyear*]])	Determines the time interval between two dates.	Long
DatePart(*interval, date*[, *firstdayofweek*[, *firstweekofyear*]])	Returns the specified part of a date.	Integer
DateSerial(*year, month, day*)	Converts the specified date to a serial number.	Date
DateValue(*date*)	Converts a string to a date.	Date
Day(*date*)	Returns a whole number between 1 and 31 representing the day of the month.	Integer
Hour(*time*)	Returns a whole number between 0 and 23 representing the hour of the day.	Integer
Minute(*time*)	Returns a whole number between 0 and 59 representing the minute of the hour.	Integer
Month(*date*)	Returns a whole number between 1 and 12 representing the month of the year.	Integer
Now	Returns the current system date and time.	Date
Second(*time*)	Returns a whole number between 0 and 59 representing the second of the minute.	Integer
Time	Returns the current system time.	Date
Timer	Indicates the number of seconds that have elapsed since midnight	Single
TimeSerial(*hour, minute, second*)	Creates a time using the specified hour, minute, and second values.	Date
TimeValue(*time*)	Converts a time to the serial number used to store time.	Date
WeekDay(*date, [firstdayofweek]*)	Returns a whole number representing the first day of the week.	Integer
Year(*date*)	Returns a whole number representing the year portion of a date	Integer

continued →

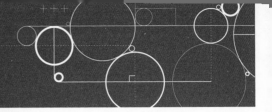

VBA Function Quick Reference *(continued)*

File and Folder Handling Functions

FUNCTION	DESCRIPTION	RETURNS
CurDir(*drive*)	Returns the current path.	String
Dir[(*pathname*[, *attributes*])]	Returns the name of the file, directory, or folder that matches the specified pattern.	String
EOF(*filenumber*)	Returns -1 when the end of a file has been reached.	Integer
FileAttr(*filenumber, returntype*)	Indicates the file mode used for files opened with the Open statement.	Long
FileDateTime(*pathname*)	Indicates the date and time when a file was last modified.	Date
FileLen(*pathname*)	Indicates the length of a file in bytes.	Long
FreeFile(*rangenumber*)	Returns the next file number available for use by the Open statement.	Integer
GetAttr(*pathname*)	Returns a whole number representing the attributes of a file, directory, or folder.	Integer
Input(*number*, [#]*filenumber*)	Returns a string containing the indicated number of characters from the specified file.	String
Loc(*filenumber*)	Indicates the current read/write position in an open file.	Long
LOF(*filenumber*)	Returns the size in bytes of a file opened using the Long Open statement.	Long
Seek(*filenumber*)	Specifies the current read/write position with a file opened with the Open statement.	Long

Financial Functions

FUNCTION	DESCRIPTION	RETURNS
DDB(*cost, salvage, life, period*[, *factor*])	Specifies the depreciation value for an asset during a specific time frame.	Double
FV(*rate, nper, pmt*[, *pv*[, *type*]])	Determines the future value of an annuity based on periodic fixed payments.	Double
IPmt(*rate, per, nper, pv*[, *fv*[, *type*]])	Determines the interest payment on an annuity for a specific period of time.	Double
IRR(*values()*, [, *guess*])	Determines the internal rate of returns for a series of cash flows.	Double
MIRR(*values()*, *finance_rate, reinvest_rate*)	Returns the modified interest rate of returns for a series of periodic cash flows	Double

VBA Function Quick Reference *(continued)*

Financial Functions (continued)

FUNCTION	DESCRIPTION	RETURNS
NPer(*rate, pmt, pv*[, *fv*[, *type*]])	Returns the number of periods for an annuity.	Double
NPV(*rate, values*())	Returns the net present value of an investment.	Double
Pmt(*rate, nper, pv*[, *fv*[, *type*]])	Returns the payment amount for an annuity based on fixed payments.	Double
PPmt(*rate, per, nper, pv*[, *fv*[, *type*]])	Returns the principal payment amount for an annuity.	Double
PV(*rate, nper, pmt*[, *fv*[, *type*]])	Returns the present value of an annuity.	Double
Rate(*nper, pmt, pv*[, *fv*[, *type*[, *guess*]]])	Returns the interest rate per period for an annuity.	Double
SLN(*cost, salvage, life*)	Determines the straight-line depreciation of an asset for a single period.	Double
SYD(*cost, salvage, life, period*)	Determines the sum-of-years' digits depreciation of an asset for a specified period.	Double

Information Functions

FUNCTION	DESCRIPTION	RETURNS
CVErr(*errornumber*)	Returns a user-defined error number.	Variant
Error[(*errornumber*)]	Returns the error message for the specified error number.	String
IsArray(*varname*)	Indicates whether a variable contains an array.	Boolean
IsDate(*expression*)	Indicates whether an expression contains a date.	Boolean
IsEmpty(*expression*)	Indicates whether a variable has been initialized.	Boolean
IsError(*expression*)	Indicates whether an expression is an error value.	Boolean
IsMissing(*argname*)	Indicates whether an optional argument was passed to a procedure.	Boolean
IsNull(*expression*)	Indicates whether an expression contains no valid data.	Boolean
IsNumeric(*expression*)	Indicates whether an expression is a number.	Boolean
IsObject(*identifier*)	Indicates whether a variable references an object.	Boolean
TypeName(*varname*)	Specifies the variable type.	String
VarType(*varname*)	Specifies the subtype of a variable.	Integer

continued ➡

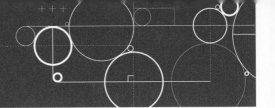

VBA Function Quick Reference *(continued)*

Interaction Functions

FUNCTION	DESCRIPTION	RETURNS
Choose(*index, choice-1,* [*choice-2, ...*])	Selects and returns a value from a list of arguments.	Mixed
DoEvents()	Yields execution so the operating system can process other events.	Integer
Iif(*expr, truepart, falsepart*)	Evaluates the expression and returns either the truepart or falsepart parameter value.	Mixed
InputBox(*prompt*[, *title*] [, *default*] [, *xpos*] [, *ypos*] [, *helpfile, context*])	Displays a dialog box prompting the user for input.	String
GetAllSettings(*appname, section*)	Returns a list of key settings and their values from the Windows Registry.	Variant
GetObject([*pathname*][, *class*])	Returns a reference to an object provided by an ActiveX Component.	Variant
GetSetting(*appname, section, key*[, *default*])	Returns a key setting value from an application's entry in the Windows registry.	Variant
MsgBox(*prompt*[, *buttons*] [, *title*] [, *helpfile, context*])	Displays a message box and returns a value representing the button pressed by the user	Integer
Partition(*number, start, stop, interval*)	Indicates where a number occurs within a series of ranges.	String
QBColor(*color*)	Returns the RGB color code for the specified color.	Long
Switch(*expr-1, value-1*[, *expr-2, value-2 ...*])	Evaluates a list of expressions and returns the value associated with the first True expression.	Variant
RGB(*red, green, blue*)	Returns a number representing the RGB color value.	Long

Mathematical Functions

FUNCTION	DESCRIPTION	RETURNS
Abs(*number*)	Returns the absolute value of a number.	Mixed
Atn(*number*)	Returns the arctangent of a number.	Double
Cos(*number*)	Returns the cosine of an angle.	Double

Mathematical Functions (continued)

FUNCTION	DESCRIPTION	RETURNS
Exp(*number*)	Returns the base of the natural logarithms raised to a power.	Double
Fix(*number*)	Returns the integer portion of a number. With negative values, returns the first negative value greater than or equal to the number.	Integer
Int(*number*)	Returns the integer portion of a number. With negative values, returns the first negative number less than or equal to the number	Integer
Log(*number*)	Returns the natural logarithm of a number.	Double
Round(*expression* [, *numdecimalplaces*])	Rounds a number to the specified number of decimal places.	Mixed
Rnd[(*number*)]	Returns a random number between 0 and 1.	Single
Sgn(*number*)	Returns 1 for a number greater than 0, 0 for a value of 0, and -1 for a number less than zero.	Integer
Sin(*number*)	Specifies the sine of an angle.	Double
Sqr(*number*)	Specifies the square root of a number.	Double
Tan(*number*)	Specifies the tangent of an angle.	Double

String Manipulation Functions

FUNCTION	DESCRIPTION	RETURNS
nStr([*start*,]*string1*, *string2* [, *compare*])	Specifies the position of one string within another string.	Long
InStrRev(*stringcheck*, *stringmatch*[, *start*[, *compare*]])	Specifies the position of one string within another starting at the end of the string.	Long
LCase(*string*)	Converts a string to lowercase.	String
Left(*string, length*)	Returns the specified number of characters from the left side of a string.	String
Len(*string* | *varname*)	Determines the number of characters in a string.	Long
LTrim(*string*)	Trims spaces from the left side of a string.	String
Mid(*string, start*[, *length*])	Returns the specified number of characters from the center of a string.	String
Right(*string, length*)	Returns the specified number of characters from the right side of a string.	String
RTrim(*string*)	Trims spaces from the right side of a string.	String
Space(*number*)	Creates a string with the specified number of spaces.	String

continued

continued ➡

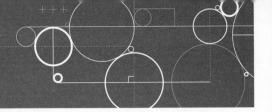

VBA Function Quick Reference *(continued)*

String Manipulation Functions (continued)

FUNCTION	DESCRIPTION	RETURNS
Spc(*n*)	Positions output when printing to a file.	String
Str(*number*)	Returns a string representation of a number.	String
StrComp(*string1*, *string2*[, *compare*])	Returns a value indicating the result of a string comparison.	Integer
StrConv(*string, conversion, LCID*)	Converts a string to the specified format.	String
String(*number, character*)	Creates a string by repeating a character the specified number of times.	String
Tab[(*n*)]	Positions output when printing to a file.	String
Trim(*string*)	Trims spaces from left and right of a string.	String
UCase(*string*)	Converts a string to uppercase.	String

VBA Function Constants and Characters

vbMsgBoxStyle Constants (MsgBox Function)

CONSTANT	VALUE	DESCRIPTION
vbAbortRetryIgnore	2	Displays Abort, Retry, and Ignore buttons.
vbApplicationModal	0	Creates application modal message box.
vbCritical	16	Displays Critical Message icon.
vbDefaultButton1	0	Makes first button default.
vbDefaultButton2	256	Makes second button default.
vbDefaultButton3	512	Makes third button default.
vbDefaultButton4	768	Makes fourth button default.
vbExclamation	48	Displays Warning Message icon.
vbInformation	64	Displays Information Message icon.
vbMsgBoxHelpButton	16384	Adds a Help button.

vbMsgBoxStyle Constants (MsgBox Function) (continued)

CONSTANT	VALUE	DESCRIPTION
vbMsgBoxRight	524288	Right aligns text in the box.
vbMsgBoxRtlReading	1048576	Used only with Hebrew and Arabic systems for right-to-left reading.
vbMsgBoxSetForeground	65536	Makes message box the foreground window.
vbOKCancel	1	Displays OK and Cancel buttons.
vbOKOnly	0	Displays only the OK button.
vbQuestion	32	Displays Warning Query icon.
vbRetryCancel	5	Displays Retry and Cancel buttons.
vbSystemModal	4096	Creates a system modal message box.
vbYesNo	4	Displays Yes and No buttons.
vbYesNoCancel	3	Displays Yes, No, and Cancel buttons.

vbDayOfWeek Constants

CONSTANT	VALUE	DESCRIPTION
vbUseSystemDayofWeek	0	Uses the system defined first day of week.
vbSunday	1	Sunday (default).
vbMonday	2	Monday.
vbTuesday	3	Tuesday.
vbWednesday	4	Wednesday.
vbThursday	5	Thursday.
vbFriday	6	Friday.
vbSaturday	7	Saturday.

vbFirstWeekOfYear Constants

CONSTANT	VALUE	DESCRIPTION
vbUseSystem	0	Uses system defined first week of year.
vbFirstJan1	1	Starts with week in which January 1 occurs (default).
vbFirstFourDays	2	Starts with the first week that has at least four days in the new year.
vbFirstFullWeek	3	Starts with first full week of the year.

continued →

VBA Function Constants and Characters *(continued)*

Format Function Characters

DATE/TIME CHARACTERS	DISPLAYS
d	Day with no leading zero.
ddd	Three-letter abbreviation of day (Sun. – Sat.).
dddd	Full day name (Sunday).
ddddd	Complete date using short date format.
dddddd	Complete date using long date format.
w	Day of week as number (1 for Sunday).
ww	Week of year as number.
m	Month with no leading zero.
mmm	Three letter abbreviation of month (Jan.-Dec.).
mmmm	Complete month name.
q	Quarter of year.
y	Day of year as number.
yy	Year as 2-digit number.
yyyy	Year as 4-digit number.
h	Hour with no leading zero.
n	Minutes with no leading zero.
s	Seconds with no leading zero.
ttttt	Complete time using system time format.
c	Date as **dddddd** and time as **ttttt**.

Format Function Predefined Formats

FORMAT	DESCRIPTION
General Date	Uses general date format.
Long Date	Uses system-defined long date, such as Tuesday, August 7, 2007.
Medium Date	Uses the medium date format, such as 07-Aug-07.
Short Date	Uses system-defined short date, such as 8/7/2007.
Long Time	Uses system-defined long time, such as 5:45:30 P.M.
Medium Time	Uses the medium time format, such as 05:45 P.M.
Short Time	Uses the short time format, such as 17:45.

Format Function Predefined Formats (continued)

FORMAT	DESCRIPTION
General Number	Uses the general number format.
Currency	Places the appropriate currency symbol in front of the number.
Fixed	Uses a fixed decimal format.
Standard	Uses standard formatting.
Percent	Converts the expression to a percentage.
Scientific	Displays the expression using scientific notation.
Yes/No	Converts the expression to a Yes or No value.
True/False	Converts the expression to a True or False value.
On/Off	Converts the expression to an On or Off value.

Excel Object Model Constants

XlColumnDataType Constants

CONSTANT	VALUE	DESCRIPTION
xlDMYFormat	4	DMY format date.
xlDYMFormat	7	DYM format date.
xlEMDFormat	10	EMD format date.
xlGeneralFormat	1	General format.
xlMDYFormat	3	MDY format date.
xlMYDFormat	6	MYD format date.
xlSkipColumn	9	Skip Column.
xlTextFormat	2	Text format.
xlYDMFormat	8	YDM format date.
xlYMDFormat	5	YMD format date.

XlFileFormat Constants

CONSTANT	VALUE	DESCRIPTION
xlAddIn	18	Excel add-in.
xlAddIn8	18	Excel 2007 Add-In
xlCSV	6	Comma-separated values format.
xlCSVMac	22	Macintosh comma-separated values format.

continued

continued →

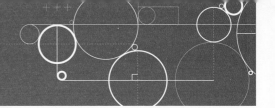

Excel Object Model Constants *(continued)*

XlFileFormat Constants (continued)

CONSTANT	VALUE	DESCRIPTION
xlCSVMSDOS	24	MSDOS comma-separated values format.
xlCSVWindows	23	MS Windows comma-separated values format.
xlCurrentPlatformText	-4158	Text file based on current operating system.
xlDBF2	7	DBase II format.
xlDBF3	8	DBase III format.
xlDBF4	11	DBase IV format.
xlDIF	9	Data interchange format.
xlExcel12	50	Excel 12 format.
xlExcel2	16	Excel 2
xlExcel2FarEast	27	Excel 2.0 format – Far East version.
xlExcel3	29	Excel 3.0 format.
xlExcel4	33	Excel 4.0 format.
xlExcel4Workbook	35	Excel 4.0 workbook format.
xlExcel5	39	Excel 5.0 format.
xlExcel7	39	Excel 97 format.
xlExcel9597	43	Excel 95 – 97 format.
xlHtml	44	HTML format.
xlIntlAddIn	26	Excel international Add-in.
xlIntlMacro	25	Excel international macro.
xlOpenXMLAddin	55	Open XML Add-In.
xlOpenXMLTemplate	54	Open XML Template.
xlOpemXMLTemplateMacroEnabled	53	Open XML Template Macro Enabled.
xlOpenXMLWorkbook	51	Open XML Workbook.
xlOpenXMLWorkbookzMacroEnabled	52	Open XML Workbook Enabled.
xlSYLK	2	Symbolic link format.
xlTemplate	17	Template file format.
xlTemplate8	17	Template.
xlTextMac	19	Macintosh text file format.
xlTextMSDOS	21	MSDOS text file format.
xlTextPrinter	36	Text file created for a printer (.prn).
xlTextWindows	20	MS Window text file format.

XlFileFormat Constants (continued)

CONSTANT	VALUE	DESCRIPTION
xlUnicodeText	42	Unicode text file format.
xlWebArchive	45	Web archive format (.mht).
xlWJ2WD1	14	WJ2WD1
xlWJ3	40	WJ3
xlWJ3FM3	41	WJ3FJ3
xlWK1	5	Lotus 2.x format.
xlWK1ALL	31	Lotus 2.x .all format.
xlWK1FMT	30	Lotus 2.x .fmt format.
xlWK3	15	Lotus 3.x format.
xlWK3FM3	32	Lotus 3.x and Lotus 1-2-3 for Windows format.
xlWK4	38	Lotus 4.0 format.
xlWKS	4	MS Works file format.
xlWorkBookDefault	51	Workbook default
xlWorkbookNormal	-4143	Excel workbook format.
xlWorks2FarEast	28	MS Works file – Far East format.
xlWQ1	34	Quattro Pro for MSDOS format.
xlXMLSpreadsheet	46	XML format.

MsoFileType Constants

CONSTANT	VALUE	DESCRIPTION
msoFileTypeAllFiles	1	All file types.
msoFileTypeBinders	6	Microsoft Office Binder file.
msoFileTypeCalendarItem	11	Microsoft Outlook Calendar item.
msoFileTypeContactItem	12	Microsoft Outlook Contact item.
msoFileTypeDatabases	7	Database files.
msoFileTypeDataConnectionFiles	17	Database connection files.
msoFileTypeDesignerFiles	22	Designer files.
msoFileTypeDocumentImagingFiles	20	Document imaging files.
msoFileTypeExcelWorkbooks	4	Microsoft Excel Workbooks.
msoFileTypeJournalItem	14	Journal items.
msoFileTypeMailItem	10	Microsoft Outlook Mail message.
msoFileTypeNoteItem	13	Microsoft Outlook Note item.
msoFileTypeOfficeFiles	2	All Microsoft Office file types.

continued

continued →

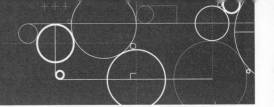

Excel Object Model Constants *(continued)*

MsoFileTypeConstant (continued)

CONSTANT	VALUE	DESCRIPTION
msoFileTypeOutlookItems	9	Microsoft Outlook files.
msoFileTypePhotoDrawFiles	16	Microsoft PhotoDraw files.
msoFileTypePowerPointPresentations	5	Microsoft PowerPoint files.
msoFileTypeProjectFiles	19	Microsoft Project files.
msoFileTypePublisherFiles	18	Microsoft Publisher files.
msoFileTypeTaskItem	15	Microsoft Outlook Task item.
msoFileTypeTemplates	8	Template files.
msoFileTypeVisioFiles	21	Visio files.
msoFileTypeWebPages	23	Web pages including .htm, .asp, and .mht files.
msoFileTypeWordDocuments	3	Microsoft Word documents.

XlChartType Constants

CONSTANT	VALUE	CHART TYPE
xl3DArea	-4098	3D Area.
xl3DAreaStacked	78	3D Stacked Area.
xl3DAreaStacked100	79	100% Stacked Area.
xl3DBarClustered	60	3D Clustered Bar.
xl3DBarStacked	61	3D Stacked Bar.
xl3DBarStacked100	62	3D 100% Stacked Bar.
xl3DColumn	-4100	3D Column.
xl3DColumnClustered	54	3D Clustered Column.
xl3DColumnStacked	55	3D Stacked Column.
xl3DColumnStacked100	56	3D 100% Stacked Column.
xl3DLine	-4101	3D Line.
xl3DPie	-4102	3D Pie.
xl3DPieExploded	70	Exploded 3D Pie.
xlArea	1	Area.
xlAreaStacked	76	Stacked Area.
xlAreaStacked100	77	100% Stacked Area.
xlBarClustered	57	Clustered Bar.

XlChartType Constants (continued)

CONSTANT	VALUE	CHART TYPE
xlBarOfPie	71	Bar of Pie.
xlBarStacked	58	Stacked Bar.
xlBarStacked100	59	100% Stacked Bar.
xlBubble	15	Bubble.
xlBubble3DEffec	87	Bubble with 3D effects.
xlColumnClustered	51	Clustered Column.
xlColumnStacked	52	Stacked Column.
xlColumnStacked100	53	100% Stacked Column.
xlConeBarClustered	102	Clustered Cone Bar.
xlConeBarStacked	103	Stacked Cone Bar.
xlConeBarStacked100	104	100% Stacked Cone Bar.
xlConeCol	105	3D Cone Column.
xlConeColClustered	99	Clustered Cone Column.
xlConeColStacked	100	Stacked Cone Column.
xlConeColStacked100	101	100% Stacked Cone Column.
xlCylinderBarClustered	95	Clustered Cylinder Bar.
xlCylinderBarStacked	96	Stacked Cylinder Bar.
xlCylinderBarStacked100	97	100% Stacked Cylinder Bar.
xlCylinderCol	98	3D Cylinder Column.
xlCylinderColClustered	92	Clustered Cone Column.
xlCylinderColStacked	93	Stacked Cone Column.
xlCylinderColStacked100	94	100% Stacked Cylinder Column.
xlDoughnut	-4120	Doughnut.
xlDoughnutExploded	80	Exploded Doughnut.
xlLine	4	Line.
xlLineMarkers	65	Line with Markers.
xlLineMarkersStacked	66	Stacked Line with Markers.
xlLineMarkersStacked100	67	100% Stacked Line with Markers.
xlLineStacked	63	Stacked Line.
xlLineStacked100	64	100% Stacked Line.
xlPie	5	Pie.
xlPieExploded	69	Exploded Pie.
xlPieOfPie	68	Pie of Pie.
xlPyramidBarClustered	109	Clustered Pyramid Bar.

continued

continued

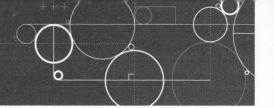

Excel Object Model Constants *(continued)*

XlChartType Constants (continued)

CONSTANT	VALUE	CHART TYPE
xlPyramidBarStacked	110	Stacked Pyramid Bar.
xlPyramidBarStacked100	111	100% Stacked Pyramid Bar.
xlPyramidCol	112	3D Pyramid Column.
xlPyramidColClustered	106	Clustered Pyramid Column.
xlPyramidColStacked	107	Stacked Pyramid Column.
xlPyramidColStacked100	108	100% Stacked Pyramid Column.
xlRadar	-4151	Radar.
xlRadarFilled	82	Filled Radar.
xlRadarMarkers	81	Radar with Data Markers.
xlStockHLC	88	High-Low-Close.
xlStockOHLC	89	Open-High-Low-Close.
xlStockVHLC	90	Volume-High-Low-Close.
xlStockVOHLC	91	Volume-Open-High-Low-Close.
xlSurface	83	3D Surface.
xlSurfaceTopView	85	Top View Surface.
xlSurfaceTopViewWireframe	86	Top View Wireframe Surface.
xlSurfaceWireframe	84	3D Surface Wireframe.
xlXYScatter	-4169	Scatter.
xlXYScatterLines	74	Scatter with Lines.
xlXYScatterLinesNoMarkers	75	Scatter with Lines and No Data Markers.
xlXYScatterSmooth	72	Scatter with Smoothed Lines.
xlXYScatterSmoothNoMarkers	73	Scatter with Smoothed Lines and No Data Markers.

XlLineStyle Constants

CONSTANT	VALUE	DESCRIPTION
xlContinuous	1	Continuous solid line.
xlDash	-4155	Dashed line.
xlDashDot	4	Line with the pattern dash dot.
xlDashDotDot	5	Line with the pattern dash dot dot.
xlDot	-4118	Dotted line.

Excel Object Model Constants *(continued)*

XlLineStyle Constants (continued)

CONSTANT	VALUE	DESCRIPTION
xlDouble	-4119	Double solid line.
xlSlantDashDot	13	Slanted line with the pattern dash dot.
xlineStyleNone	-4142	No line.

XlBorderWeight Constants

CONSTANT	VALUE	DESCRIPTION
xlHairline	1	Creates a very thin line.
xlMedium	-4138	Creates a medium width line.
xlThick	4	Creates a thick line.
xlThin	2	Creates a thin line.

XlPattern Constants

CONSTANT	VALUE	DESCRIPTION
xlPatternAutomatic	-4105	System default.
xlPatternChecker	9	Checkered pattern.
xlPatternCrissCross	16	Criss-cross pattern.
xlPatternDown	-4121	Downward pattern.
xlPatternGray25	-4124	25% gray pattern.
xlPatternGray50	-4125	50% gray pattern.
xlPatternGray75	-4126	75% gray pattern.
xlPatternGrid	15	Grid pattern.
xlPatternHorizontal	-4128	Horizontal pattern.
xlPatternLightHorizontal	11	Light horizontal pattern.
xlPatternLightVertical	12	Light vertical pattern.
xlPatternLightDown	13	Light downward pattern.
xlPatternLightUp	14	Light upward pattern.
xlPatternNone	-4142	No pattern.
xlPatternSemiGray75	10	75% semi-gray pattern.
xlPatternSolid	1	Solid color, no pattern.
xlPatternUp	-4162	Upward pattern.
xlPatternVertical	-4166	Vertical pattern.

Ribbon Controls Quick Reference

XML Controls

XML controls specific to the Ribbon.

CONTROL	DESCRIPTION	COMMON ATTRIBUTES	CHILDREN
customUI	The root tag for Ribbon customizations.	None	commands, ribbon
commands	Globally repurposed commands.	None	command
command	Represents the command that you are repurposing.	enabled, getEnabled, idMso (required), onAction	contextualTabs, officeMenu, qat, tabs
contextualTabs	The contextual tabs that display in Excel. For example, the Chart tools.	None	tabSet
tabSet	A collection of tab controls.	getVisible, idMso (required), visible	tab
qat	The Quick Access Toolbar. Used only in the start from scratch mode.	None	documentControls, sharedControls
sharedControls	Controls shared across documents. In general, you should use documentControls, not sharedControls.	None	button, control, separator
documentControls	Controls specific to a document.	None	button, control, separator
officeMenu	Microsoft Office menu controls.	None	button, checkbox, control, dynamicMenu, gallery, menu, menuSeparator, splitButton, toggleButton
tabs	Container for tab controls.	None	tab
tab	A tab on the Ribbon.	getKeytip, getLabel, getVisible, id, idMso, idQ, insertAfterMso, insertAfterQ, insertBeforeMso, insertBeforeQ, keytip, label, tag, visible	group
group	A group on a tab on the Ribbon.	getImage, getImageMso, getKeytip, getLabel, getScreentip, getSupertip, getVisible, id, idMso, idQ, image, imageMso, insertAfterMso, insertAfterQ, insertBeforeMso, insertBeforeQ, keytip, label, screentip, supertip, visible	box, button, buttonGroup, checkBox, comboBox, control, dialogBoxLauncher, dropDown, editBox, gallery, labelControl, menu, separator, splitButton, toggleButton

CONTROL	DESCRIPTION	COMMON ATTRIBUTES	CHILDREN
box	Use to arrange controls within a group.	getVisible, id, idQ, insertAfterMso, insertAfterQ, insertBeforeMso, insertBeforeQ, visible	box, button, buttonGroup, checkBox, comboBox, control, dropdown, dynamicMenu, editBox, gallery, labelControl, menu, splitButton, toggleButton
button	Use to represent a button control.	description, enabled, getDescription, getEnabled, getImage, getImageMso, getKeytip, getLabel, getScreentip, getShowImage, getShowLabel, getSize, getSupertip, getVisible, id, idMso, idQ, image, imageMso, insertAfterMso, insertAfterQ, insertBeforeMso, insertBeforeQ, keytip, label, onAction, screentip, showImage, showLabel, size, supertip, tag, visible	None
buttonGroup	Use to create a grouping of buttons.	getVisible, id, idQ, insertAfterMso, insertAfterQ, insertBeforeMso, insertBeforeQ, visible	button, control, dynamicMenu, gallery, menu, splitButton, toggleButton
checkbox	Use to create a check box control.	description, enabled, getDescription, getEnabled, getKeytip, getLabel, getScreentip, getSupertip, getVisible, id, idMso, idQ, insertAfterMso, insertAfterQ, insertBeforeMso, insertBeforeQ, keytip, label, onAction, screentip, supertip, tag, visible	None
comboBox	Use to create a combo box control.	enabled, getEnabled, getImage, getImageMso, getKeytip, getLabel, getScreentip, getShowImage, getShowLabel, getSupertip, getVisible, id, idMso, idQ, image, imageMso, insertAfterMso, insertAfterQ, insertBeforeMso, insertBeforeQ, label, screentip, showImage, showLabel, supertip, tag, visible, Shared with editBox: getText, maxLength, onChange, sizeString	item
dialogBox Launcher	Use to create a dialog box launcher for a group. A group control can only have one dialog box launcher, the control must contain a button control, and must be the final element in the group element.	None	button (required)

continued

continued ➡

XML Basic Controls *(continued)*

CONTROL	DESCRIPTION	COMMON ATTRIBUTES	CHILDREN
dropdown	Use to create a drop-down list box.	enabled, getEnabled, getImage, getImageMso, getKeytip, getLabel, getScreentip, getShowImage, getShowLabel, getSupertip, getVisible, id, idMso, idQ, image, imageMso, insertAfterMso, insertAfterQ, insertBeforeMso, insertBeforeQ, keytip, label, onAction, screentip, showImage, showLabel, supertip, tag, visible Shared with comboBox: getItemCount, getItemID, getItemImage, getItemLabel, getItemScreentip, getItemSupertip, showItemImage, Shared with editBox: sizeString	item
dynamicMenu	Use to create a menu at run time.	description, enabled, getDescription, getEnabled, getImage, getImageMso, getKeytip, getLabel, getScreentip, getShowImage, getShowLabel, getSize, getSupertip, getVisible, id, idMso, idQ, image, imageMso, insertAfterMso, insertAfterQ, insertBeforeMso, insertBeforeQ, keytip, label, screentip, showImage, showLabel, supertip, tag, visible	Same as a menu, but is populated by using the getContent callback.
editBox	Use to create an edit box control.	enabled, getEnabled, getImage, getImageMso, getKeytip, getLabel, getScreentip, getShowImage, getShowLabel, getSupertip, getVisible, id, idMso, idQ, image, imageMso, insertAfterMso, insertAfterQ, insertBeforeMso, insertBeforeQ, keytip, label, screentip, showImage, showLabel, supertip, tag, visible	None
gallery	Use to create a gallery control.	description, enabled, getDescription, getEnabled, getImage, getImageMso, getKeytip, getLabel, getScreentip, getShowImage, getShowLabel, getSize,getSupertip, getVisible, id, idMso, idQ, image, imageMso, insertAfterMso, insertAfterQ, insertBeforeMso, insertBeforeQ, keytip, label, onAction, screentip, showImage, showLabel, size, supertip, tag, visible, Shared with comboBox: getItemCount, getItemID, getItemImage, getItemLabel, getItemScreentip, getItemSupertip, showItemImage, showItemLabel, Shared with dropDown: getSelectedItemID, getSelectedItem Index Shared with editBox: sizeString	item, button. Buttons must be listed after the items, and all buttons appear at the bottom of the gallery.
item	A static gallery, dropDown, or comboBox item. If you specify static items, you cannot also specify dynamic items.	id, image, imageMso, label, screentip, supertip	None

XML Basic Controls *(continued)*

CONTROL	DESCRIPTION	COMMON ATTRIBUTES	CHILDREN
labelControl	Use to create a label control.	enabled, getEnabled, getLabel, getScreentip, getShowLabel, getSupertip, getVisible, id, idMso, idQ, insertAfterMso, insertAfterQ, insertBeforeMso, insertBeforeQ, label, screentip, showLabel, supertip, tag, visible	None
menu	Use to create a menu control.	description, enabled, getDescription, getEnabled, getImage, getImageMso, getKeytip, getLabel, getScreentip, getShowImage, getShowLabel, getSize, getSupertip, getVisible, id, idMso, idQ, image, imageMso, insertAfterMso, insertAfterQ, insertBeforeMso, insertBeforeQ, keytip, label, screentip, showImage, showLabel, size, supertip, tag, visible	button, checkBox, control, dynamicMenu, gallery, menu, menuSeparator, splitButton, toggleButton
menu Separator	Use to create a separator line (which can optionally include a text label) between menu items.	id, idQ, insertAfterMso, insertAfterQ, insertBeforeMso, insertBeforeQ	None
separator	Use to create a separator line between controls.	getVisible, id, idQ, insertAfterMso, insertAfterQ, insertBeforeMso, insertBeforeQ, visible	None
splitButton	Use to create a split button control.	enabled, getEnabled, getKeytip, getShowLabel, getSize, getSupertip, getVisible, id, idMso, idQ, insertAfterMso, insertAfterQ, insertBeforeMso, insertBeforeQ, keytip, showLabel (determines whether the button or toggle button control displays its label), size, supertip, tag, visible	button or toggleButton (required, only one permitted, and must appear before the menu): The main button for the split button control menu (required, and only one permitted): The menu of a split button control.
toggleButton	Use to create a toggle button control.	description, enabled, getDescription, getEnabled, getImage, getImageMso, getKeytip, getLabel, getPressed, getScreentip, getShowImage, getShowLabel, getSize, getSupertip, getVisible, id, idMso, idQ, image, imageMso, insertAfterMso, insertAfterQ, insertBeforeMso, insertBeforeQ, keytip, label, onAction, screentip, showImage, showLabel, size, supertip, tag, visible	None

continued ➡

Ribbon Controls Quick Reference (continued)

Attributes and Methods of Ribbon Controls

The following tables list the attributes and methods related to specific ribbon controls.

CONTROL	ATTRIBUTE OR METHOD	TYPE OR ACTION	DESCRIPTION
customUI	xmlns	String	You must set xmlns to http://schemas.microsoft.com/office/2006/01/customui
customUI	onLoad	callback	As the Ribbon load passes a Ribbon parameter to the callback procedure. This enables the associated code to store a reference to the Ribbon for later use.
customUI	loadImage	callback	Use to create a procedure to load all of the images required by the Ribbon.

CONTROL	ATTRIBUTE	VALUES	DESCRIPTION
ribbon	startFromScratch	True, False, 1, 0	Set to True, to hide built-in Ribbon tabs and display a minimal File menu.

CONTROL	ATTRIBUTE	VALUES	DESCRIPTION
box	boxStyle	Horizontal, Vertical	Sets the flow of the controls inside a box.

CONTROL	ATTRIBUTE	TYPE OR ACTION	DESCRIPTION
checkBox	getPressed	callback	Use to specify whether the checkBox control is pressed.

CONTROL	METHOD	ATTRIBUTE OR METHOD	DESCRIPTION
comboBox	getItemCount	callback	Returns the number of items in a comboBox.
comboBox	getItemID	callback	Returns the ID of for the item.
comboBox	getItemImage	callback	Returns the image for the item.
comboBox	getItemLabel	callback	Returns the label of for the item.
comboBox	getItemScreentip	callback	Returns the ScreenTip of for the item.
comboBox	getItemSupertip	callback	Returns the Enhanced ScreenTip for the item.
comboBox	showItemImage	True, False, 1, 0	Specifies whether to display the item image.

CONTROL	METHOD	ACTION	DESCRIPTION
dropdown	getSelectedItemID	callback	Asks for the item that should be selected by ID. Specify either this attribute or the getSelectedItemIndex attribute, but not both.
dropdown	getSelectedItemIndex	callback	Asks for the item that should be selected by index. Specify either this attribute or the getSelectedItemId attribute, but not both.
dropdown	showItemLabel	True, False, 1, 0	Indicates whether items should display labels.

Attributes and Methods of Ribbon Controls *(continued)*

CONTROL	METHOD	ACTION	DESCRIPTION
dynamicMenu	getContent	callback	Returns an XML string that contains the contents of the dynamic menu.

CONTROL	ATTRIBUTE OR METHOD	TYPE OR ACTION	DESCRIPTION
editBox	getText	callback	Returns the text that displays in the edit box.
editBox	maxLength	Integer	The maximum number of characters that a user can type in an edit box.
editBox	onChange	callback	Called when the value in the edit box changes.
editBox	sizeString	String	A string, such as "wwwwwwwwww". Determines the size of an edit box.

CONTROL	ATTRIBUTE OR METHOD	TYPE OR ACTION	DESCRIPTION
gallery	columns	Integer	The number of columns in a gallery.
gallery	getItemHeight	callback	Requests the height of items, in pixels.
gallery	getItemWidth	callback	Requests the width of items, in pixels.
gallery	itemHeight	Integer	The height of items, in pixels.
gallery	itemWidth	Integer	The width of items, in pixels.
gallery	rows	Integer	The number of rows in a gallery.

CONTROL	ATTRIBUTE	VALUES	DESCRIPTION
menu	itemSize	Normal, Large	The size of an item. The Description property shows for Large menu items.

CONTROL	ATTRIBUTE	TYPE OR ACTION	DESCRIPTION
menuSeparator	title	String	The text for this separator.
menuSeparator	getTitle	callback	Callback for this separator's text.

CONTROL	ATTRIBUTE	TYPE OR ACTION	DESCRIPTION
toggleButton	getPressed	callback	Enables you to specify whether the toggle button control is pressed.

continued →

Ribbon Controls Quick Reference (continued)

Callbacks

The following table lists all of the callbacks used by RibbonX.

CONTROL	CALLBACK NAME	SIGNATURES
(several controls)	getDescription	Sub GetDescription (control As IRibbonControl, ByRef description)
(several controls)	getEnabled	Sub GetEnabled (control As IRibbonControl, ByRef enabled)
(several controls)	getImage	Sub GetImage (control As IRibbonControl, ByRef image)
(several controls)	getImageMso	Sub GetImageMso (control As IRibbonControl, ByRef imageMso)
(several controls)	getLabel	Sub GetLabel (control As IRibbonControl, ByRef label)
(several controls)	getKeytip	Sub GetKeytip (control As IRibbonControl, ByRef label)
(several controls)	getSize	Sub GetSize (control As IRibbonControl, ByRef size)
(several controls)	getScreentip	Sub GetScreentip (control As IRibbonControl, ByRef screentip)
(several controls)	getSupertip	Sub GetSupertip (control As IRibbonControl, ByRef screentip)
(several controls)	getVisible	Sub GetVisible (control As IRibbonControl, ByRef visible)
button	getShowImage	Sub GetShowImage (control As IRibbonControl, ByRef showImage)
button	getShowLabel	Sub GetShowLabel (control As IRibbonControl, ByRef showLabel)
button	onAction – repurposed	Sub OnAction (control As IRibbonControl, byRef CancelDefault)
button	onAction	Sub OnAction (control As IRibbonControl)
checkBox	getPressed	Sub GetPressed (control As IRibbonControl, ByRef returnValue)
checkBox	onAction	Sub OnAction (control As IRibbonControl, pressed As Boolean)(pvarfPressed)
comboBox	getItemCount	Sub GetItemCount (control As IRibbonControl, ByRef count)
comboBox	getItemID	Sub GetItemID (control As IRibbonControl, index As Integer, ByRef id)
comboBox	getItemImage	Sub GetItemImage (control As IRibbonControl, index As Integer, ByRef image)
comboBox	getItemLabel	Sub GetItemLabel (control As IRibbonControl, index As Integer, ByRef label)
comboBox	getItemScreenTip	Sub GetItemScreenTip (control As IRibbonControl, index As Integer, ByRef screentip)
comboBox	getItemSuperTip	Sub GetItemSuperTip (control As IRibbonControl, index As Integer, ByRef supertip)
comboBox	getText	Sub GetText (control As IRibbonControl, ByRef text)
comboBox	onChange	Sub OnChange (control As IRibbonControl, text As String)
customUI	loadImage	Sub LoadImage (imageId As string, ByRef image)
customUI	onLoad	Sub OnLoad (ribbon As IRibbonUI)
dropDown	getItemCount	Sub GetItemCount (control As IRibbonControl, ByRef count)

CONTROL	CALLBACK NAME	SIGNATURES
dropDown	getItemID	Sub GetItemID (control As IRibbonControl, index As Integer, ByRef id)
dropDown	getItemImage	Sub GetItemImage (control As IRibbonControl, index As Integer, ByRef image)
dropDown	getItemLabel	Sub GetItemLabel (control As IRibbonControl, index As Integer, ByRef label)
dropDown	getItemScreenTip	Sub GetItemScreenTip (control As IRibbonControl, index As Integer, ByRef screenTip)
dropDown	getItemSuperTip	Sub GetItemSuperTip (control As IRibbonControl, index As Integer, ByRef superTip)
dropDown	getSelectedItemID	Sub GetSelectedItemID (control As IRibbonControl, ByRef index)
dropDown	getSelectedItemIndex	Sub GetSelectedItemIndex (control As IRibbonControl, ByRef index)
dropDown	onAction	Sub OnAction (control As IRibbonControl, selectedId As String, selectedIndex As Integer)
dynamicMenu	getContent	Sub GetContent (control As IRibbonControl, ByRef content)
editBox	getText	Sub GetText (control As IRibbonControl, ByRef text)
editBox	onChange	Sub OnChange (control As IRibbonControl, text As String)
gallery	getItemCount	Sub GetItemCount (control As IRibbonControl, ByRef count)
gallery	getItemHeight	Sub getItemHeight (control As IRibbonControl, ByRef height)
gallery	getItemID	Sub GetItemID (control As IRibbonControl, index As Integer, ByRef id)
gallery	getItemImage	Sub GetItemImage (control As IRibbonControl, index As Integer, ByRef image)
gallery	getItemLabel	Sub GetItemLabel (control As IRibbonControl, index As Integer, ByRef label)
gallery	getItemScreenTip	Sub GetItemScreenTip (control As IRibbonControl, index as Integer, ByRef screen)
gallery	getItemSuperTip	Sub GetItemSuperTip (control As IRibbonControl, index as Integer, ByRef screen)
gallery	getItemWidth	Sub getItemWidth (control As IRibbonControl, ByRef width)
gallery	getSelectedItemID	Sub GetSelectedItemID (control As IRibbonControl, ByRef index)
gallery	getSelectedItemIndex	Sub GetSelectedItemIndex (control As IRibbonControl, ByRef index)
gallery	onAction	Sub OnAction (control As IRibbonControl, selectedId As String, selectedIndex As Integer)
menuSeparator	getTitle	Sub GetTitle (control As IRibbonControl, ByRef title)
toggleButton	getPressed	Sub GetPressed (control As IRibbonControl, ByRef returnValue)
toggleButton	onAction	Sub OnAction (control As IRibbonControl, pressed As Boolean, byRef cancelDefault)
toggleButton	onAction	Sub OnAction (control As IRibbonControl, pressed As Boolean)

continued ➡

Attributes

The following table lists all of the Ribbon attributes used by
RibbonX.

ATTRIBUTE	TYPE OR VALUE	DESCRIPTION
description	String	When the itemSize attribute is set to large, sets the description text that displays in menus.
enabled	true, false, 0, 1	Enables controls.
getContent	callback	Retrieves XML content that describes the menu. Used with a dynamic menu.
getDescription	callback	Returns the control description.
getEnabled	callback	Returns the control enabled state.
getImage	callback	Returns the image.
getImageMso	callback	Uses a control ID to returns a built-in control icon.
getItemCount	callback	Returns the number of items in a combo box, drop-down list, or gallery.
getItemID	callback	Returns the ID for a specific item in a combo box, drop-down list, or gallery.
getItemImage	callback	Returns the image for a specific item in a combo box, drop-down list, or gallery.
getItemLabel	callback	Returns the label for a specific item in a combo box, drop-down list, or gallery.
getItemScreentip	callback	Returns the ScreenTip for a specific item in a combo box, drop-down list, or gallery.
getItemSupertip	callback	Returns the Enhanced ScreenTip for a specific item in a combo box, drop-down list, or gallery.
getKeytip	callback	Returns the KeyTip.
getLabel	callback	Returns the label.
getPressed	callback	When used with a toggle button, gets a value that indicates whether the state is pressed or not pressed. When used with a checkbox, gets a value that indicates whether the state is selected or cleared.
getScreentip	callback	Returns the ScreenTip.
getSelectedItemID	callback	For a drop-down list or gallery, gets the ID of the selected item.
getSelectedItemIndex	callback	For a drop-down list or gallery, gets the index of the selected item.
getShowImage	callback	Returns a value that sets whether to display the control image.
getShowLabel	callback	Returns a value that sets whether to display the control label.
getSize	callback	Returns a value that sets the size of a control (normal or large).
getSupertip	callback	Returns a value that sets the Enhanced ScreenTip for a control.
getText	callback	For a text box or edit box, gets the text to display in the edit portion of the control.

ATTRIBUTE	TYPE OR VALUE	DESCRIPTION
getTitle	callback	For a menu separator, sets the text to display (rather than a horizontal line).
getVisible	callback	Returns the value that determines whether the control is visible.
id	String	A user-defined unique identifier for a control. If you define an id, do not assign an idMso or an idQ.
idMso	control id	Built-in control ID. If you define an idMso, do not assign an id or an idQ.
idQ	qualified id	Qualified control ID, prefixed with a namespace identifier. If you define an idQ, do not assign an idMso or an id.
image	String	Sets the image for a control.
imageMso	control id	Sets the identifier for a built-in image.
insertAfterMso	control id	Specifes the identifier for the built-in control after which the control is positioned.
insertAfterQ	qualified id	Specifies the identifier of a qualified control (that is, the control whose idQ property was specified) after which the control is positioned.
insertBeforeMso	control id	Specifies the identifier for the built-in control before the control is positioned.
insertBeforeQ	qualified id	Specifies the identifier of a qualified control (that is, a control whose idQ property was specified) before which the control is positioned.
itemSize	large, normal	Sets the size for the items in the menu.
keytip	String	Sets the KeyTip for the control. KeyTips display when the user presses the ALT key plus a letter.
label	String	Sets the label for the control.
onAction	callback	Called when the user clicks the control.
onChange	callback	Called when the user commits text in an edit box or combo box.
screentip	String	Sets the control's ScreenTip.
showImage	true, false, 0, 1	Specifed whether the control's image displays.
showItemImage	true, false, 0, 1	In a combo box, drop-down list, or gallery, specifies whether each item's image shows.
showItemLabel	true, false, 0, 1	In a combo box, drop-down list, or gallery, specifies whether to show each item's label.
showLabel	true, false, 0, 1	Specifies whether the control's label shows.
size	large, normal	Sets the size of the control.
sizeString	String	Sets a string, such as "MMMMM". The string sets the width of the control.
supertip	String	Sets the Enhanced ScreenTip for the control. An EnhancedScreenTip is a longer screen tip.
tag	String	Sets user-defined text that enables you to store information about the control that is not pertinent to any other specific property.
title	String	Used with a menu separator. Sets the text displayed (rather than a horizontal line).
visible	true, false, 0, 1	Determines whether the control is visible.

INDEX

Symbols

& (ampersand), concatenation operator, 58
' (apostrophe), comment indicator, 48
* (asterisk)
  multiplication operator, 56
  wildcard character, 150
\ (backslash), integer division operator, 56
^ (caret), exponential operator, 56
:= (colon, equal sign), assigning argument values, 73
= (equal sign), equals operator, 70, 86
> (greater than), greater than operator, 86
>= (greater than, equal), greater than or equal to operator, 86
< (less than), less than operator, 86
<= (less than, equal), less than or equal to operator, 86
- (minus sign), subtraction operator, 56
+ (plus sign)
  addition operator, 56
  concatenation operator, 58
(pound signs), error indicator, 201
? (question mark)
  in debugging, 128
  wildcard character, 150
/ (slash), division operator, 56
_ (underscore), continuation character, 105
< > (angle brackets), not equal operator, 86

A

absolute references, 4, 9
Activate method, 145, 175
ActiveSheet property, 67
Add method, 148–149, 152–153, 242–245, 248–249
AddComment method, 206–207
add-ins
  Conditional Sum Wizard, 280
  converting Ribbon to, 237
  converting workbooks to, 276–277
  creating, 276–277
  Data Analysis Toolpak, 280
  deleting, 281
  digital signatures, 279
  distributing, 277
  downloading, 280
  Euro Currency Tools, 280
  installing, 280–281
  loading, 282–283

naming, 278–279
open, checking for, 145
password protection, 278–279
protecting, 278–279
Solver, 280
standard with Excel, 280
third-party, 279, 280
viruses, 279
AddItem method, 226
AddToMru parameter, 134–135
AllowEdit property, 183
ampersand (&), concatenation operator, 58
And operator, 87
angle brackets (< >), not equal operator, 86
apostrophe ('), comment indicator, 48
application events, 261
Application objects, 62
arguments, 45, 72–73
Array function, 80–81
arrays, 76–85, 94–95, 303. *See also* variables
asterisk (*)
  multiplication operator, 56
  wildcard character, 150
attributes, of objects. *See* properties
attributes, XML, 284
Auto Data Tips option, 35
Auto Indent option, 35
Auto List Member option, 35
Auto Quick Info option, 35
Auto Syntax Check option, 35
AutoFill method, 208–209
AutoFit method, 201
automation. *See* macros
Axis methods, 256–257

B

backslash (\), integer division operator, 56
backups, 38, 164
.bas file extension, 38
BeforeClose event, 264–265
BeforeSave event, 266–267
bold fonts, 177
Boolean data types, 50
BorderAround method, 212–213
borders, 203, 212–213, 319
Break mode, 123–124
breakpoints, 122–123
buttons, 107, 236–237. *See also* form controls

INDEX

INDEX

INDEX

INDEX

For more professional instruction in a visual format, try these.

All designed for visual learners—just like you!

Read Less–Learn More®

Visual®

Excel Data Analysis
2nd Edition

Your visual blueprint™ for analyzing data, charts, and PivotTables

Data analysis tools on CD-ROM!

ISBN-10: 0-7645-9780-9
ISBN-13: 978-0-7645-9780-0

Ajax

Your visual blueprint™ for creating rich Internet applications

Bonus! Companion Web site includes all code used in the book

ISBN-10: 0-470-04306-7
ISBN-13: 978-0-470-04306-6

Excel PivotTables and PivotCharts

Your visual blueprint for creating dynamic spreadsheets

ISBN-10: 0-471-78489-3
ISBN-13: 978-0-471-78489-0

For a complete listing of *Visual Blueprint*™ titles and other Visual books, go to wiley.com/go/visual

Visual®
An Imprint of ⊕**WILEY**
Now you know.